P9-CIU-210

SB Shojo Beat

yona of the Dawn

1

Story & Art by

Mizuho Kusanagi

Yona of the Dawn

Volume 1

CONTENTS

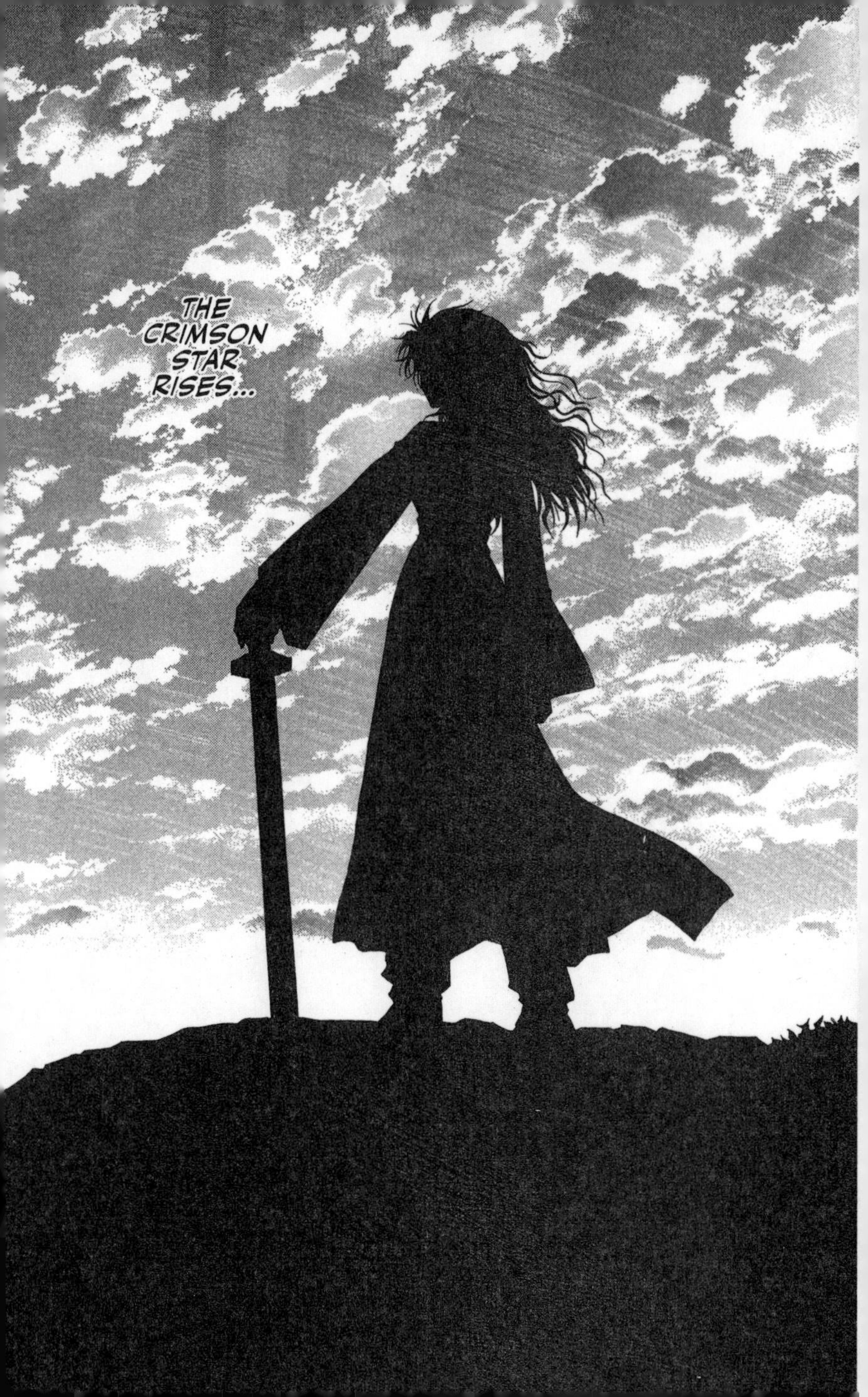
THE CRIMSON STAR RISES...

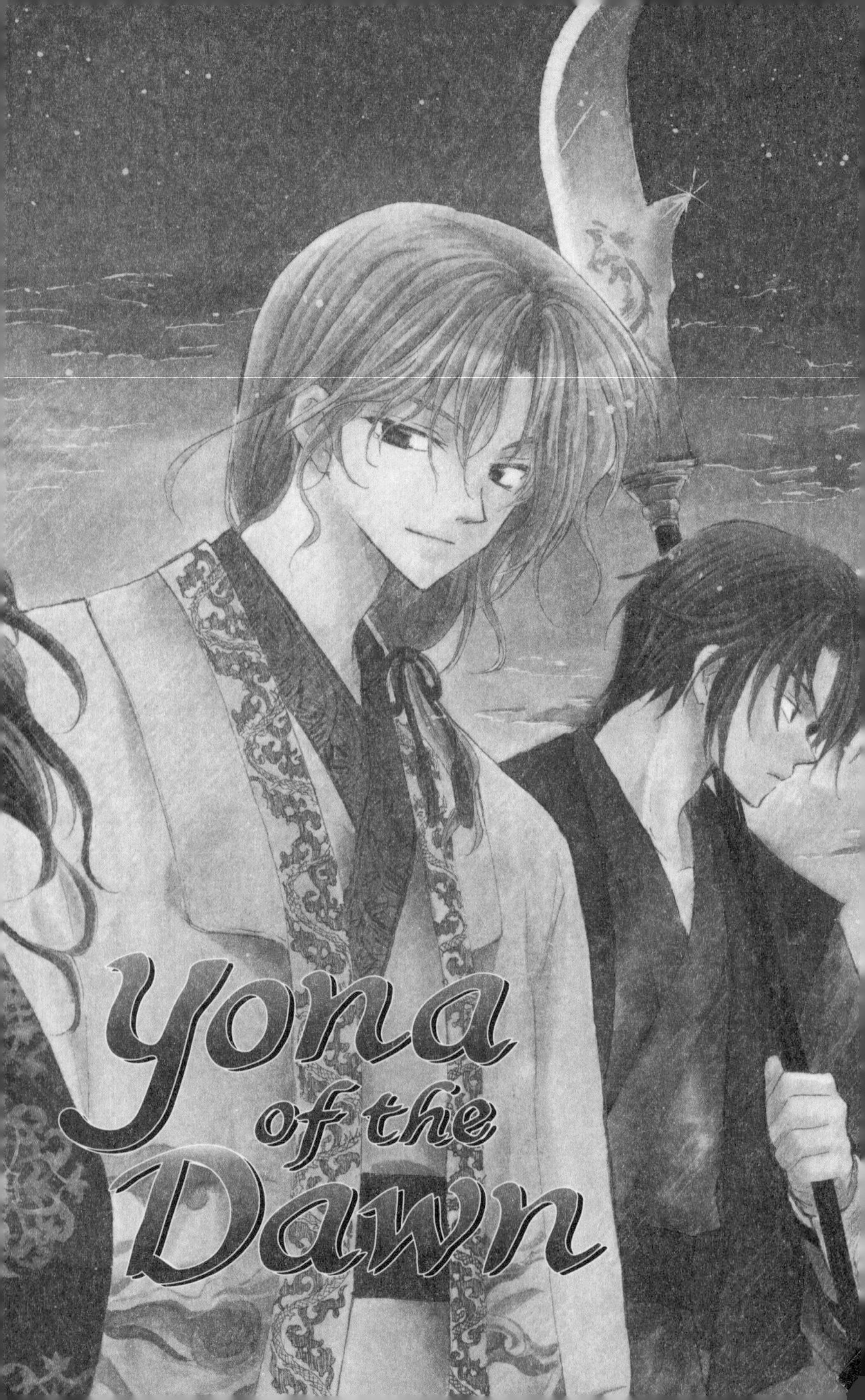
Yona of the Dawn

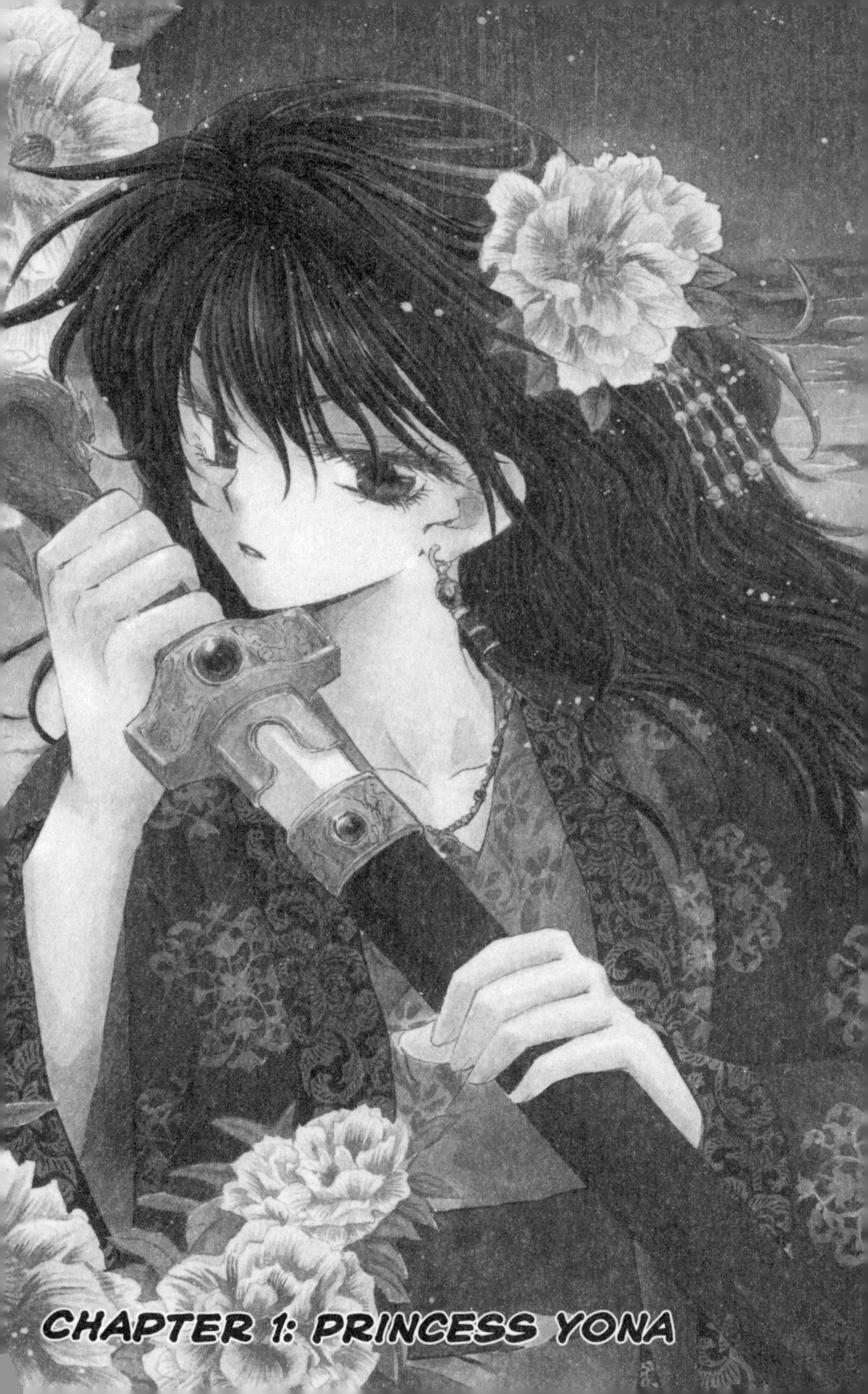

CHAPTER 1: PRINCESS YONA

Yona
of the
Dawn

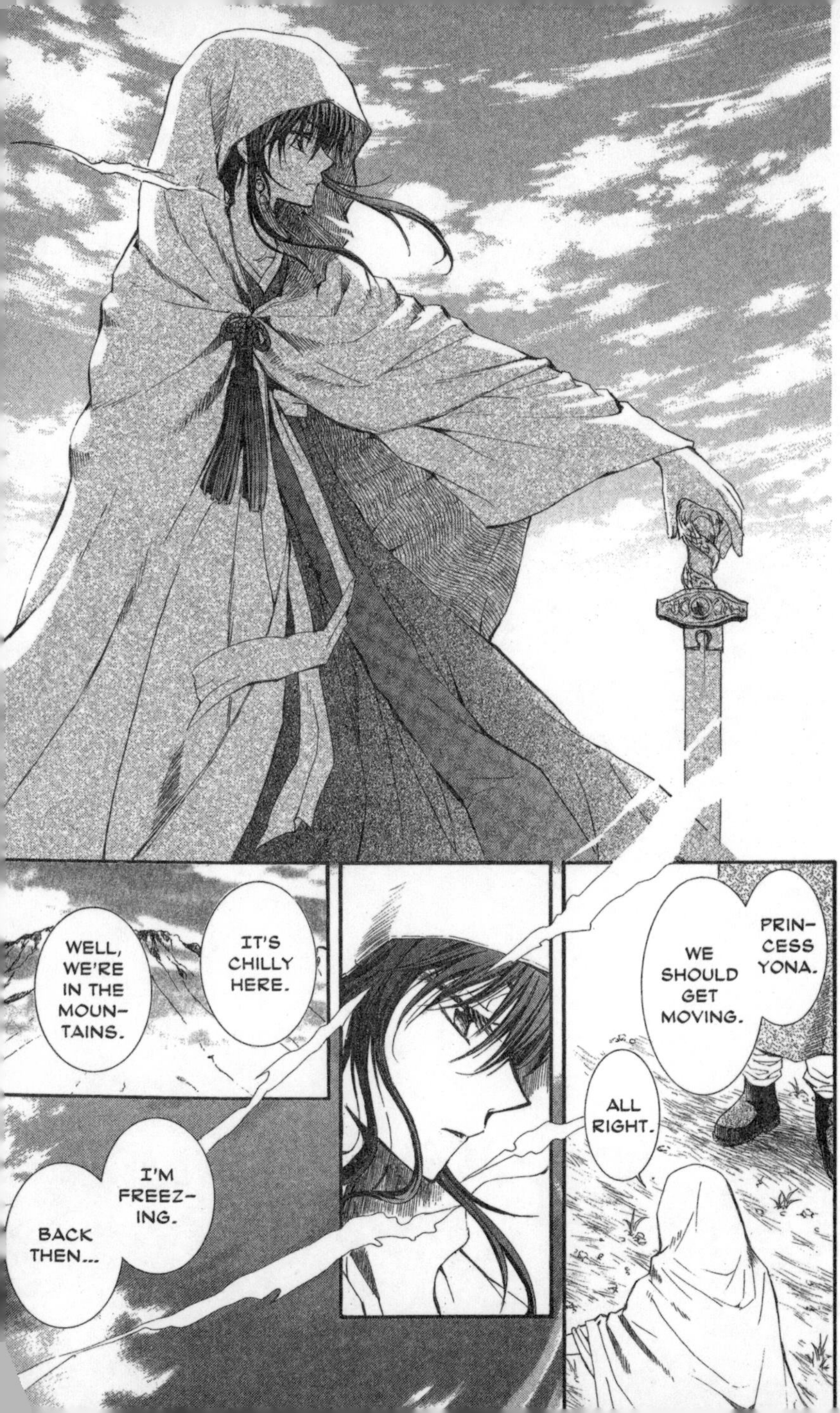
PRINCESS YONA.
WE SHOULD GET MOVING.
ALL RIGHT.
IT'S CHILLY HERE.
WELL, WE'RE IN THE MOUNTAINS.
I'M FREEZING.
BACK THEN...

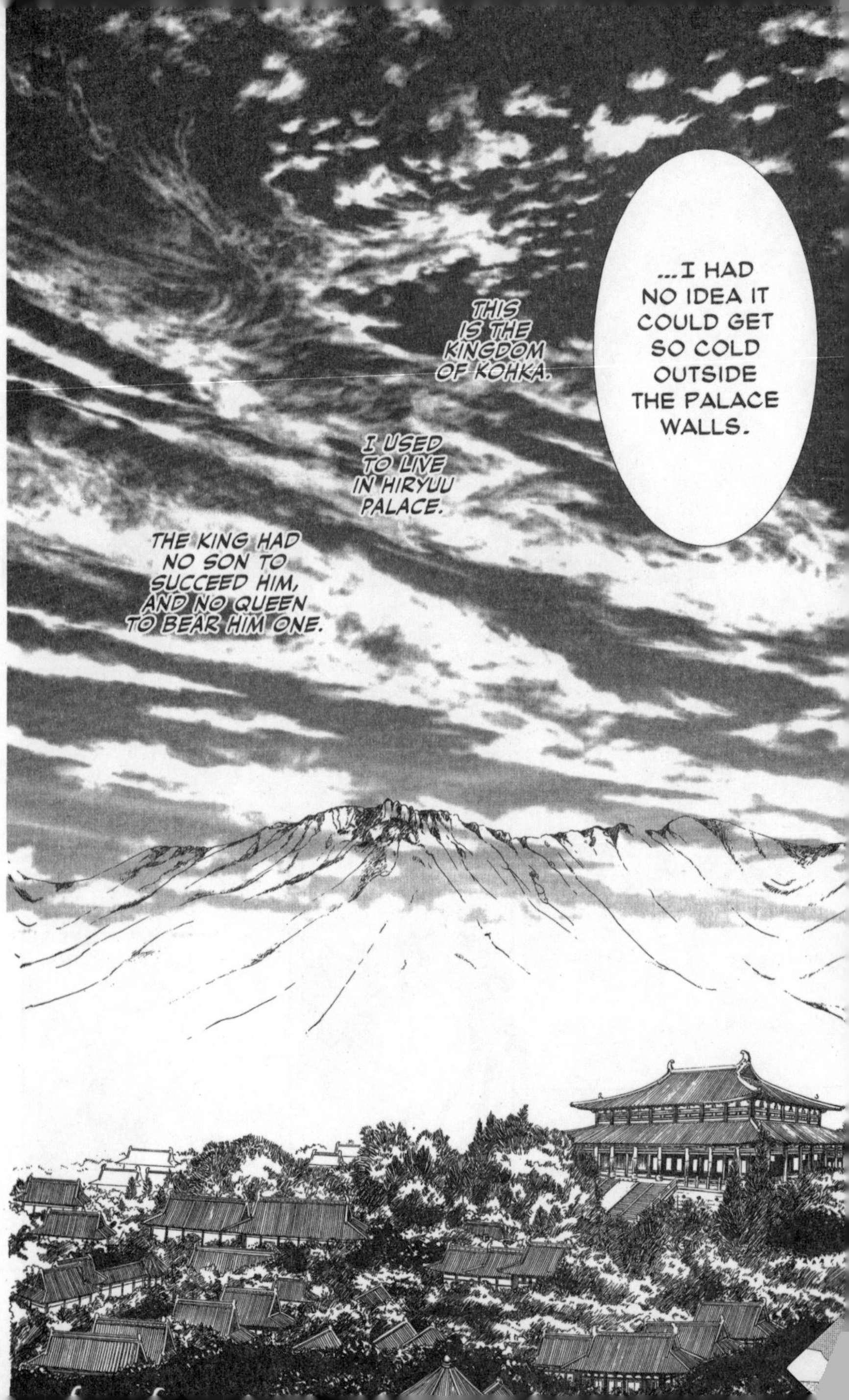
...I HAD NO IDEA IT COULD GET SO COLD OUTSIDE THE PALACE WALLS.
THIS IS THE KINGDOM OF KOHKA.
I USED TO LIVE IN HIRYUU PALACE.
THE KING HAD NO SON TO SUCCEED HIM, AND NO QUEEN TO BEAR HIM ONE.

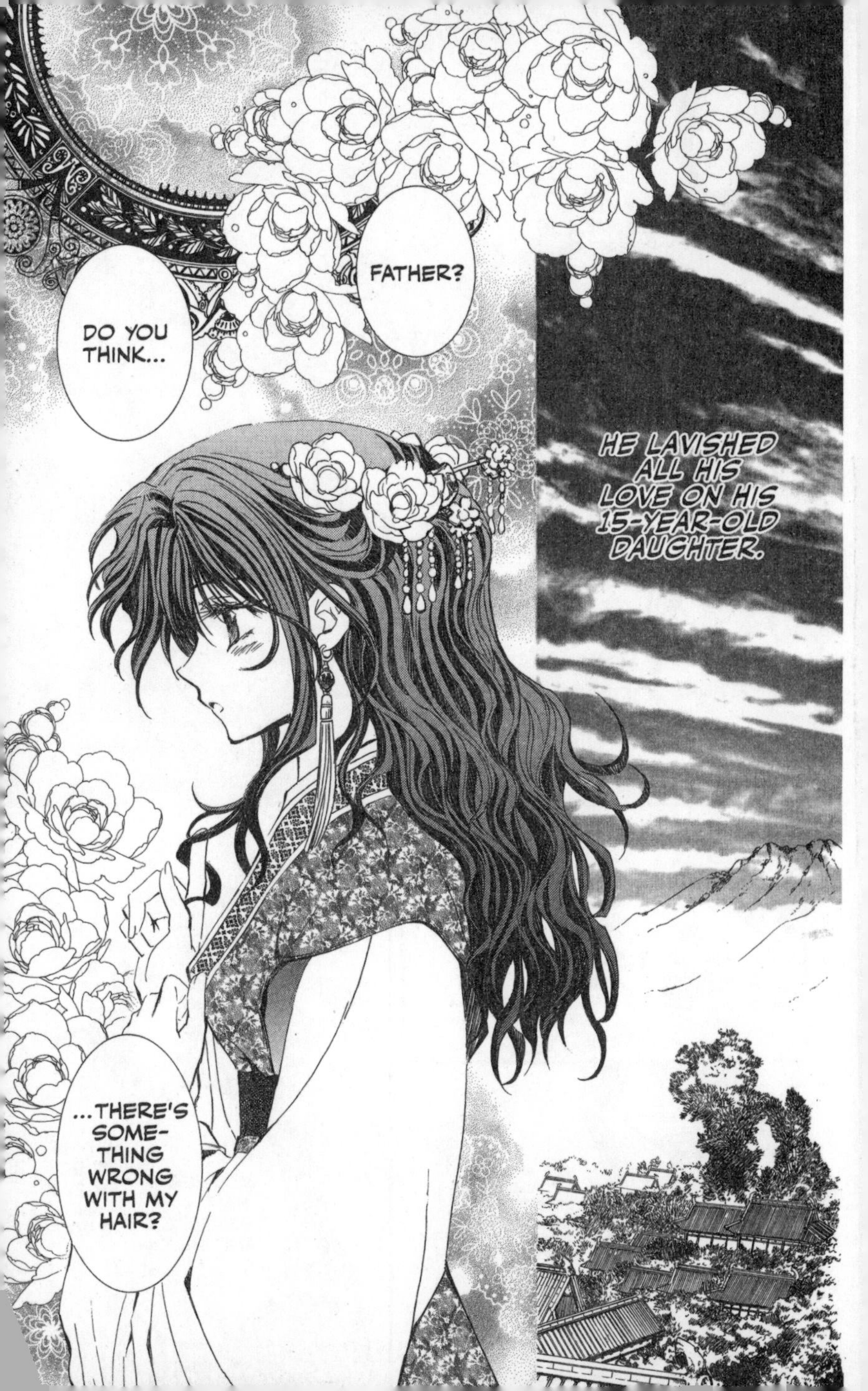
HE LAVISHED ALL HIS LOVE ON HIS 15-YEAR-OLD DAUGHTER.
FATHER?
DO YOU THINK...
...THERE'S SOME-THING WRONG WITH MY HAIR?

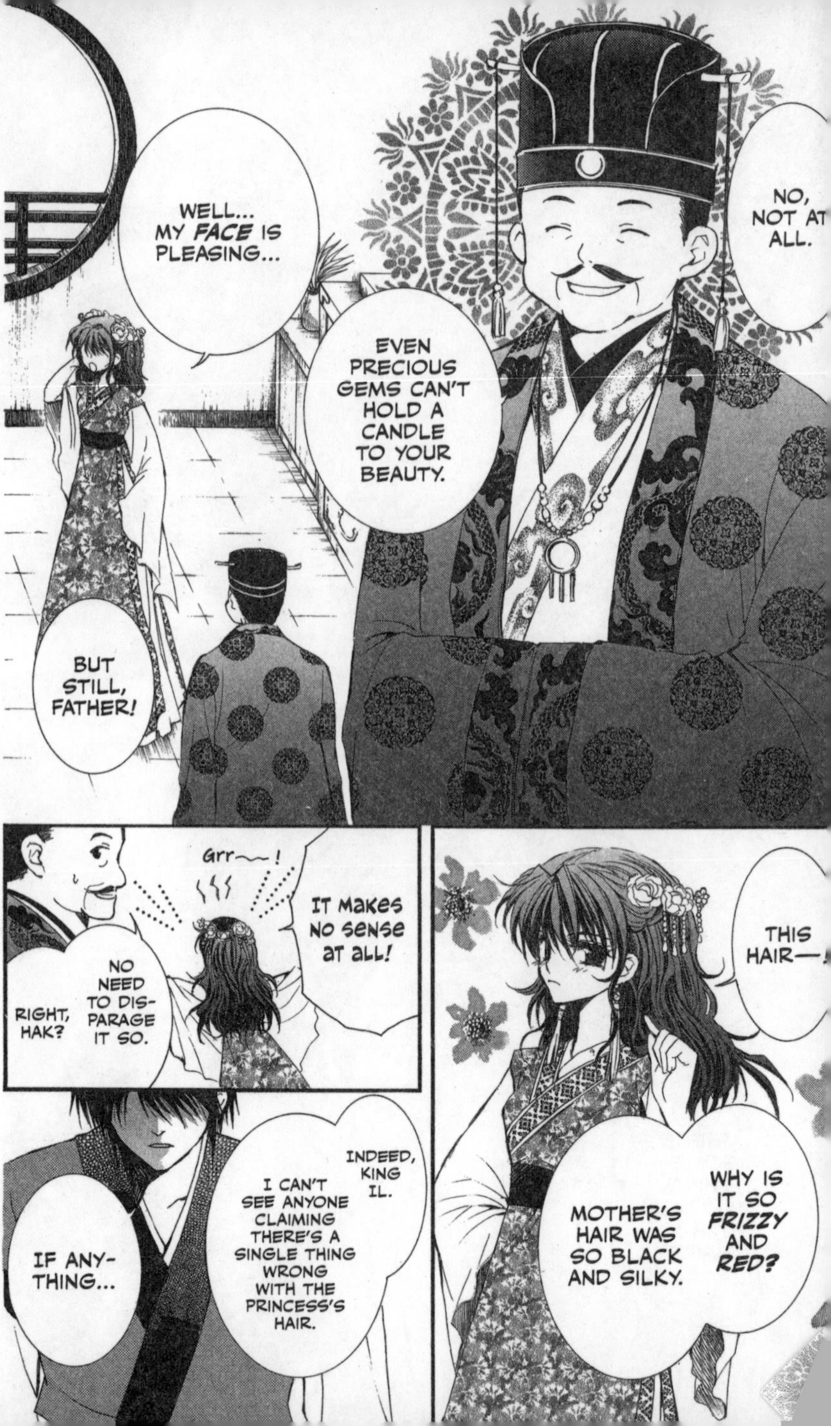
NO, NOT AT ALL.
EVEN PRECIOUS GEMS CAN'T HOLD A CANDLE TO YOUR BEAUTY.
WELL... MY *FACE* IS PLEASING...
BUT STILL, FATHER!
THIS HAIR—!
WHY IS IT SO *FRIZZY* AND *RED?*
MOTHER'S HAIR WAS SO BLACK AND SILKY.
Grr~~!
IT MAKES NO SENSE AT ALL!
NO NEED TO DIS-PARAGE IT SO.
RIGHT, HAK?
INDEED, KING IL.
I CAN'T SEE ANYONE CLAIMING THERE'S A SINGLE THING WRONG WITH THE PRINCESS'S HAIR.
IF ANY-THING...

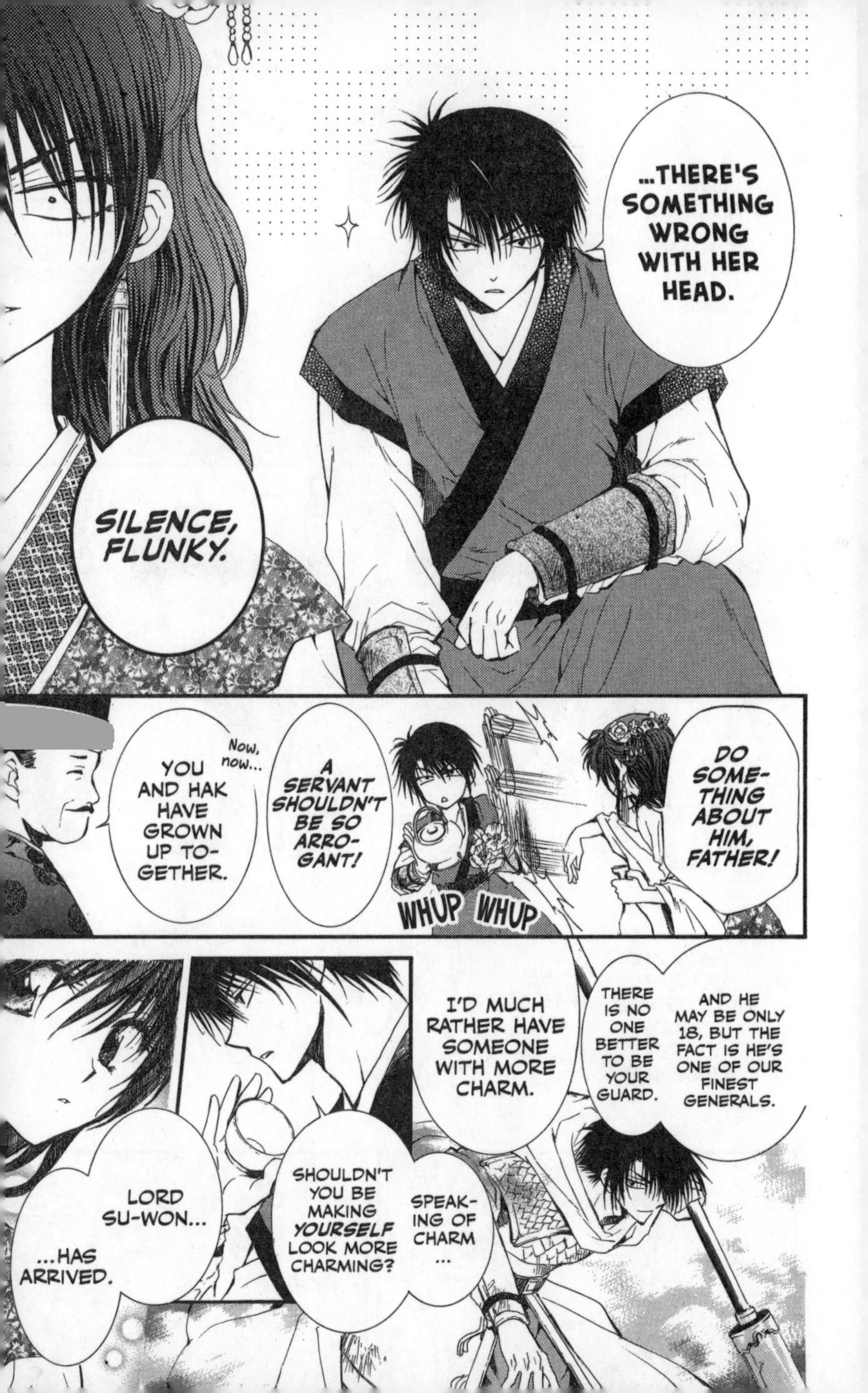
...THERE'S SOMETHING WRONG WITH HER HEAD.
SILENCE, FLUNKY.
DO SOMETHING ABOUT HIM, FATHER!
WHUP WHUP
A SERVANT SHOULDN'T BE SO ARROGANT!
Now, now...
YOU AND HAK HAVE GROWN UP TOGETHER.
AND HE MAY BE ONLY 18, BUT THE FACT IS HE'S ONE OF OUR FINEST GENERALS.
THERE IS NO ONE BETTER TO BE YOUR GUARD.
I'D MUCH RATHER HAVE SOMEONE WITH MORE CHARM.
SPEAKING OF CHARM...
SHOULDN'T YOU BE MAKING *YOURSELF* LOOK MORE CHARMING?
LORD SU-WON...
...HAS ARRIVED.

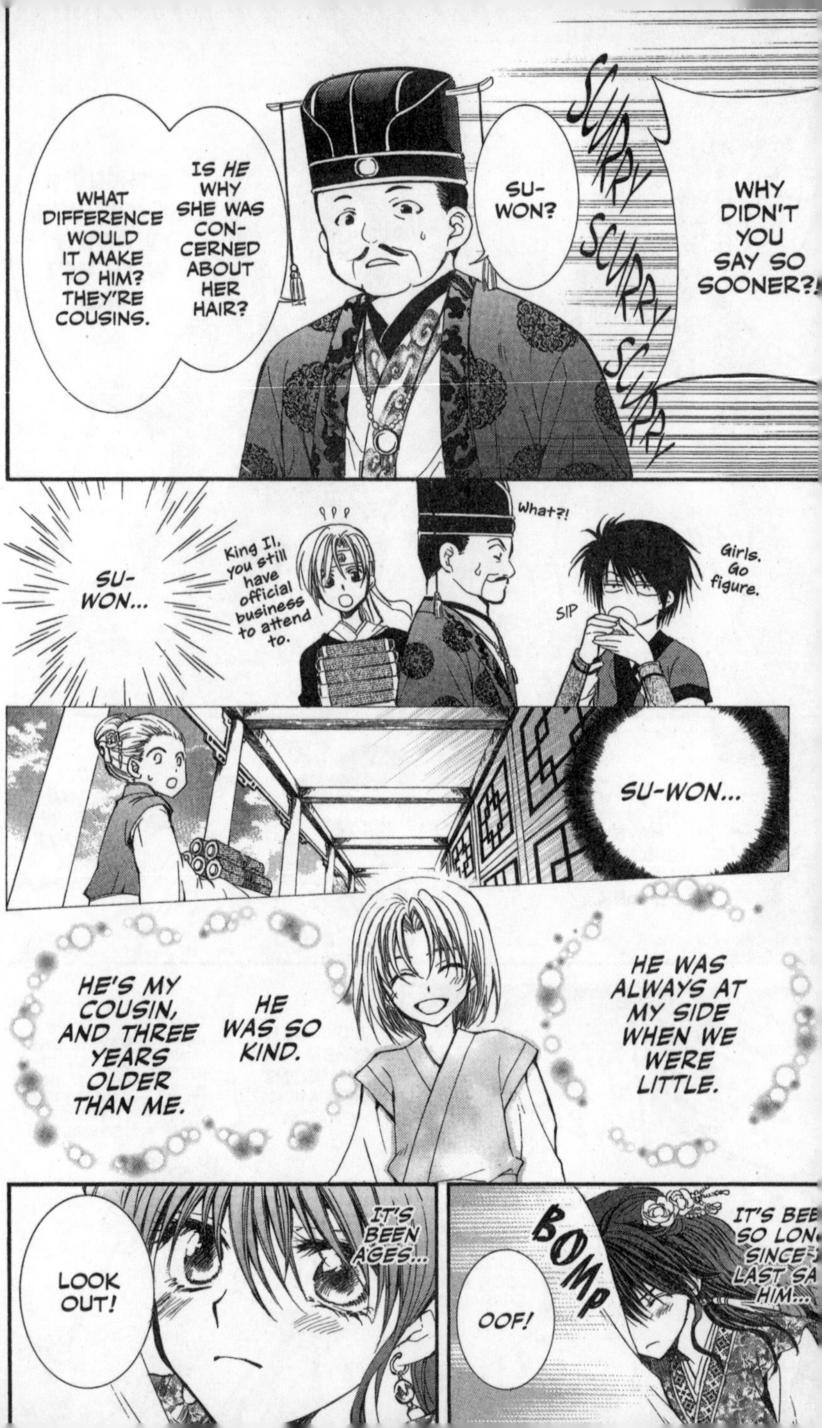
WHY DIDN'T YOU SAY SO SOONER?!
SCURRY SCURRY SCURRY SCURRY
SU-WON?
IS HE WHY SHE WAS CONCERNED ABOUT HER HAIR?
WHAT DIFFERENCE WOULD IT MAKE TO HIM? THEY'RE COUSINS.
Girls. Go figure.
SIP
What?!
King Il, you still have official business to attend to.
SU-WON...
SU-WON...
HE WAS ALWAYS AT MY SIDE WHEN WE WERE LITTLE.
HE WAS SO KIND.
HE'S MY COUSIN, AND THREE YEARS OLDER THAN ME.
IT'S BEE SO LON SINCE LAST SA HIM...
BOMP
OOF!
IT'S BEEN AGES...
LOOK OUT!

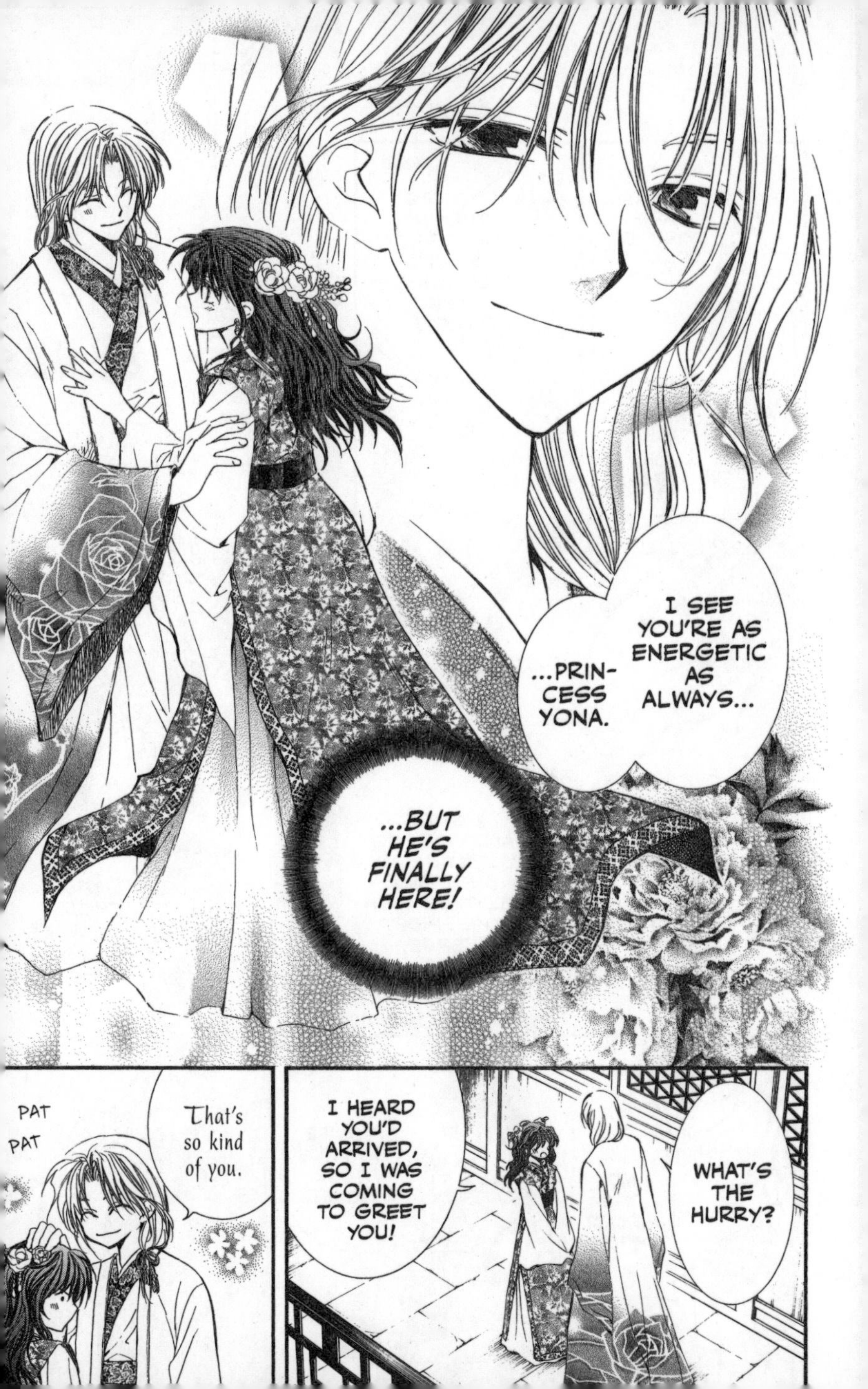
I SEE YOU'RE AS ENERGETIC AS ALWAYS... ...PRINCESS YONA.
...BUT HE'S FINALLY HERE!
WHAT'S THE HURRY?
I HEARD YOU'D ARRIVED, SO I WAS COMING TO GREET YOU!
That's so kind of you.
PAT
PAT

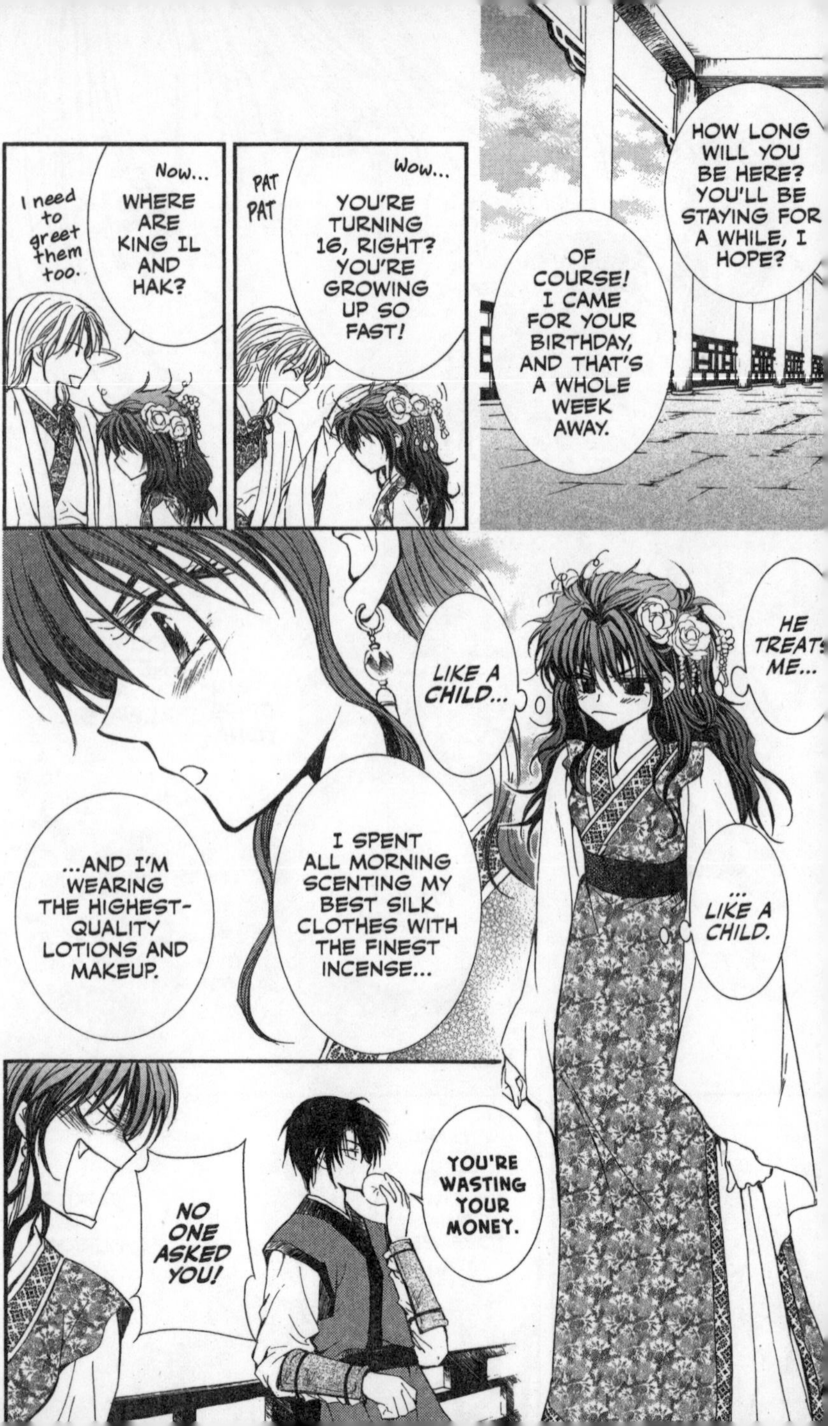

HOW LONG WILL YOU BE HERE? YOU'LL BE STAYING FOR A WHILE, I HOPE?
OF COURSE! I CAME FOR YOUR BIRTHDAY, AND THAT'S A WHOLE WEEK AWAY.
Wow...
YOU'RE TURNING 16, RIGHT? YOU'RE GROWING UP SO FAST!
PAT PAT
Now...
WHERE ARE KING IL AND HAK?
I need to greet them too.
HE TREATS ME...
... LIKE A CHILD.
LIKE A CHILD...
I SPENT ALL MORNING SCENTING MY BEST SILK CLOTHES WITH THE FINEST INCENSE...
...AND I'M WEARING THE HIGHEST-QUALITY LOTIONS AND MAKEUP.
YOU'RE WASTING YOUR MONEY.
NO ONE ASKED YOU!

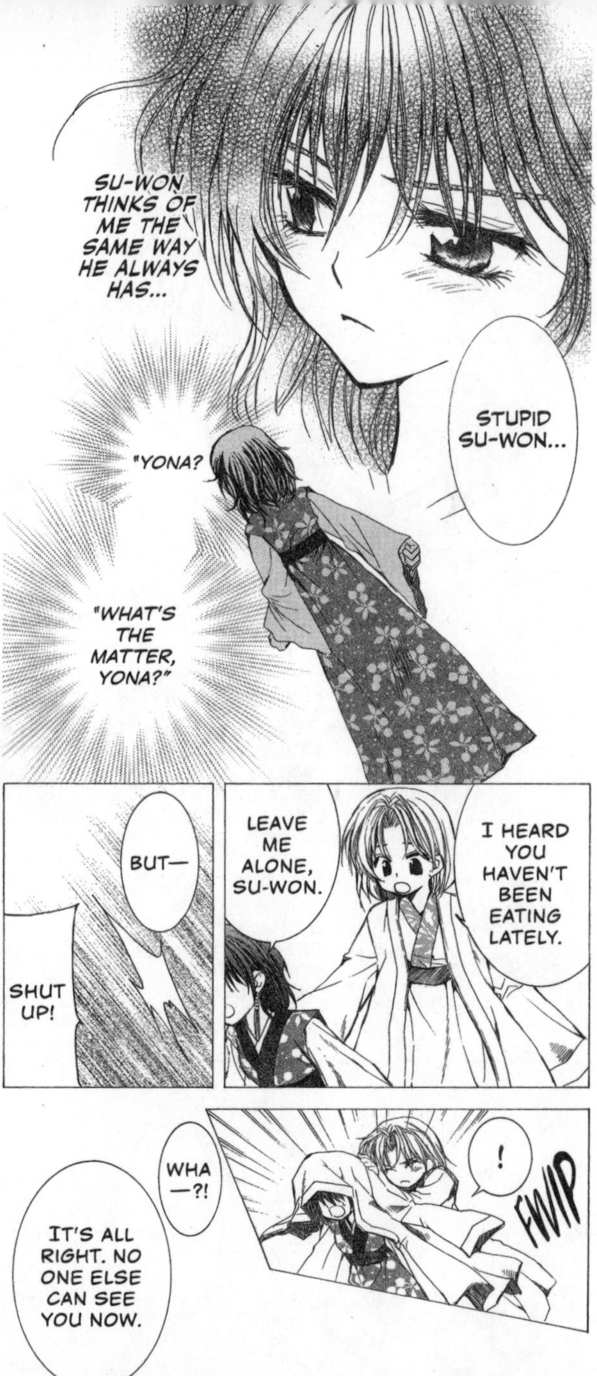
SU-WON THINKS OF ME THE SAME WAY HE ALWAYS HAS...
STUPID SU-WON...
"YONA?
"WHAT'S THE MATTER, YONA?"
I HEARD YOU HAVEN'T BEEN EATING LATELY.
LEAVE ME ALONE, SU-WON.
BUT—
SHUT UP!
!
FWIP
WHA—?!
IT'S ALL RIGHT. NO ONE ELSE CAN SEE YOU NOW.

Hello! It's lovely to meet you. I'm Mizuho Kusanagi. Thank you for picking up the first volume of *Yona of the Dawn*! This time around, I'm trying to create a fantasy series.

After *NG Life* ended, I had no idea I'd be writing a story like this! I've always dreamed of writing a fantasy series starring a girl, but I never thought I'd get a chance to do it, so I'm very grateful for this opportunity. It's my job to flesh out this basic framework I'm starting with, and I'll do my best to bring it to life! I hope you enjoy it.

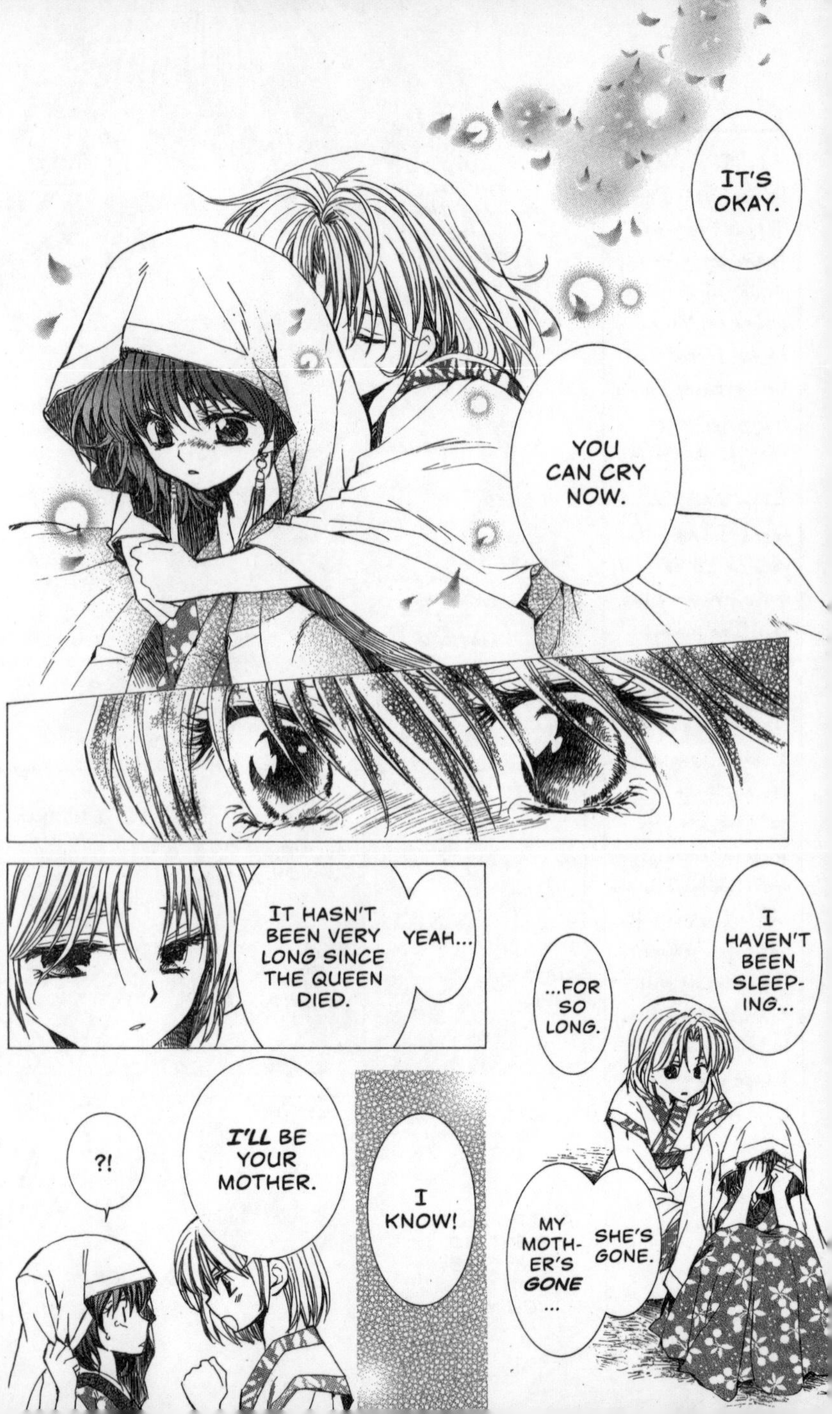
IT'S OKAY.
YOU CAN CRY NOW.
I HAVEN'T BEEN SLEEPING...
...FOR SO LONG.
SHE'S GONE.
MY MOTHER'S *GONE* ...
YEAH...
IT HASN'T BEEN VERY LONG SINCE THE QUEEN DIED.
I KNOW!
I'LL BE YOUR MOTHER.
?!

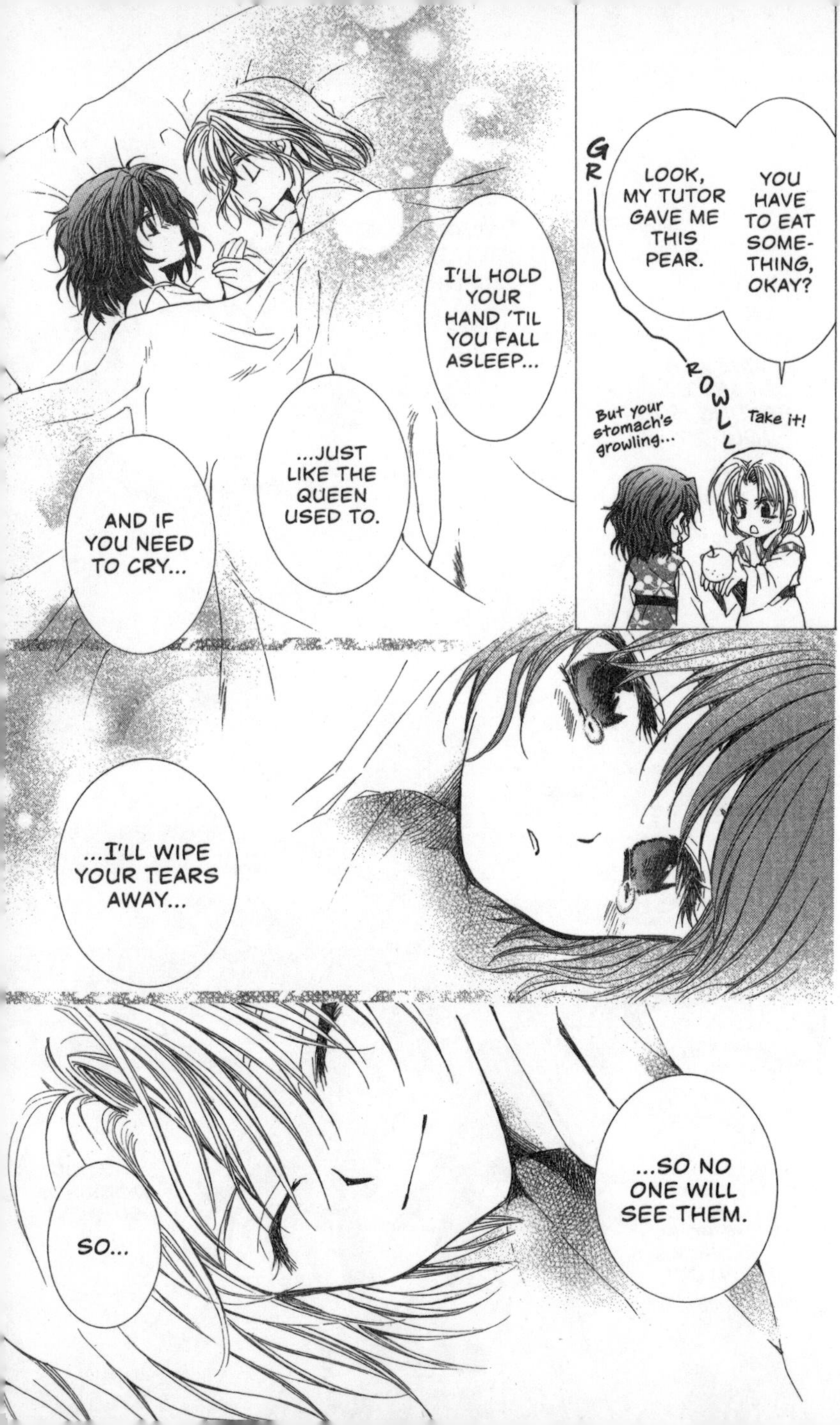
YOU HAVE TO EAT SOMETHING, OKAY?
LOOK, MY TUTOR GAVE ME THIS PEAR.
GRROWLL
Take it!
But your stomach's growling...
I'LL HOLD YOUR HAND 'TIL YOU FALL ASLEEP...
...JUST LIKE THE QUEEN USED TO.
AND IF YOU NEED TO CRY...
...I'LL WIPE YOUR TEARS AWAY...
...SO NO ONE WILL SEE THEM.
SO...

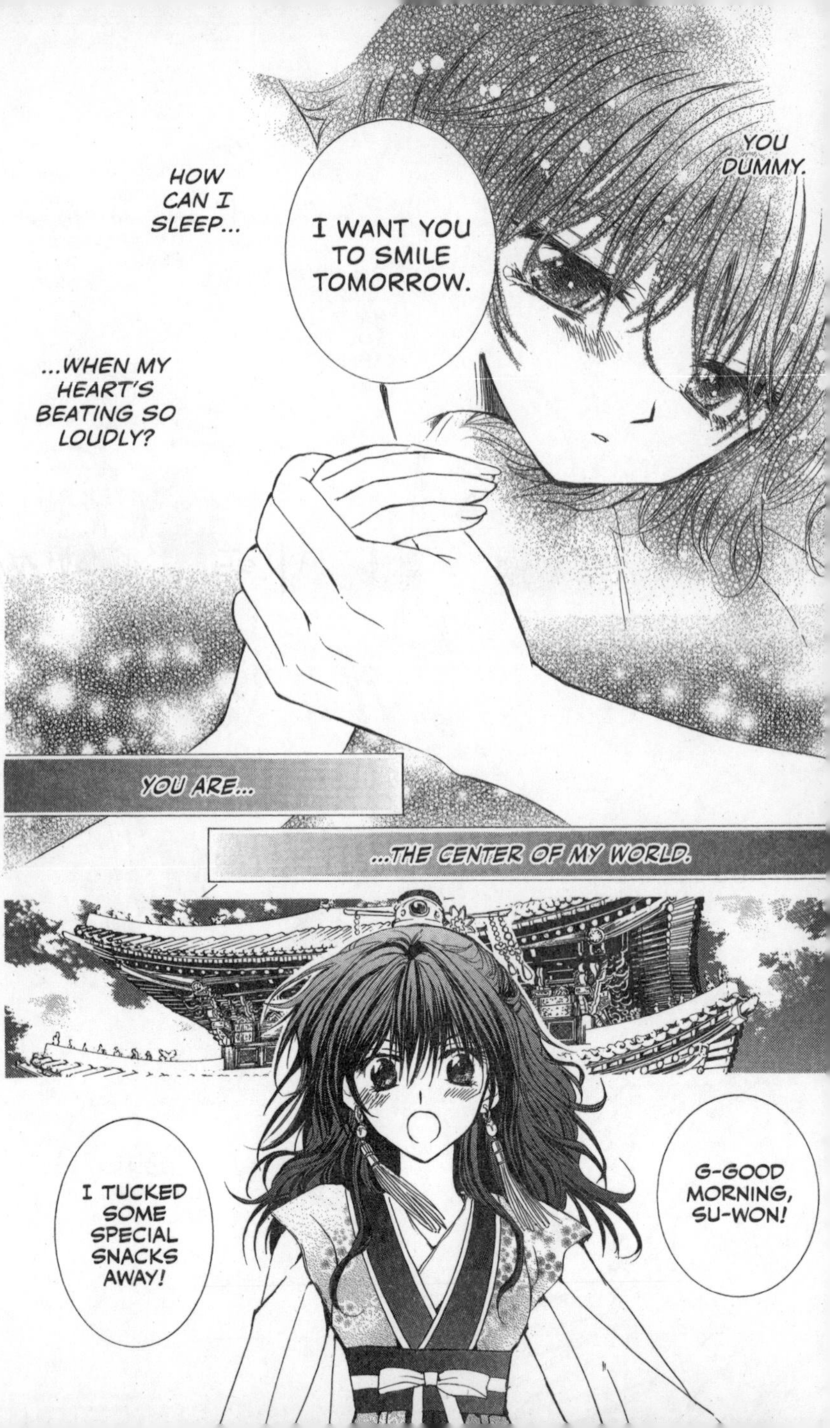
YOU DUMMY.
I WANT YOU TO SMILE TOMORROW.
HOW CAN I SLEEP...
...WHEN MY HEART'S BEATING SO LOUDLY?
YOU ARE...
...THE CENTER OF MY WORLD.
G-GOOD MORNING, SU-WON!
I TUCKED SOME SPECIAL SNACKS AWAY!

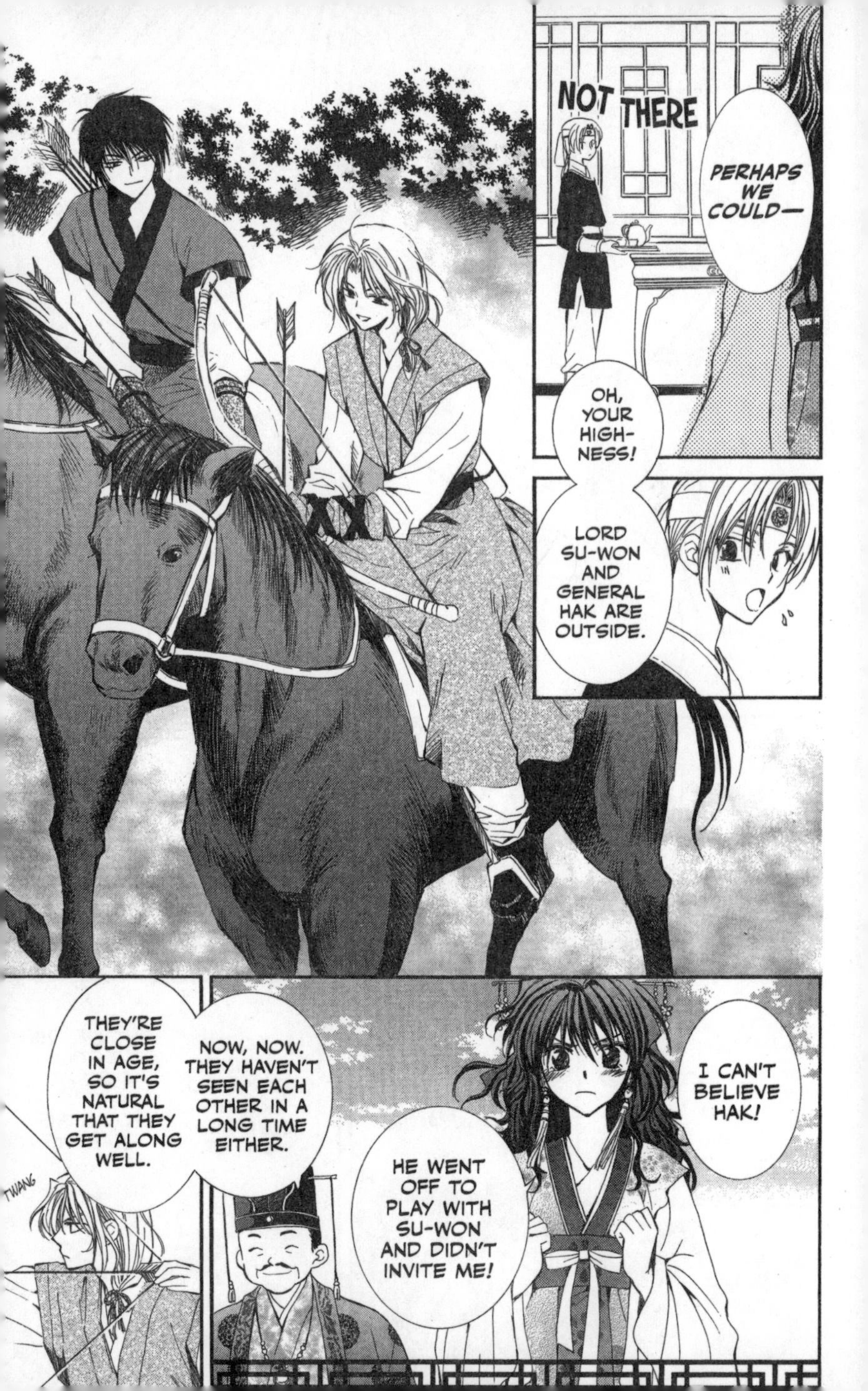
PERHAPS WE COULD—
NOT THERE
OH, YOUR HIGHNESS!
LORD SU-WON AND GENERAL HAK ARE OUTSIDE.
I CAN'T BELIEVE HAK!
HE WENT OFF TO PLAY WITH SU-WON AND DIDN'T INVITE ME!
NOW, NOW. THEY HAVEN'T SEEN EACH OTHER IN A LONG TIME EITHER.
THEY'RE CLOSE IN AGE, SO IT'S NATURAL THAT THEY GET ALONG WELL.
TWANG

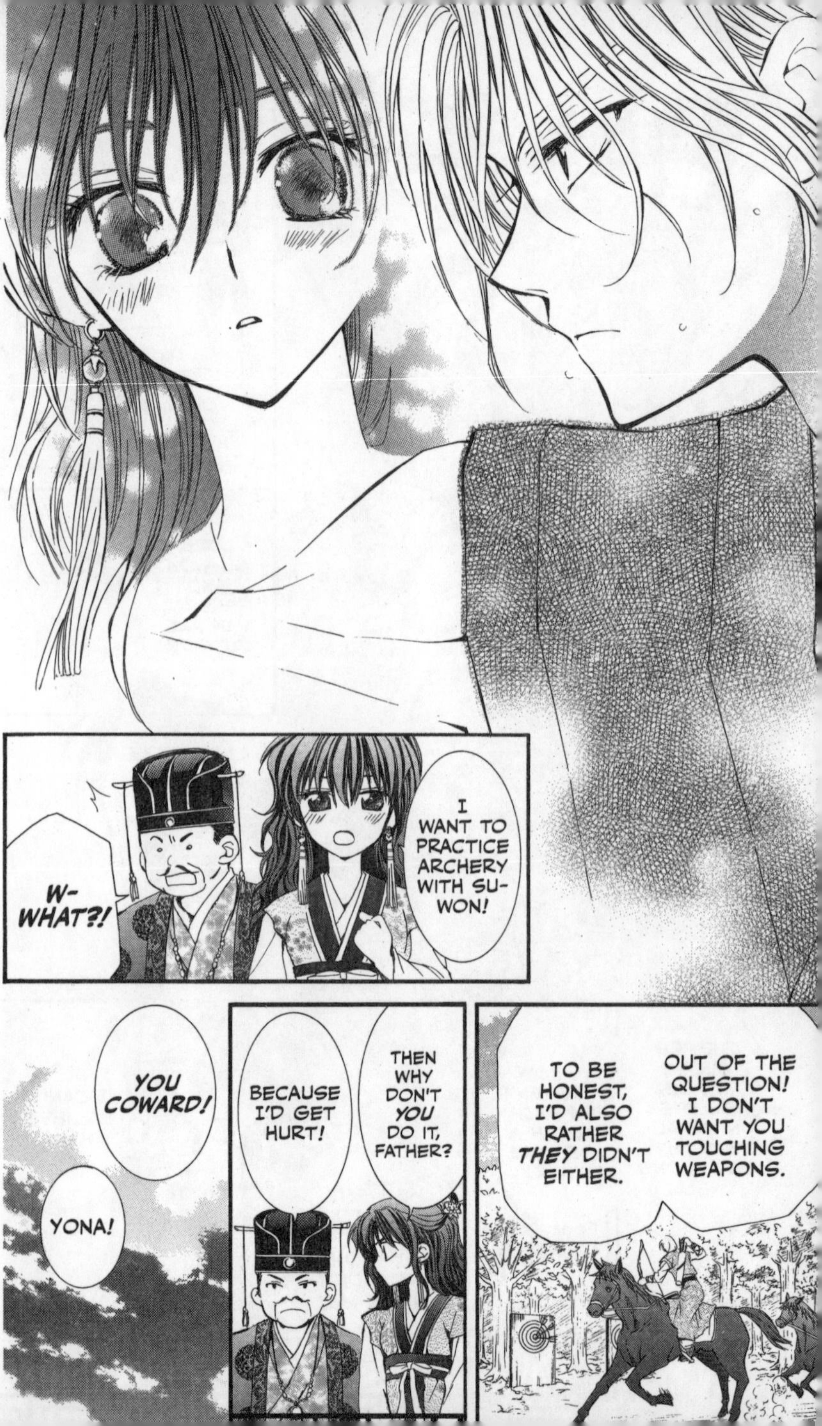
I WANT TO PRACTICE ARCHERY WITH SU-WON!
W-WHAT?!
OUT OF THE QUESTION! I DON'T WANT YOU TOUCHING WEAPONS.
TO BE HONEST, I'D ALSO RATHER THEY DIDN'T EITHER.
THEN WHY DON'T YOU DO IT, FATHER?
BECAUSE I'D GET HURT!
YOU COWARD!
YONA!

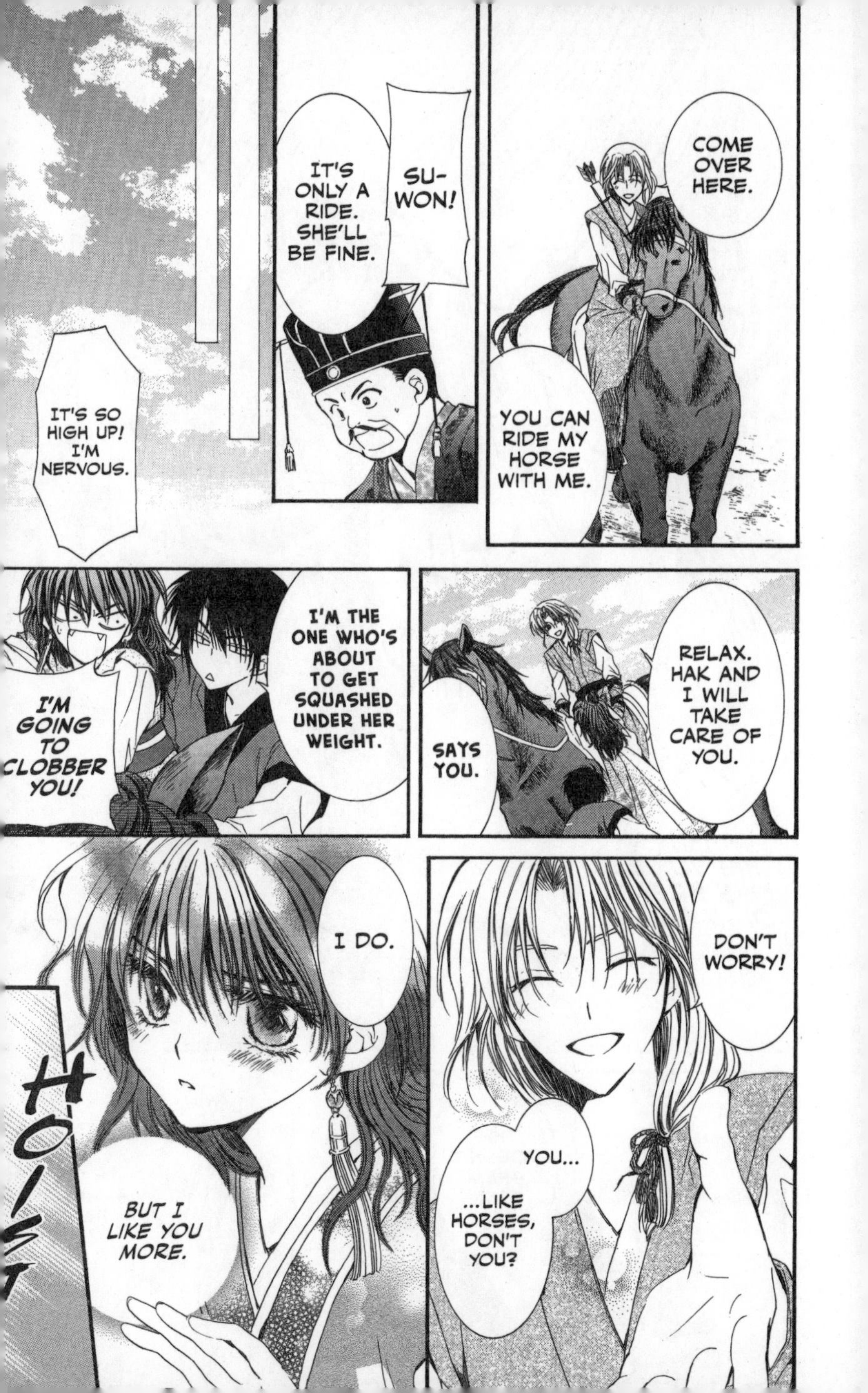
COME OVER HERE.
YOU CAN RIDE MY HORSE WITH ME.
SU-WON!
IT'S ONLY A RIDE. SHE'LL BE FINE.
IT'S SO HIGH UP! I'M NERVOUS.
RELAX. HAK AND I WILL TAKE CARE OF YOU.
SAYS YOU.
I'M THE ONE WHO'S ABOUT TO GET SQUASHED UNDER HER WEIGHT.
I'M GOING TO CLOBBER YOU!
DON'T WORRY!
YOU...
...LIKE HORSES, DON'T YOU?
I DO.
BUT I LIKE YOU MORE.
HOIST

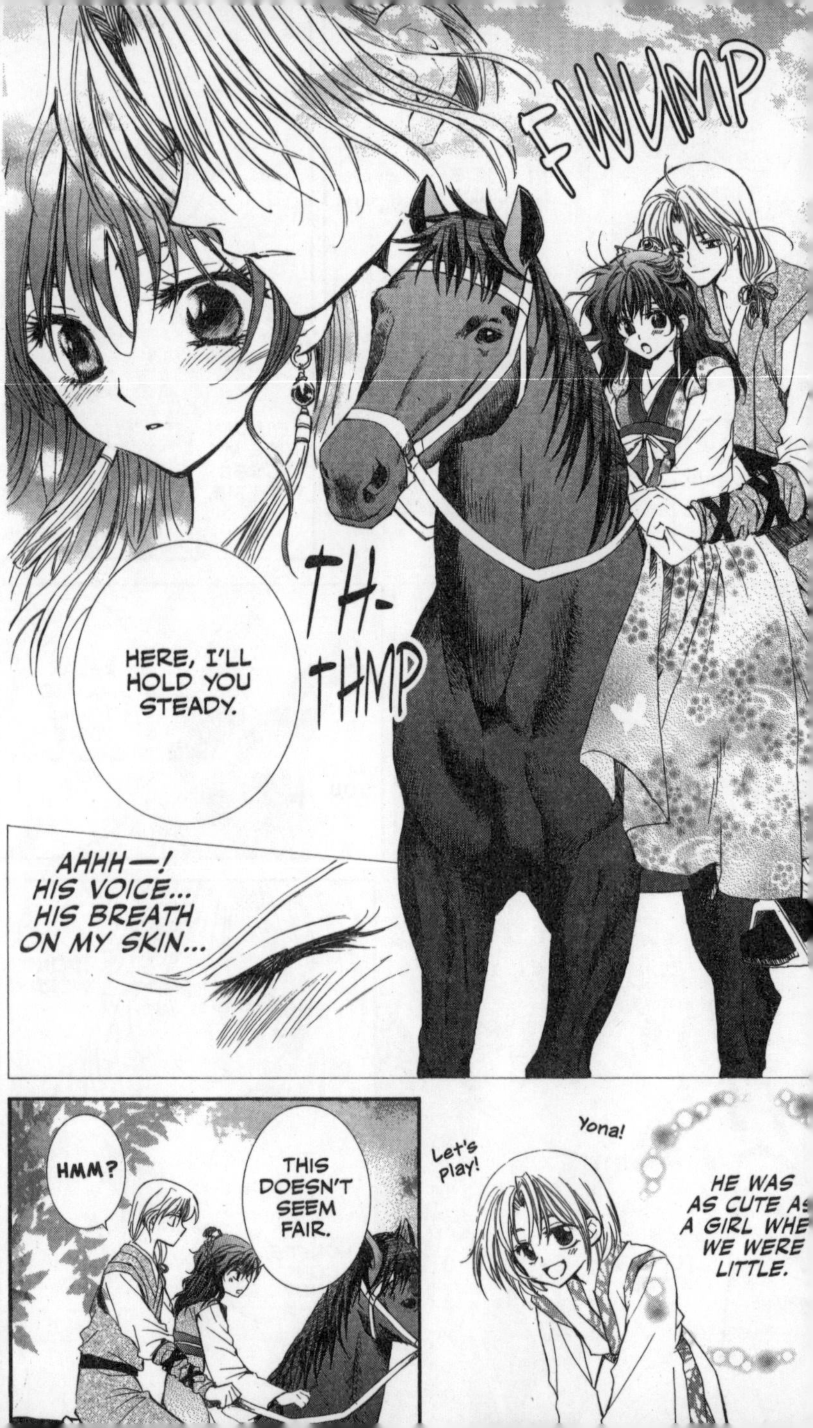
FWUMP
TH-THMP
HERE, I'LL HOLD YOU STEADY.
AHHH—! HIS VOICE... HIS BREATH ON MY SKIN...
Yona!
Let's play!
HE WAS AS CUTE AS A GIRL WHE WE WERE LITTLE.
THIS DOESN'T SEEM FAIR.
HMM?

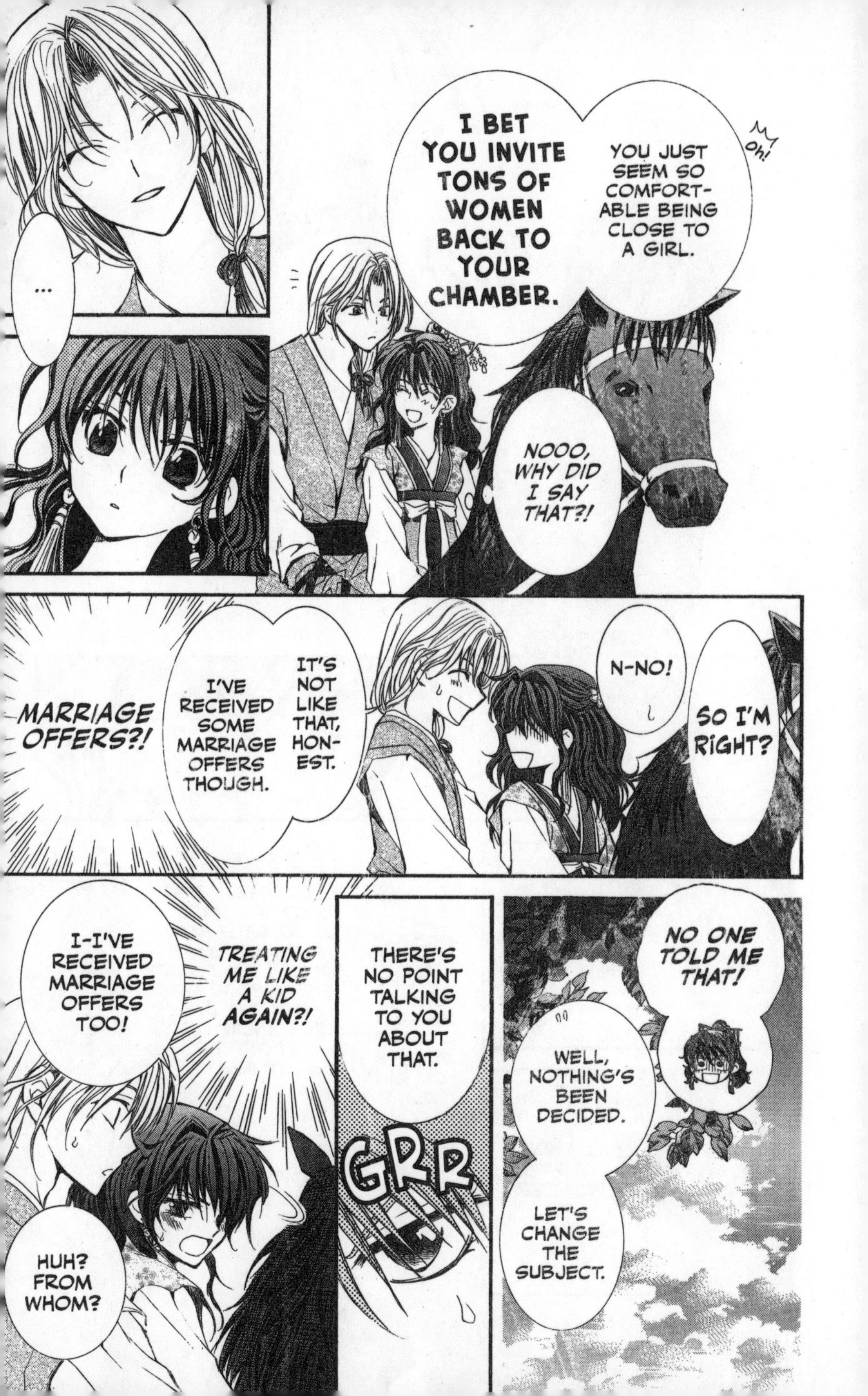
Oh!
YOU JUST SEEM SO COMFORT-ABLE BEING CLOSE TO A GIRL.
I BET YOU INVITE TONS OF WOMEN BACK TO YOUR CHAMBER.
NOOO, WHY DID I SAY THAT?!
...
SO I'M RIGHT?
N-NO!
IT'S NOT LIKE THAT, HON-EST.
I'VE RECEIVED SOME MARRIAGE OFFERS THOUGH.
MARRIAGE OFFERS?!
NO ONE TOLD ME THAT!
WELL, NOTHING'S BEEN DECIDED.
LET'S CHANGE THE SUBJECT.
THERE'S NO POINT TALKING TO YOU ABOUT THAT.
GRR
TREATING ME LIKE A KID AGAIN?!
I-I'VE RECEIVED MARRIAGE OFFERS TOO!
HUH? FROM WHOM?

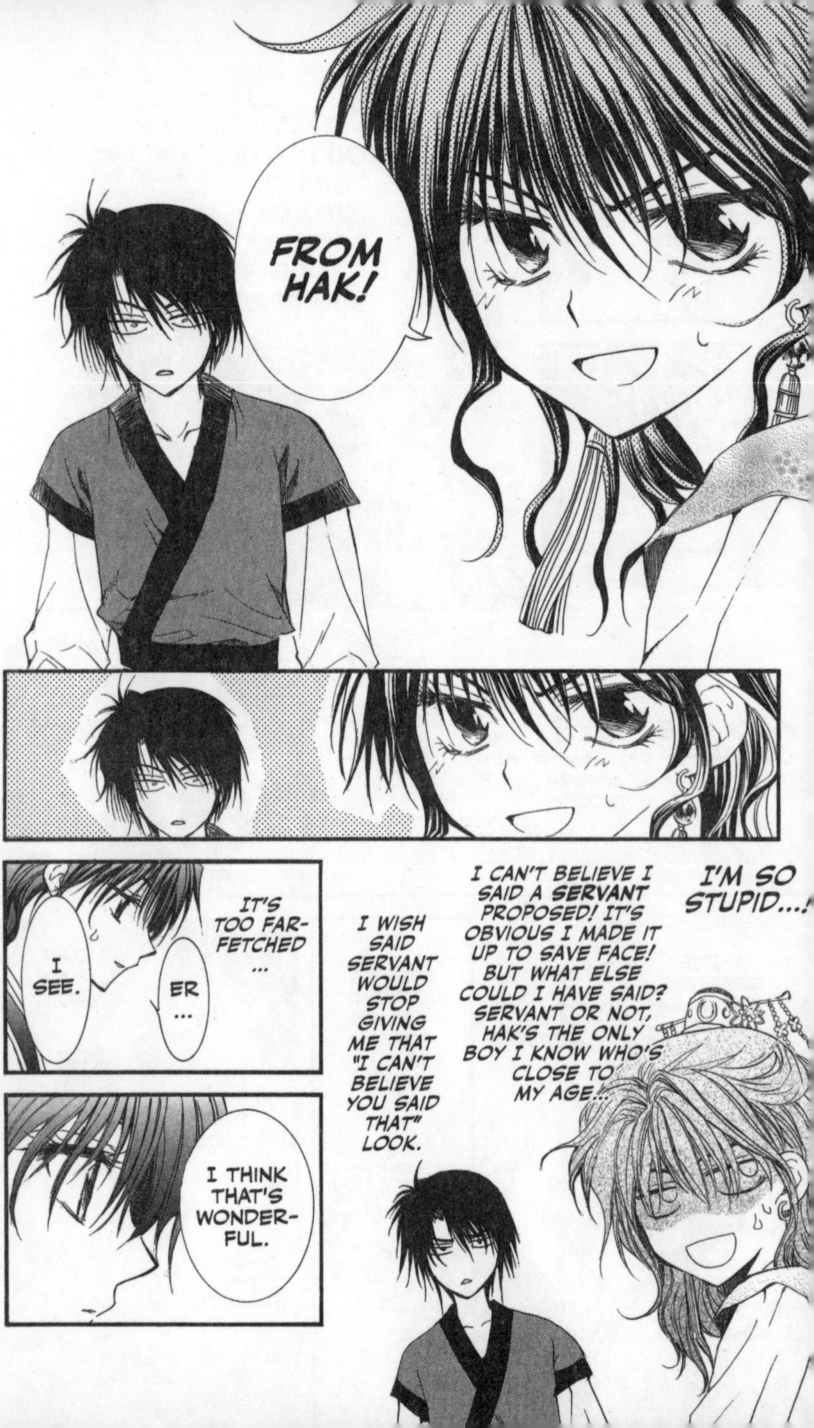
FROM HAK!
I'M SO STUPID...!
I CAN'T BELIEVE I SAID A SERVANT PROPOSED! IT'S OBVIOUS I MADE IT UP TO SAVE FACE! BUT WHAT ELSE COULD I HAVE SAID? SERVANT OR NOT, HAK'S THE ONLY BOY I KNOW WHO'S CLOSE TO MY AGE...
I WISH SAID SERVANT WOULD STOP GIVING ME THAT "I CAN'T BELIEVE YOU SAID THAT" LOOK.
IT'S TOO FAR-FETCHED ...
ER ...
I SEE.
I THINK THAT'S WONDERFUL.

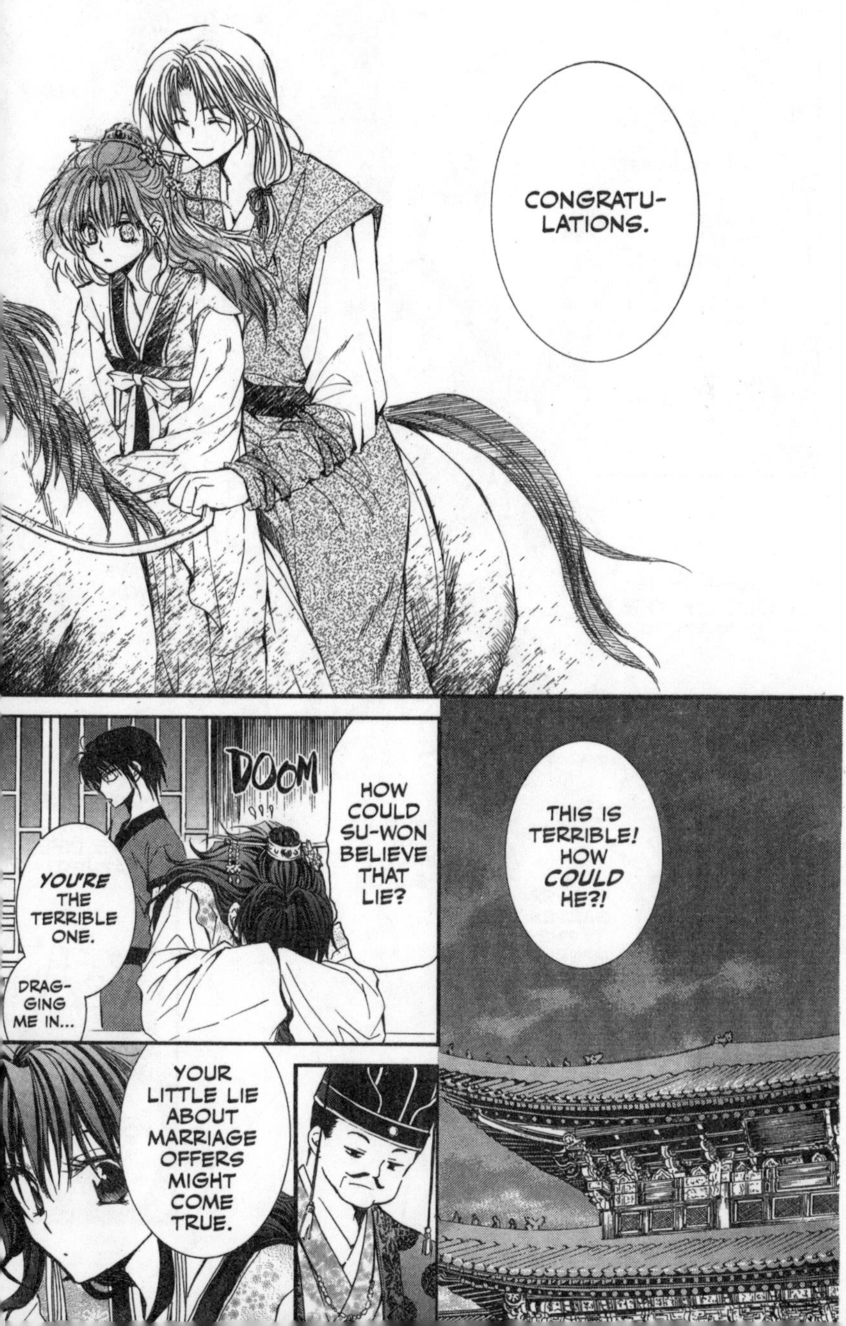
CONGRATU-LATIONS.
THIS IS TERRIBLE! HOW *COULD* HE?!
DOOM
HOW COULD SU-WON BELIEVE THAT LIE?
YOU'RE THE TERRIBLE ONE.
DRAG-GING ME IN...
YOUR LITTLE LIE ABOUT MARRIAGE OFFERS MIGHT COME TRUE.

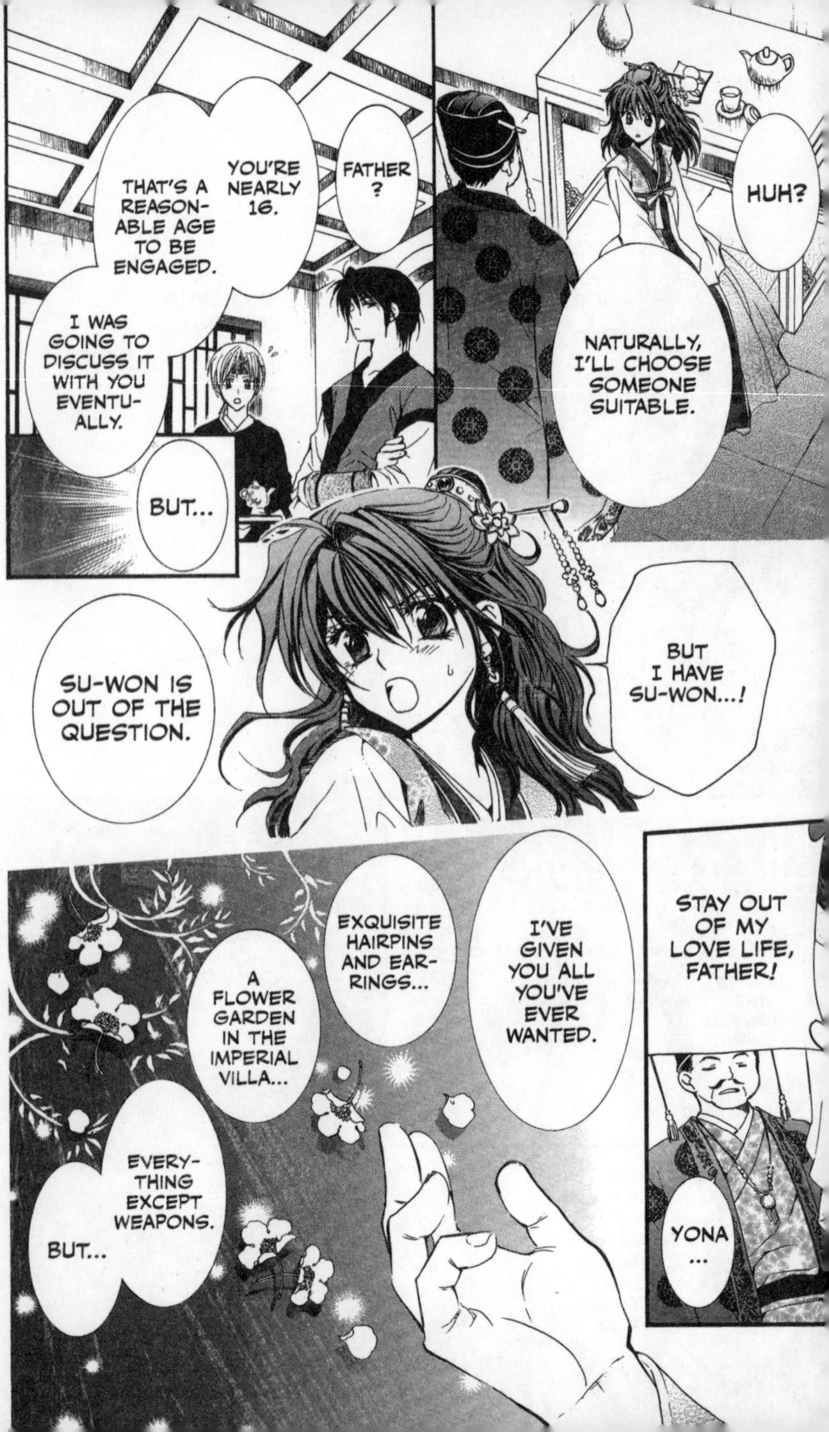
HUH?
NATURALLY, I'LL CHOOSE SOMEONE SUITABLE.
FATHER?
YOU'RE NEARLY 16.
THAT'S A REASON-ABLE AGE TO BE ENGAGED.
I WAS GOING TO DISCUSS IT WITH YOU EVENTU-ALLY.
BUT...
BUT I HAVE SU-WON...!
SU-WON IS OUT OF THE QUESTION.
STAY OUT OF MY LOVE LIFE, FATHER!
YONA...
I'VE GIVEN YOU ALL YOU'VE EVER WANTED.
EXQUISITE HAIRPINS AND EAR-RINGS...
A FLOWER GARDEN IN THE IMPERIAL VILLA...
EVERY-THING EXCEPT WEAPONS.
BUT...

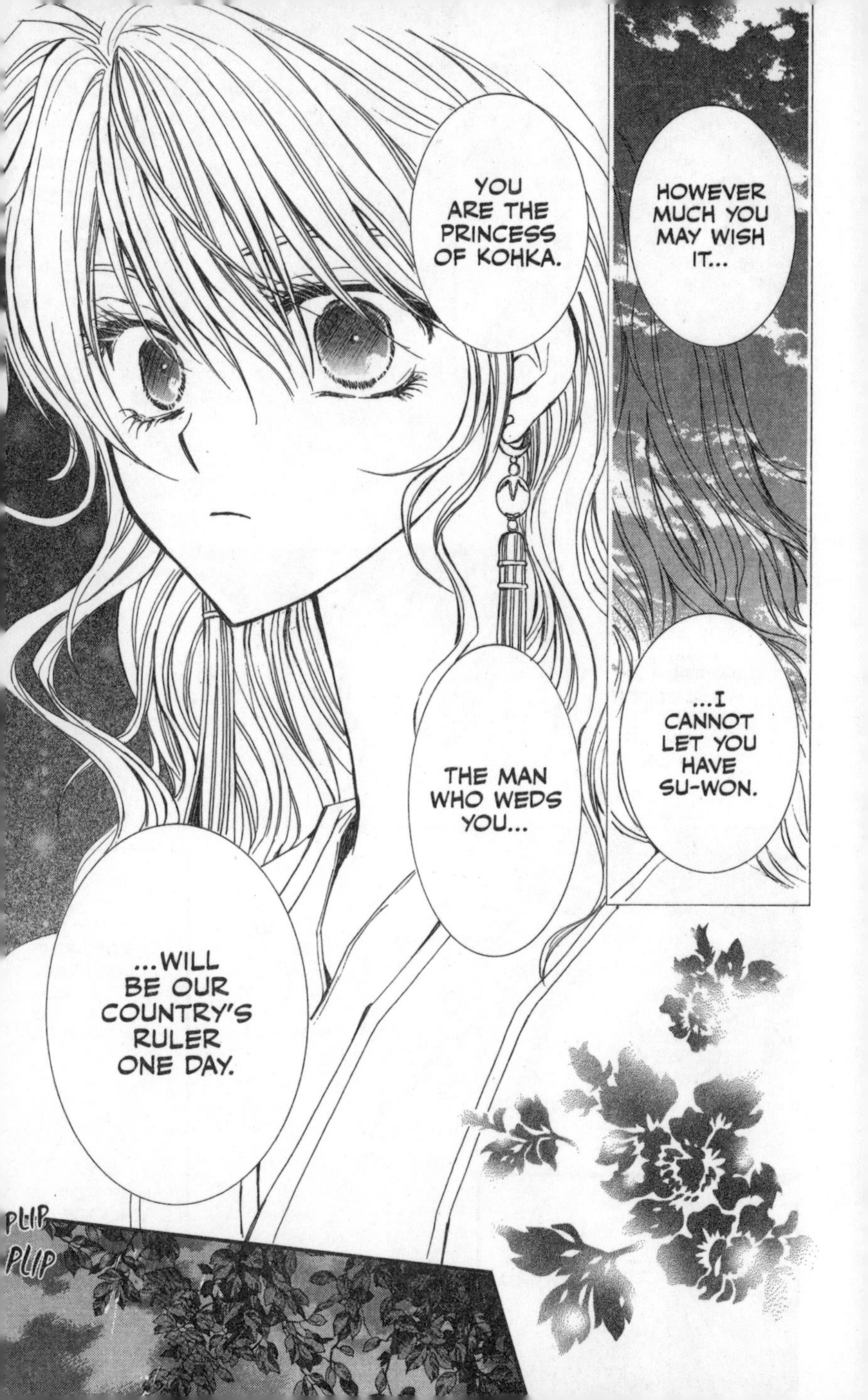
HOWEVER MUCH YOU MAY WISH IT...
...I CANNOT LET YOU HAVE SU-WON.
YOU ARE THE PRINCESS OF KOHKA.
THE MAN WHO WEDS YOU...
...WILL BE OUR COUNTRY'S RULER ONE DAY.
PLIP PLIP

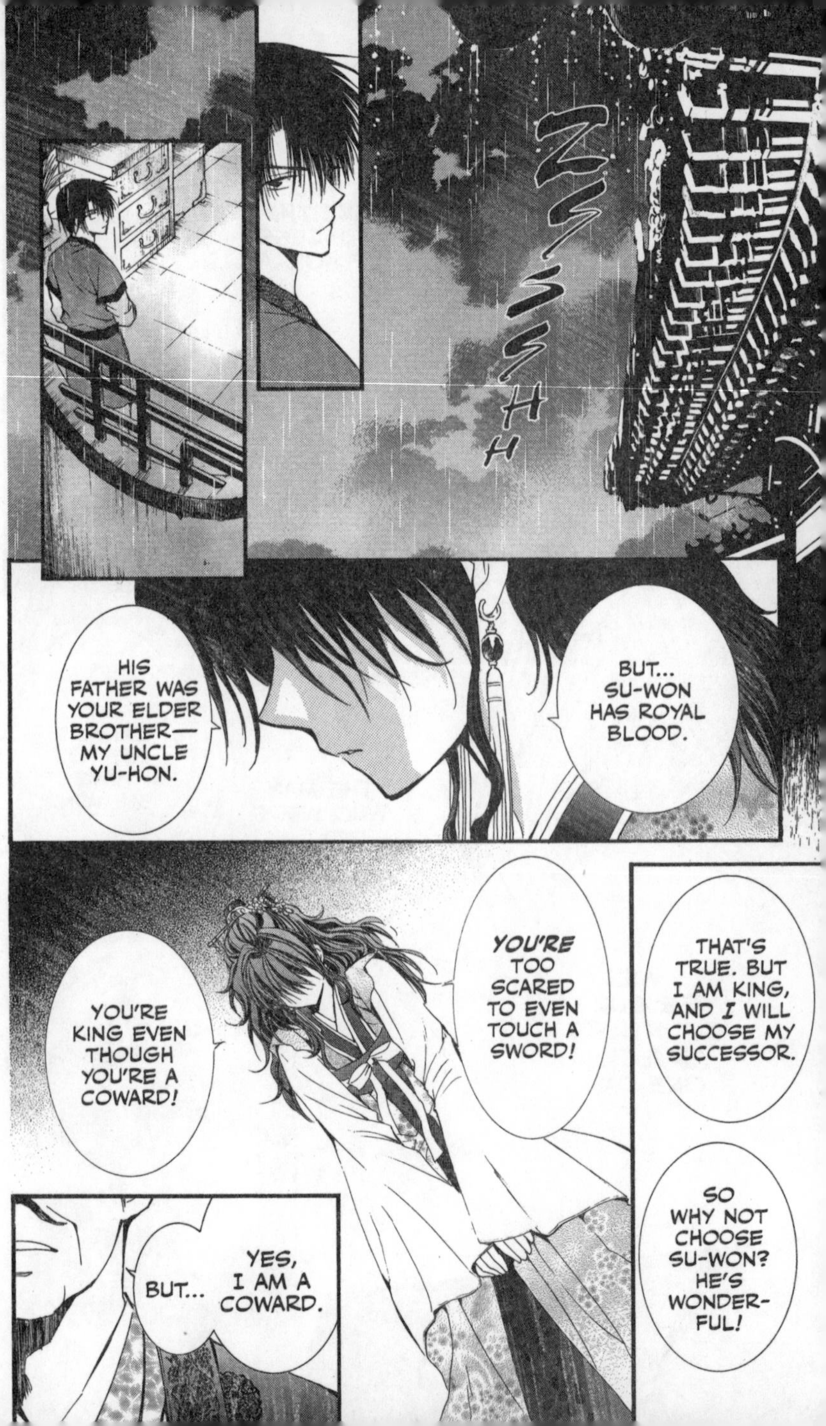
ZSSSHHH
BUT... SU-WON HAS ROYAL BLOOD.
HIS FATHER WAS YOUR ELDER BROTHER— MY UNCLE YU-HON.
THAT'S TRUE. BUT I AM KING, AND *I* WILL CHOOSE MY SUCCESSOR.
SO WHY NOT CHOOSE SU-WON? HE'S WONDER-FUL!
YOU'RE TOO SCARED TO EVEN TOUCH A SWORD!
YOU'RE KING EVEN THOUGH YOU'RE A COWARD!
YES, I AM A COWARD.
BUT...

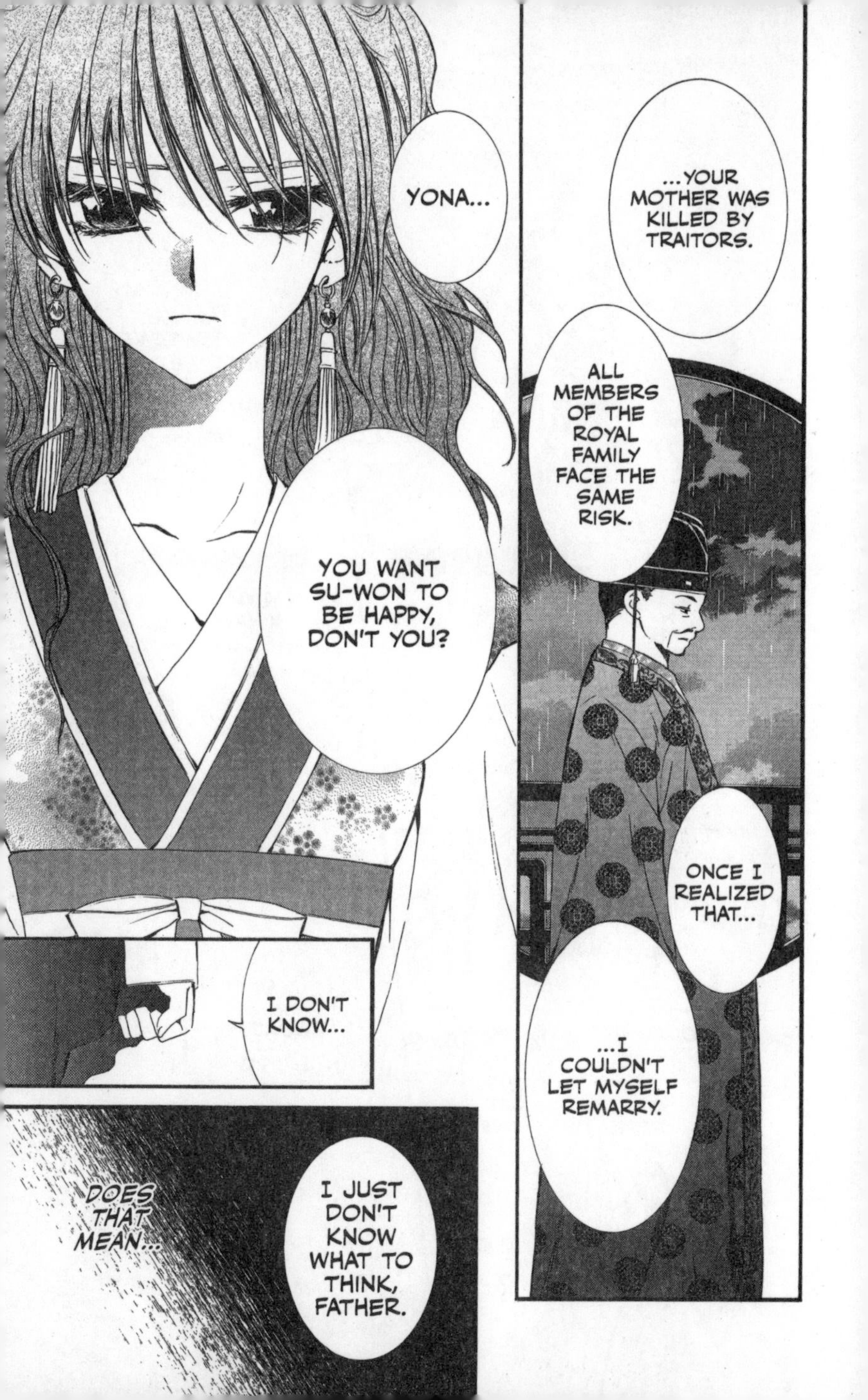
...YOUR MOTHER WAS KILLED BY TRAITORS.
ALL MEMBERS OF THE ROYAL FAMILY FACE THE SAME RISK.
ONCE I REALIZED THAT...
...I COULDN'T LET MYSELF REMARRY.
YONA...
YOU WANT SU-WON TO BE HAPPY, DON'T YOU?
I DON'T KNOW...
I JUST DON'T KNOW WHAT TO THINK, FATHER.
DOES THAT MEAN...

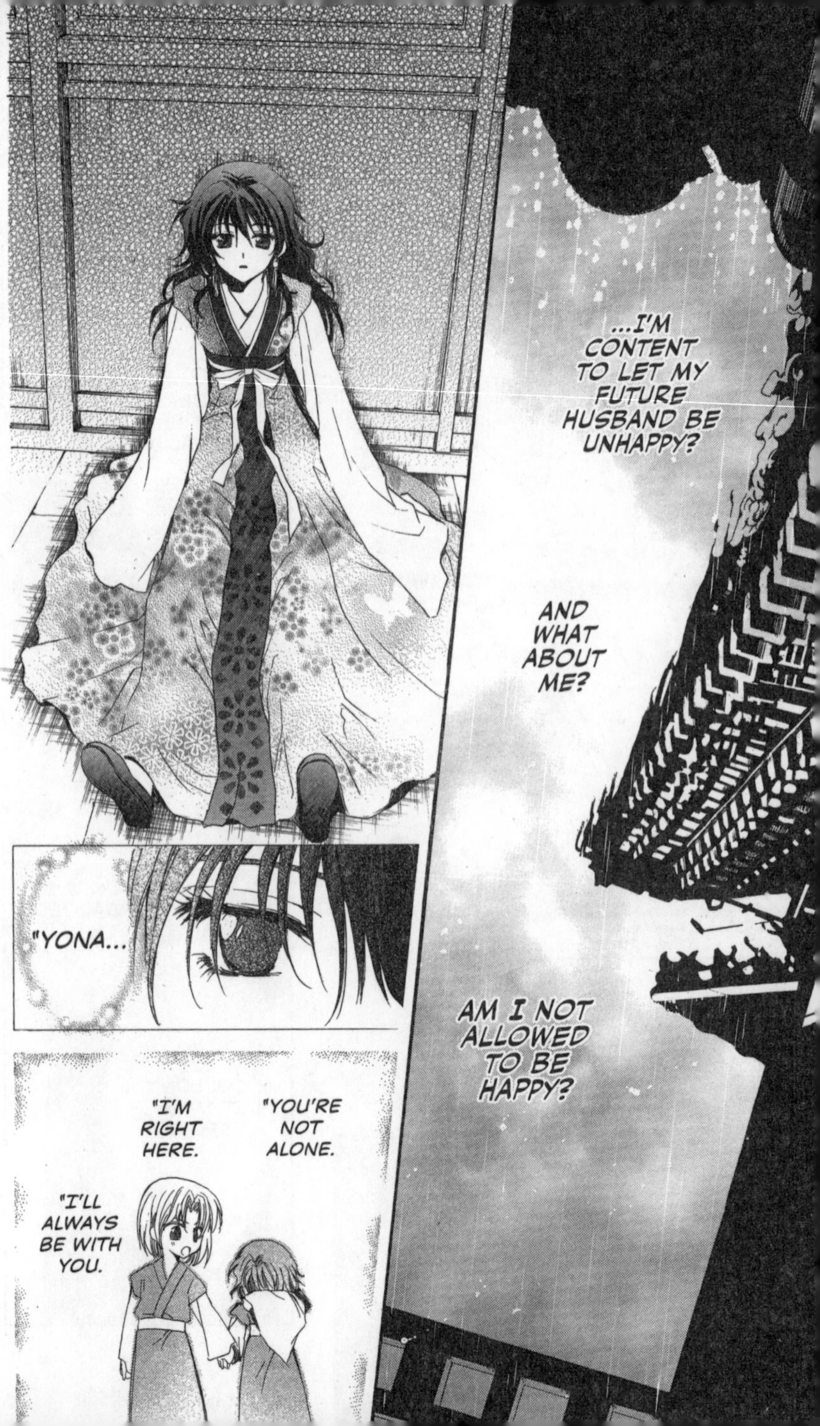
...I'M CONTENT TO LET MY FUTURE HUSBAND BE UNHAPPY?
AND WHAT ABOUT ME?
AM I NOT ALLOWED TO BE HAPPY?
"YONA...
"YOU'RE NOT ALONE.
"I'M RIGHT HERE.
"I'LL ALWAYS BE WITH YOU.

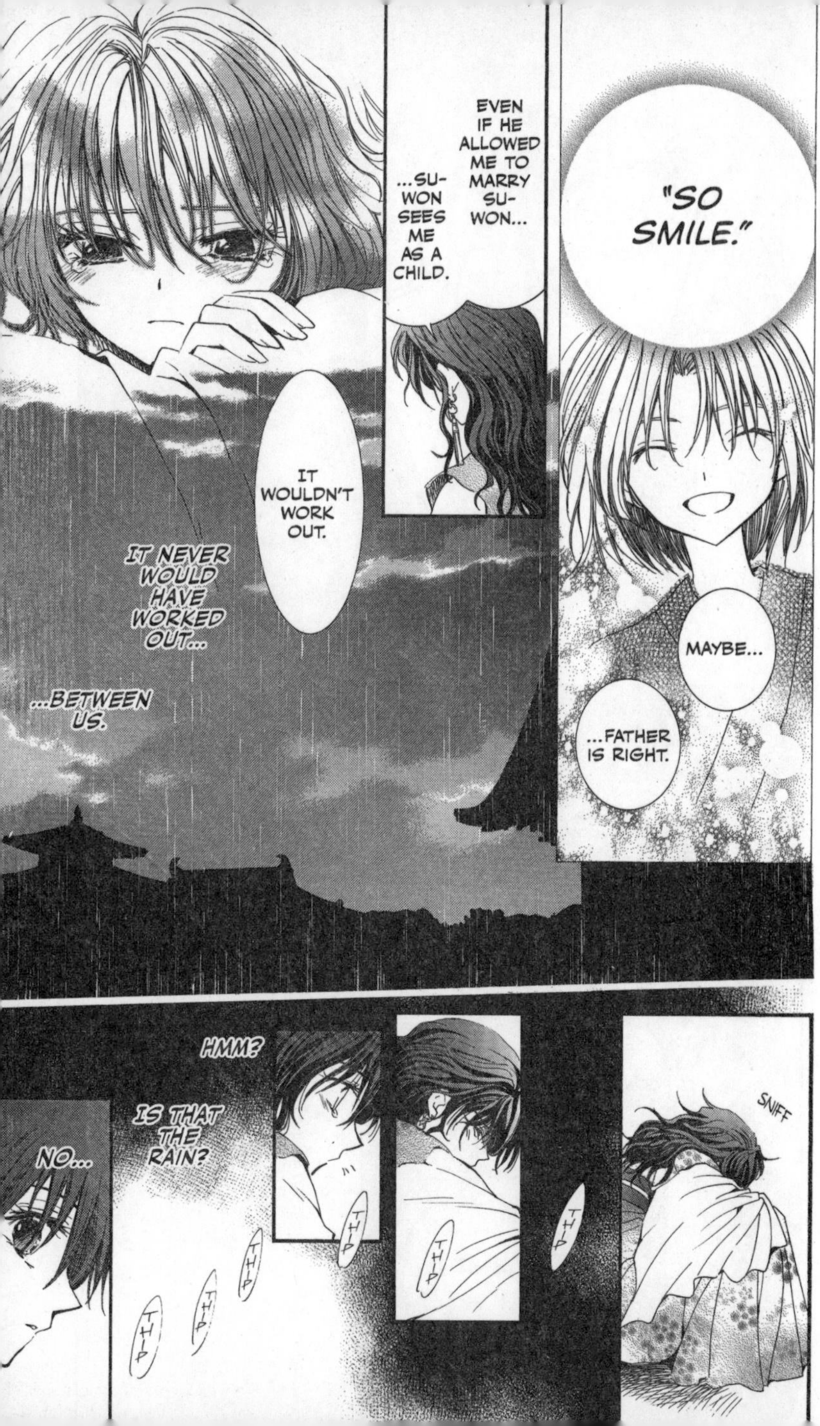
"SO SMILE."
MAYBE...
...FATHER IS RIGHT.
EVEN IF HE ALLOWED ME TO MARRY SU-WON...
...SU-WON SEES ME AS A CHILD.
IT WOULDN'T WORK OUT.
IT NEVER WOULD HAVE WORKED OUT...
...BETWEEN US.
SNIFF
THIP
THIP
HMM?
IS THAT THE RAIN?
THIP
NO...
THIP
THIP
THIP

IT'S FOOTSTEPS...

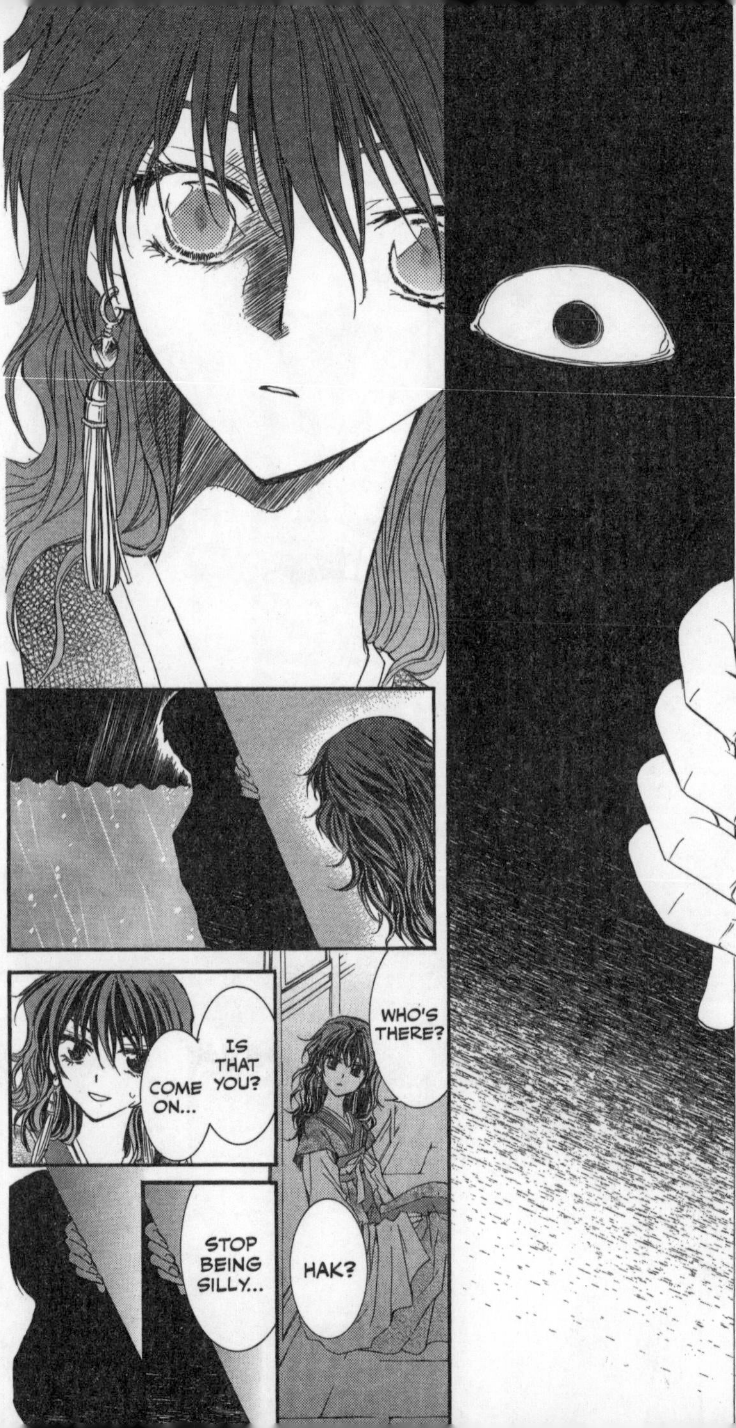
WHO'S THERE?
HAK?
IS THAT YOU?
COME ON...
STOP BEING SILLY...

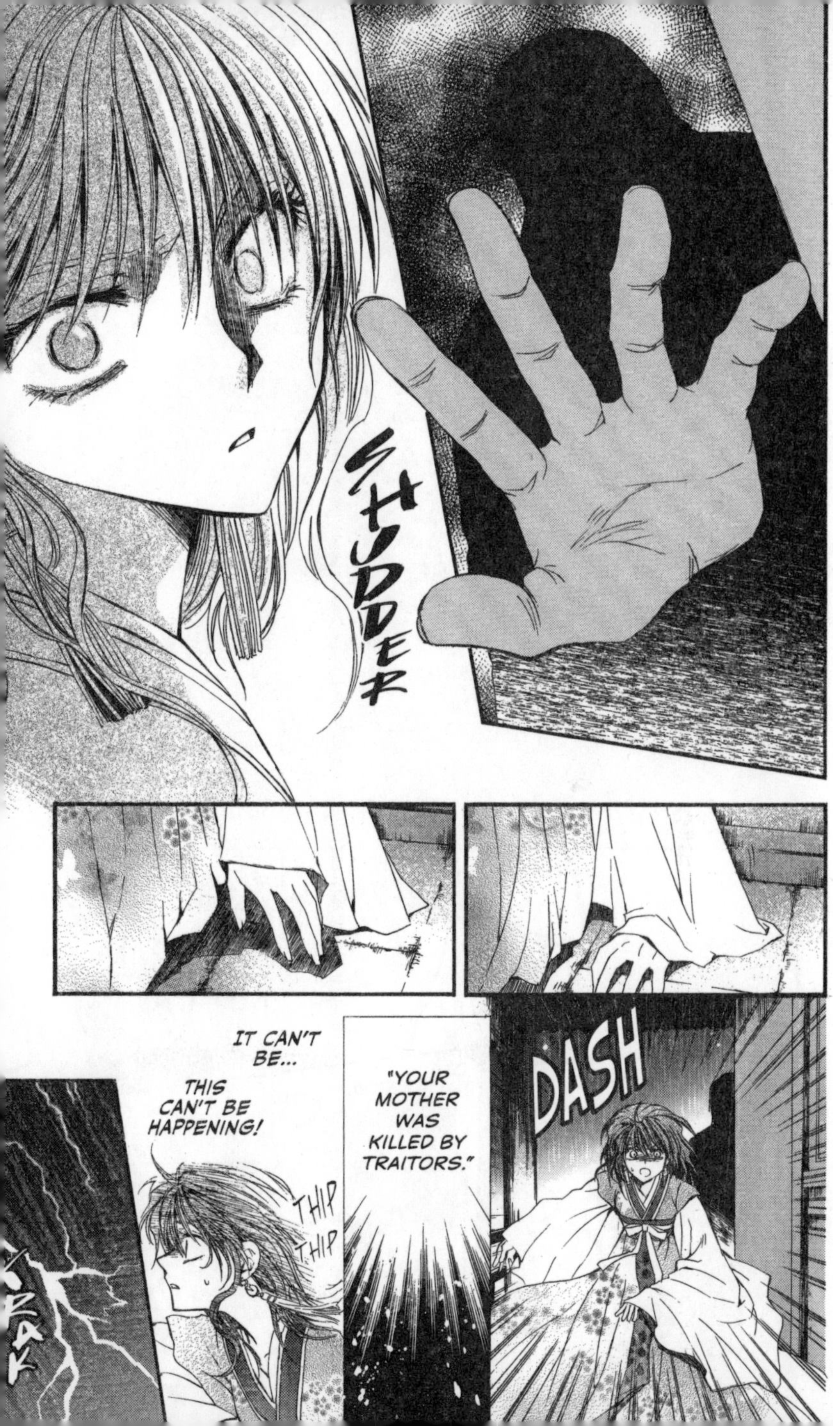
SHUDDER
DASH
"YOUR MOTHER WAS KILLED BY TRAITORS."
IT CAN'T BE...
THIS CAN'T BE HAPPENING!
THIP THIP

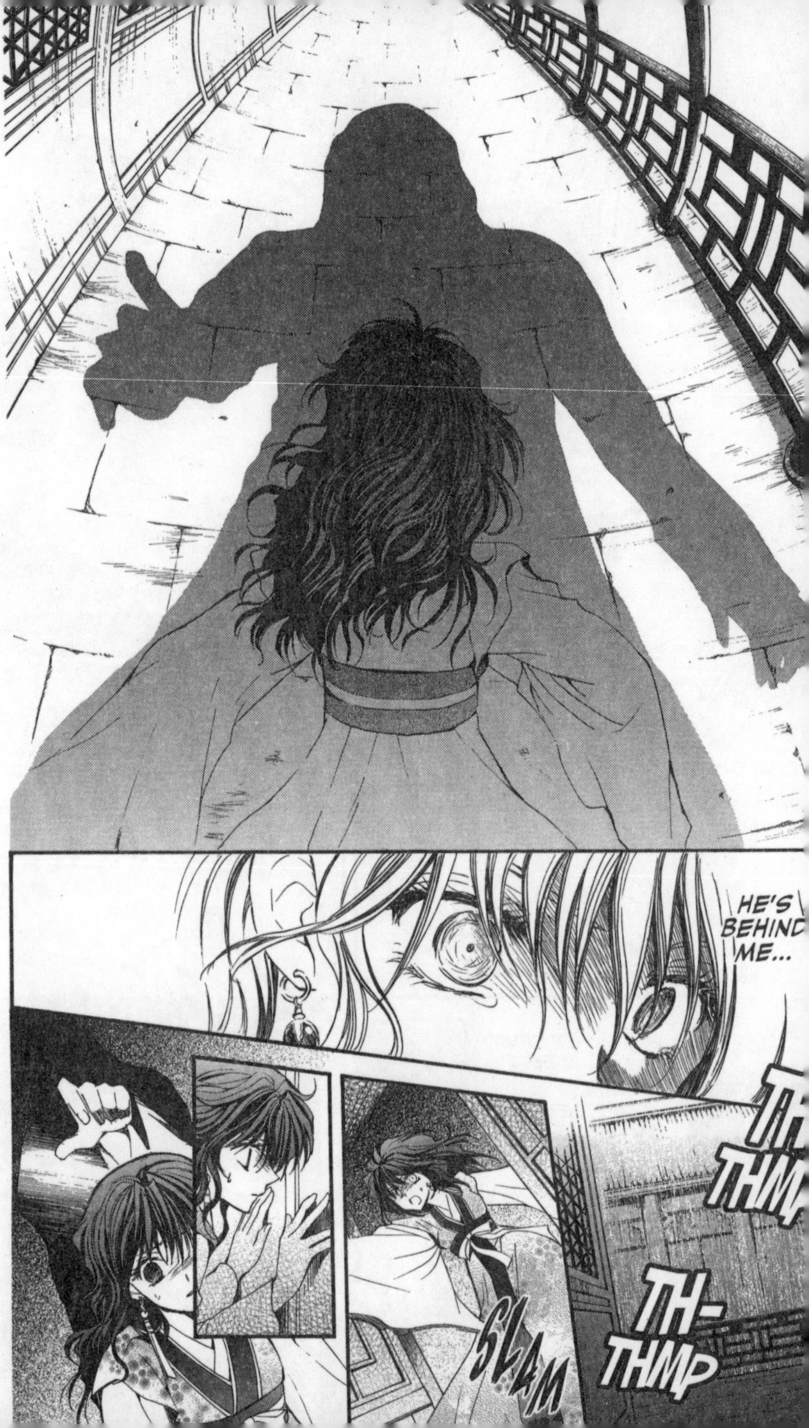
HE'S BEHIND ME...
TH-THMP
TH-THMP
SLAM

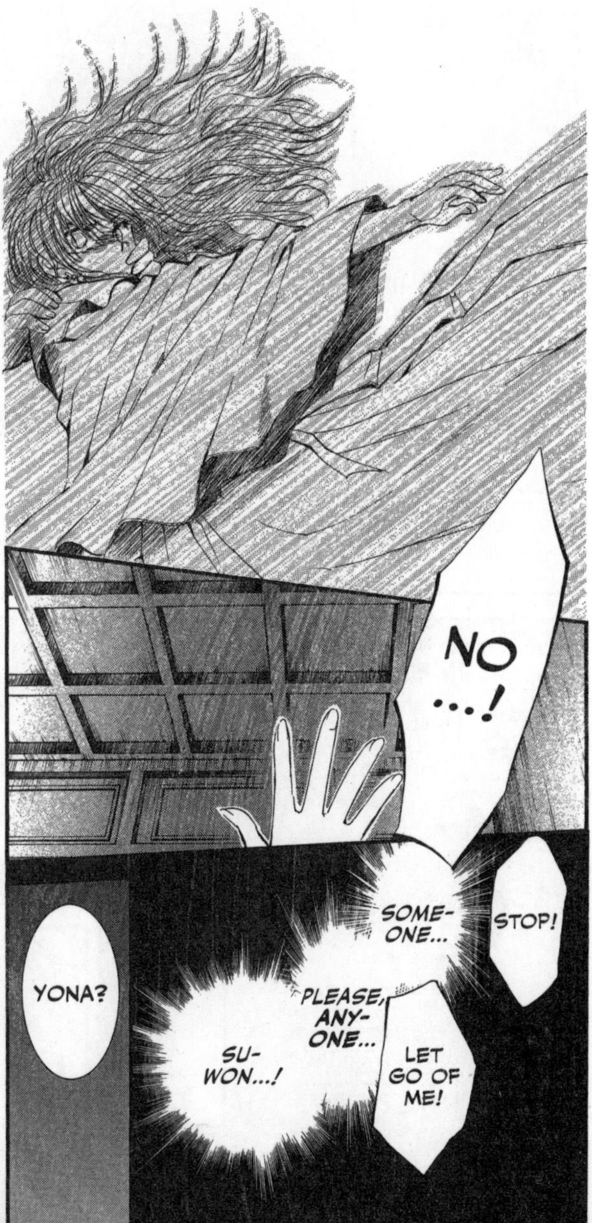
NO ...!
STOP!
SOME-ONE...
LET GO OF ME!
PLEASE, ANY-ONE...
SU-WON...!
YONA?

From my first publication through *NG Life*, my editor H and I worked together to hash out how my stories were going to go. But for *Yona* I was transferred to editor Y. Without H, I wouldn't have had *Mugen Spiral*, *Game x Rush* or *NG*, and without Y, I wouldn't have *Yona*. Thank you both!

I wasn't too sure about whether or not to do *Yona*, but editor Y gave me the encouragement I needed to go ahead with it.

I'm still pretty indecisive, but it helps that my editor makes quick decisions. I need to hang in there.

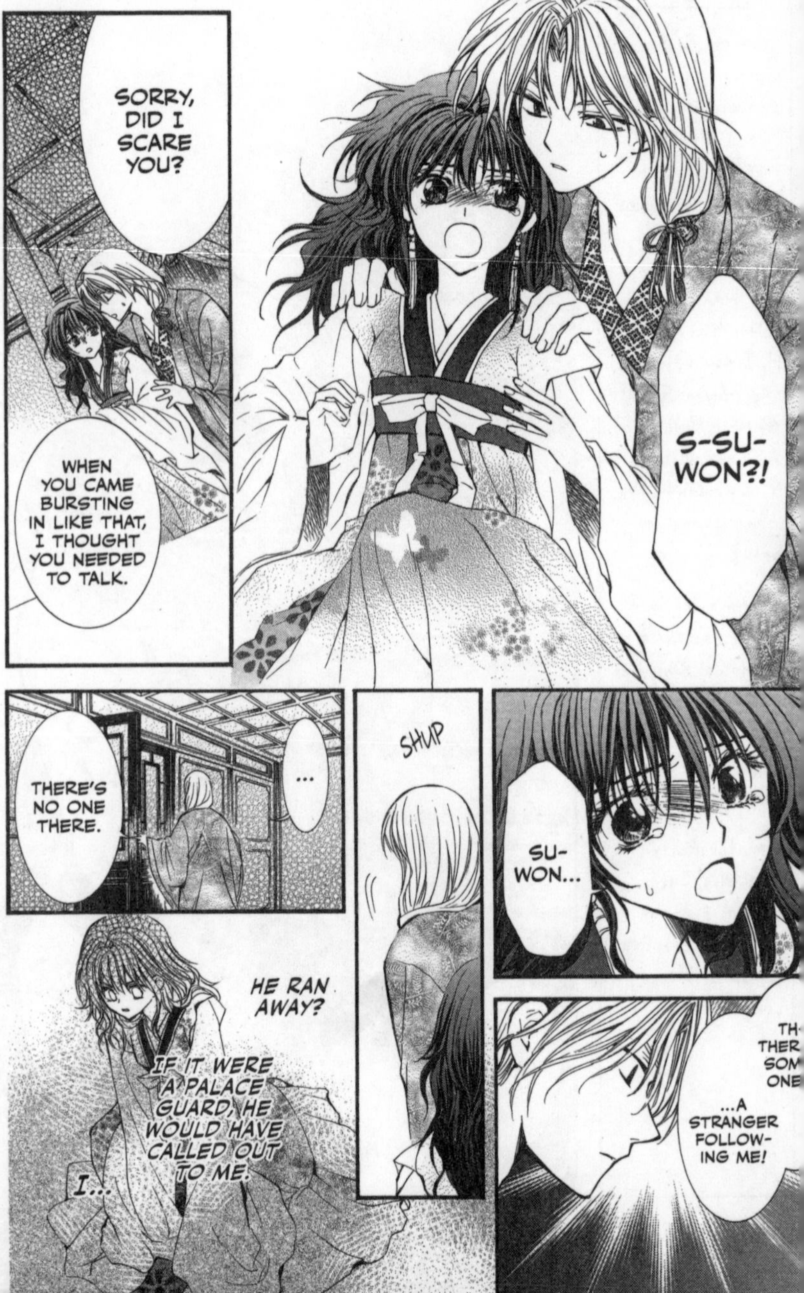
S-SU-WON?!
SORRY, DID I SCARE YOU?
WHEN YOU CAME BURSTING IN LIKE THAT, I THOUGHT YOU NEEDED TO TALK.
SU-WON...
TH- THER SOM ONE
...A STRANGER FOLLOWING ME!
SHUP
...
THERE'S NO ONE THERE.
HE RAN AWAY?
IF IT WERE A PALACE GUARD, HE WOULD HAVE CALLED OUT TO ME.
I...

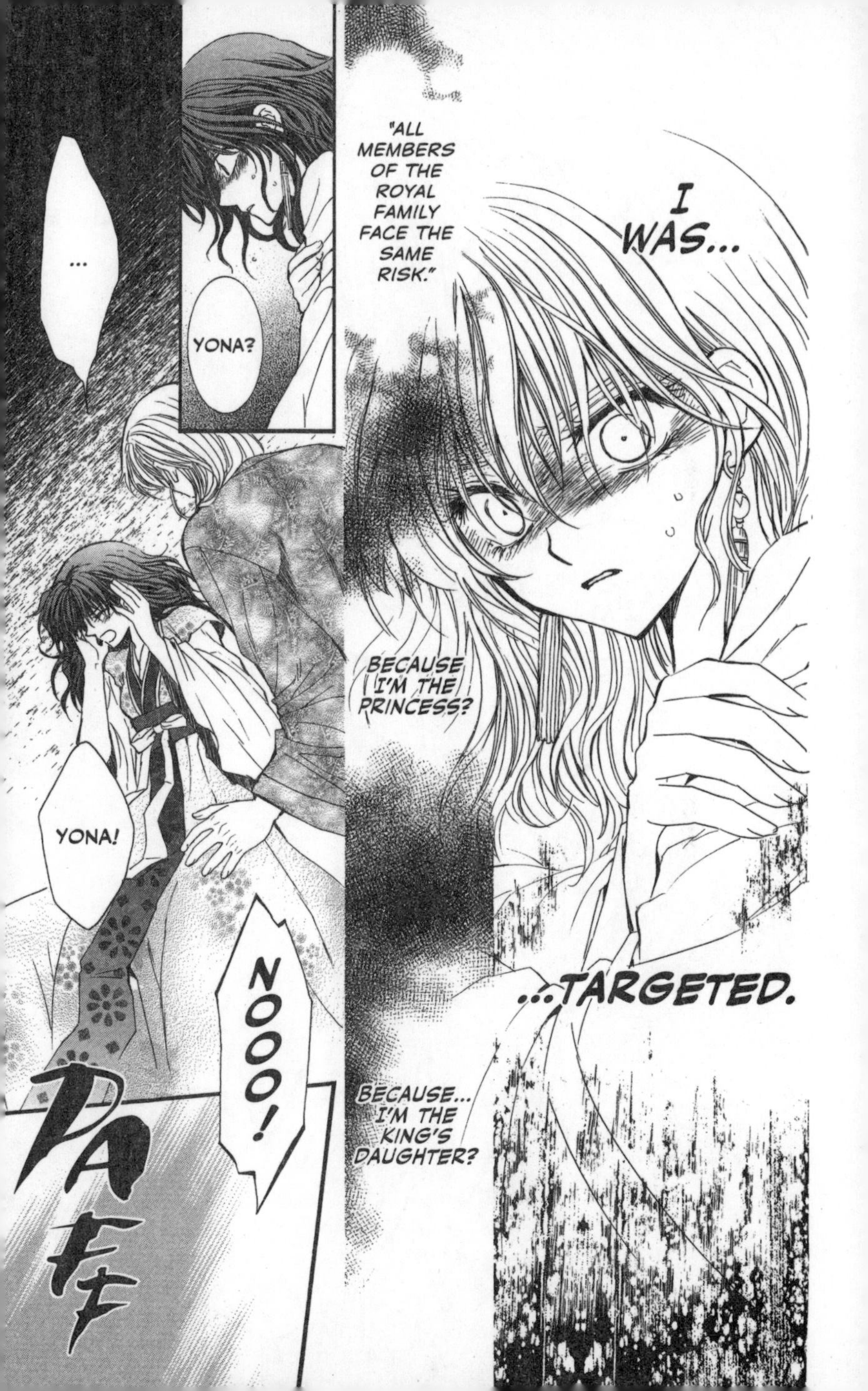
"ALL MEMBERS OF THE ROYAL FAMILY FACE THE SAME RISK."
I WAS...
BECAUSE I'M THE PRINCESS?
...TARGETED.
BECAUSE... I'M THE KING'S DAUGHTER?
YONA?
...
YONA!
NOOOO!

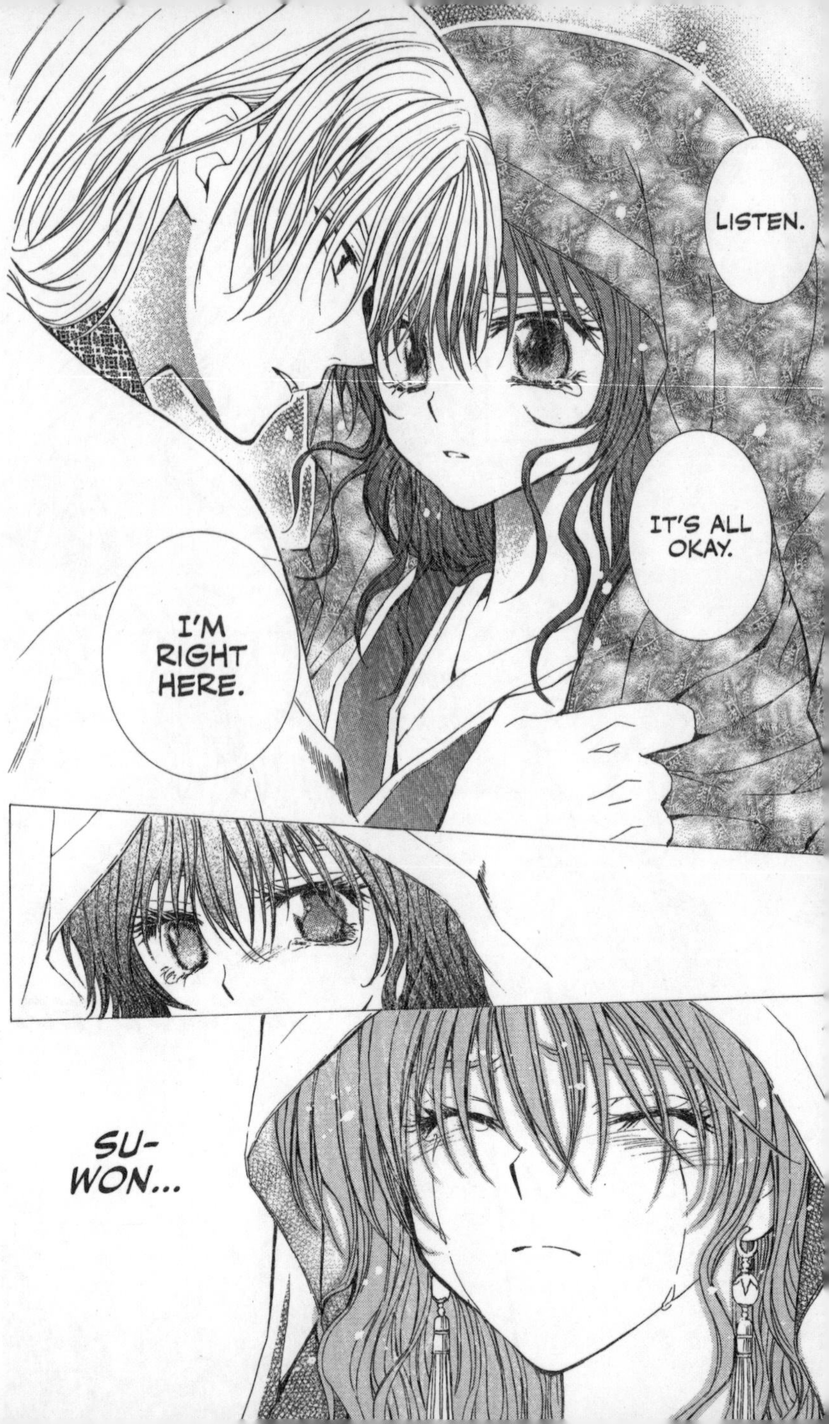
LISTEN.
IT'S ALL OKAY.
I'M RIGHT HERE.
SU-WON...

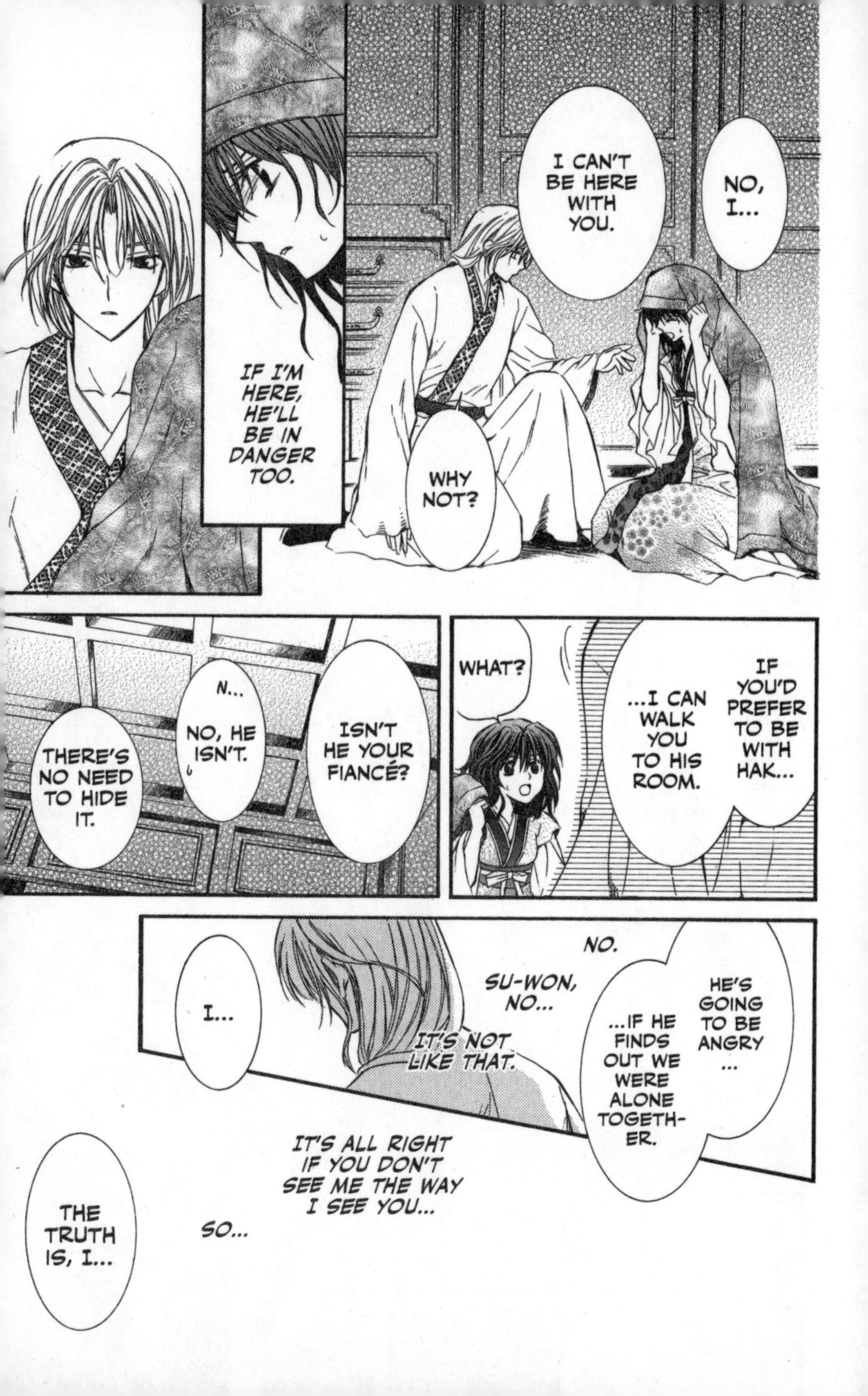
NO, I...
I CAN'T BE HERE WITH YOU.
WHY NOT?
IF I'M HERE, HE'LL BE IN DANGER TOO.
IF YOU'D PREFER TO BE WITH HAK...
...I CAN WALK YOU TO HIS ROOM.
WHAT?
ISN'T HE YOUR FIANCÉ?
N...
NO, HE ISN'T.
THERE'S NO NEED TO HIDE IT.
HE'S GOING TO BE ANGRY ...
...IF HE FINDS OUT WE WERE ALONE TOGETH-ER.
NO.
SU-WON, NO...
IT'S NOT LIKE THAT.
I...
IT'S ALL RIGHT IF YOU DON'T SEE ME THE WAY I SEE YOU...
SO...
THE TRUTH IS, I...

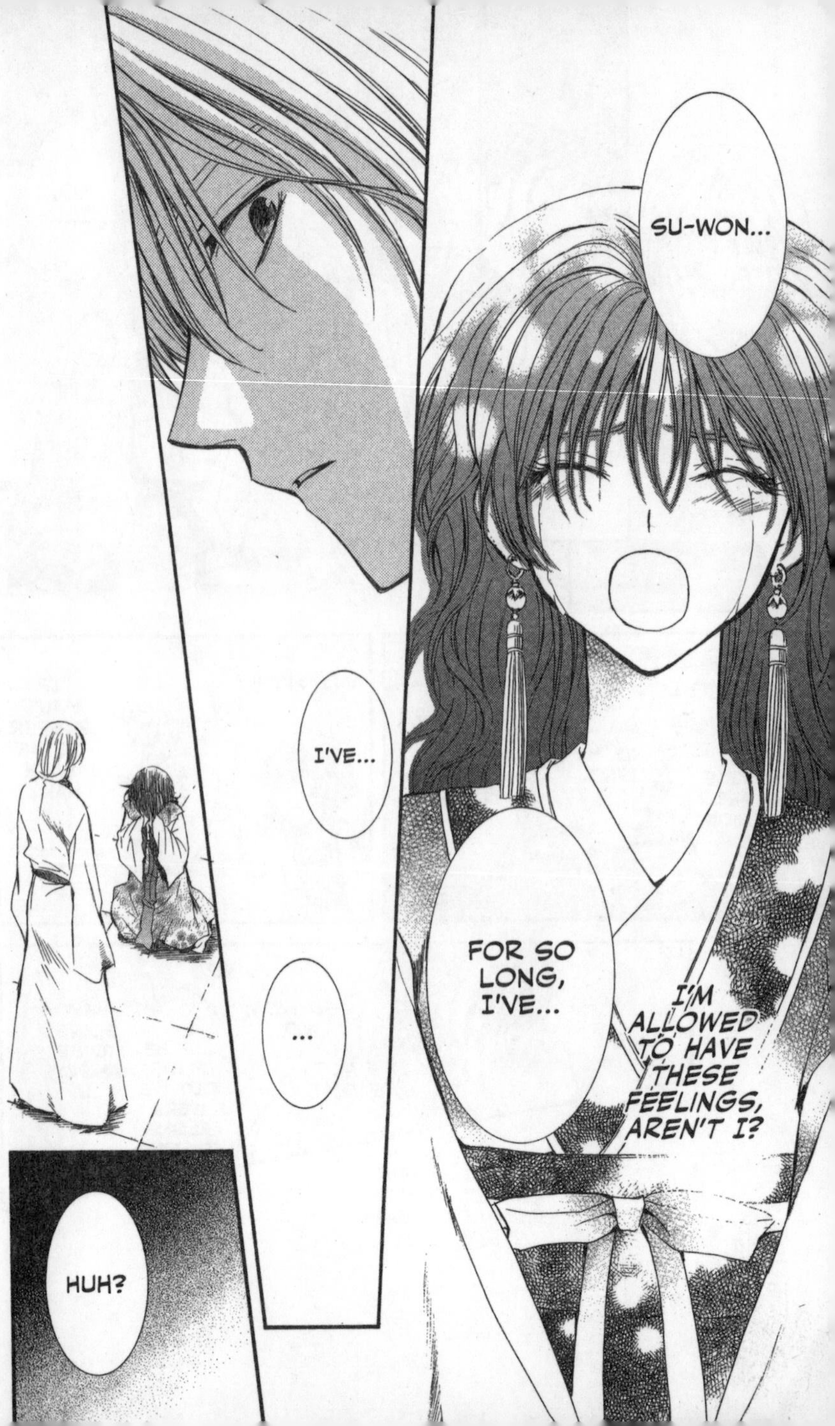
SU-WON...
FOR SO LONG, I'VE...
I'M ALLOWED TO HAVE THESE FEELINGS, AREN'T I?
I'VE...
...
HUH?

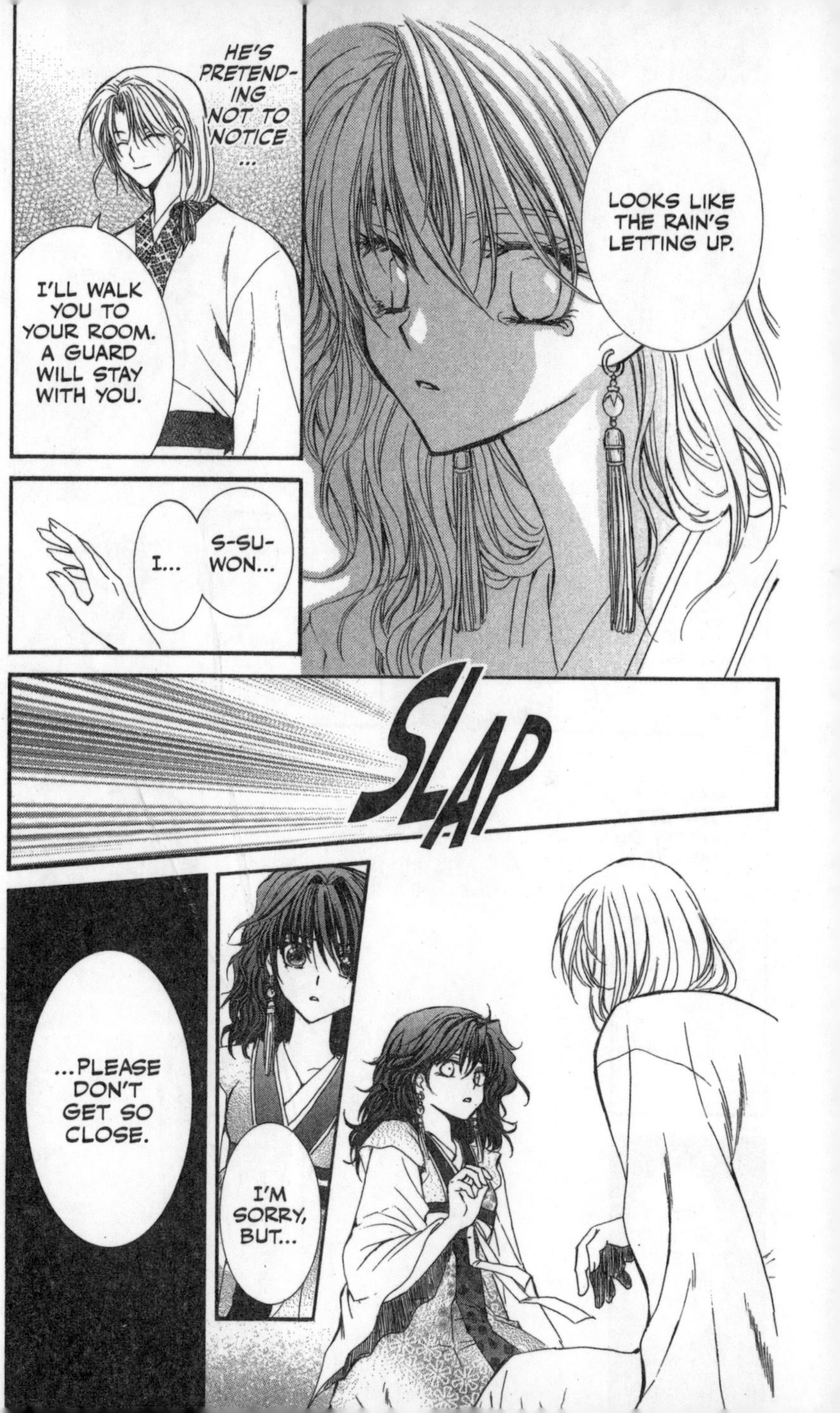
LOOKS LIKE THE RAIN'S LETTING UP.
HE'S PRETEND-ING NOT TO NOTICE ...
I'LL WALK YOU TO YOUR ROOM. A GUARD WILL STAY WITH YOU.
S-SU-WON...
I...
SLAP
I'M SORRY, BUT...
...PLEASE DON'T GET SO CLOSE.

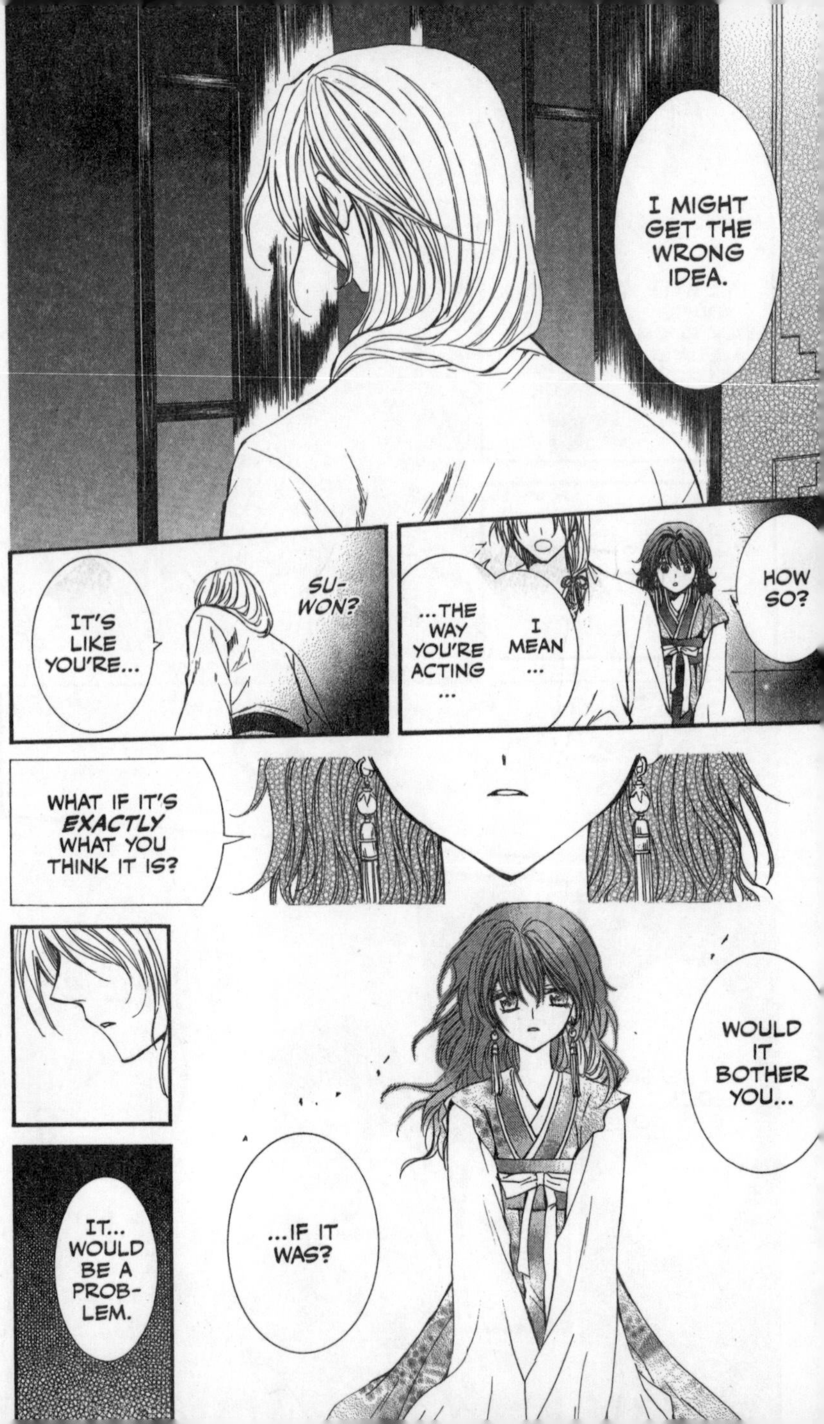
I MIGHT GET THE WRONG IDEA.
HOW SO?
I MEAN ...
...THE WAY YOU'RE ACTING ...
SU-WON?
IT'S LIKE YOU'RE...
WHAT IF IT'S *EXACTLY* WHAT YOU THINK IT IS?
WOULD IT BOTHER YOU...
...IF IT WAS?
IT... WOULD BE A PROBLEM.

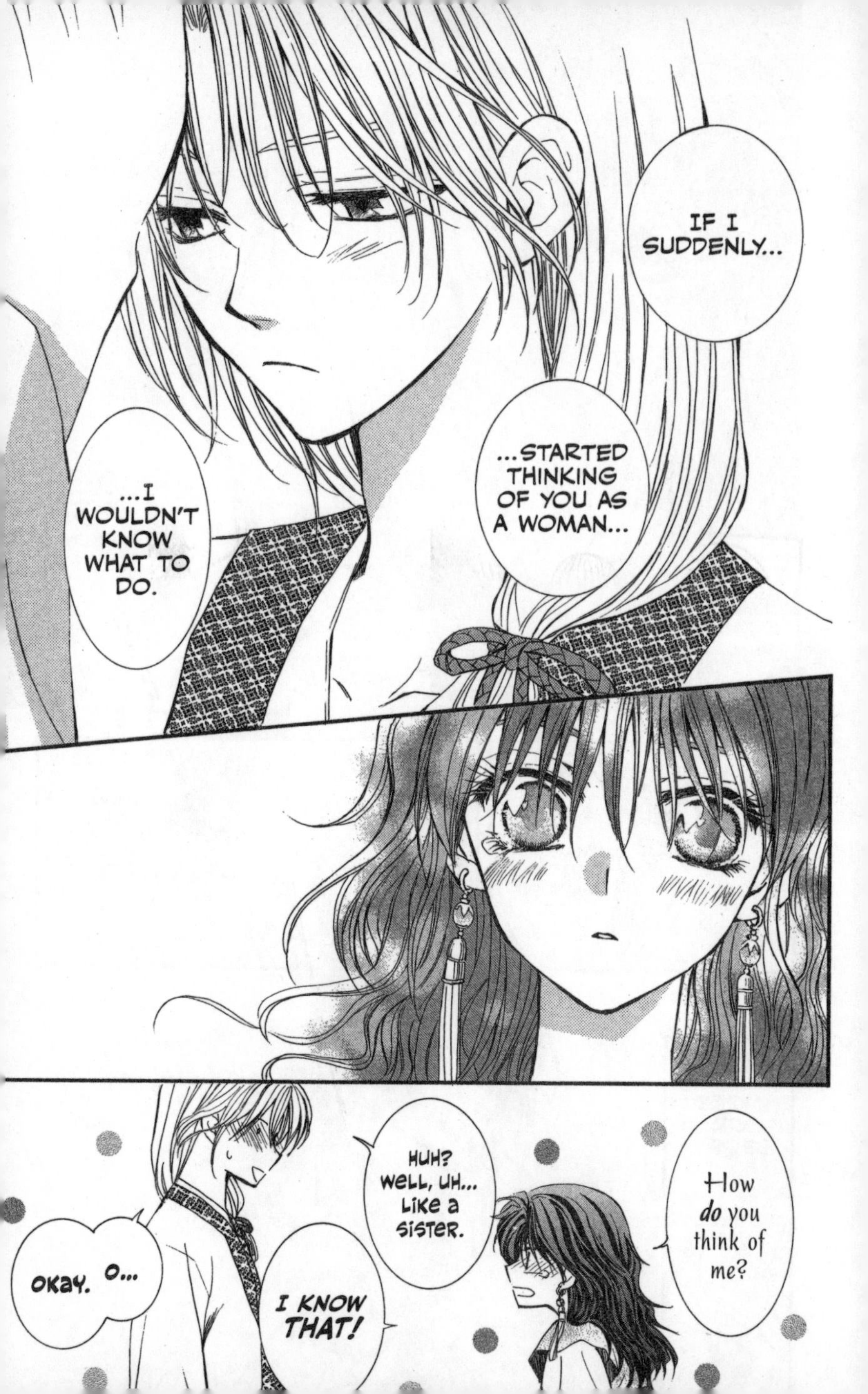
IF I SUDDENLY...
...STARTED THINKING OF YOU AS A WOMAN...
...I WOULDN'T KNOW WHAT TO DO.
How *do* you think of me?
HUH? WELL, UH... LIKE A SISTER.
I KNOW THAT!
O... OKAY.

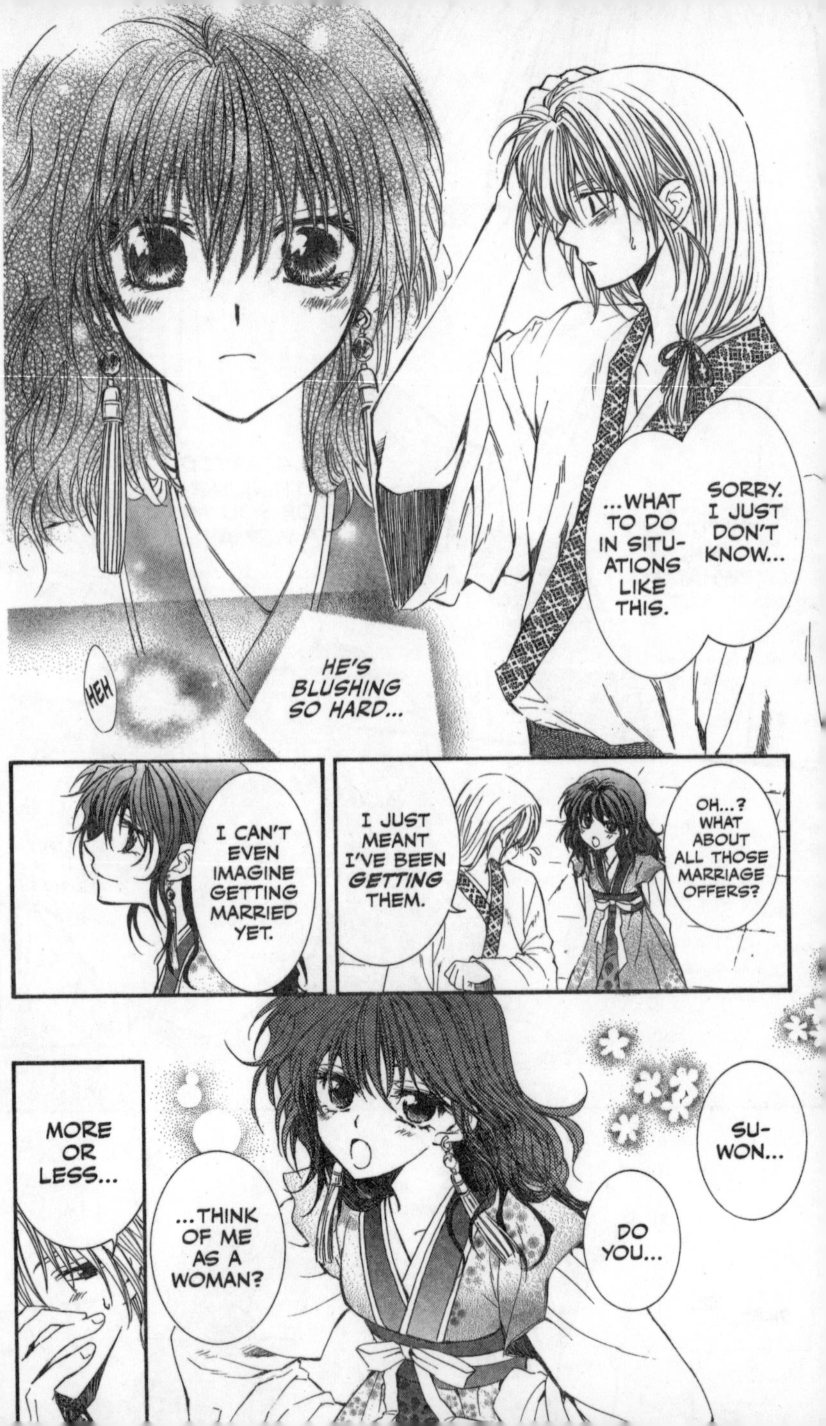
SORRY. I JUST DON'T KNOW...
...WHAT TO DO IN SITU-ATIONS LIKE THIS.
HE'S BLUSHING SO HARD...
HEH
OH...? WHAT ABOUT ALL THOSE MARRIAGE OFFERS?
I JUST MEANT I'VE BEEN *GETTING* THEM.
I CAN'T EVEN IMAGINE GETTING MARRIED YET.
SU-WON...
DO YOU...
...THINK OF ME AS A WOMAN?
MORE OR LESS...

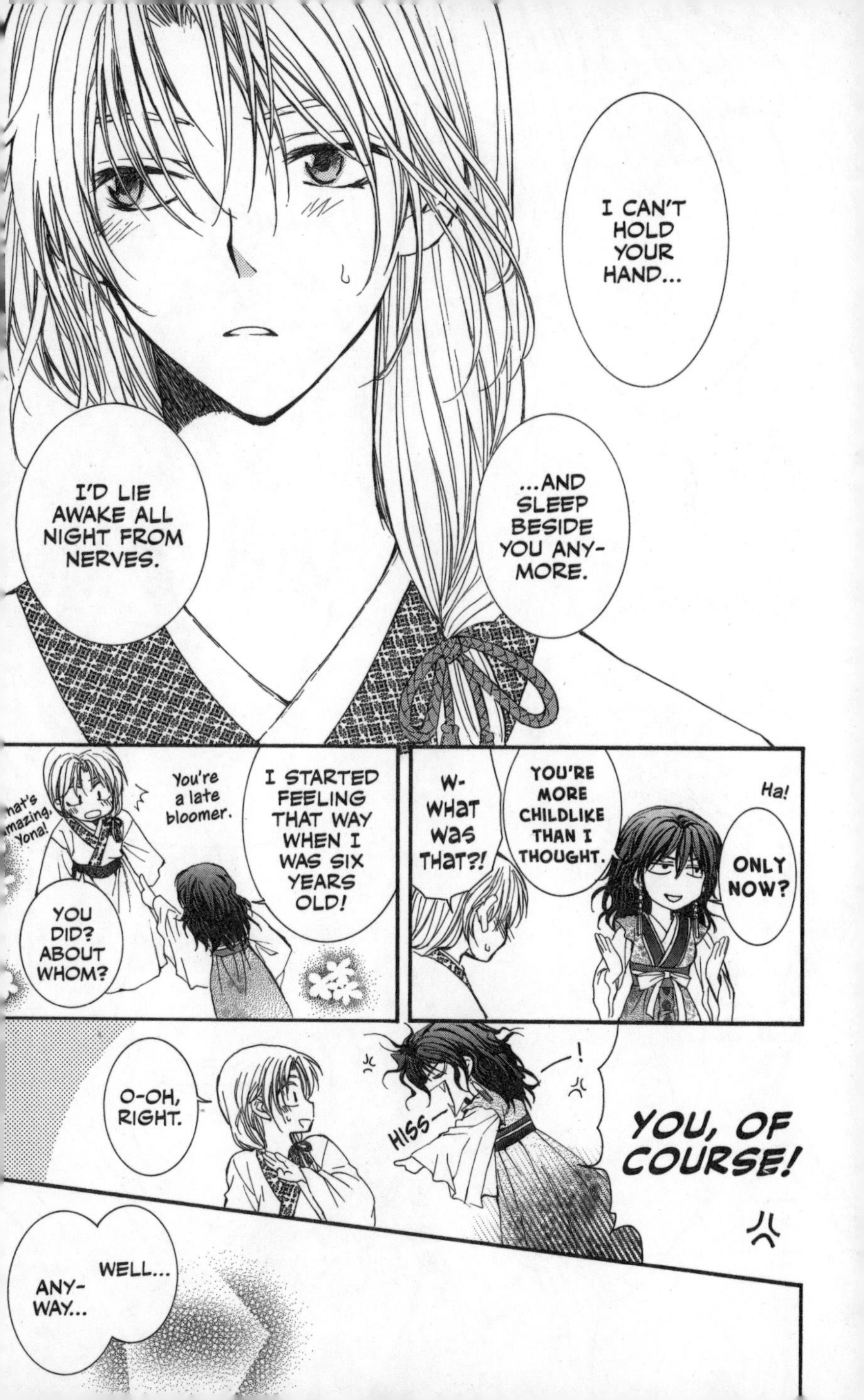
I CAN'T HOLD YOUR HAND...
...AND SLEEP BESIDE YOU ANY-MORE.
I'D LIE AWAKE ALL NIGHT FROM NERVES.
Ha!
ONLY NOW?
YOU'RE MORE CHILDLIKE THAN I THOUGHT.
W-WHAT WAS THAT?!
I STARTED FEELING THAT WAY WHEN I WAS SIX YEARS OLD!
You're a late bloomer.
hat's amazing, Yona!
YOU DID? ABOUT WHOM?
YOU, OF COURSE!
HISS—
O-OH, RIGHT.
WELL... ANY-WAY...

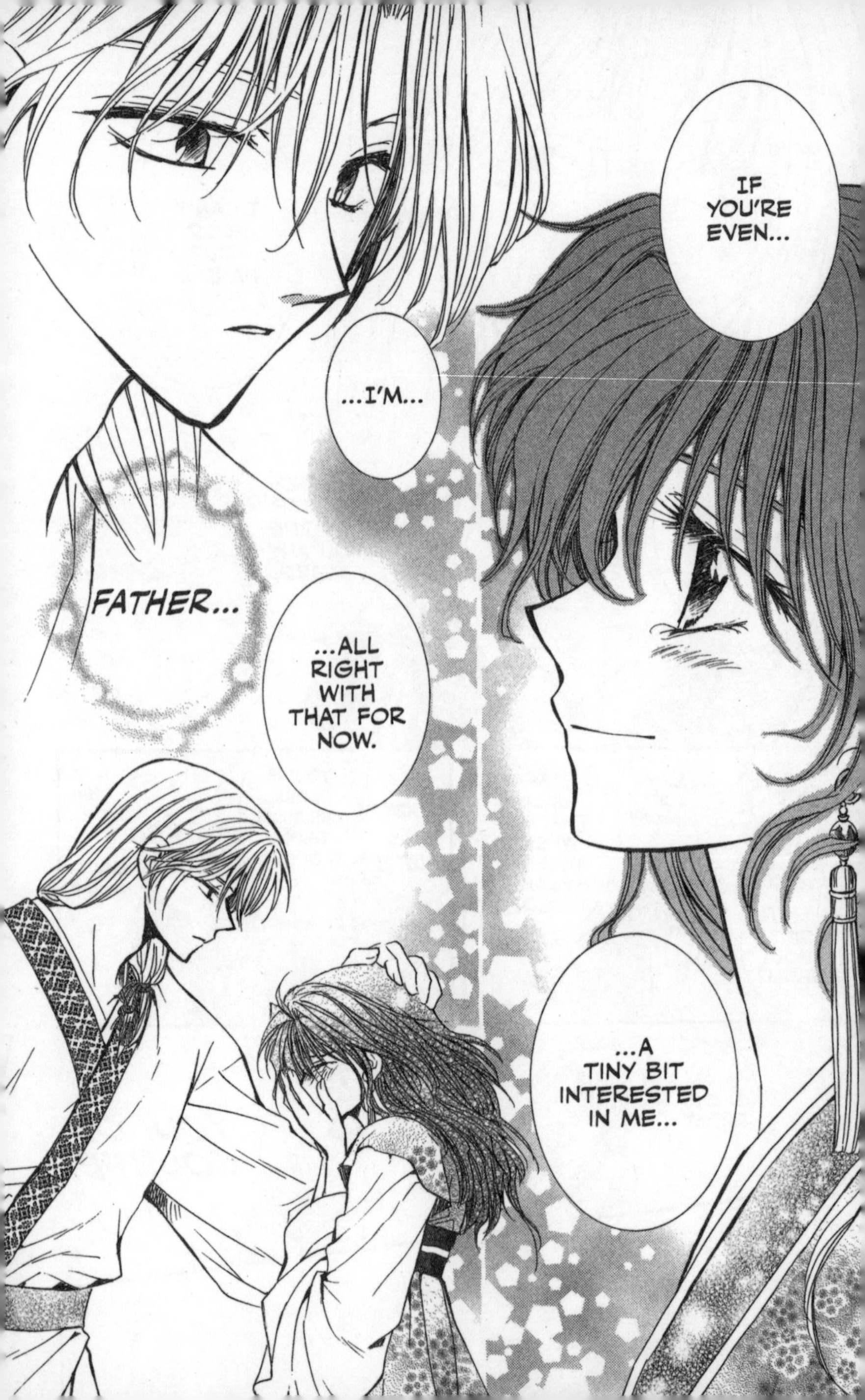
IF YOU'RE EVEN...
...A TINY BIT INTERESTED IN ME...
...I'M...
...ALL RIGHT WITH THAT FOR NOW.
FATHER...

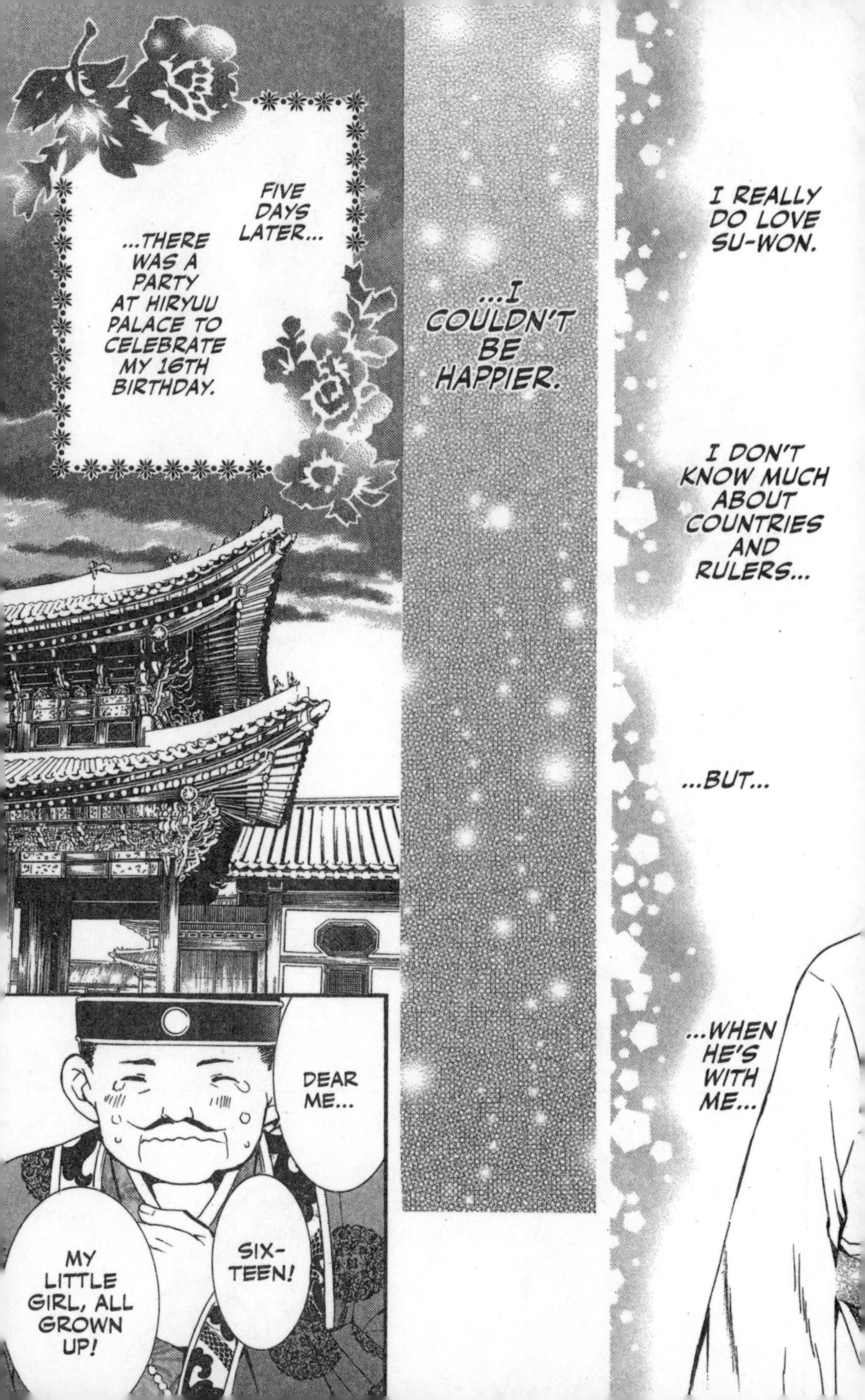
I REALLY DO LOVE SU-WON.
I DON'T KNOW MUCH ABOUT COUNTRIES AND RULERS...
...BUT...
...WHEN HE'S WITH ME...
...I COULDN'T BE HAPPIER.
FIVE DAYS LATER...
...THERE WAS A PARTY AT HIRYUU PALACE TO CELEBRATE MY 16TH BIRTHDAY.
DEAR ME...
SIXTEEN!
MY LITTLE GIRL, ALL GROWN UP!

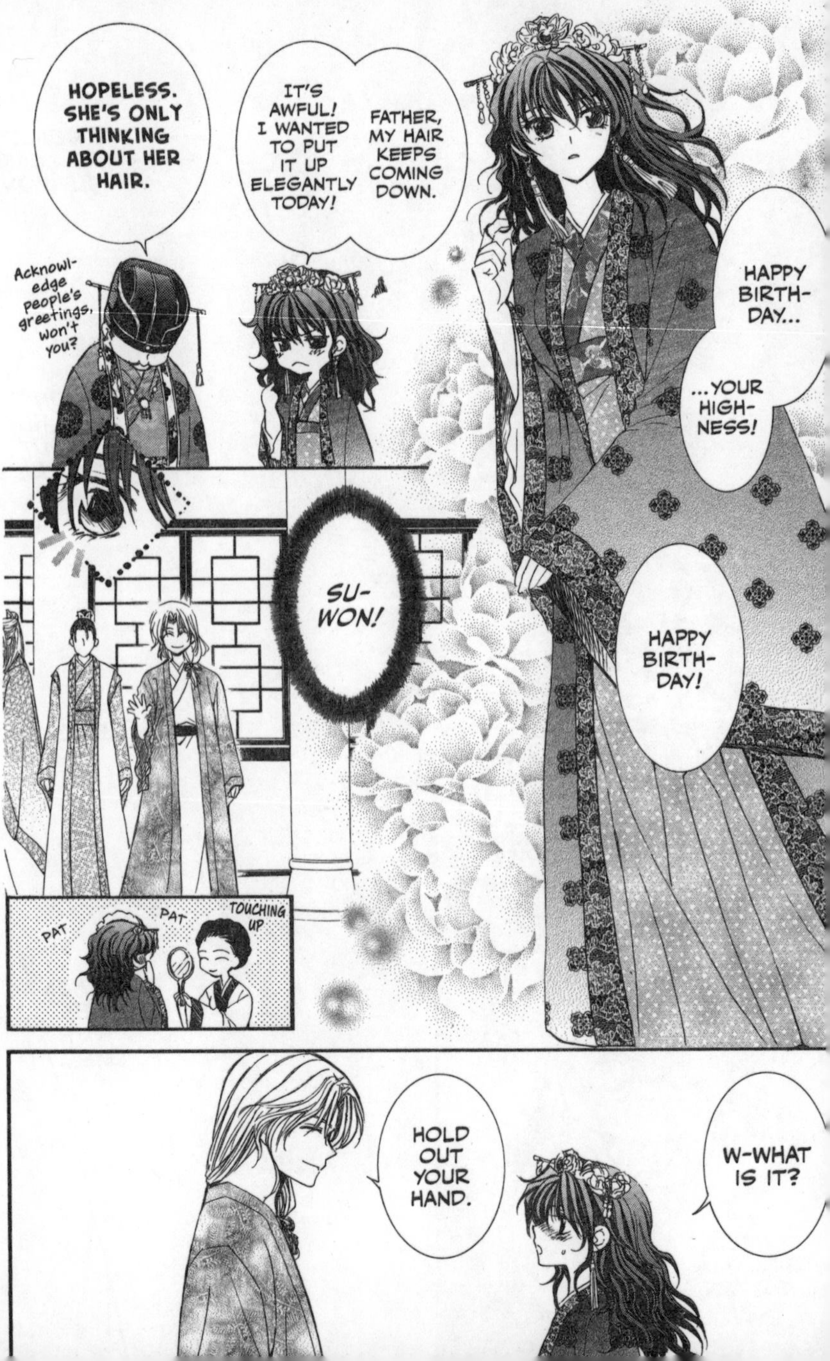
HAPPY BIRTH-DAY...
...YOUR HIGH-NESS!
HAPPY BIRTH-DAY!
FATHER, MY HAIR KEEPS COMING DOWN.
IT'S AWFUL! I WANTED TO PUT IT UP ELEGANTLY TODAY!
HOPELESS. SHE'S ONLY THINKING ABOUT HER HAIR.
Acknowl-edge people's greetings, won't you?
SU-WON!
TOUCHING UP
PAT
PAT
W-WHAT IS IT?
HOLD OUT YOUR HAND.

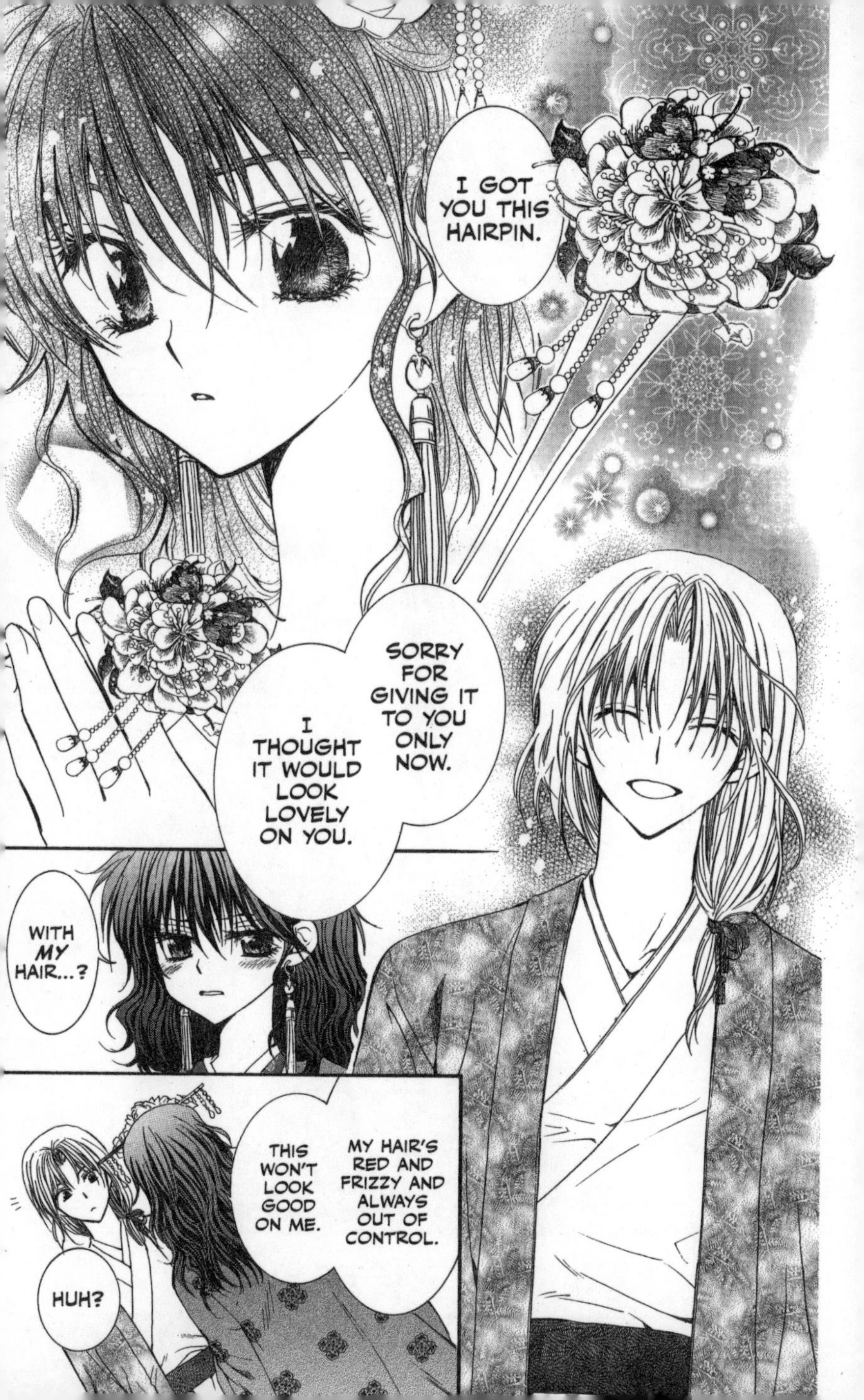
I GOT YOU THIS HAIRPIN.
SORRY FOR GIVING IT TO YOU ONLY NOW.
I THOUGHT IT WOULD LOOK LOVELY ON YOU.
WITH *MY* HAIR...?
MY HAIR'S RED AND FRIZZY AND ALWAYS OUT OF CONTROL.
THIS WON'T LOOK GOOD ON ME.
HUH?

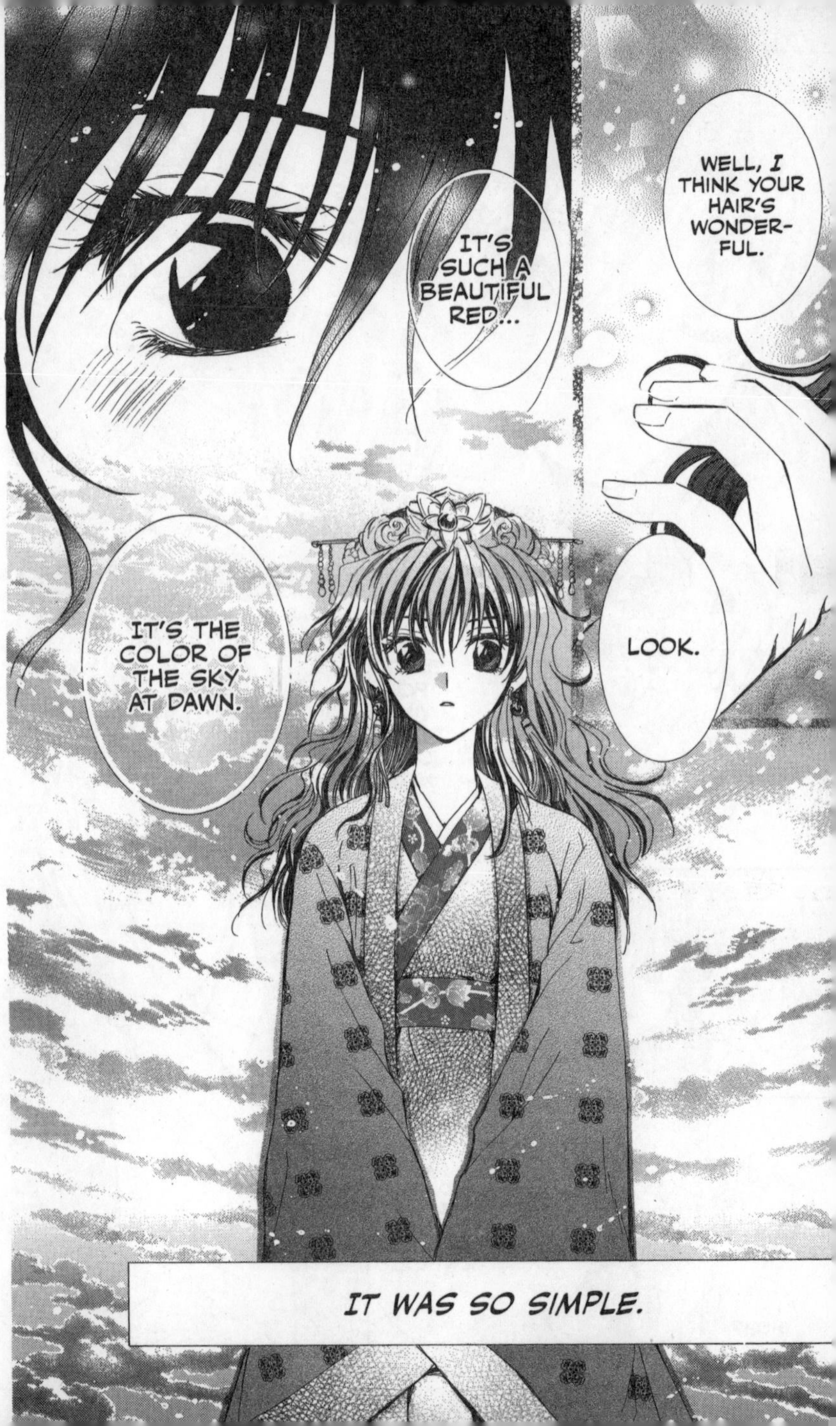
WELL, I THINK YOUR HAIR'S WONDERFUL.
LOOK.
IT'S SUCH A BEAUTIFUL RED...
IT'S THE COLOR OF THE SKY AT DAWN.
IT WAS SO SIMPLE.

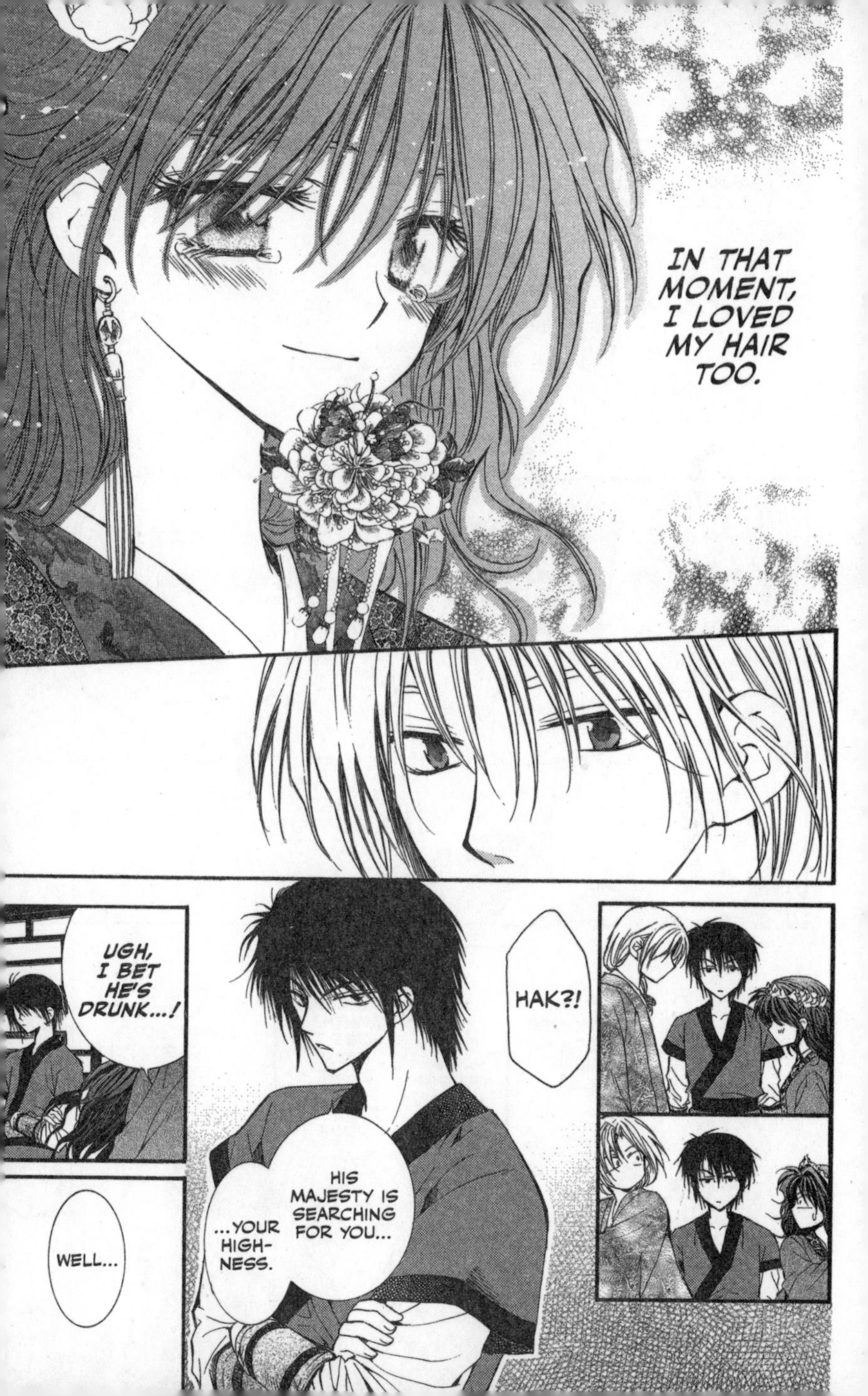
IN THAT MOMENT, I LOVED MY HAIR TOO.
HAK?!
HIS MAJESTY IS SEARCHING FOR YOU...
...YOUR HIGH-NESS.
UGH, I BET HE'S DRUNK...!
WELL...

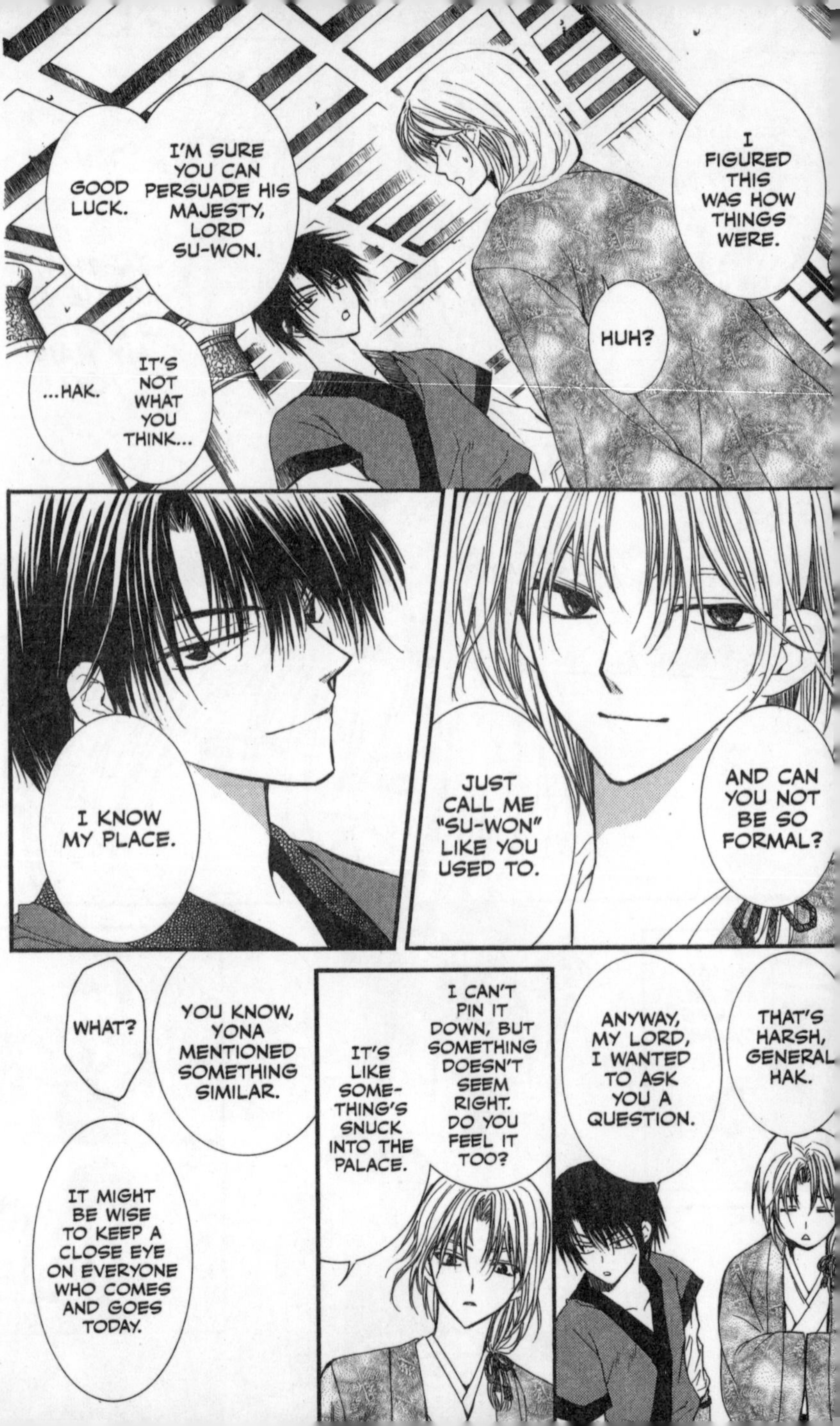
I FIGURED THIS WAS HOW THINGS WERE.
HUH?
I'M SURE YOU CAN PERSUADE HIS MAJESTY, LORD SU-WON.
GOOD LUCK.
IT'S NOT WHAT YOU THINK...
...HAK.
AND CAN YOU NOT BE SO FORMAL?
JUST CALL ME "SU-WON" LIKE YOU USED TO.
I KNOW MY PLACE.
THAT'S HARSH, GENERAL HAK.
ANYWAY, MY LORD, I WANTED TO ASK YOU A QUESTION.
I CAN'T PIN IT DOWN, BUT SOMETHING DOESN'T SEEM RIGHT. DO YOU FEEL IT TOO?
IT'S LIKE SOME-THING'S SNUCK INTO THE PALACE.
YOU KNOW, YONA MENTIONED SOMETHING SIMILAR.
WHAT?
IT MIGHT BE WISE TO KEEP A CLOSE EYE ON EVERYONE WHO COMES AND GOES TODAY.

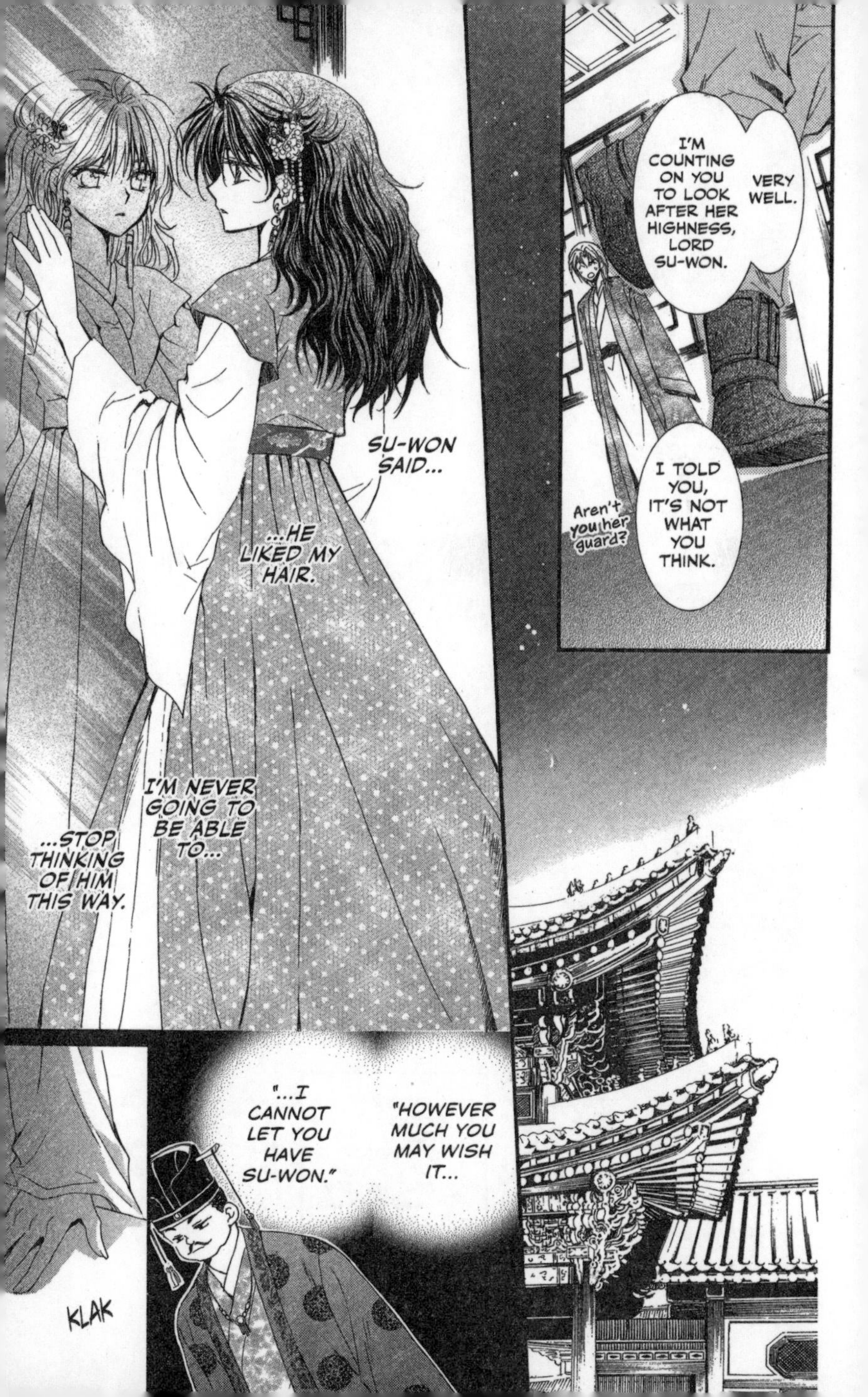
I'M COUNTING ON YOU TO LOOK AFTER HER HIGHNESS, LORD SU-WON.
VERY WELL.
I TOLD YOU, IT'S NOT WHAT YOU THINK.
Aren't you her guard?
SU-WON SAID...
...HE LIKED MY HAIR.
I'M NEVER GOING TO BE ABLE TO...
...STOP THINKING OF HIM THIS WAY.
"HOWEVER MUCH YOU MAY WISH IT...
"...I CANNOT LET YOU HAVE SU-WON."
KLAK

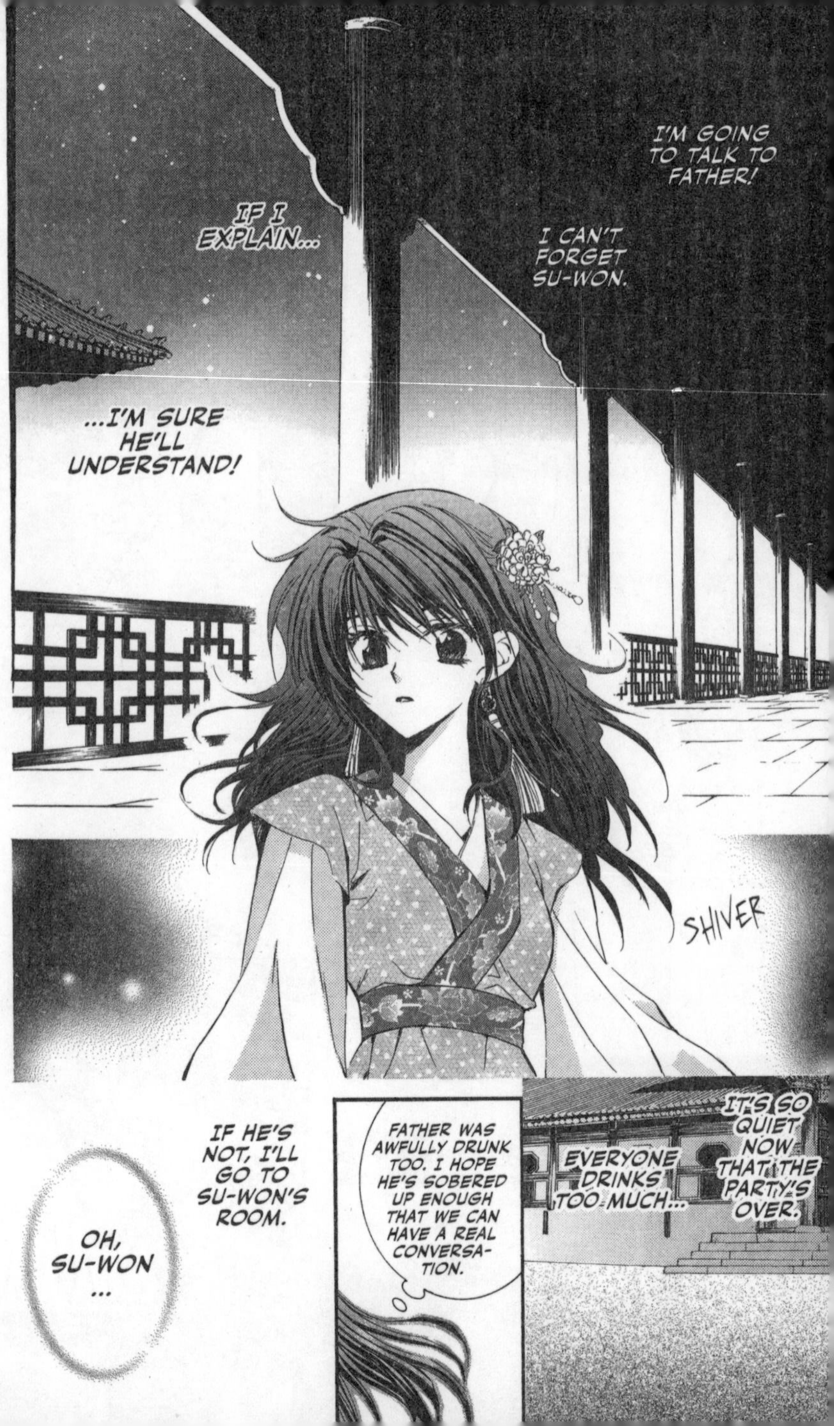
I'M GOING TO TALK TO FATHER!
I CAN'T FORGET SU-WON.
IF I EXPLAIN...
...I'M SURE HE'LL UNDERSTAND!
SHIVER
IT'S SO QUIET NOW THAT THE PARTY'S OVER.
EVERYONE DRINKS TOO MUCH...
FATHER WAS AWFULLY DRUNK TOO. I HOPE HE'S SOBERED UP ENOUGH THAT WE CAN HAVE A REAL CONVERSA-TION.
IF HE'S NOT, I'LL GO TO SU-WON'S ROOM.
OH, SU-WON ...

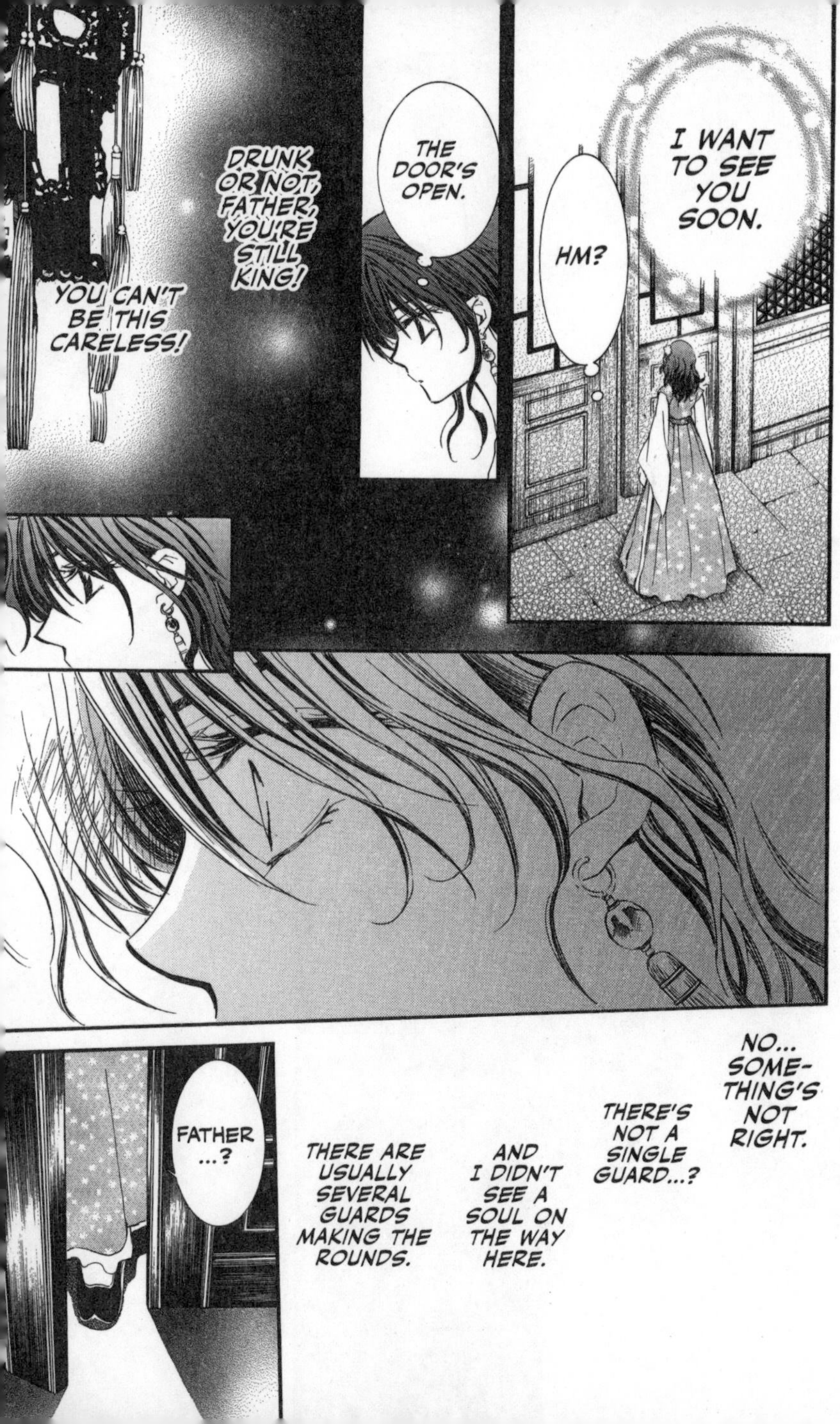
I WANT TO SEE YOU SOON.
HM?
THE DOOR'S OPEN.
DRUNK OR NOT, FATHER, YOU'RE STILL KING!
YOU CAN'T BE THIS CARELESS!
NO... SOMETHING'S NOT RIGHT.
THERE'S NOT A SINGLE GUARD...?
AND I DIDN'T SEE A SOUL ON THE WAY HERE.
THERE ARE USUALLY SEVERAL GUARDS MAKING THE ROUNDS.
FATHER ...?

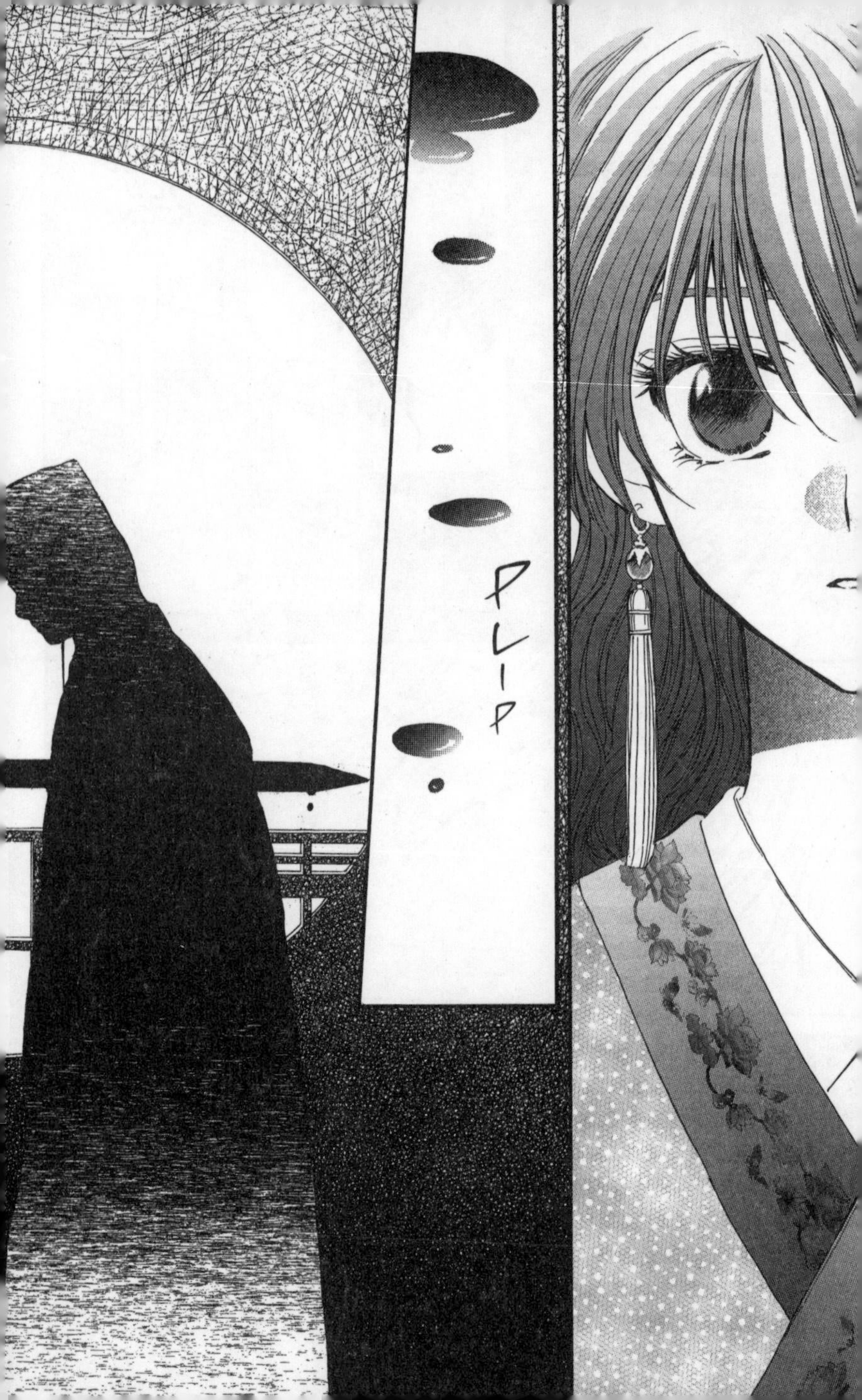
PLIP

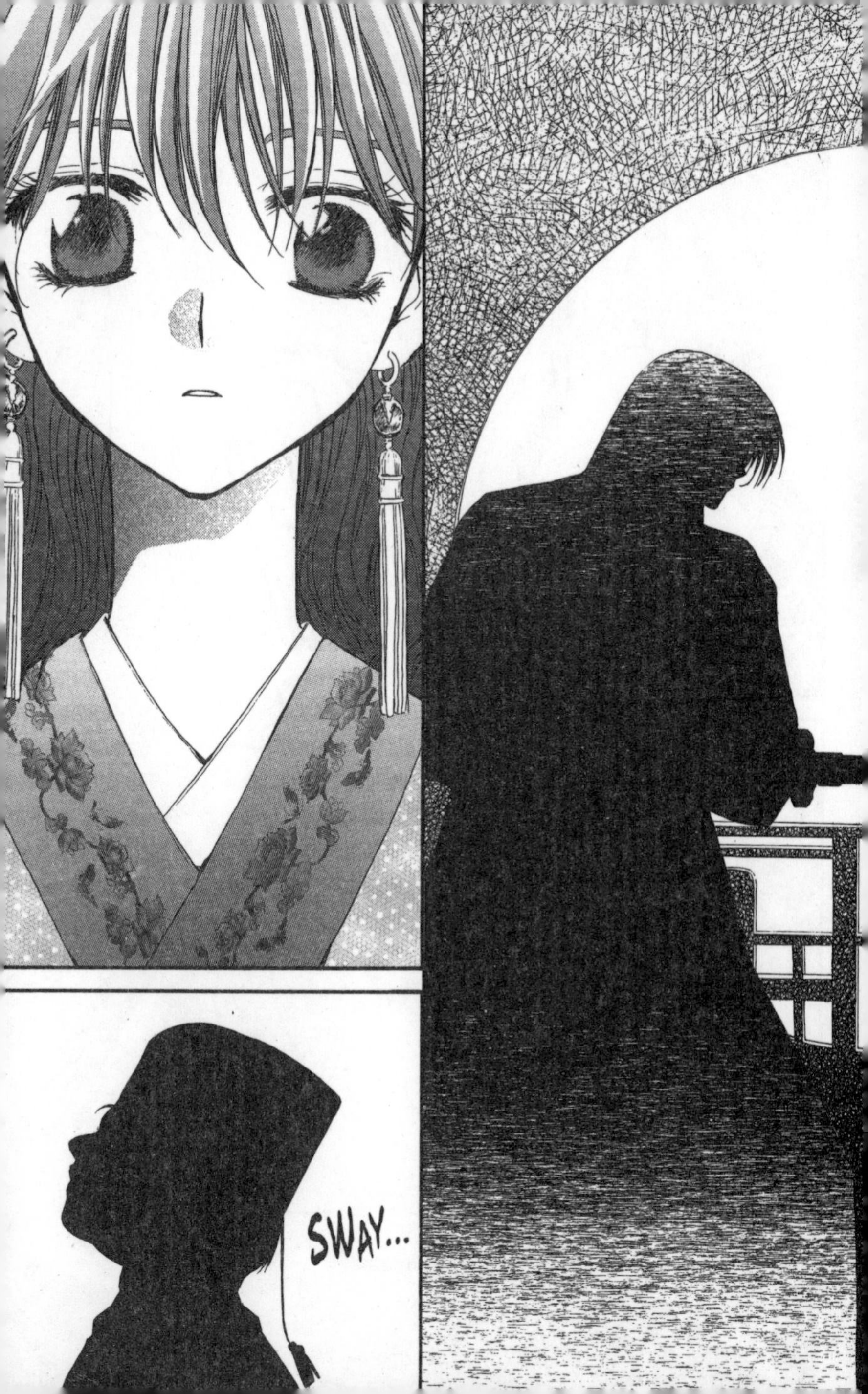
SWAY...

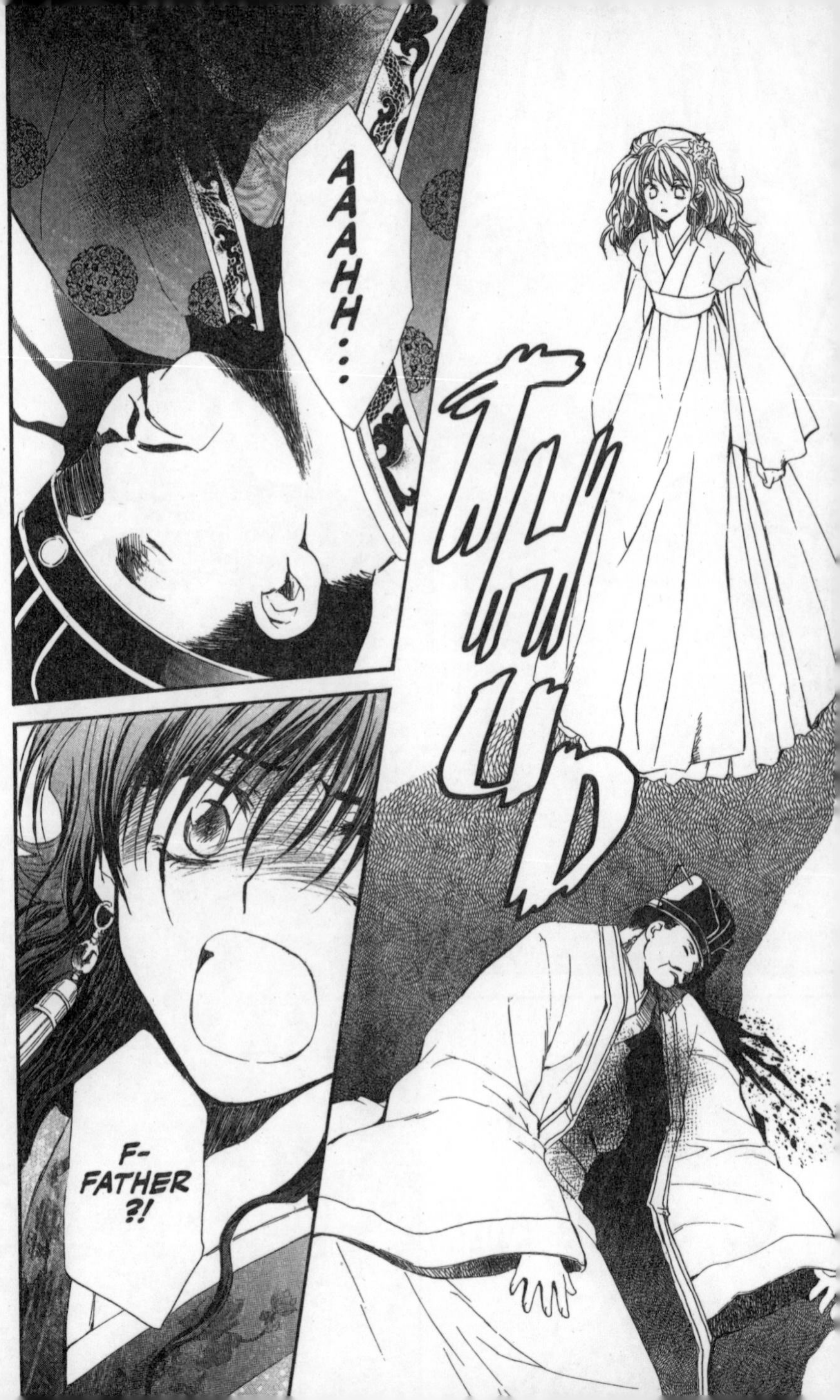
THUD
AAAHH...
F-FATHER ?!

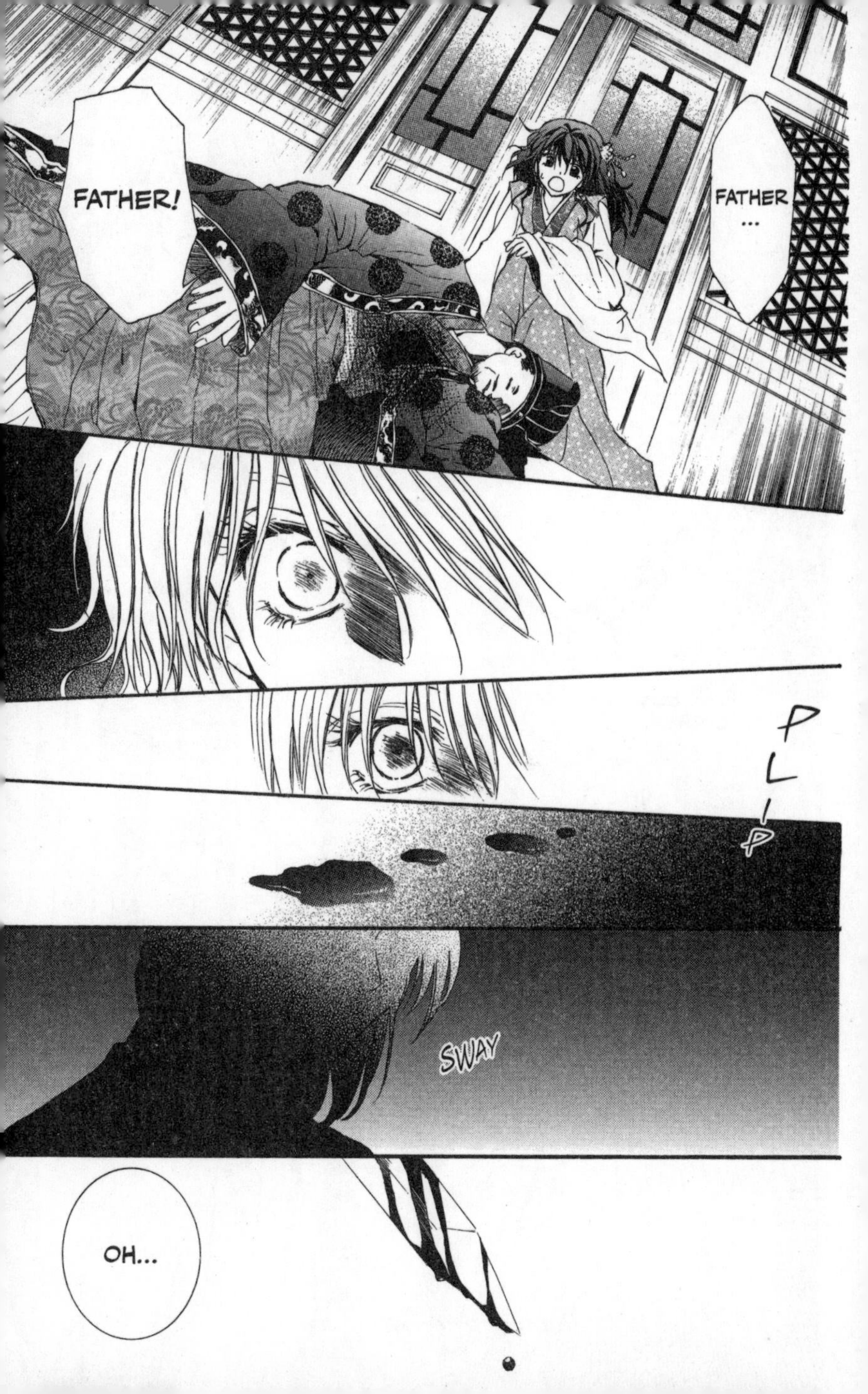
FATHER...
FATHER!
PLIP
SWAY
OH...

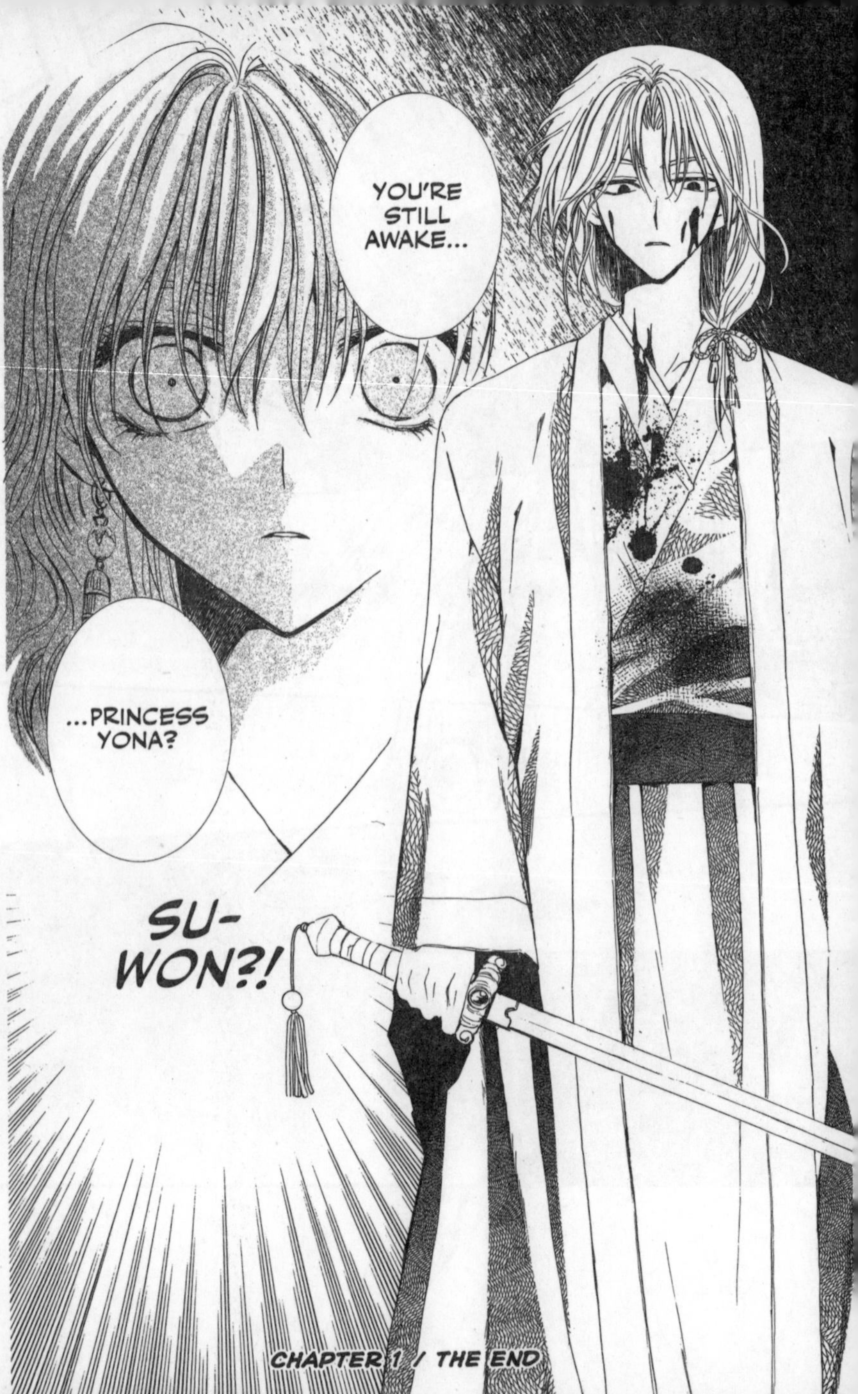
YOU'RE STILL AWAKE...
...PRINCESS YONA?
SU-WON?!
CHAPTER 1 / THE END

CHAPTER 2: SHATTERED BONDS

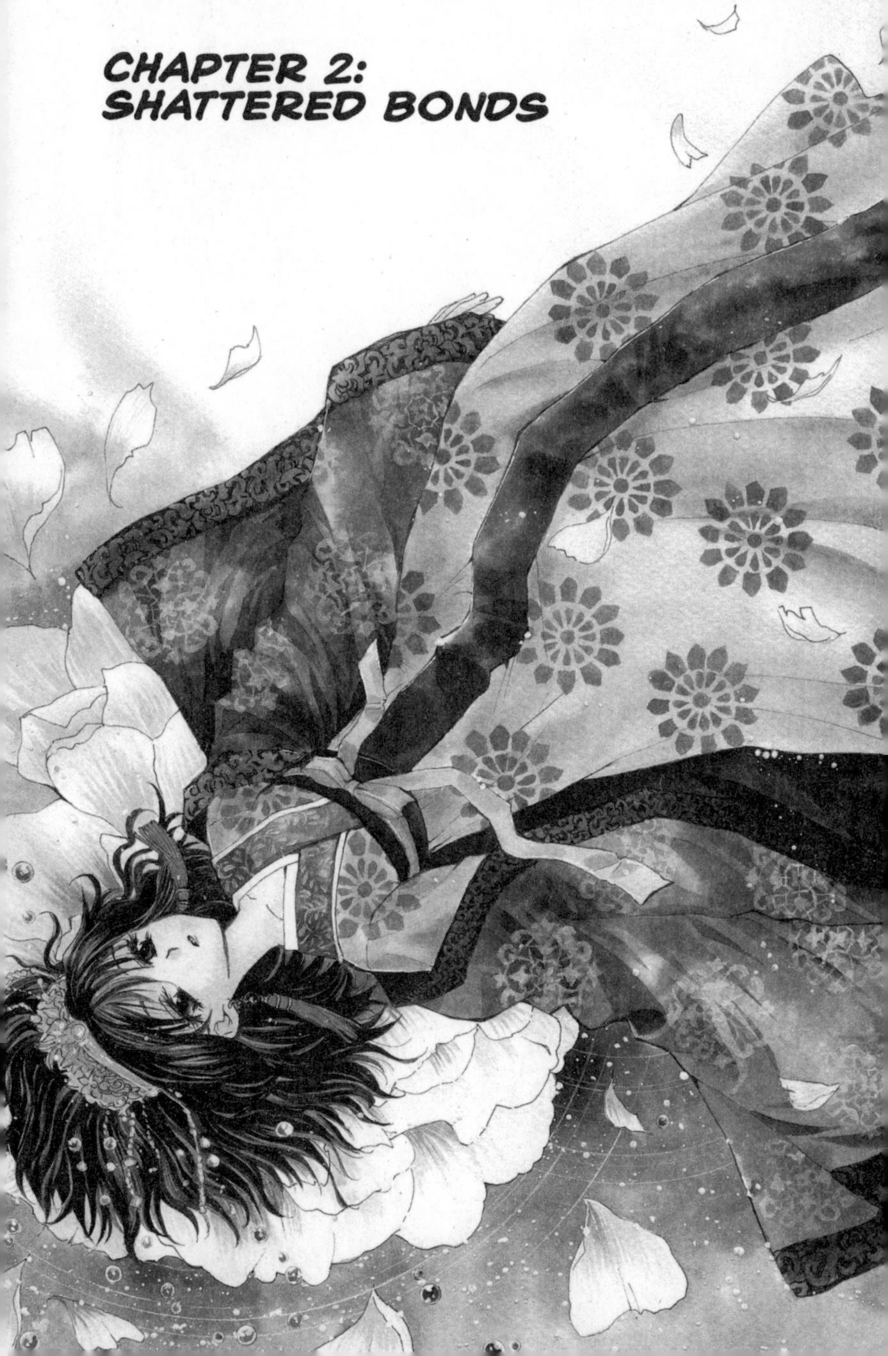

Min-su

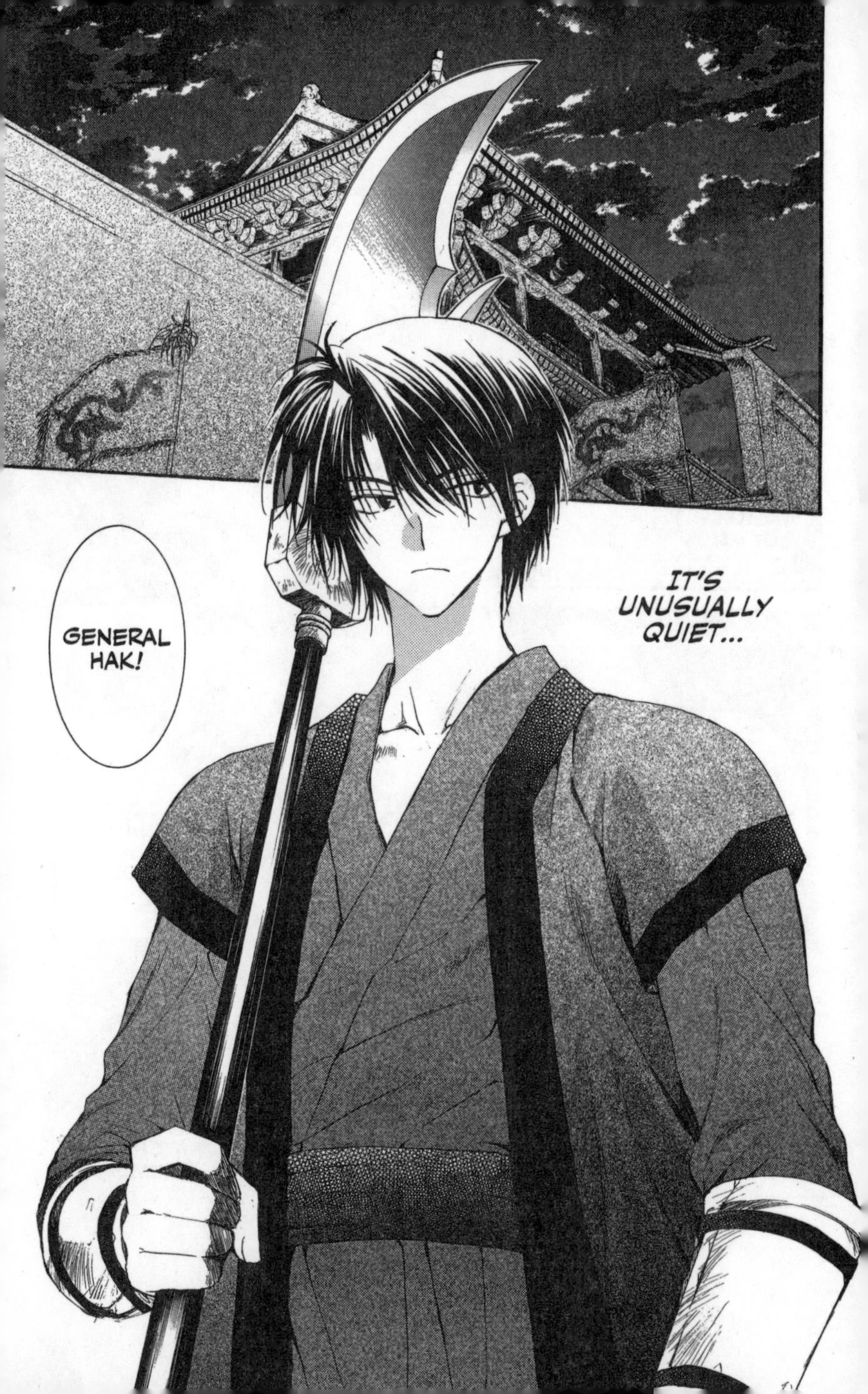
IT'S UNUSUALLY QUIET...
GENERAL HAK!

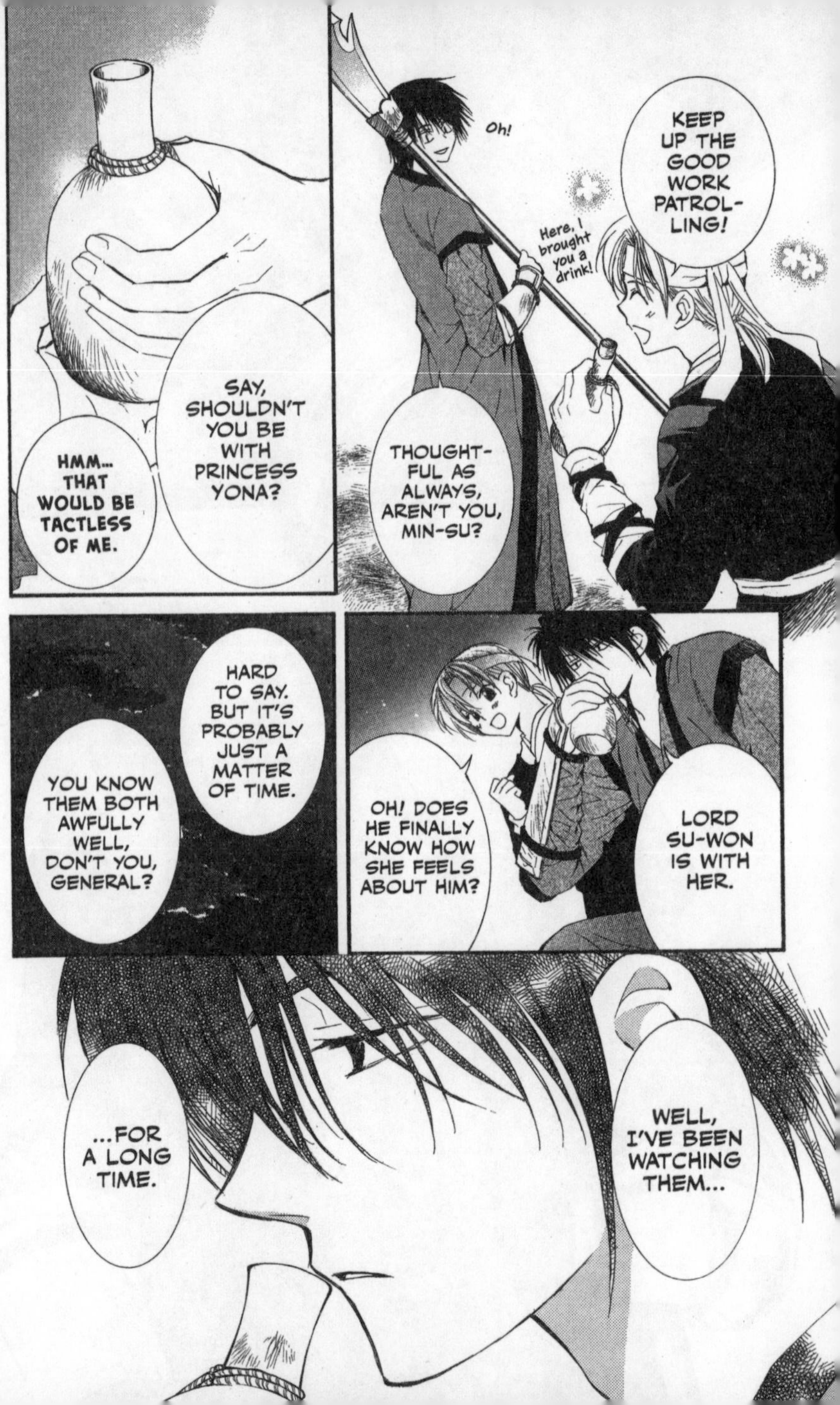
KEEP UP THE GOOD WORK PATROLLING!
Here, I brought you a drink!
Oh!
THOUGHTFUL AS ALWAYS, AREN'T YOU, MIN-SU?
SAY, SHOULDN'T YOU BE WITH PRINCESS YONA?
HMM... THAT WOULD BE TACTLESS OF ME.
LORD SU-WON IS WITH HER.
OH! DOES HE FINALLY KNOW HOW SHE FEELS ABOUT HIM?
HARD TO SAY. BUT IT'S PROBABLY JUST A MATTER OF TIME.
YOU KNOW THEM BOTH AWFULLY WELL, DON'T YOU, GENERAL?
WELL, I'VE BEEN WATCHING THEM...
...FOR A LONG TIME.

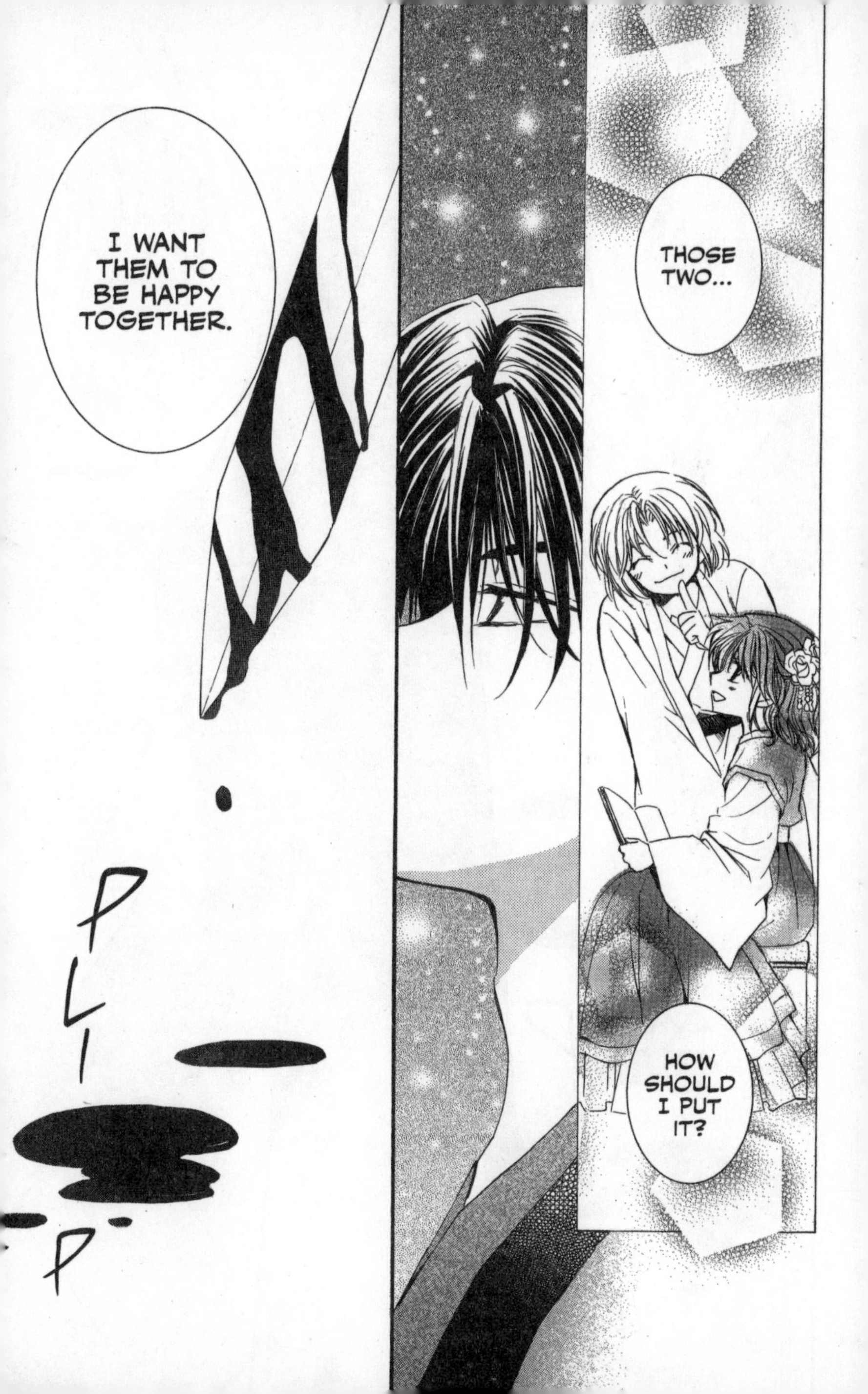
THOSE TWO...
HOW SHOULD I PUT IT?
I WANT THEM TO BE HAPPY TOGETHER.
PLIP

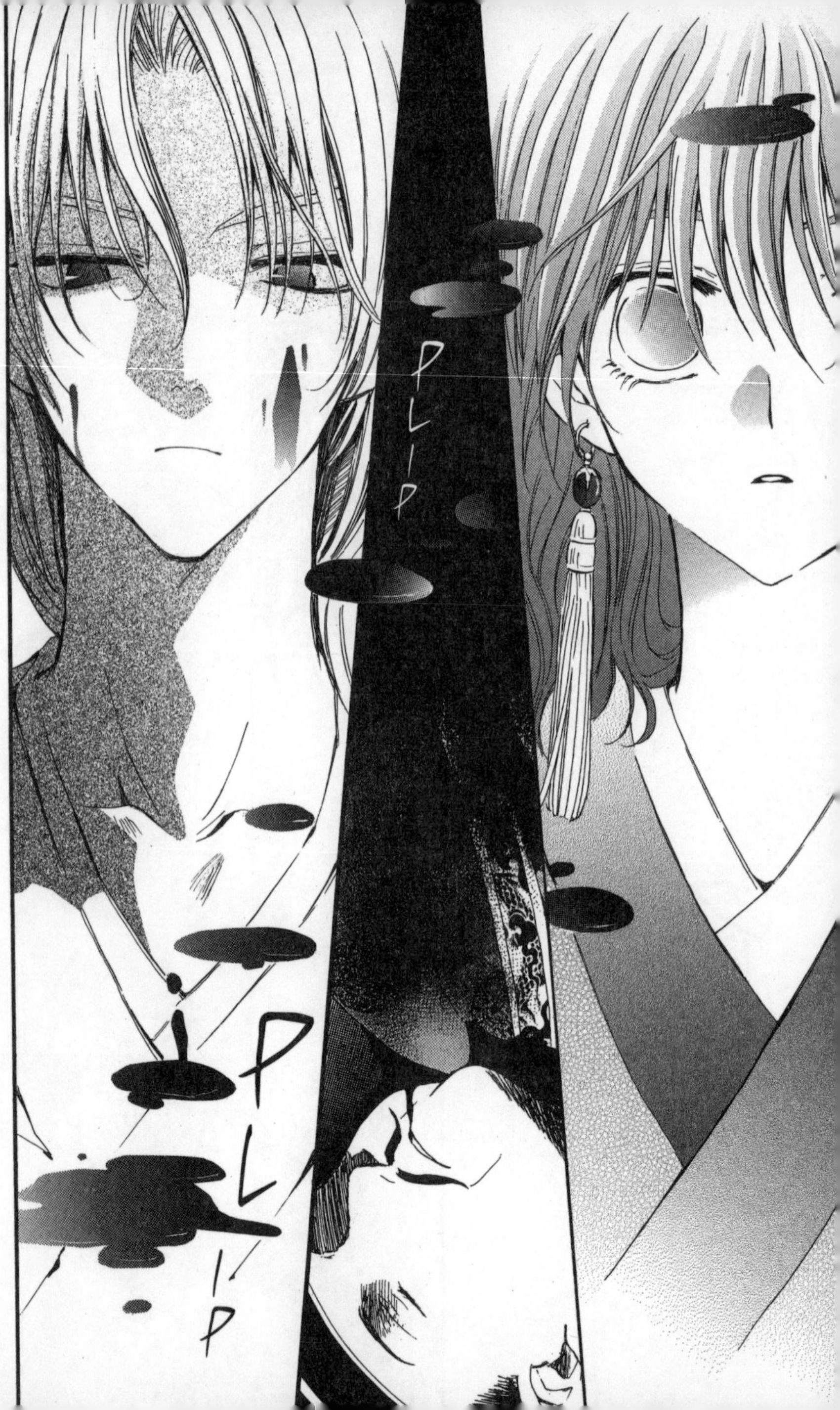
PLIP
PLIP

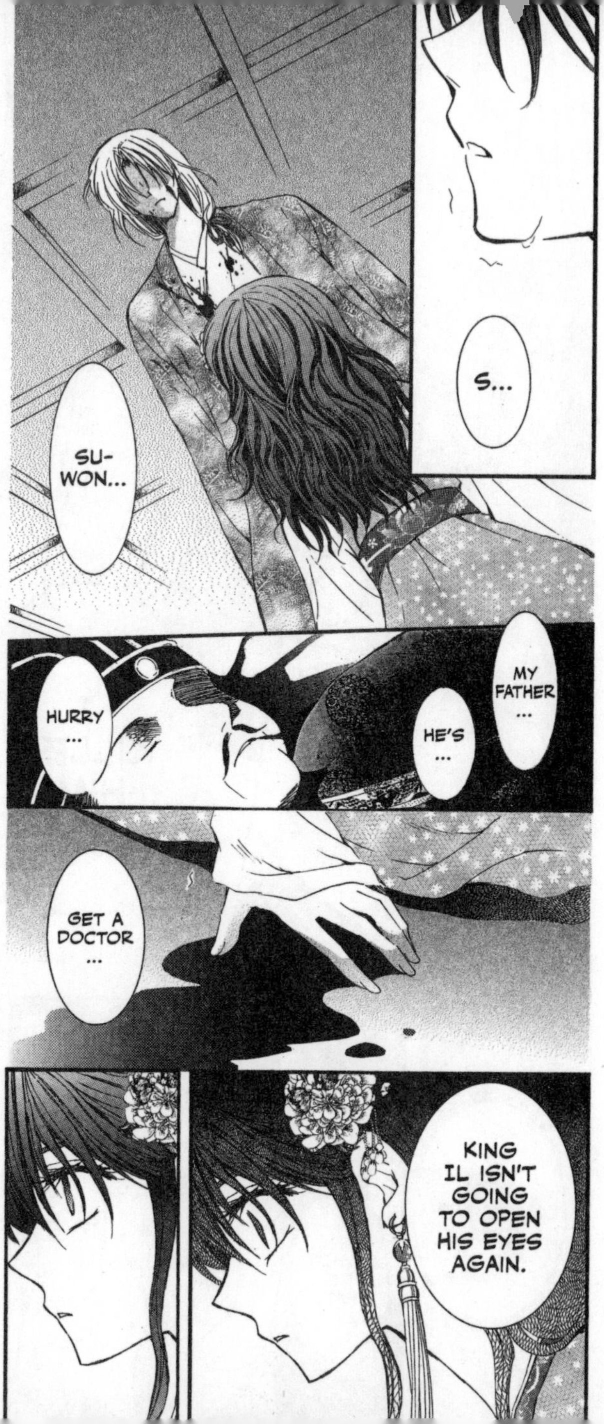
S...
SU-WON...
MY FATHER...
HE'S...
HURRY...
GET A DOCTOR...
KING IL ISN'T GOING TO OPEN HIS EYES AGAIN.

I've been blogging since around June 2009. I'm not very good at using computers or writing about myself, but I wanted someplace to provide information about my work and send messages to my readers. I got my younger sister to help me create a page.
It's full of daily life and trivial thoughts, but please check it out if you're interested! And if you have feedback about my work, I look forward to hearing it!
My blog is called "Mizuho Kusanagi's NG Life."

http://yaplog.jp/sanaginonaka/

I want to thank all of you who visit me there regularly.

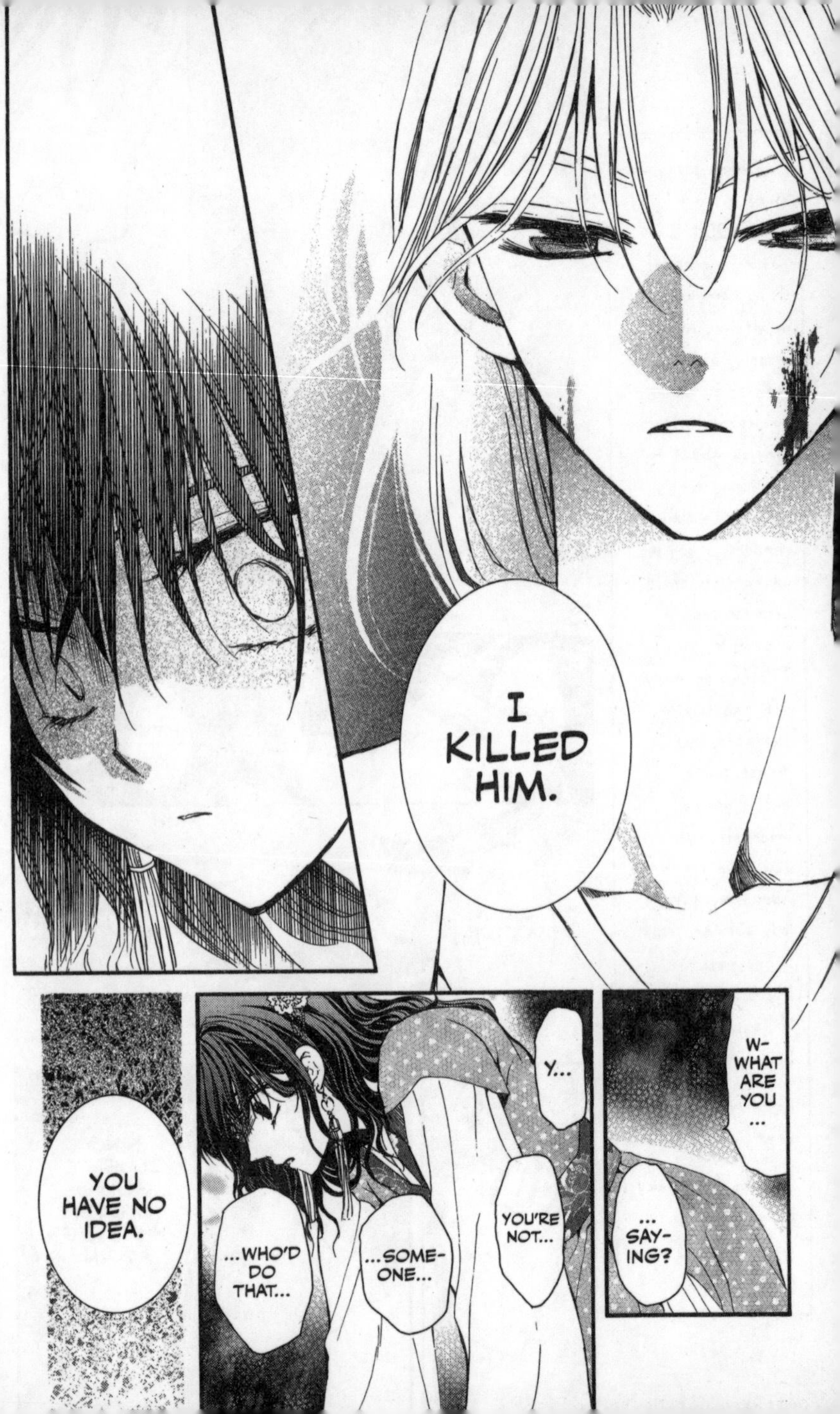
I KILLED HIM.
W-WHAT ARE YOU...
...SAY-ING?
Y...
YOU'RE NOT...
...SOME-ONE...
...WHO'D DO THAT...
YOU HAVE NO IDEA.

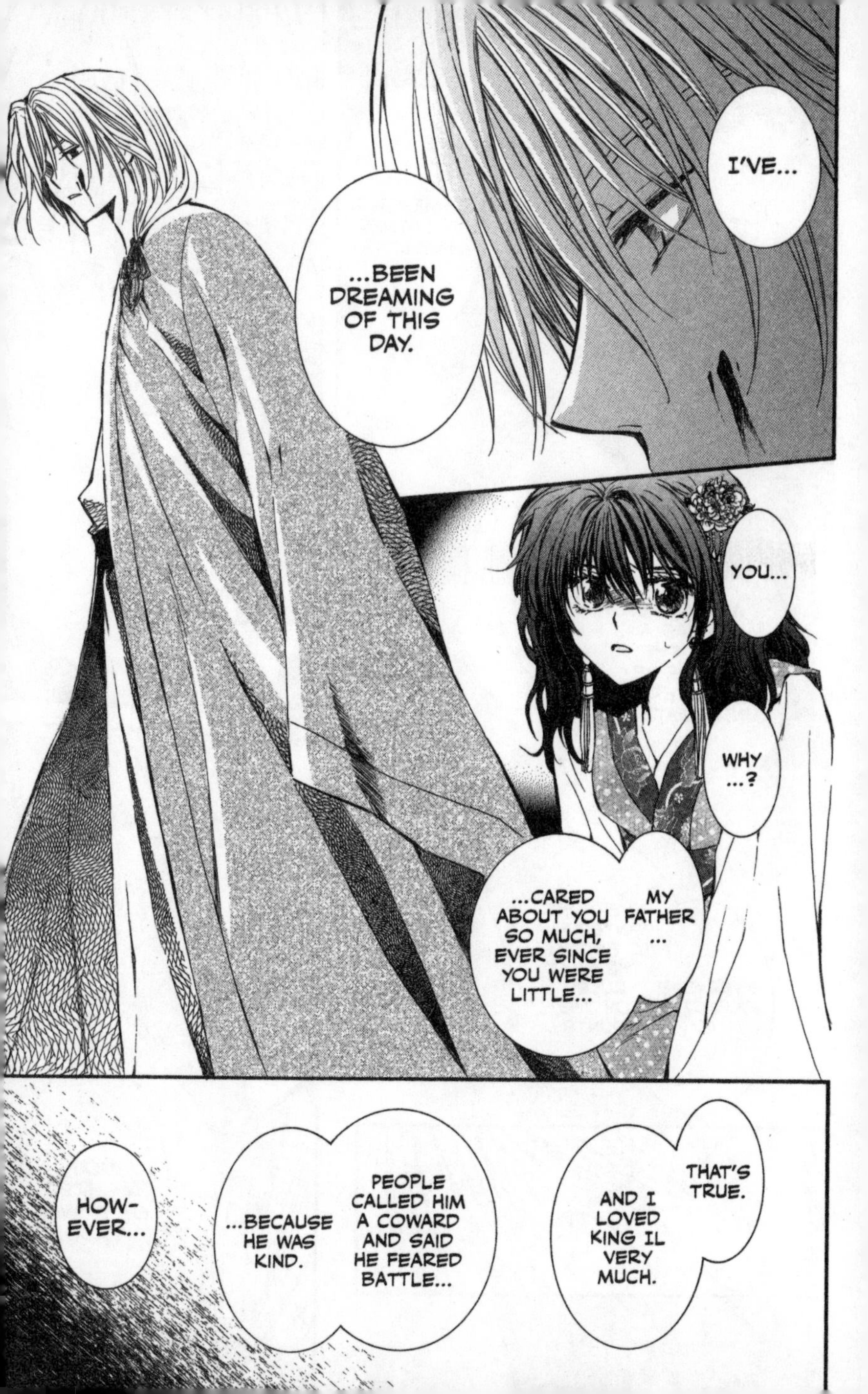

I'VE...
...BEEN DREAMING OF THIS DAY.
YOU...
WHY...?
MY FATHER...
...CARED ABOUT YOU SO MUCH, EVER SINCE YOU WERE LITTLE...
THAT'S TRUE.
AND I LOVED KING IL VERY MUCH.
PEOPLE CALLED HIM A COWARD AND SAID HE FEARED BATTLE...
...BECAUSE HE WAS KIND.
HOW-EVER...

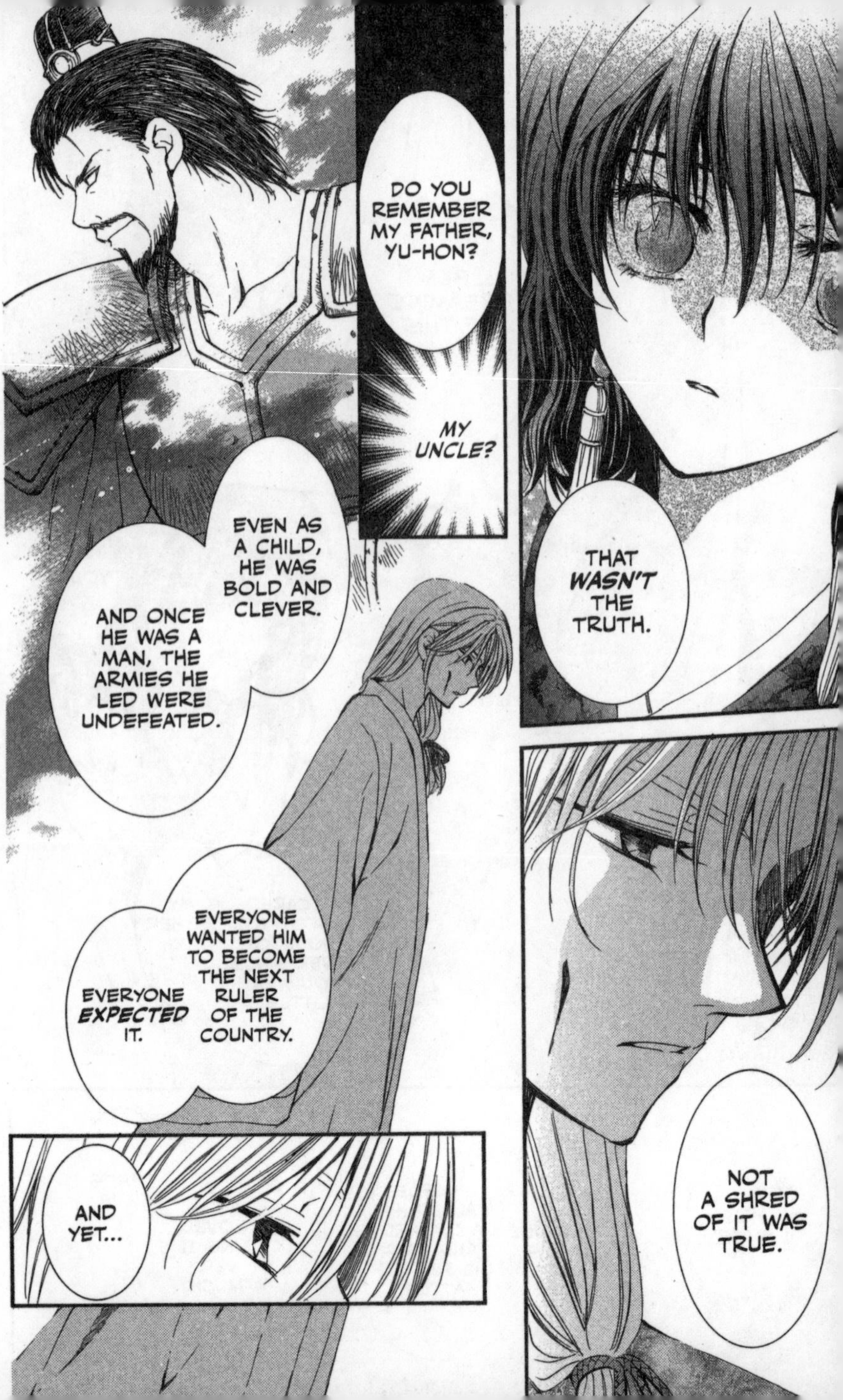
DO YOU REMEMBER MY FATHER, YU-HON?
MY UNCLE?
EVEN AS A CHILD, HE WAS BOLD AND CLEVER.
AND ONCE HE WAS A MAN, THE ARMIES HE LED WERE UNDEFEATED.
EVERYONE WANTED HIM TO BECOME THE NEXT RULER OF THE COUNTRY.
EVERYONE *EXPECTED* IT.
AND YET...
THAT *WASN'T* THE TRUTH.
NOT A SHRED OF IT WAS TRUE.

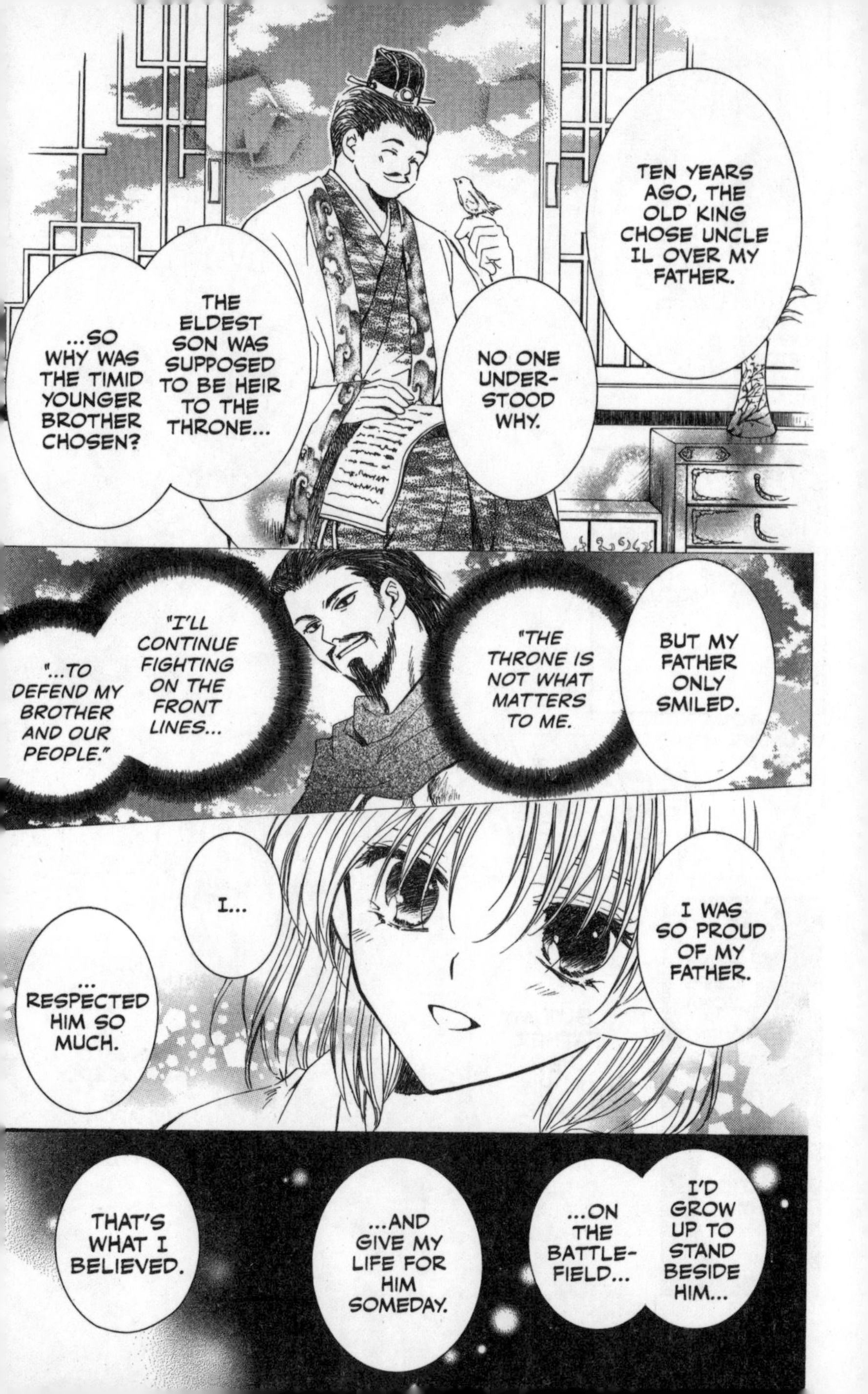
TEN YEARS AGO, THE OLD KING CHOSE UNCLE IL OVER MY FATHER.
NO ONE UNDER-STOOD WHY.
THE ELDEST SON WAS SUPPOSED TO BE HEIR TO THE THRONE...
...SO WHY WAS THE TIMID YOUNGER BROTHER CHOSEN?
BUT MY FATHER ONLY SMILED.
"THE THRONE IS NOT WHAT MATTERS TO ME.
"I'LL CONTINUE FIGHTING ON THE FRONT LINES...
"...TO DEFEND MY BROTHER AND OUR PEOPLE."
I WAS SO PROUD OF MY FATHER.
I...
...RESPECTED HIM SO MUCH.
I'D GROW UP TO STAND BESIDE HIM...
...ON THE BATTLE-FIELD...
...AND GIVE MY LIFE FOR HIM SOMEDAY.
THAT'S WHAT I BELIEVED.

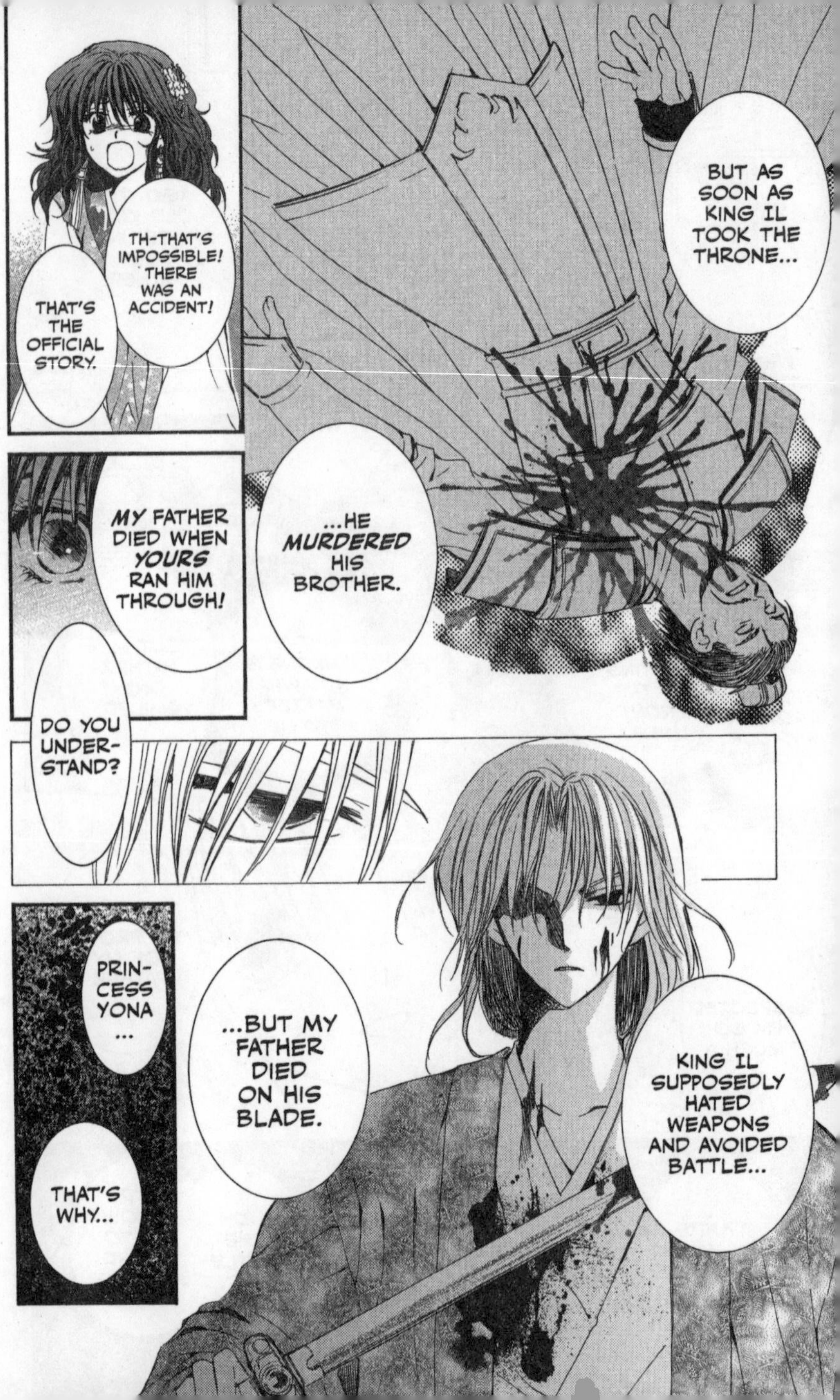
BUT AS SOON AS KING IL TOOK THE THRONE...
...HE *MURDERED* HIS BROTHER.
TH-THAT'S IMPOSSIBLE! THERE WAS AN ACCIDENT!
THAT'S THE OFFICIAL STORY.
MY FATHER DIED WHEN *YOURS* RAN HIM THROUGH!
DO YOU UNDER-STAND?
KING IL SUPPOSEDLY HATED WEAPONS AND AVOIDED BATTLE...
...BUT MY FATHER DIED ON HIS BLADE.
PRIN-CESS YONA ...
THAT'S WHY...

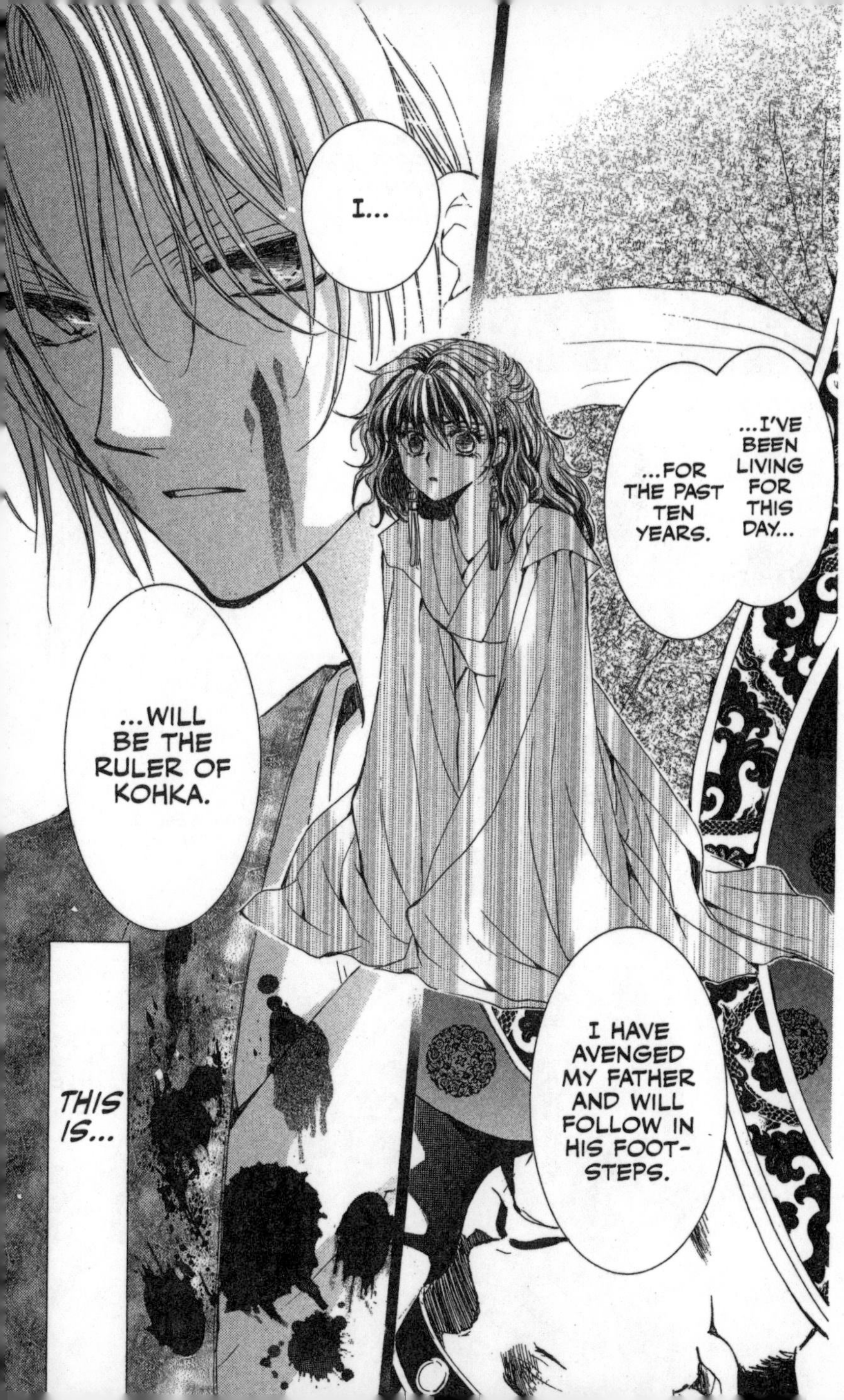
...I'VE BEEN LIVING FOR THIS DAY...
...FOR THE PAST TEN YEARS.
I HAVE AVENGED MY FATHER AND WILL FOLLOW IN HIS FOOT-STEPS.
I...
...WILL BE THE RULER OF KOHKA.
THIS IS...

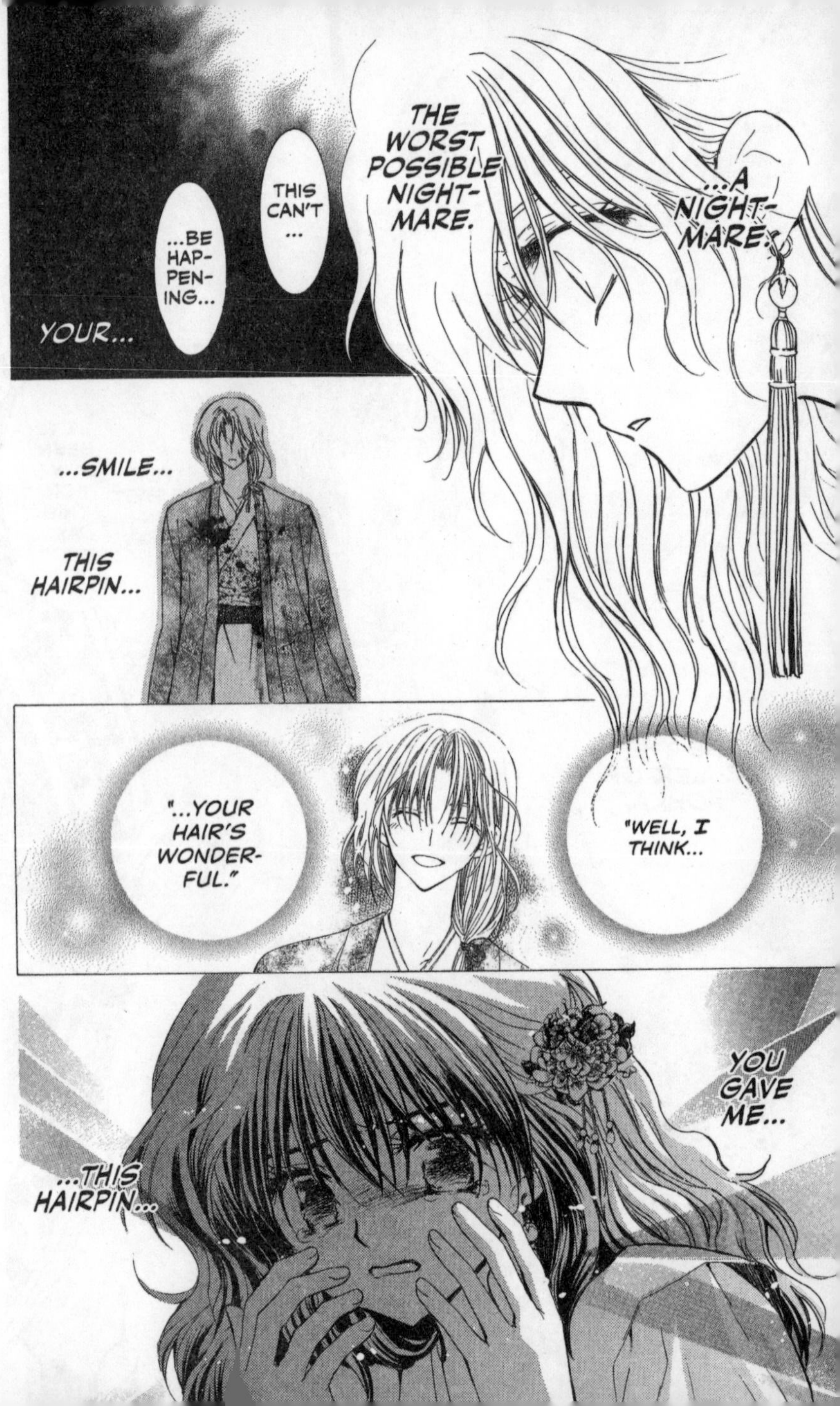
...A NIGHTMARE.
THE WORST POSSIBLE NIGHTMARE.
THIS CAN'T...
...BE HAPPENING...
YOUR...
...SMILE...
THIS HAIRPIN...
"WELL, I THINK...
"...YOUR HAIR'S WONDERFUL."
YOU GAVE ME...
...THIS HAIRPIN...

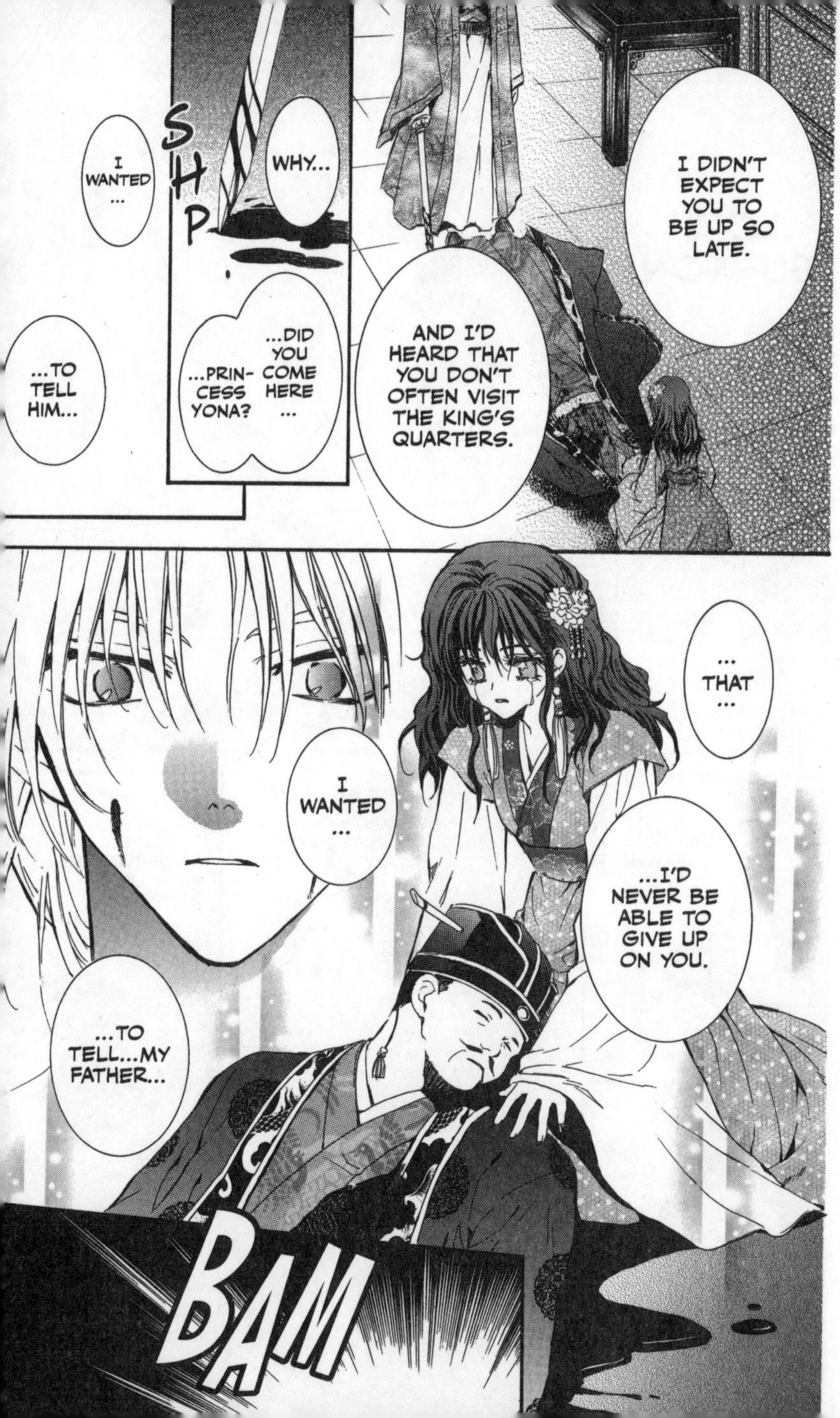
I DIDN'T EXPECT YOU TO BE UP SO LATE.
AND I'D HEARD THAT YOU DON'T OFTEN VISIT THE KING'S QUARTERS.
WHY...
SHP
...DID YOU COME HERE ...
...PRINCESS YONA?
I WANTED ...
...TO TELL HIM...
... THAT ...
I WANTED ...
...I'D NEVER BE ABLE TO GIVE UP ON YOU.
...TO TELL...MY FATHER...
BAM

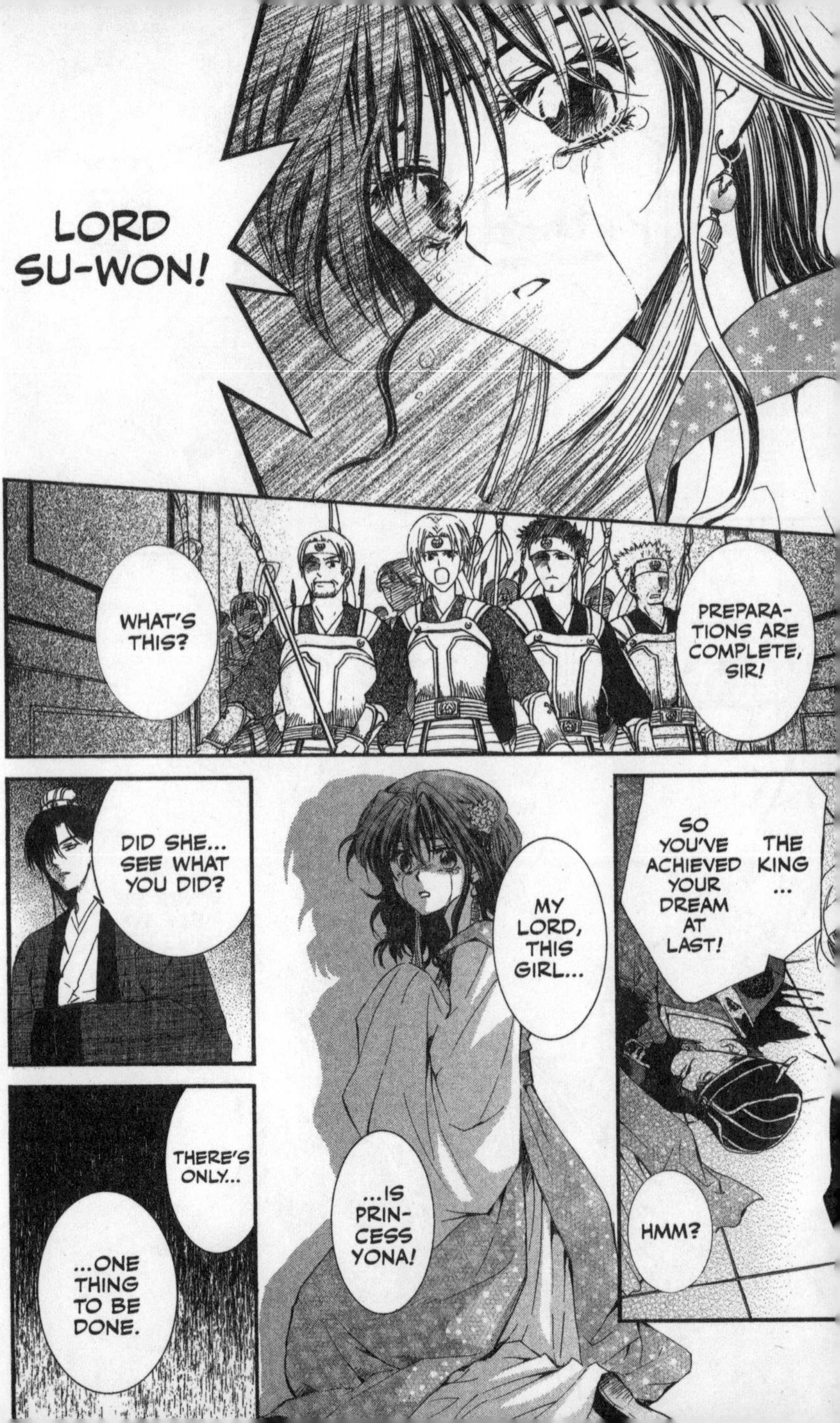
LORD SU-WON!
PREPARA-TIONS ARE COMPLETE, SIR!
WHAT'S THIS?
THE KING ...
SO YOU'VE ACHIEVED YOUR DREAM AT LAST!
HMM?
MY LORD, THIS GIRL...
...IS PRIN-CESS YONA!
DID SHE... SEE WHAT YOU DID?
THERE'S ONLY...
...ONE THING TO BE DONE.

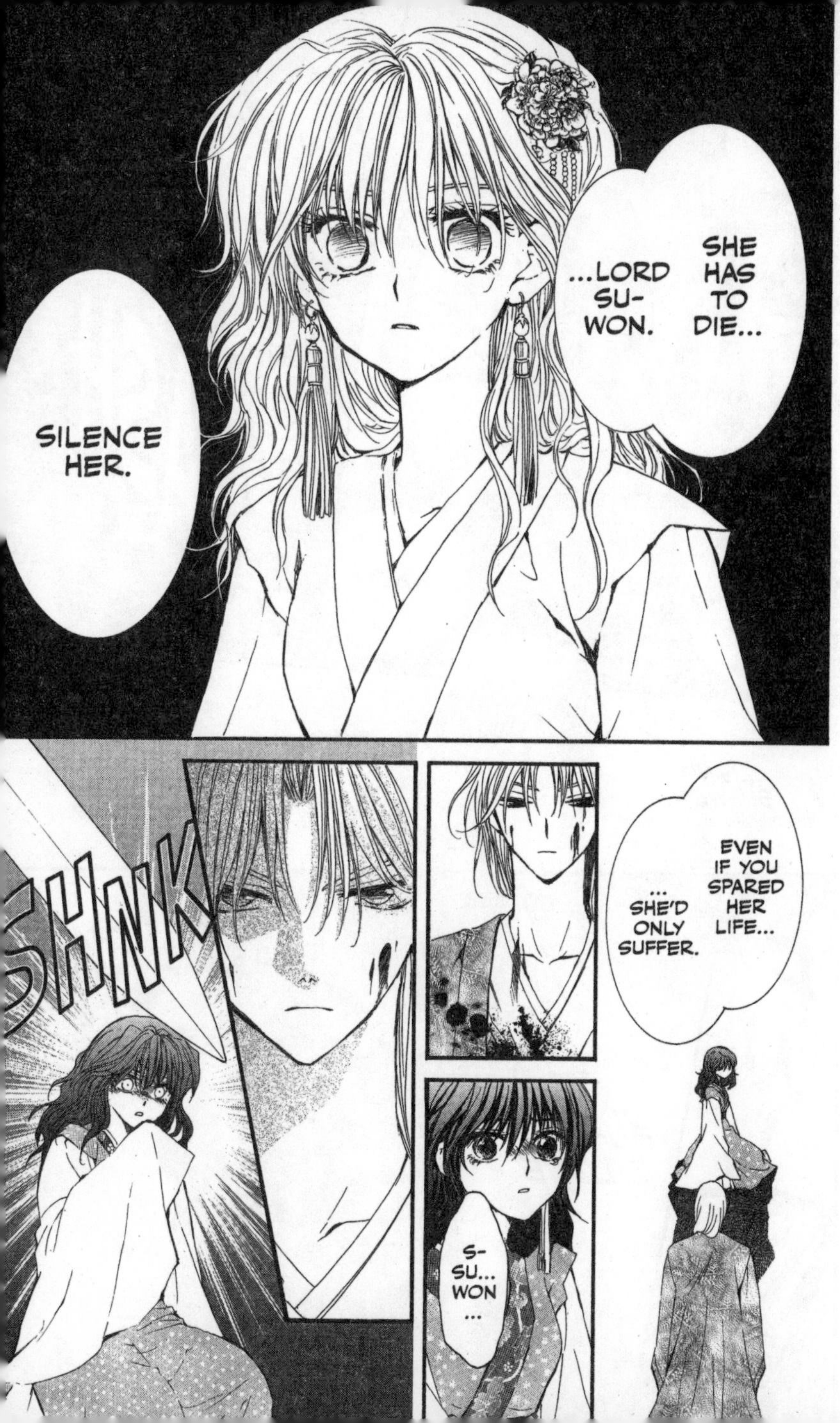
SHE HAS TO DIE...
...LORD SU-WON.
SILENCE HER.
EVEN IF YOU SPARED HER LIFE...
...SHE'D ONLY SUFFER.
S-SU...WON...
SHNK

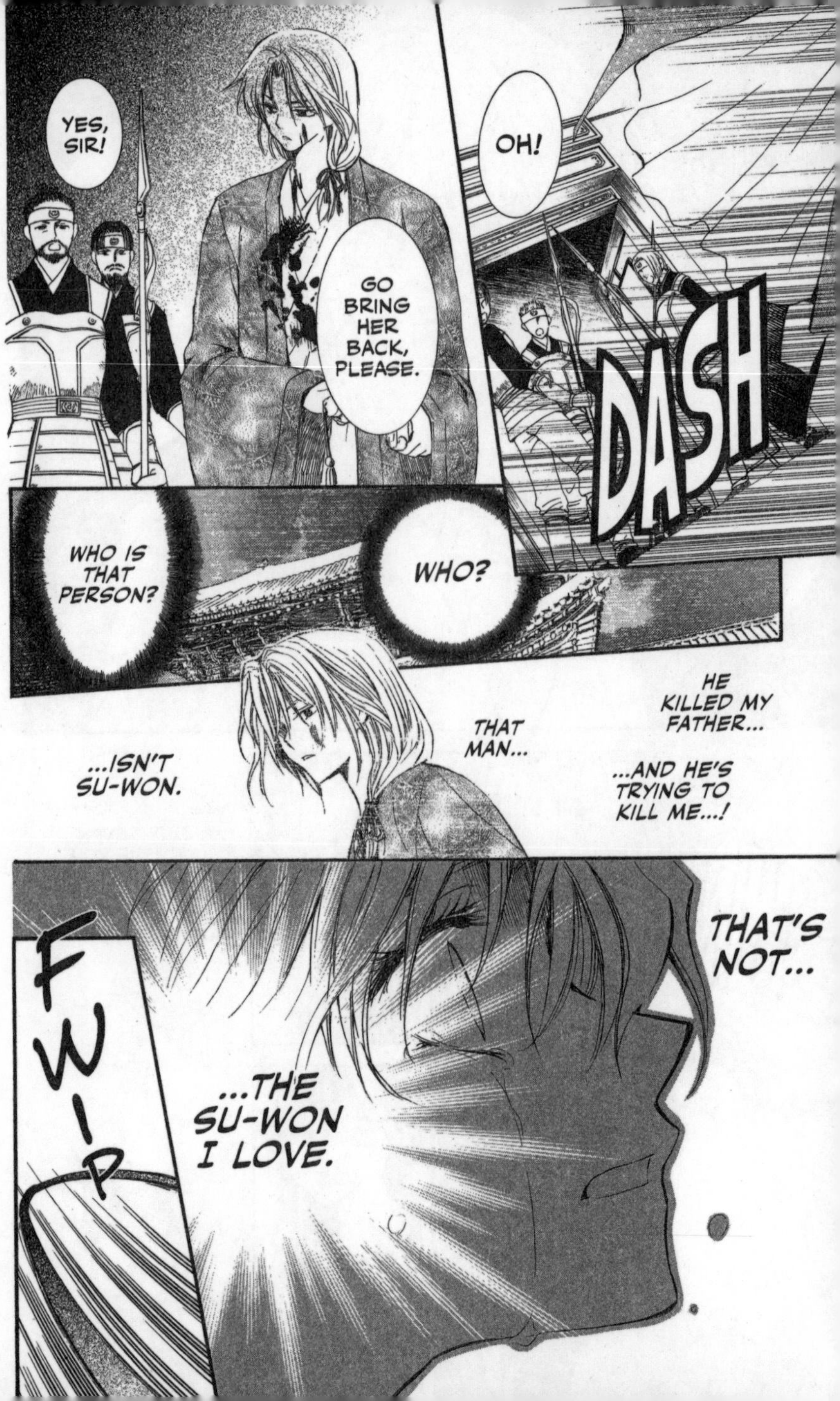
OH!
DASH
GO BRING HER BACK, PLEASE.
YES, SIR!
WHO?
WHO IS THAT PERSON?
HE KILLED MY FATHER...
...AND HE'S TRYING TO KILL ME...!
THAT MAN...
...ISN'T SU-WON.
THAT'S NOT...
...THE SU-WON I LOVE.
FWIP

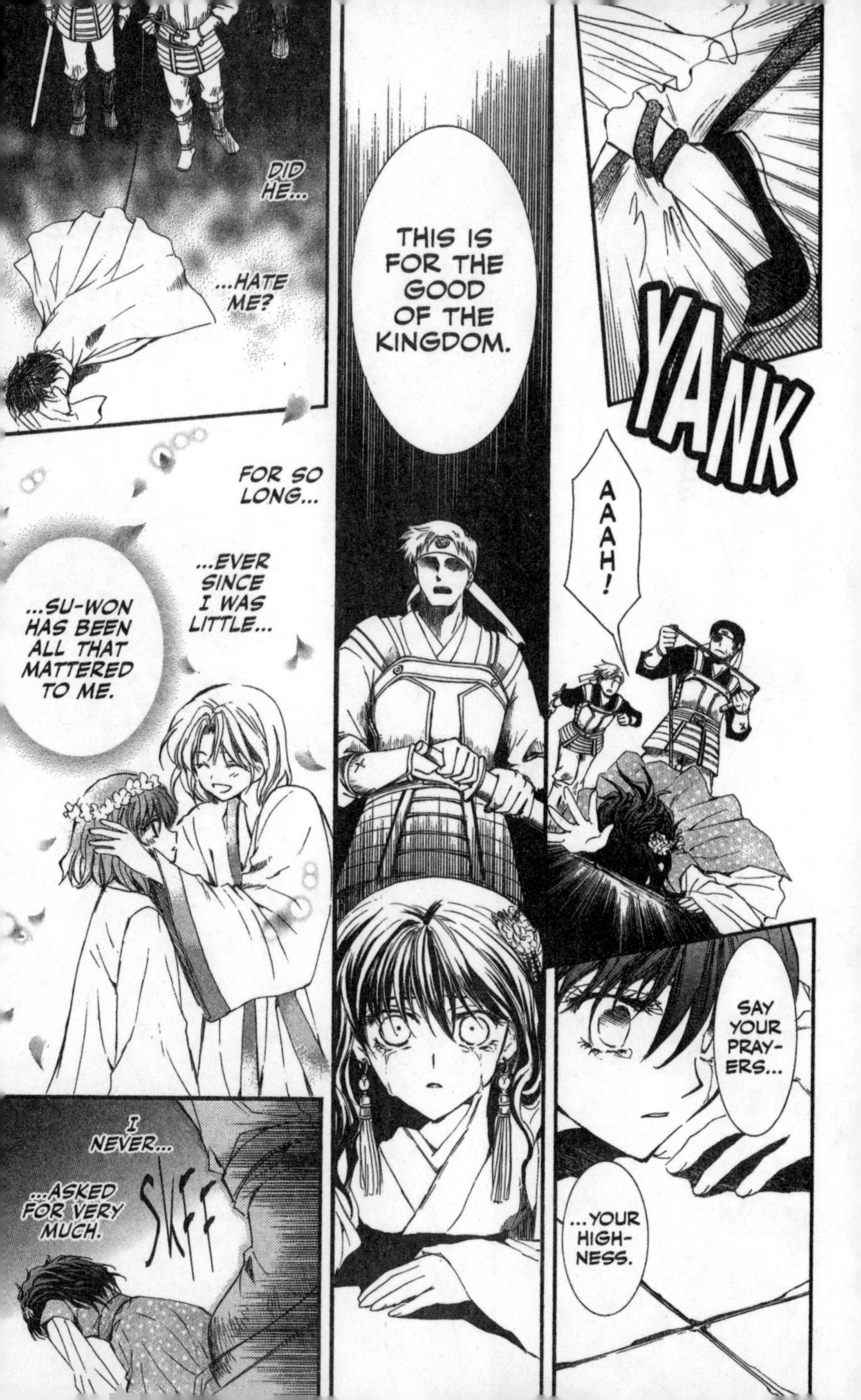
YANK
AAAAH!
SAY YOUR PRAYERS...
...YOUR HIGHNESS.
THIS IS FOR THE GOOD OF THE KINGDOM.
DID HE...
...HATE ME?
FOR SO LONG...
...EVER SINCE I WAS LITTLE...
...SU-WON HAS BEEN ALL THAT MATTERED TO ME.
I NEVER...
...ASKED FOR VERY MUCH.
SKFF

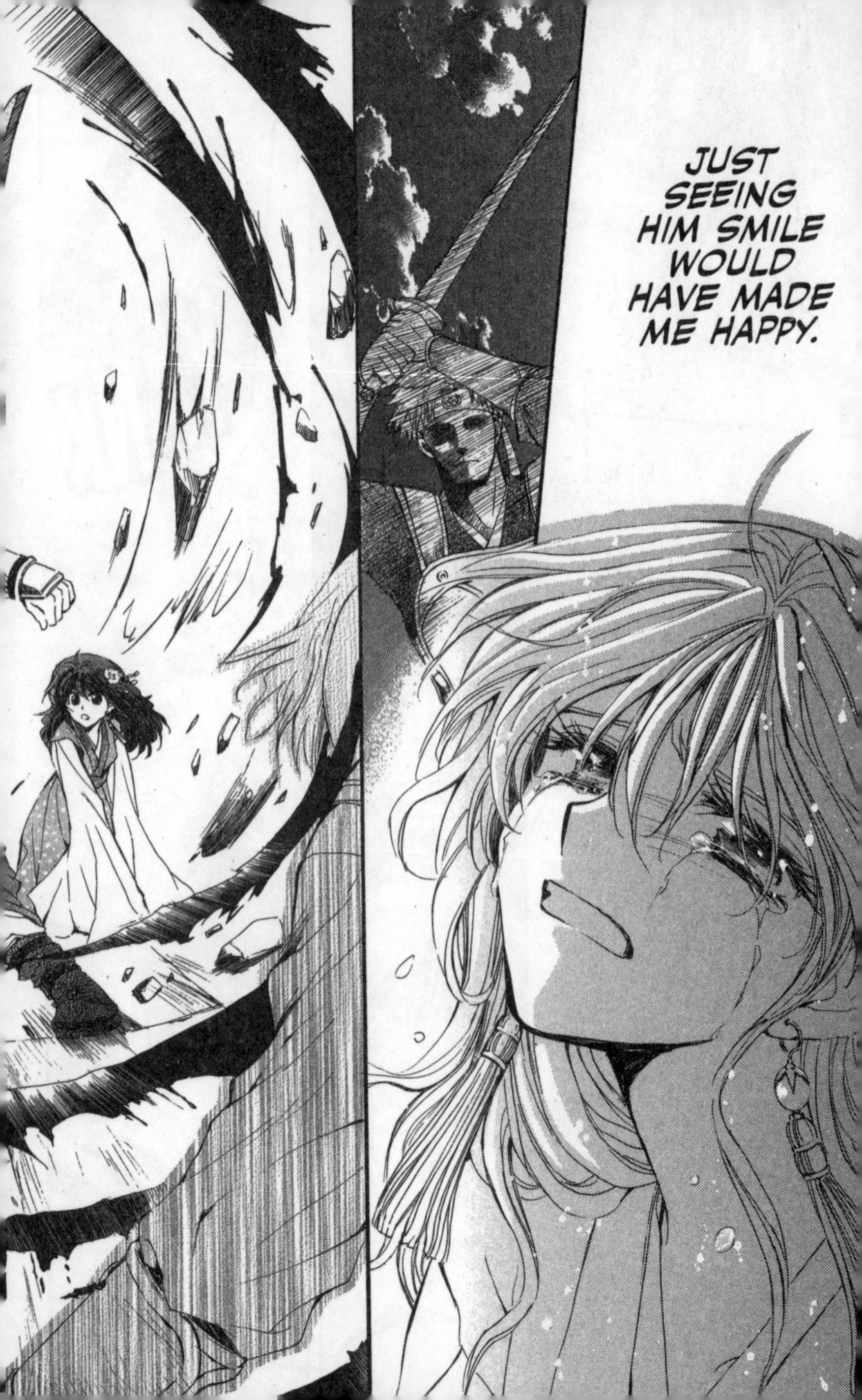
JUST SEEING HIM SMILE WOULD HAVE MADE ME HAPPY.

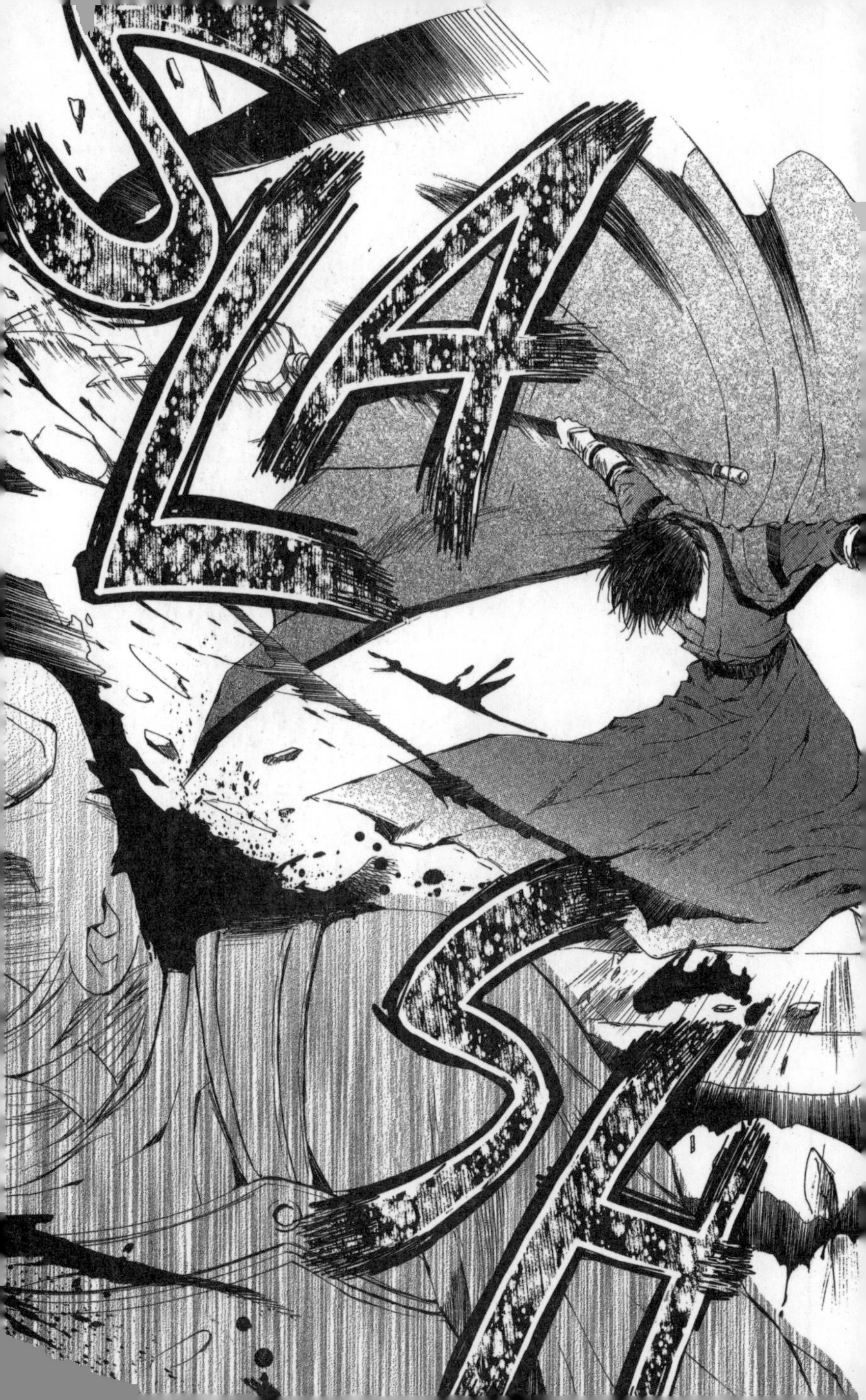
SLASH

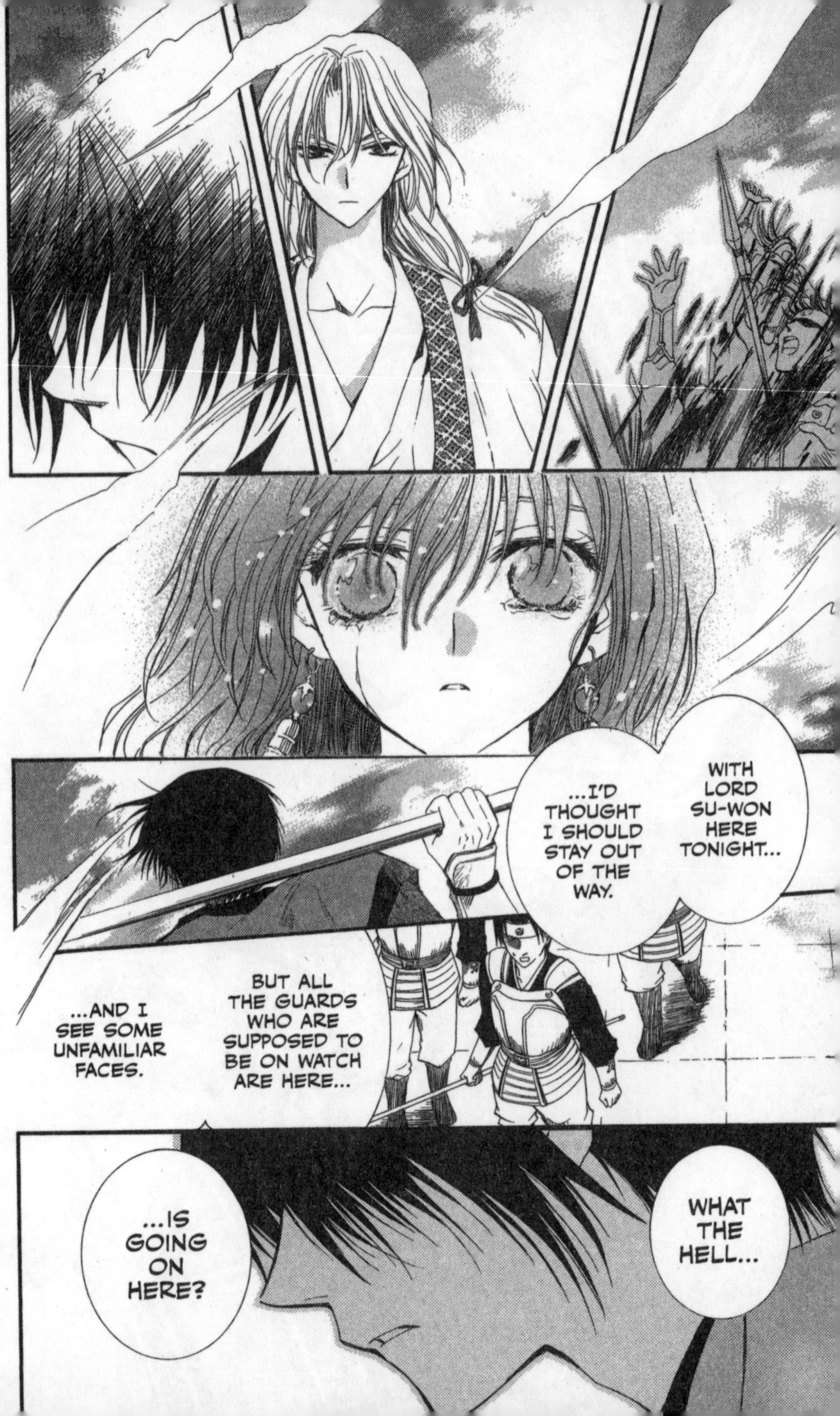
WITH LORD SU-WON HERE TONIGHT...
...I'D THOUGHT I SHOULD STAY OUT OF THE WAY.
BUT ALL THE GUARDS WHO ARE SUPPOSED TO BE ON WATCH ARE HERE...
...AND I SEE SOME UNFAMILIAR FACES.
WHAT THE HELL...
...IS GOING ON HERE?

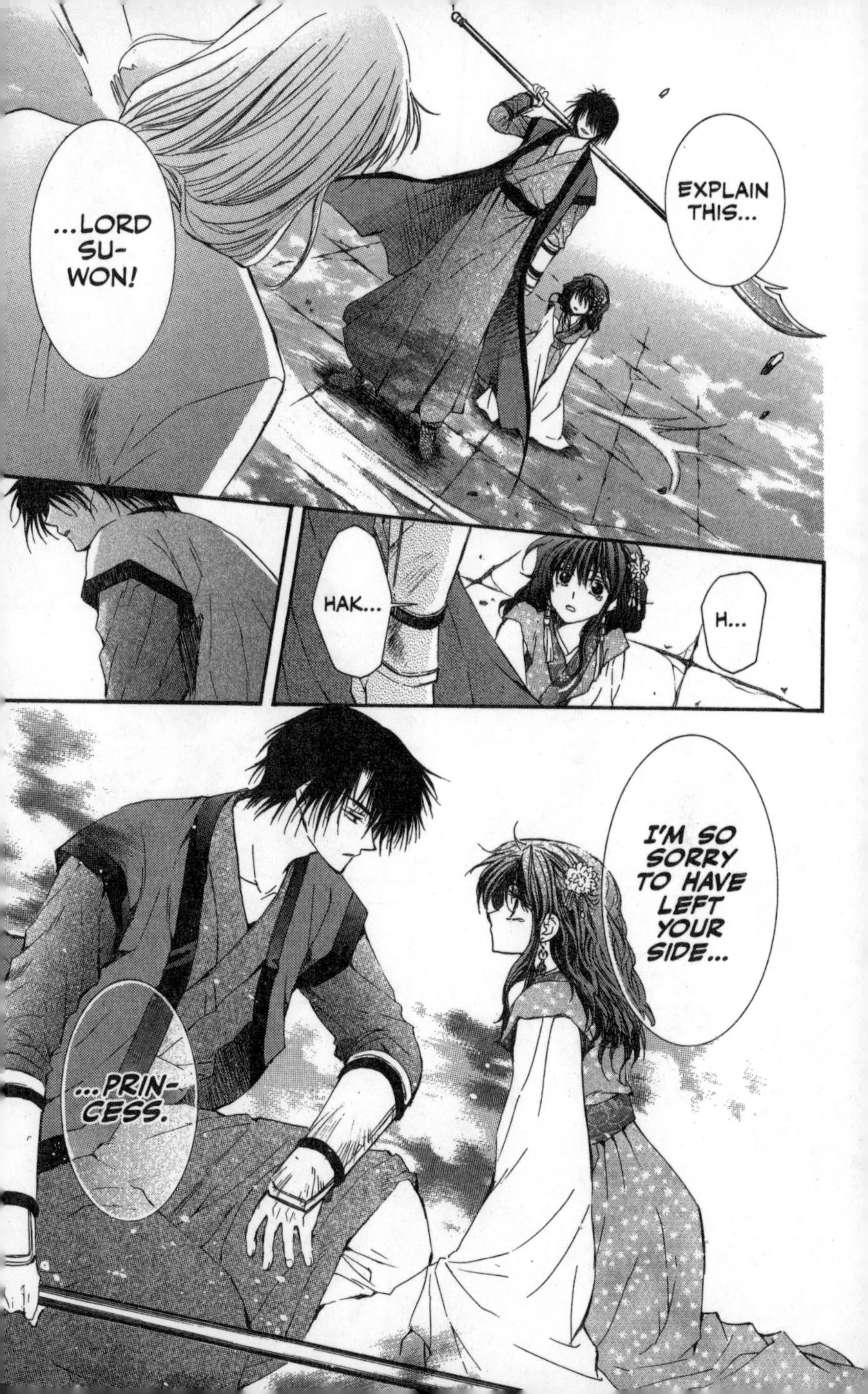
EXPLAIN THIS...
...LORD SU-WON!
H...
HAK...
I'M SO SORRY TO HAVE LEFT YOUR SIDE...
...PRINCESS.

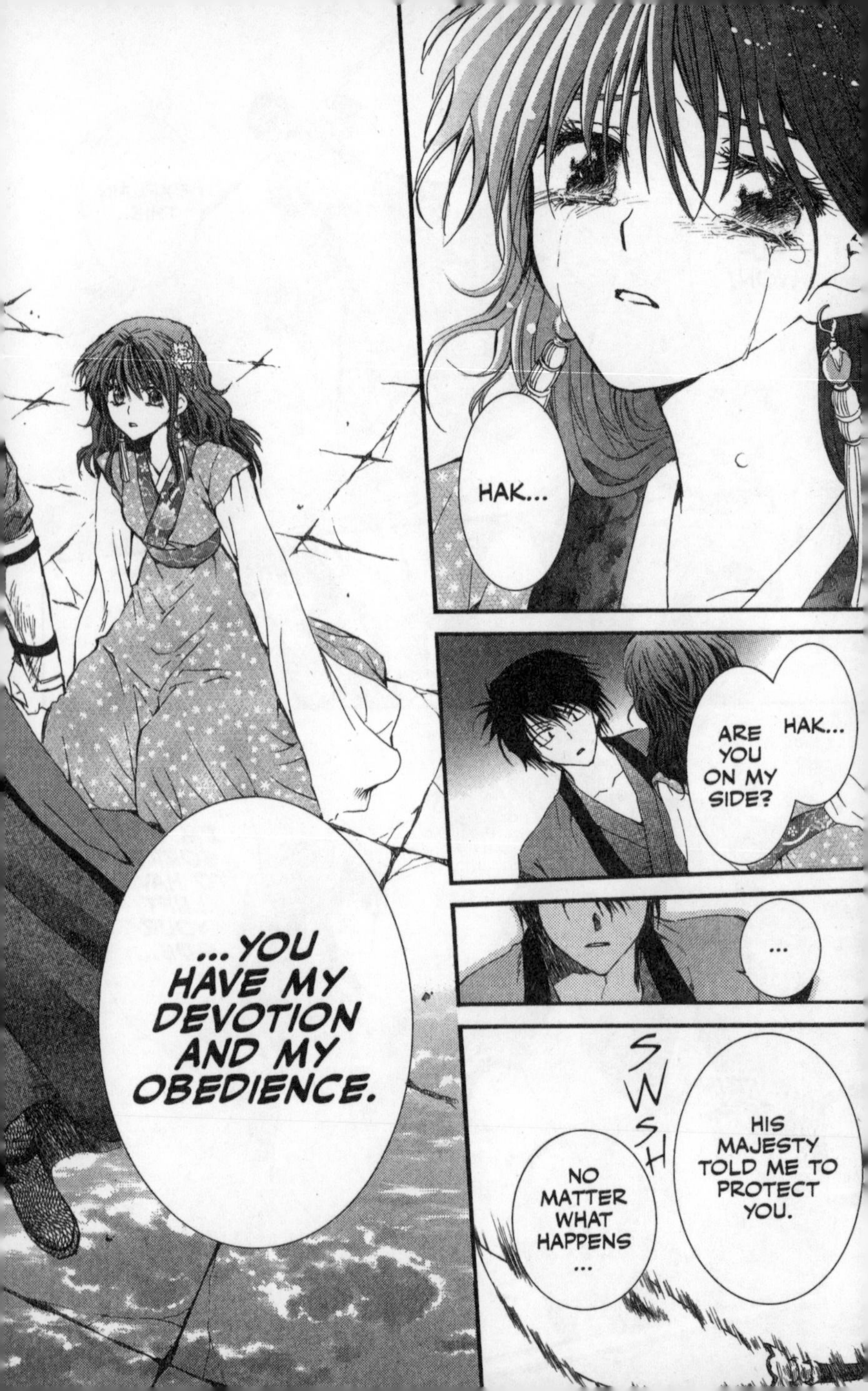
HAK...
HAK... ARE YOU ON MY SIDE?
...
HIS MAJESTY TOLD ME TO PROTECT YOU.
SWSH
NO MATTER WHAT HAPPENS ...
...YOU HAVE MY DEVOTION AND MY OBEDIENCE.

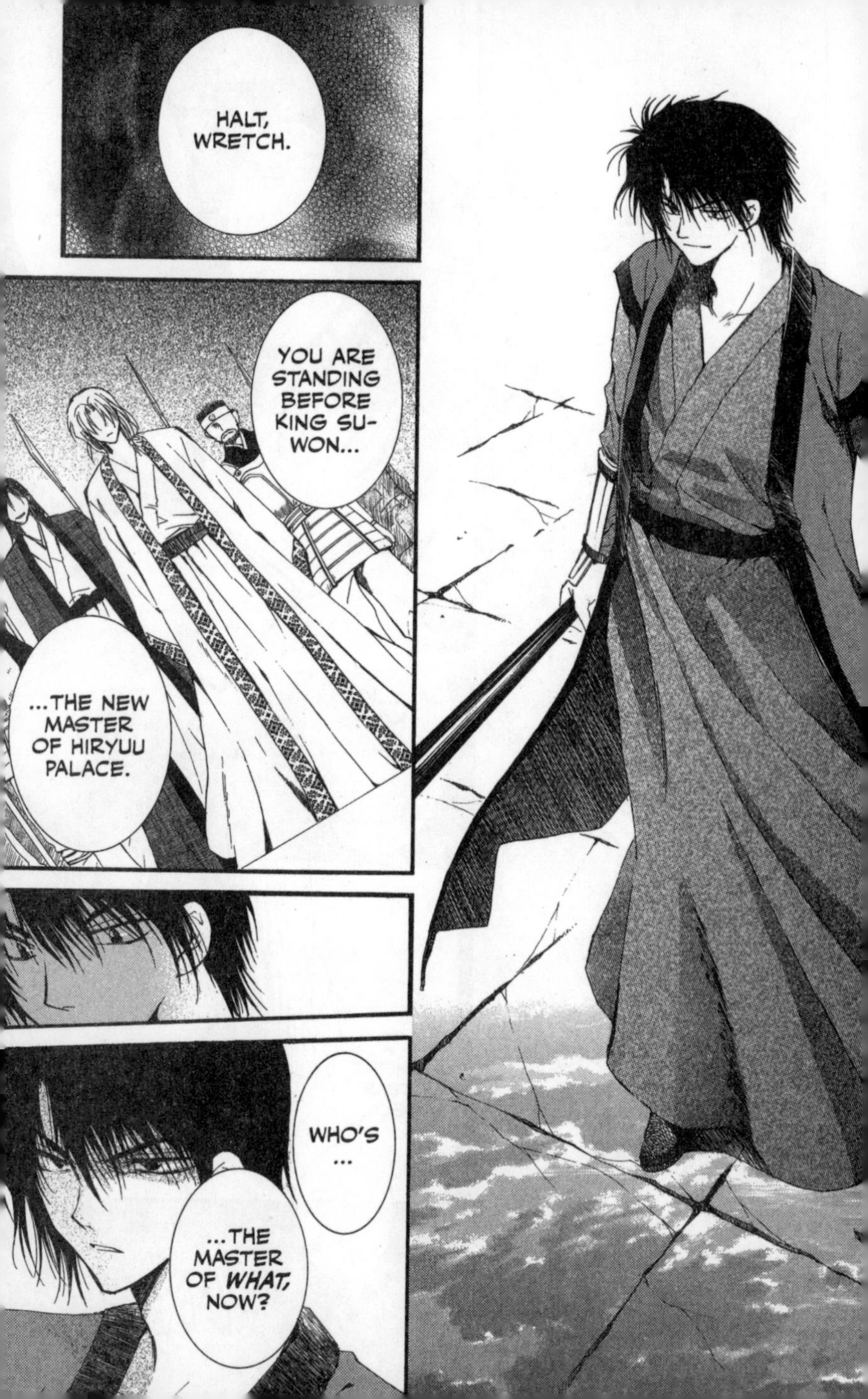
HALT, WRETCH.
YOU ARE STANDING BEFORE KING SU-WON...
...THE NEW MASTER OF HIRYUU PALACE.
WHO'S ...
...THE MASTER OF *WHAT,* NOW?

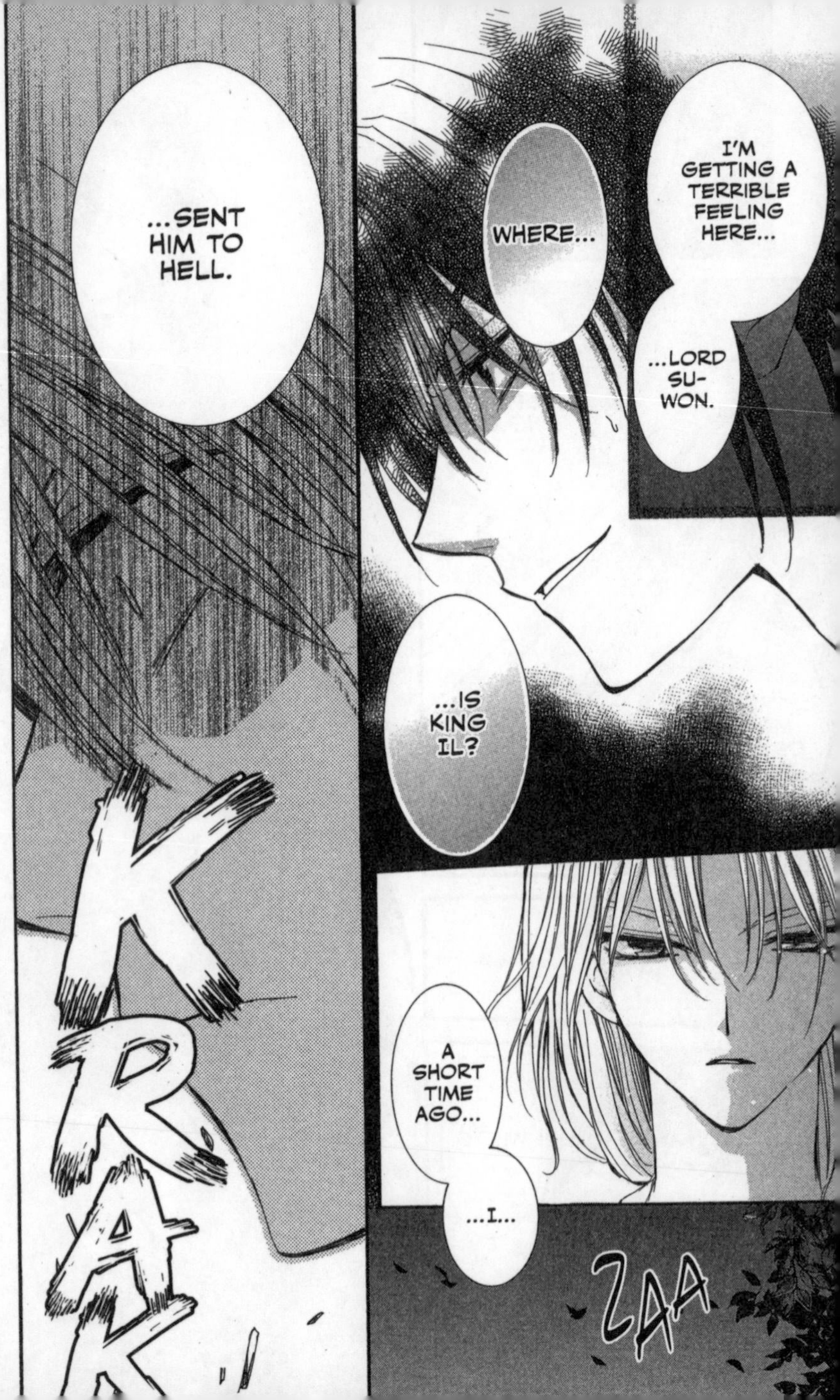
I'M GETTING A TERRIBLE FEELING HERE...
...LORD SU-WON.
WHERE...
...IS KING IL?
A SHORT TIME AGO...
...I...
ZAA
...SENT HIM TO HELL.
KRA

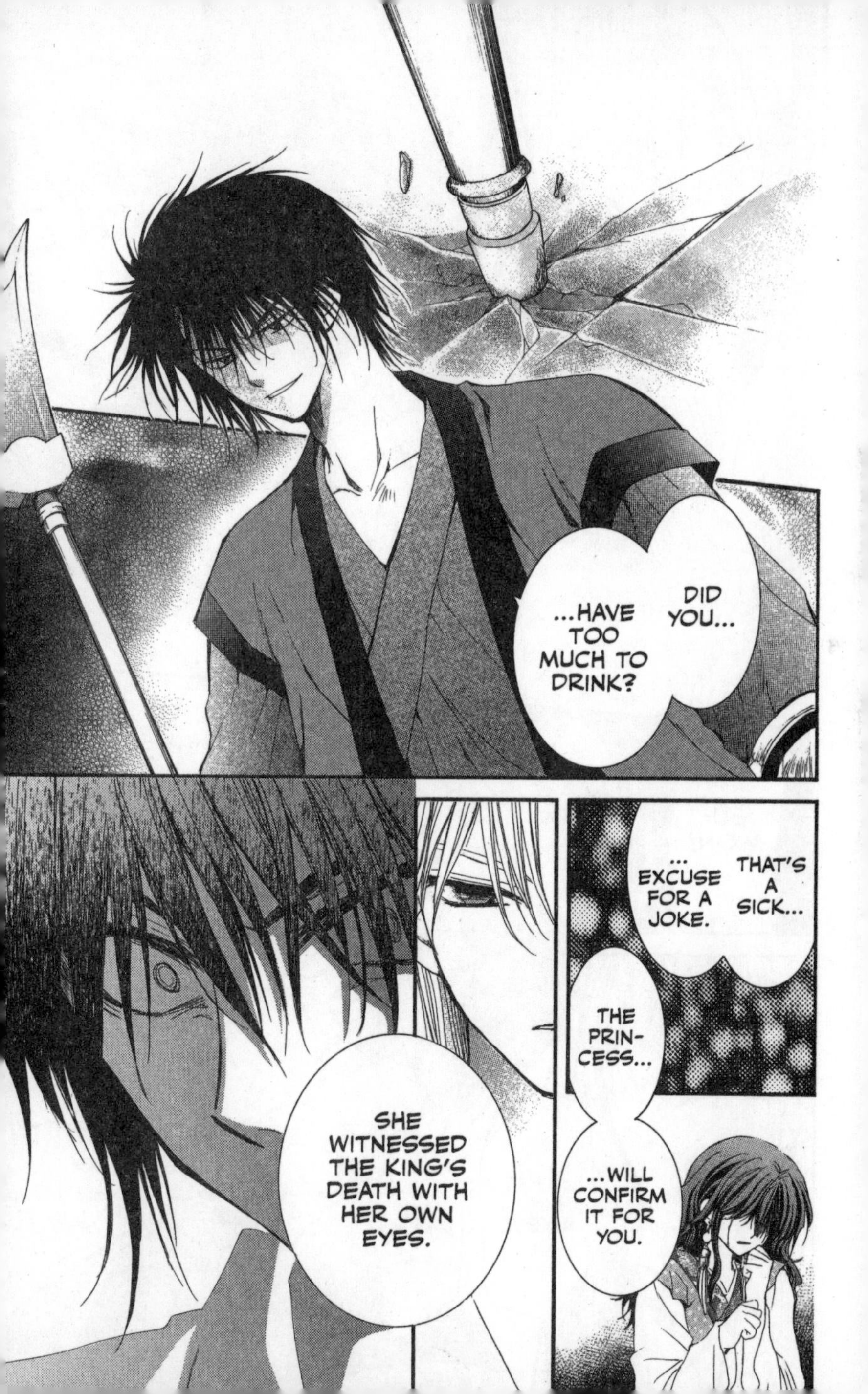
DID YOU...
...HAVE TOO MUCH TO DRINK?
THAT'S A SICK...
...EXCUSE FOR A JOKE.
THE PRINCESS...
...WILL CONFIRM IT FOR YOU.
SHE WITNESSED THE KING'S DEATH WITH HER OWN EYES.

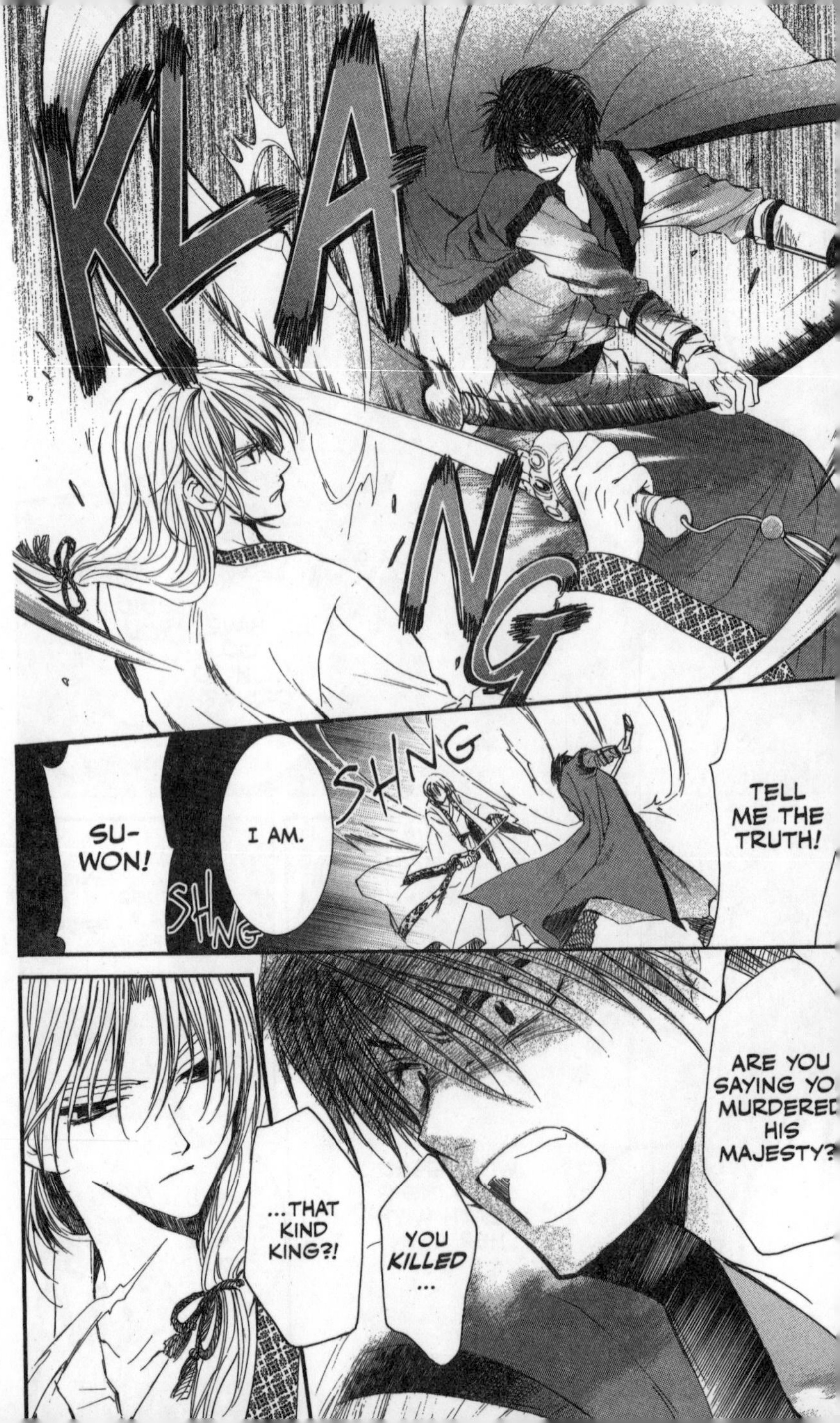
KLANG
TELL ME THE TRUTH!
SHING
I AM.
SU-WON!
SHING
ARE YOU SAYING YO MURDERE HIS MAJESTY?
YOU KILLED ...
...THAT KIND KING?!

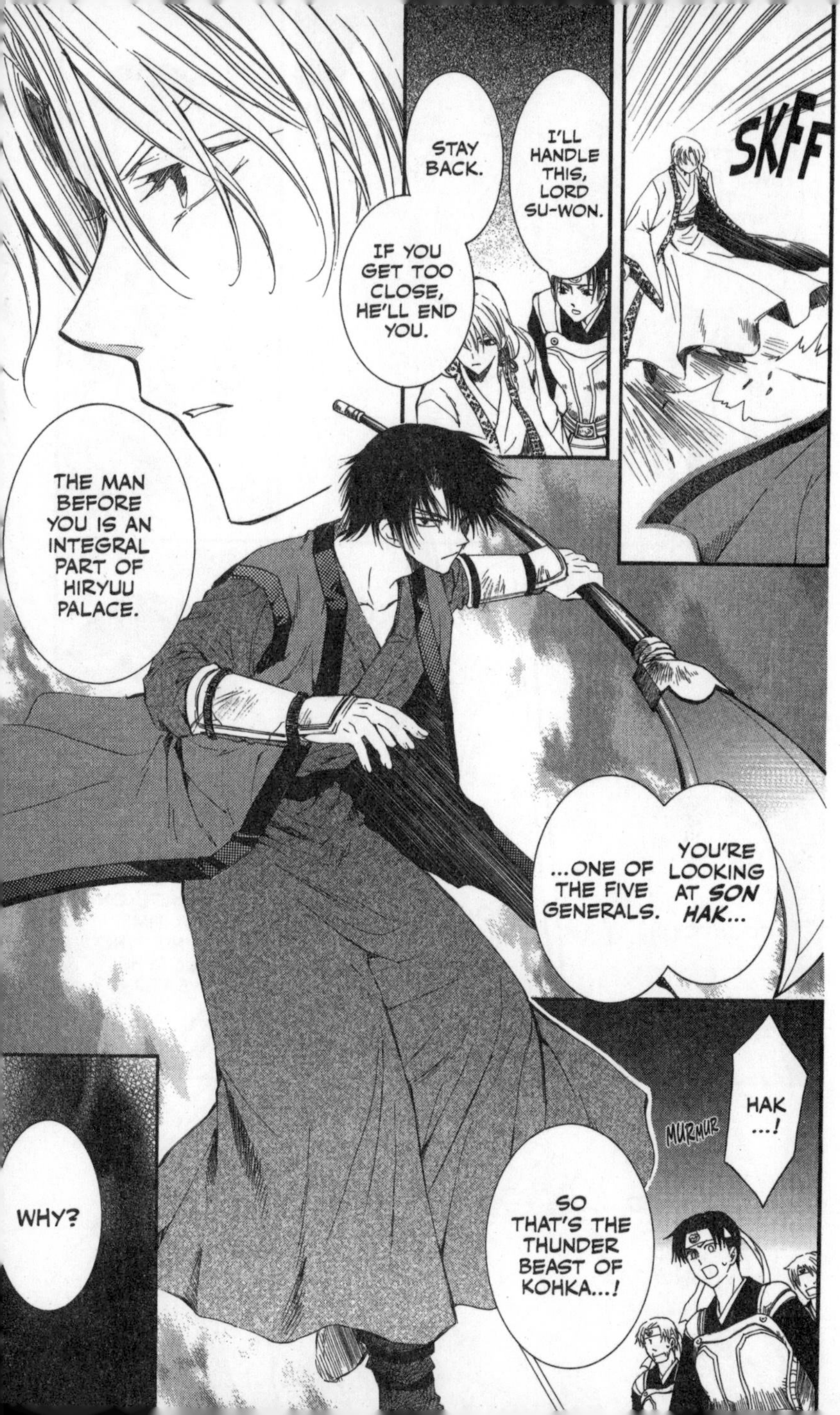
SKFF
I'LL HANDLE THIS, LORD SU-WON.
STAY BACK.
IF YOU GET TOO CLOSE, HE'LL END YOU.
THE MAN BEFORE YOU IS AN INTEGRAL PART OF HIRYUU PALACE.
YOU'RE LOOKING AT *SON HAK*...
...ONE OF THE FIVE GENERALS.
HAK ...!
MURMUR
SO THAT'S THE THUNDER BEAST OF KOHKA...!
WHY?

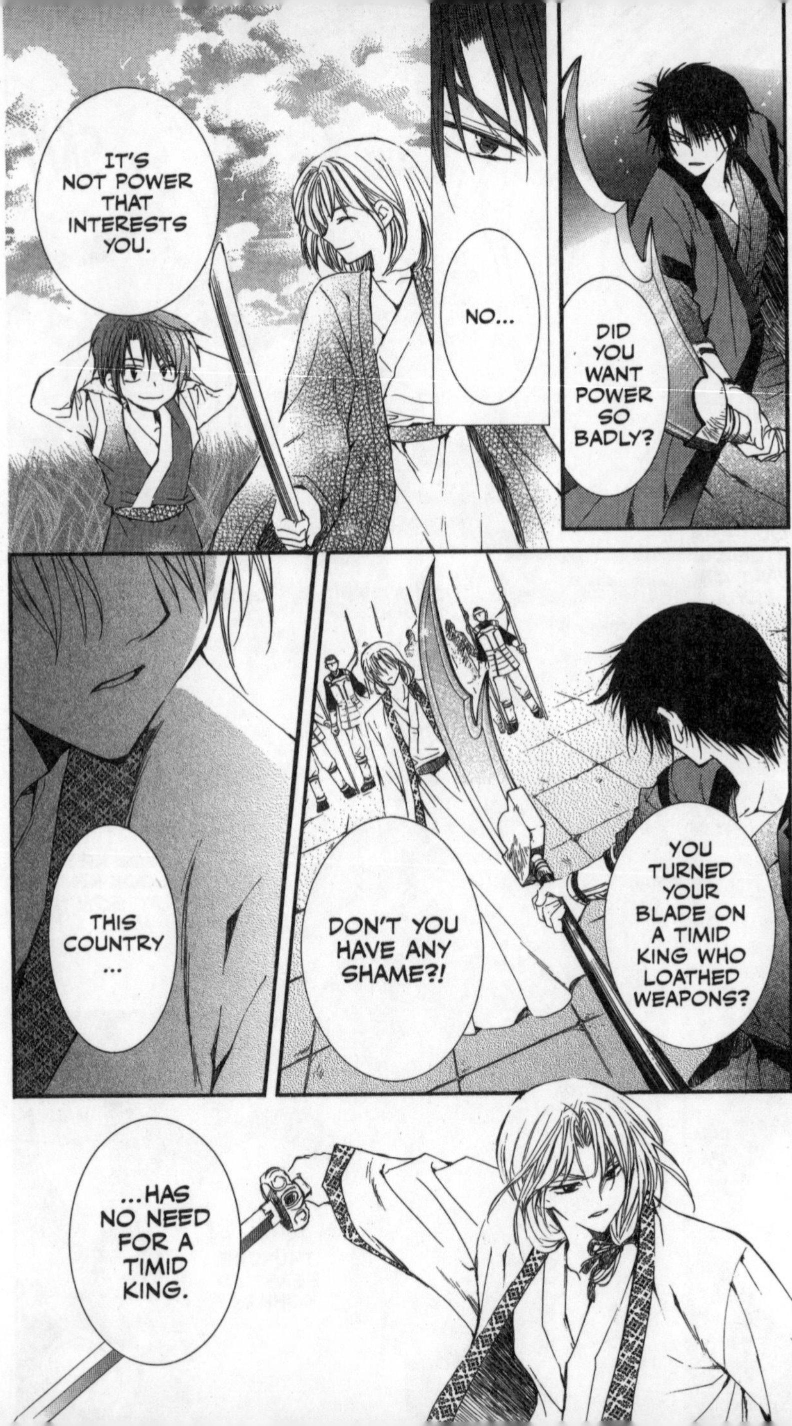
DID YOU WANT POWER SO BADLY?
NO...
IT'S NOT POWER THAT INTERESTS YOU.
YOU TURNED YOUR BLADE ON A TIMID KING WHO LOATHED WEAPONS?
DON'T YOU HAVE ANY SHAME?!
THIS COUNTRY ...
...HAS NO NEED FOR A TIMID KING.

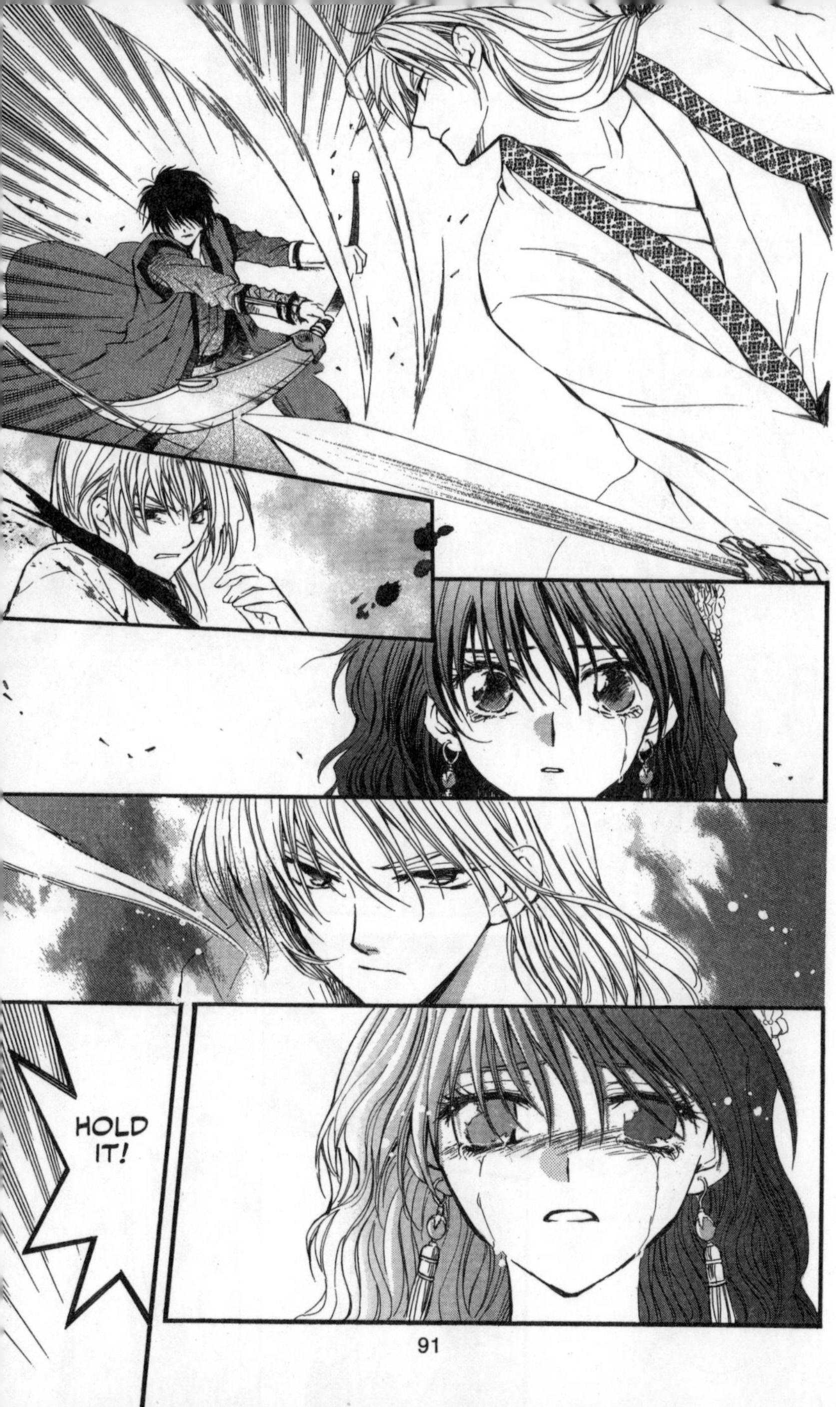
HOLD IT!

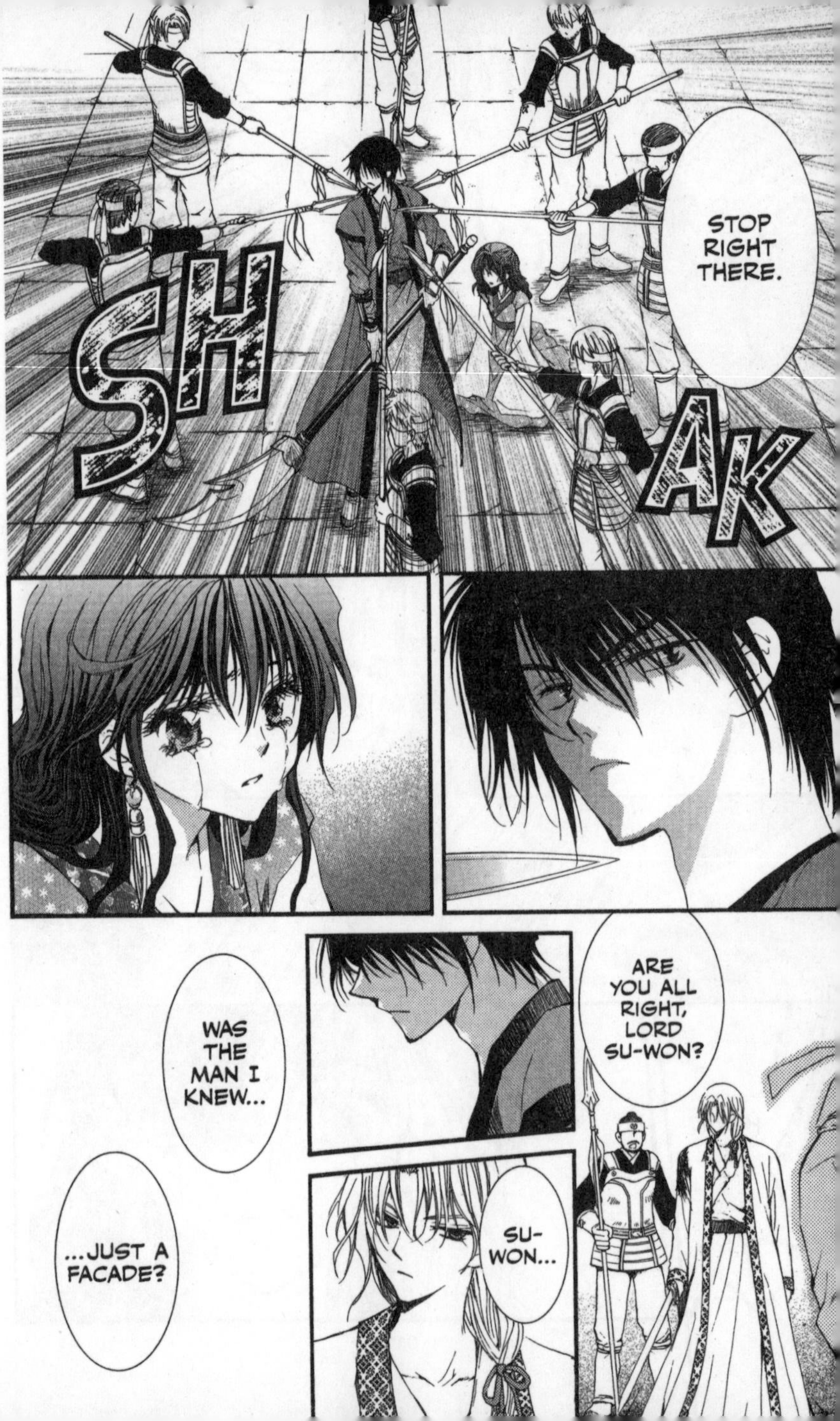
SHAK
STOP RIGHT THERE.
ARE YOU ALL RIGHT, LORD SU-WON?
WAS THE MAN I KNEW...
SU-WON...
...JUST A FACADE?

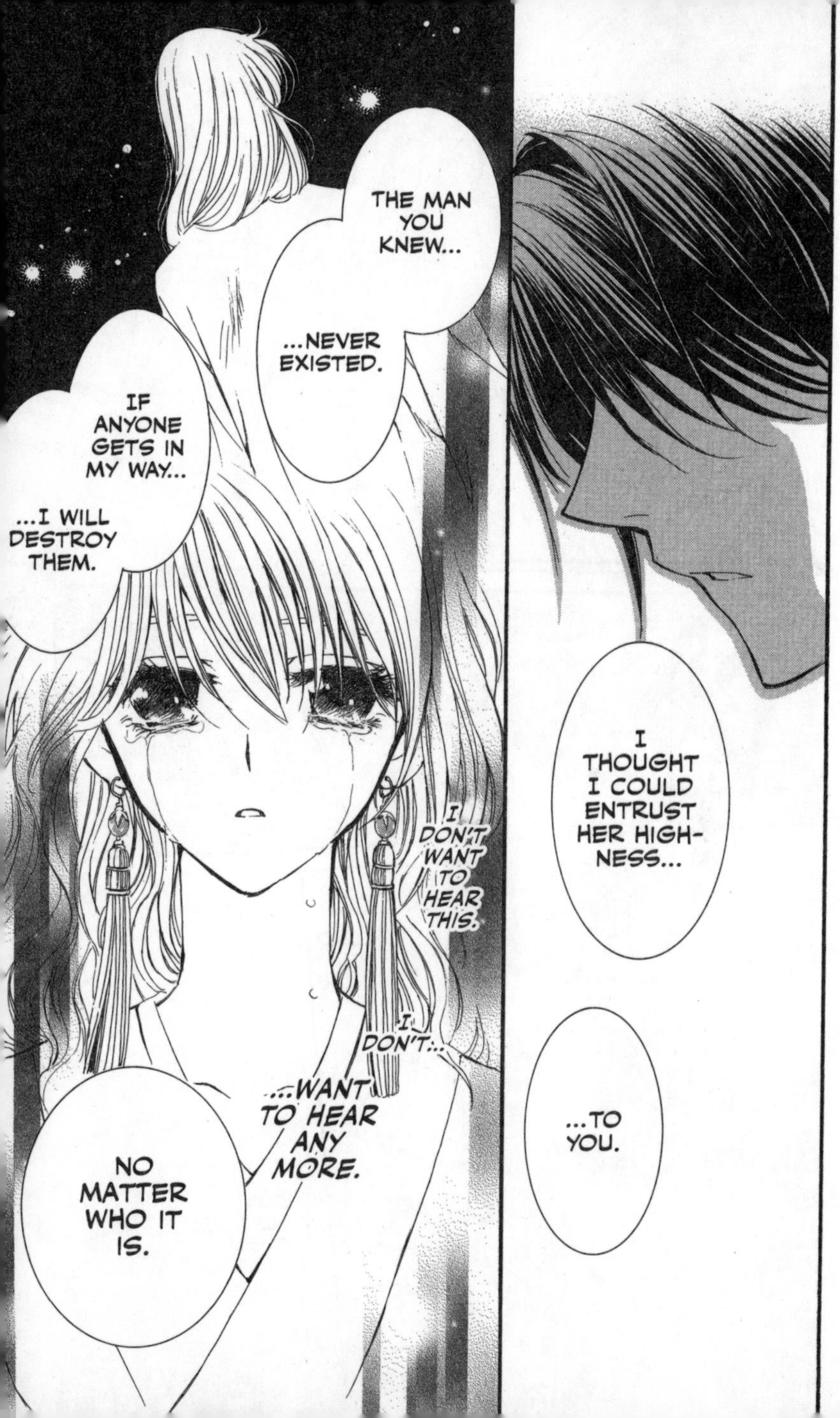
I THOUGHT I COULD ENTRUST HER HIGHNESS...
...TO YOU.
THE MAN YOU KNEW...
...NEVER EXISTED.
IF ANYONE GETS IN MY WAY...
...I WILL DESTROY THEM.
I DON'T WANT TO HEAR THIS.
I DON'T...
...WANT TO HEAR ANY MORE.
NO MATTER WHO IT IS.

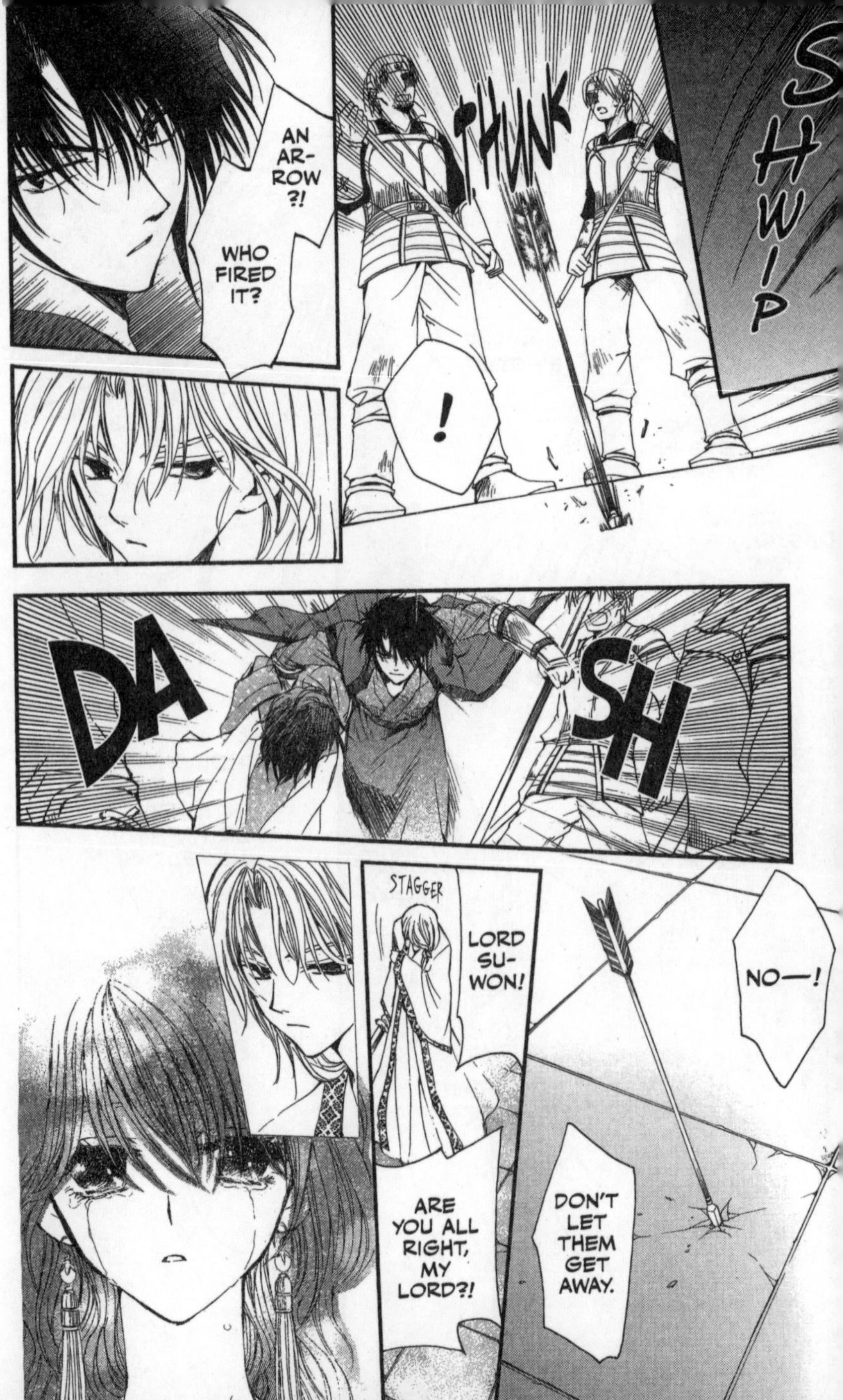
SHWIP
THUNK
!
AN AR-ROW?!
WHO FIRED IT?
DASH
NO—!
STAGGER
LORD SU-WON!
DON'T LET THEM GET AWAY.
ARE YOU ALL RIGHT, MY LORD?!

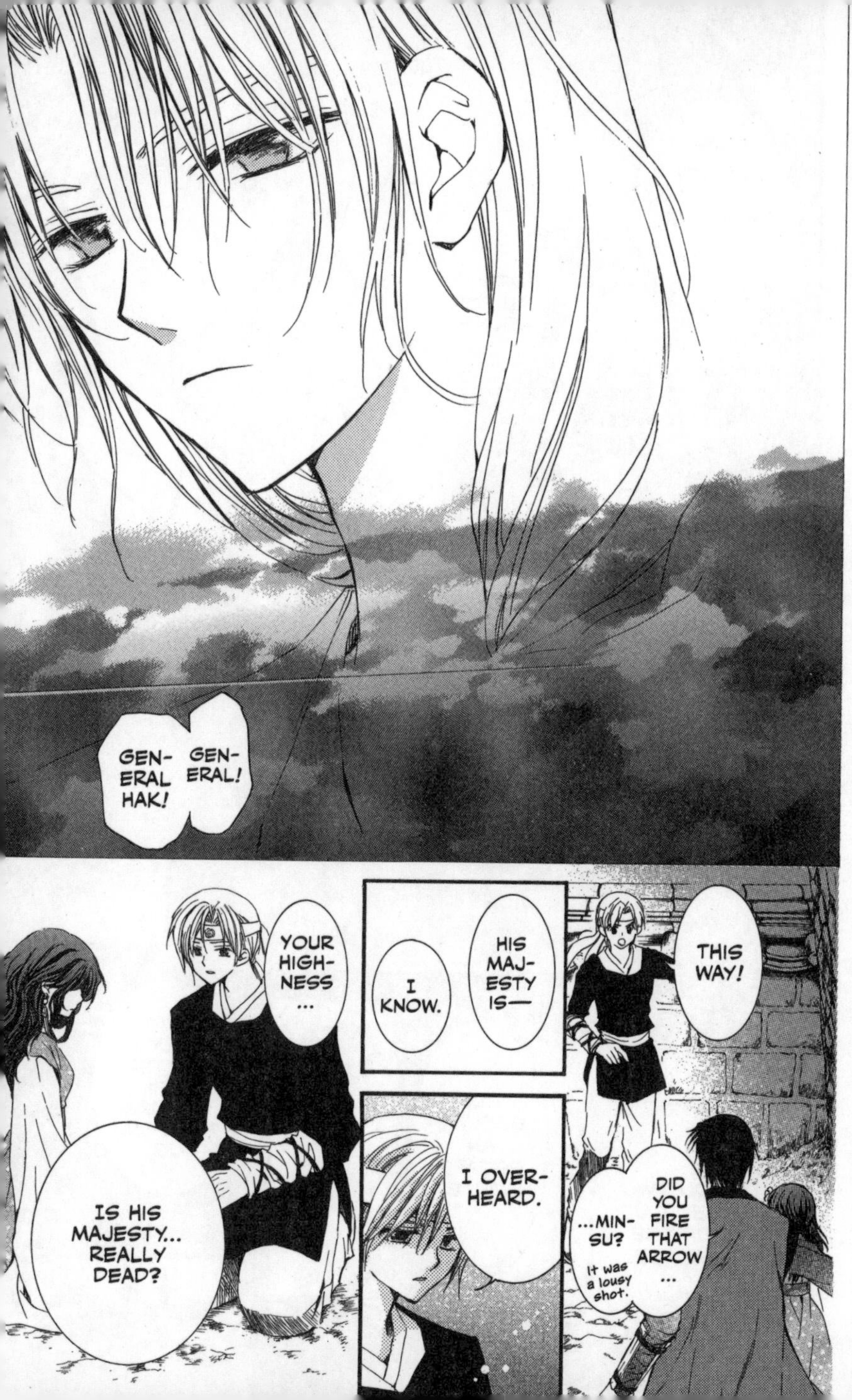
GEN-ERAL!
GEN-ERAL HAK!
THIS WAY!
DID YOU FIRE THAT ARROW ...
...MIN-SU?
It was a lousy shot.
HIS MAJ-ESTY IS—
I KNOW.
I OVER-HEARD.
YOUR HIGH-NESS ...
IS HIS MAJESTY... REALLY DEAD?

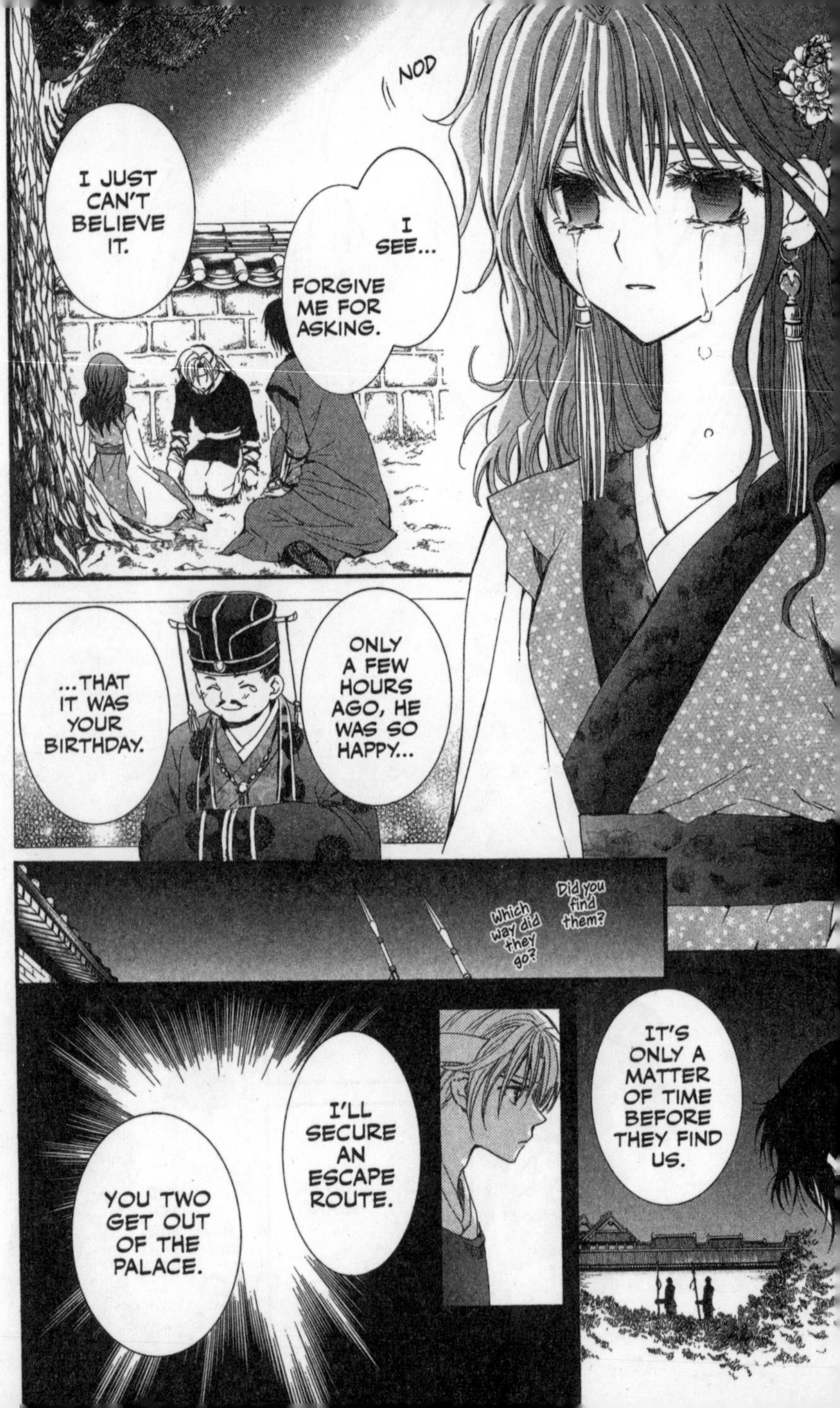
NOD
I SEE... FORGIVE ME FOR ASKING.
I JUST CAN'T BELIEVE IT.
ONLY A FEW HOURS AGO, HE WAS SO HAPPY...
...THAT IT WAS YOUR BIRTHDAY.
Did you find them?
Which way did they go?
IT'S ONLY A MATTER OF TIME BEFORE THEY FIND US.
I'LL SECURE AN ESCAPE ROUTE.
YOU TWO GET OUT OF THE PALACE.

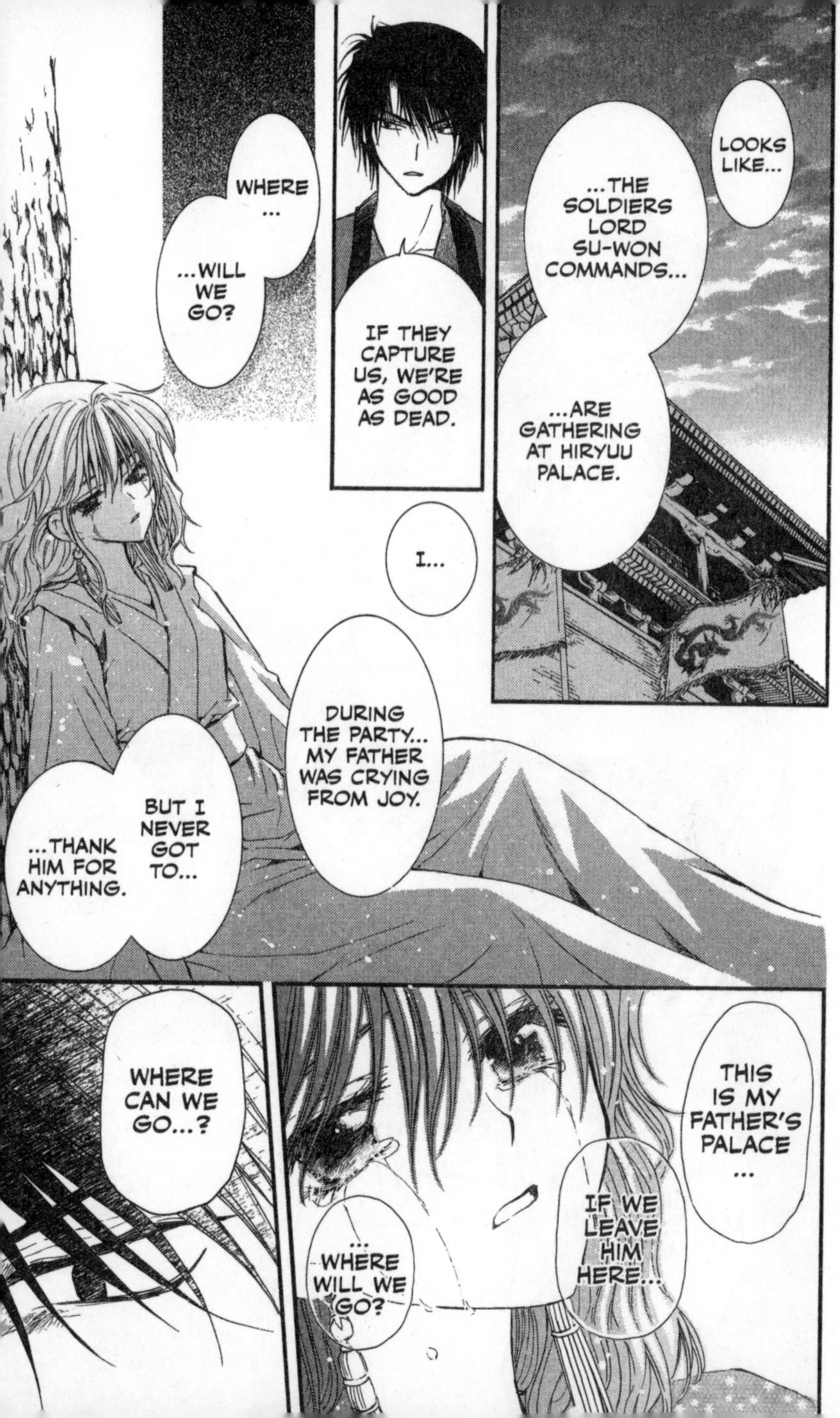
LOOKS LIKE...
...THE SOLDIERS LORD SU-WON COMMANDS...
...ARE GATHERING AT HIRYUU PALACE.
IF THEY CAPTURE US, WE'RE AS GOOD AS DEAD.
WHERE...
...WILL WE GO?
I...
DURING THE PARTY... MY FATHER WAS CRYING FROM JOY.
BUT I NEVER GOT TO...
...THANK HIM FOR ANYTHING.
THIS IS MY FATHER'S PALACE...
IF WE LEAVE HIM HERE...
...WHERE WILL WE GO?
WHERE CAN WE GO...?

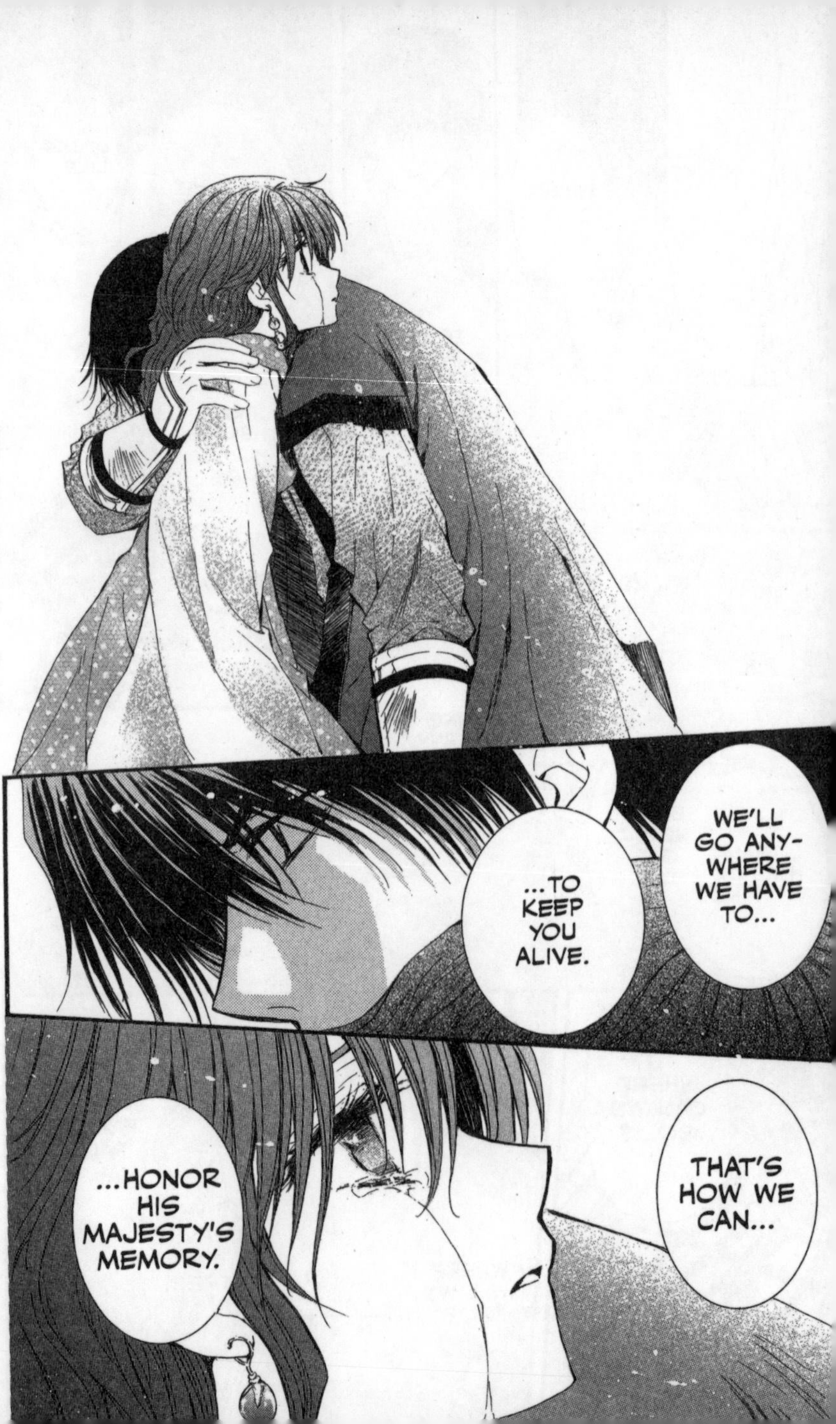
WE'LL GO ANY-WHERE WE HAVE TO...
...TO KEEP YOU ALIVE.
THAT'S HOW WE CAN...
...HONOR HIS MAJESTY'S MEMORY.

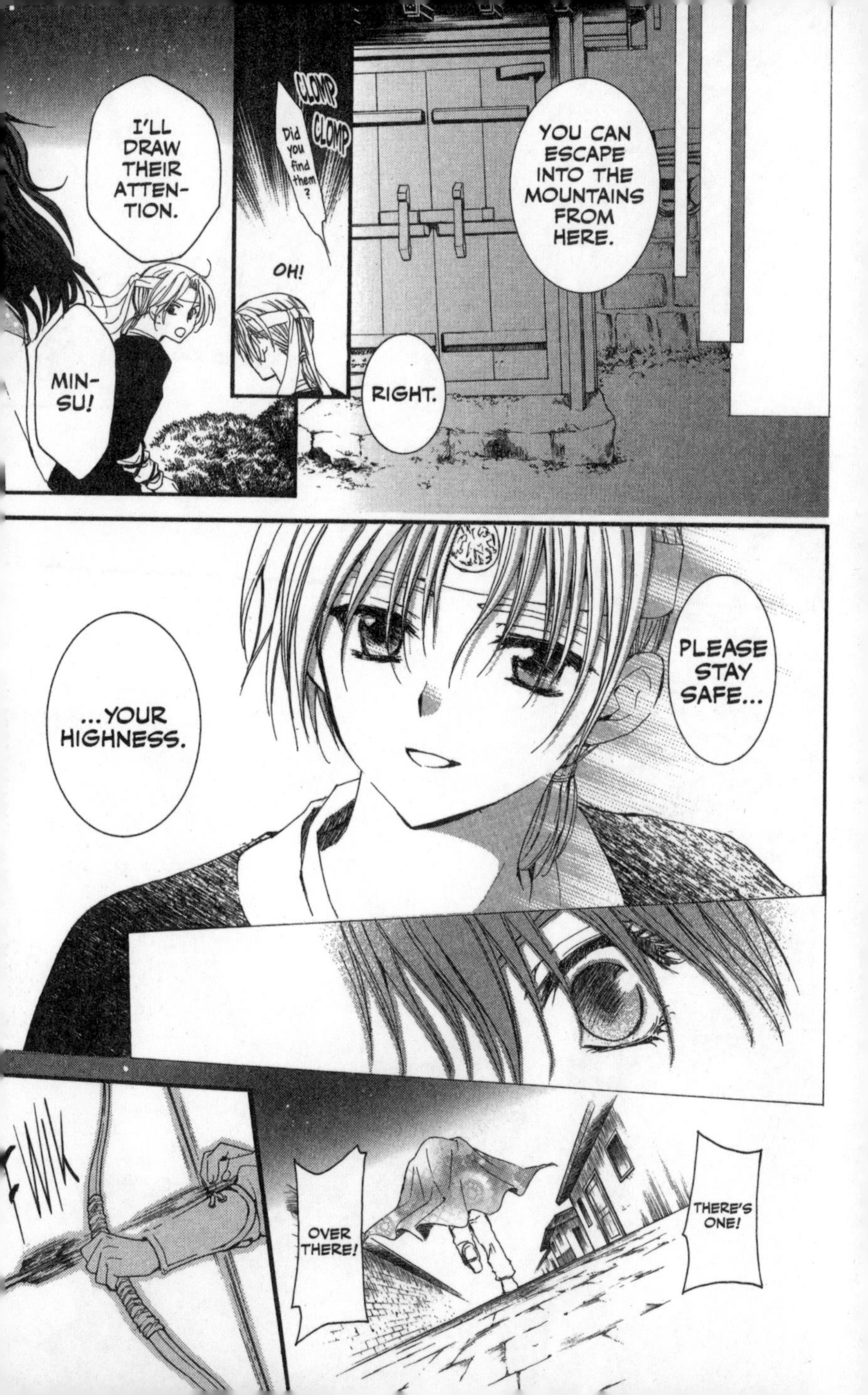
YOU CAN ESCAPE INTO THE MOUNTAINS FROM HERE.
RIGHT.
CLOMP CLOMP
Did you find them?
OH!
I'LL DRAW THEIR ATTENTION.
MIN-SU!
PLEASE STAY SAFE...
...YOUR HIGHNESS.
THERE'S ONE!
OVER THERE!
FWIK

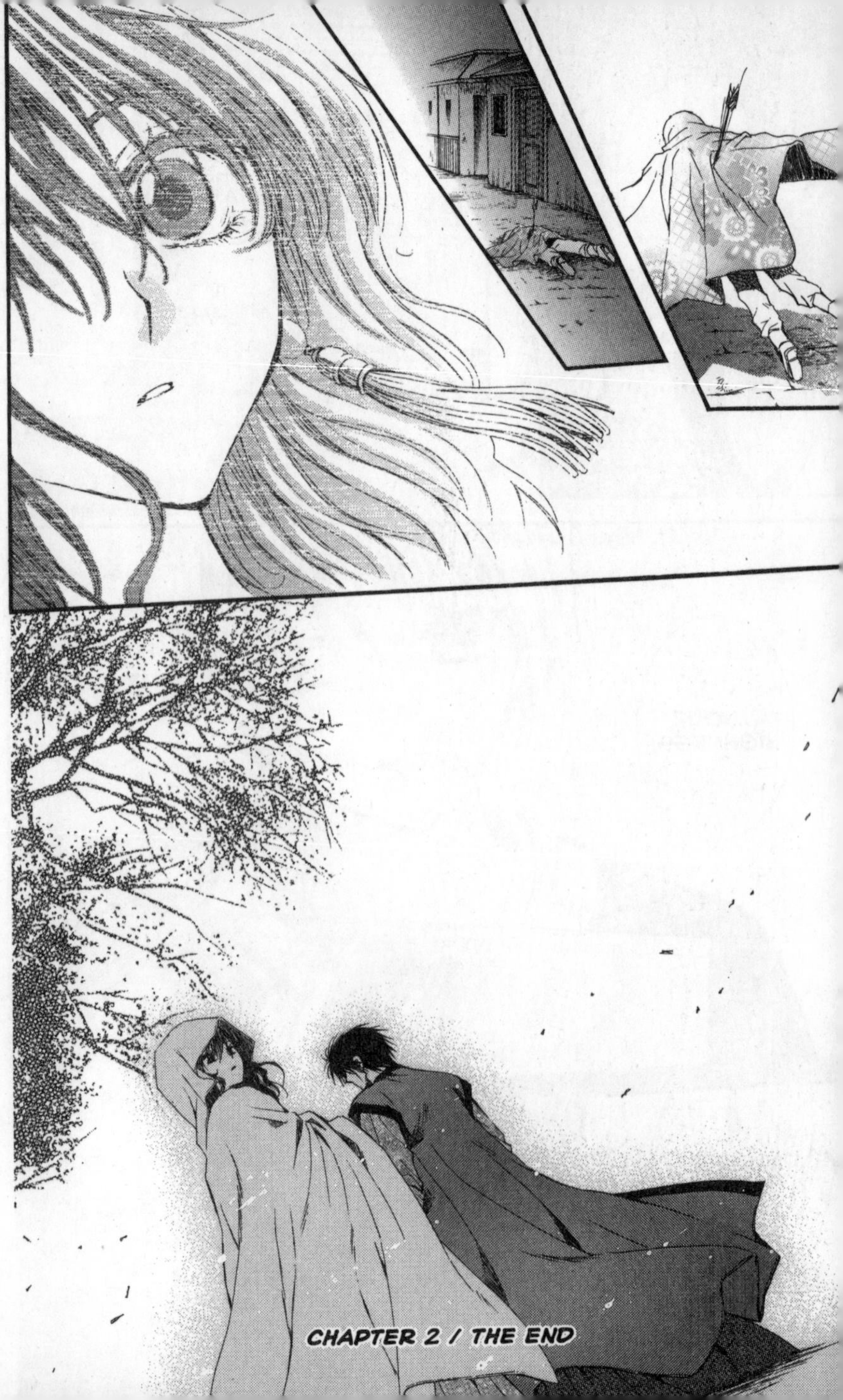
CHAPTER 2 / THE END

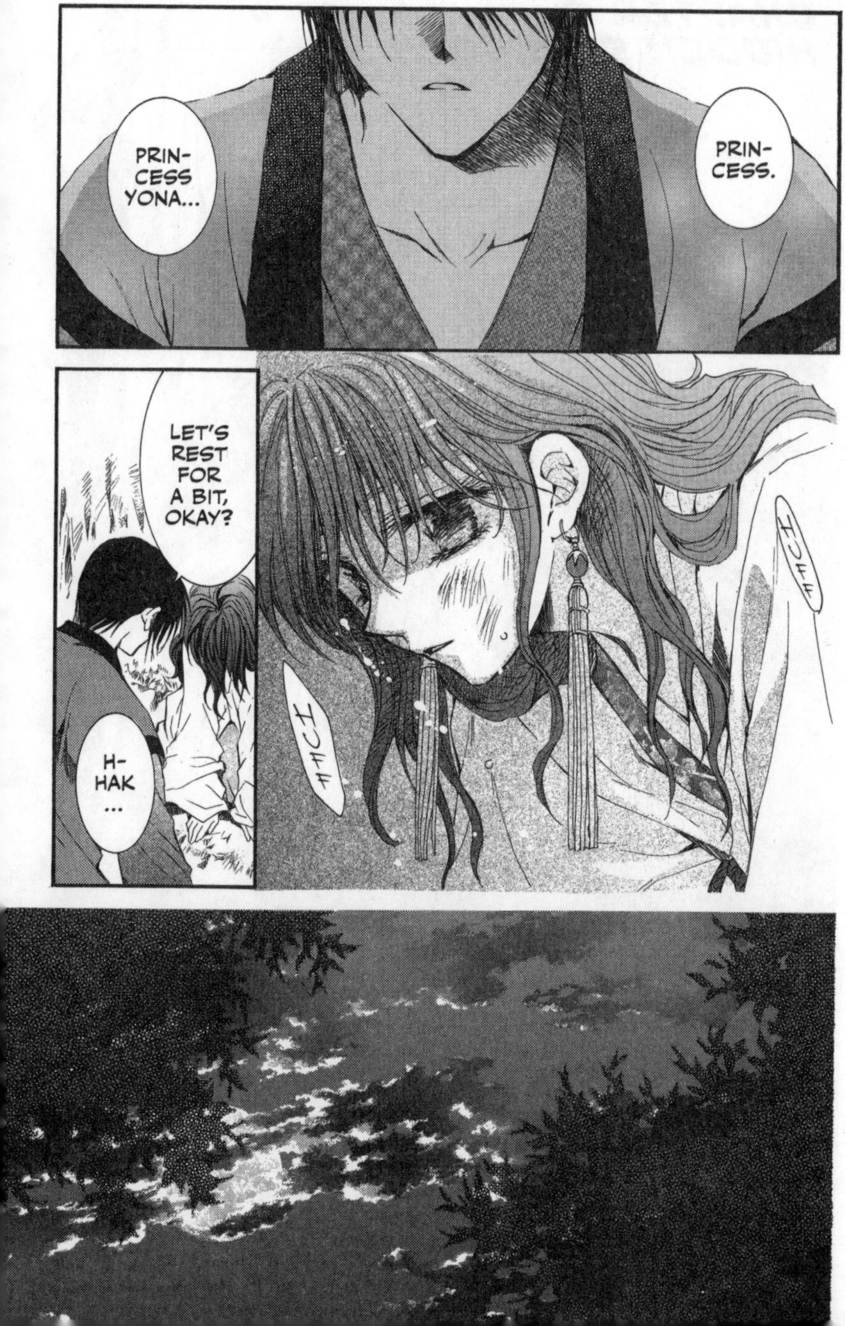

PRINCESS.
PRINCESS YONA...
HUFF
HUFF
LET'S REST FOR A BIT, OKAY?
H-HAK...

CHAPTER 3: HIDDEN STRENGTH

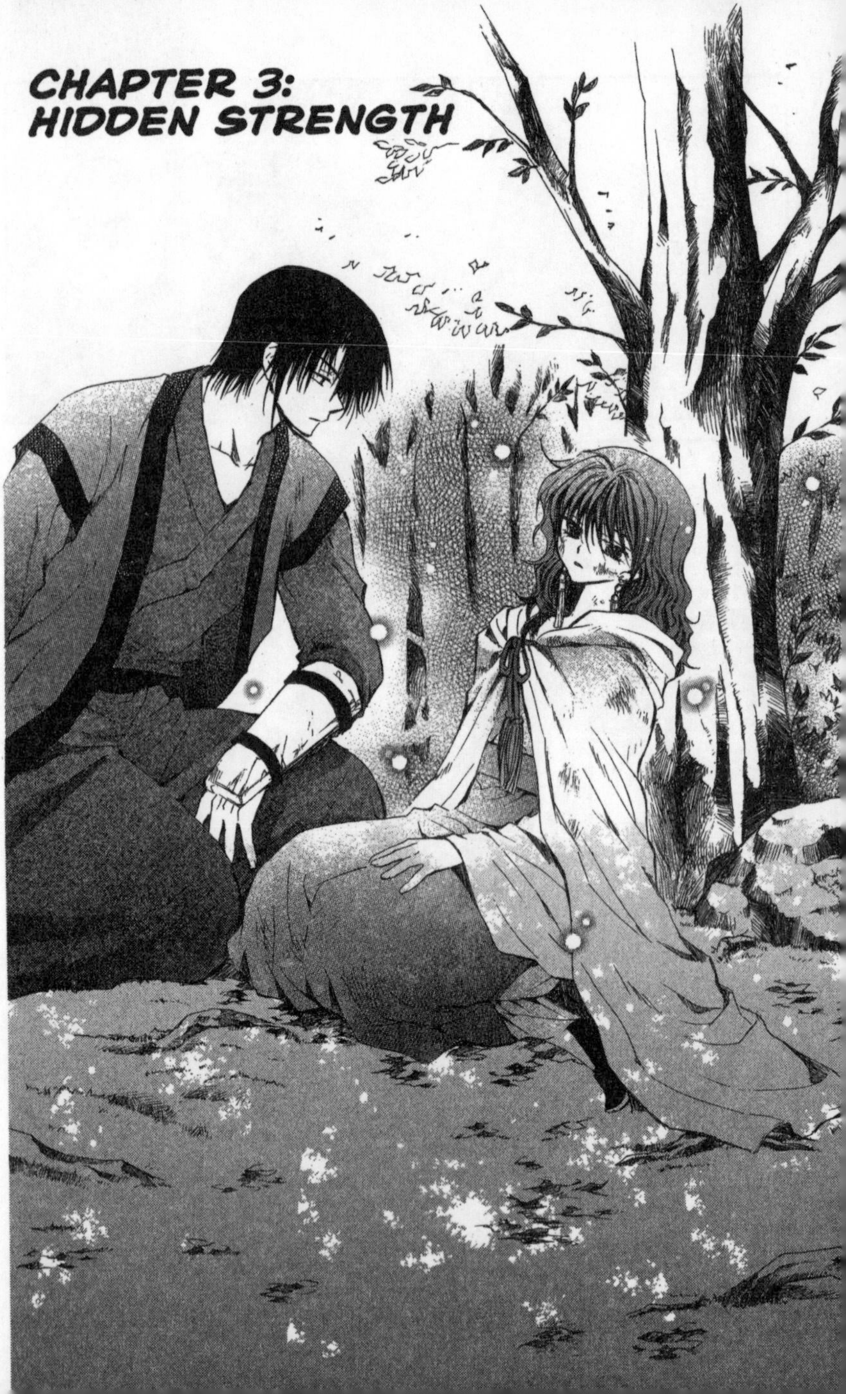

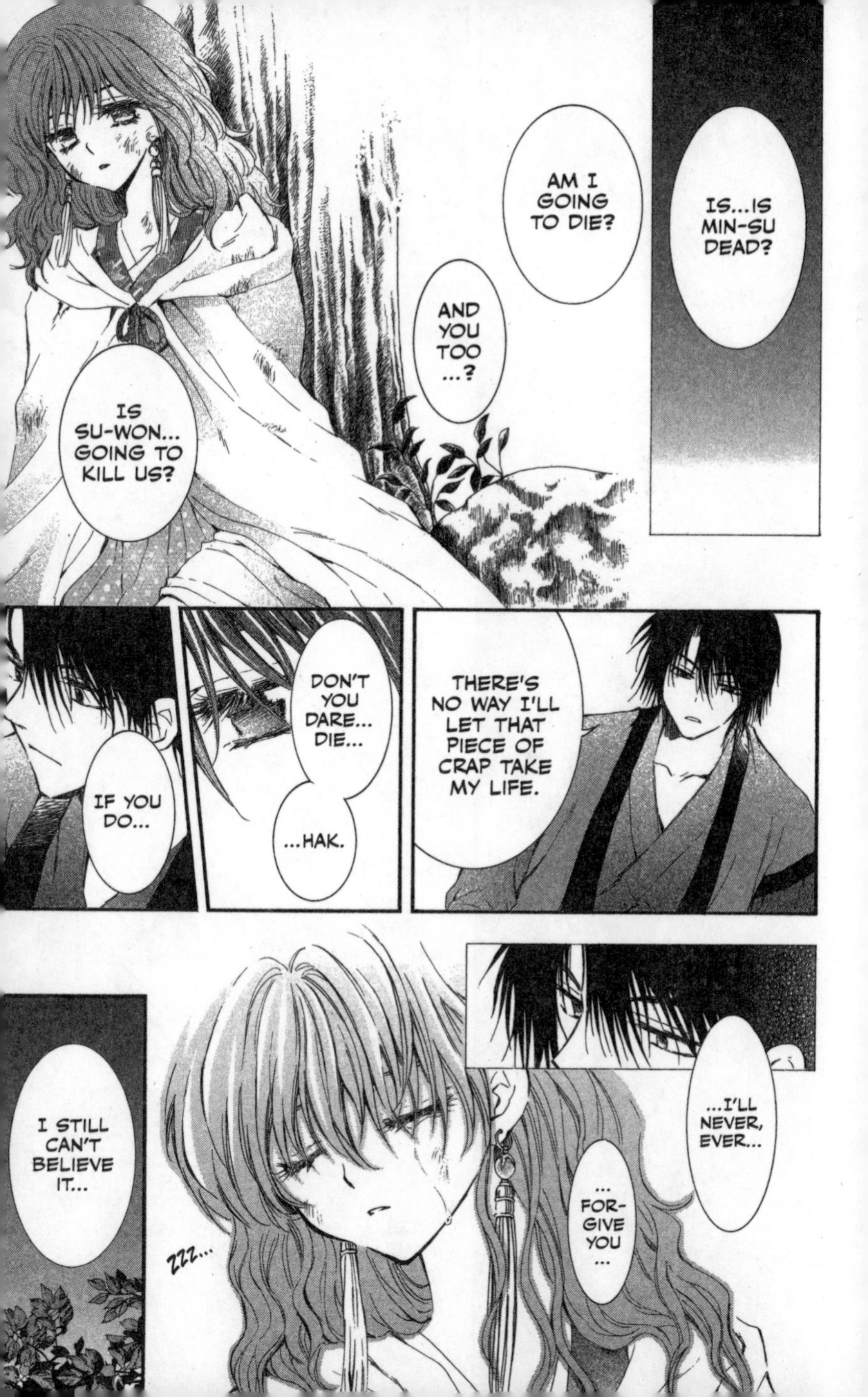
IS...IS MIN-SU DEAD?
AM I GOING TO DIE?
AND YOU TOO ...?
IS SU-WON... GOING TO KILL US?
THERE'S NO WAY I'LL LET THAT PIECE OF CRAP TAKE MY LIFE.
DON'T YOU DARE... DIE...
...HAK.
IF YOU DO...
...I'LL NEVER, EVER...
... FOR-GIVE YOU ...
ZZZ...
I STILL CAN'T BELIEVE IT...

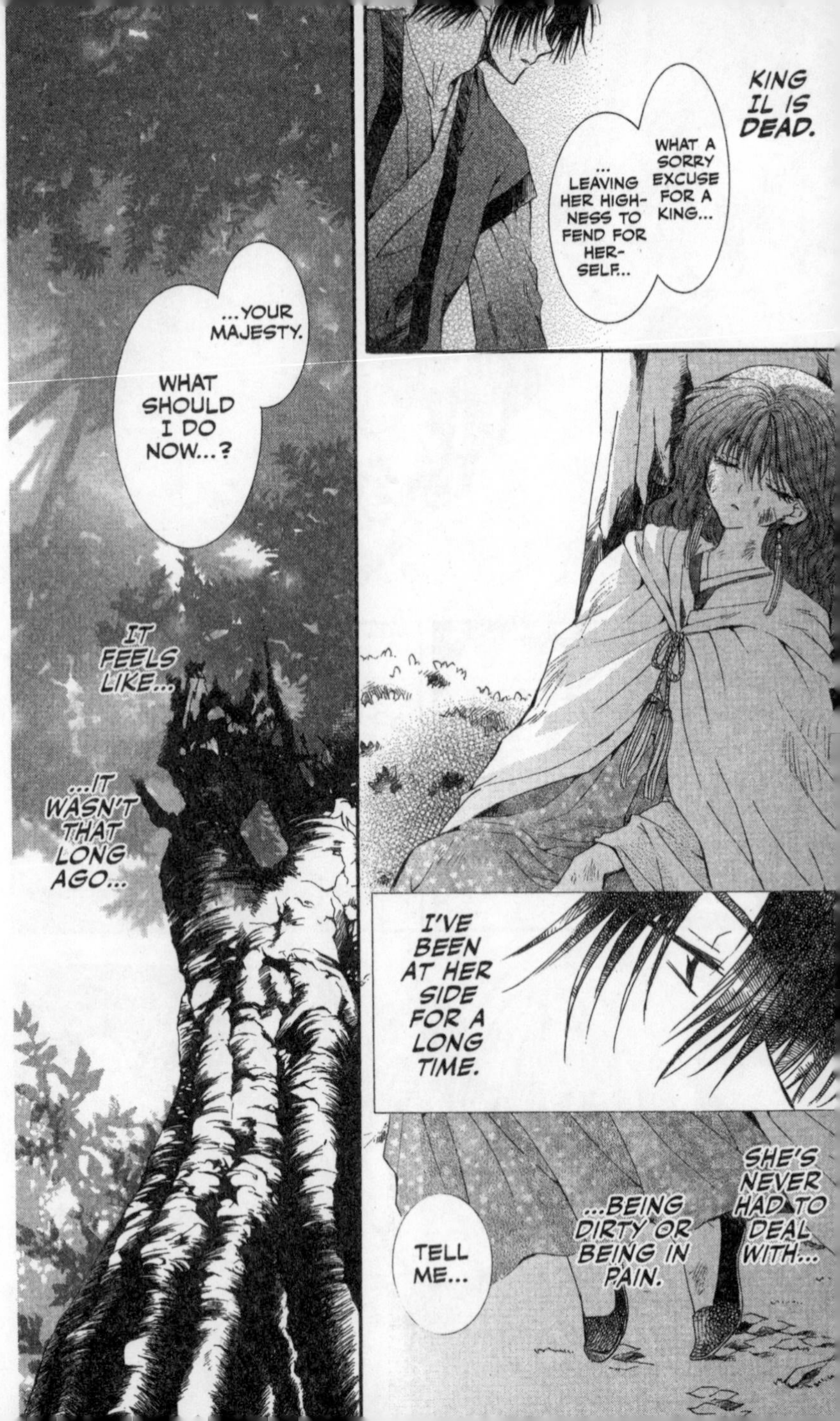
KING IL IS DEAD.
WHAT A SORRY EXCUSE FOR A KING...
...LEAVING HER HIGHNESS TO FEND FOR HERSELF...
I'VE BEEN AT HER SIDE FOR A LONG TIME.
SHE'S NEVER HAD TO DEAL WITH...
...BEING DIRTY OR BEING IN PAIN.
TELL ME...
...YOUR MAJESTY.
WHAT SHOULD I DO NOW...?
IT FEELS LIKE...
...IT WASN'T THAT LONG AGO...

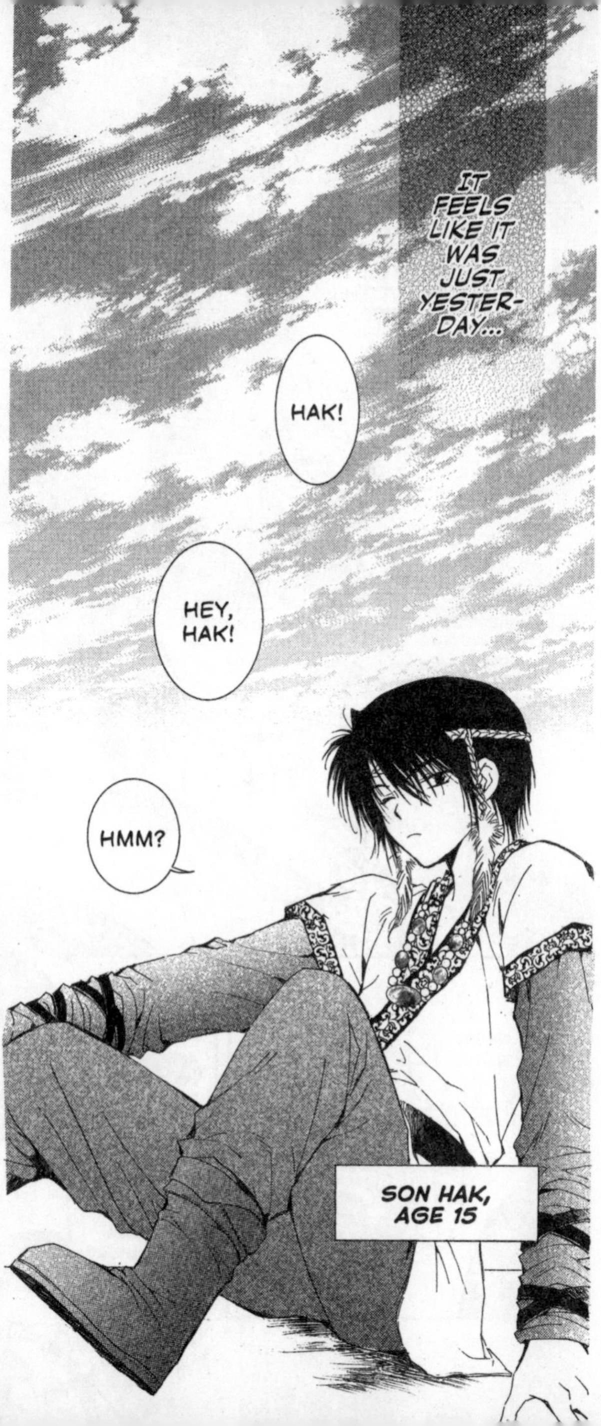
IT FEELS LIKE IT WAS JUST YESTER-DAY...
HAK!
HEY, HAK!
HMM?
SON HAK, AGE 15

Thanks to my irregular hours, I don't get a lot of exercise. (*Sweat...*)

But thanks to my mom, I have good eating habits! ♡... I love veggies, so I eat tons of salad. And I prefer Japanese cuisine over western or Chinese cuisines. ♥ I mean, I like those fine, but miso soup and natto are my comfort foods. I love noodles too!

As for what I don't like... I'm not into meat or shellfish. (But I'm fine with ground meats! I love hamburger steak and meat sauce. ♥ And pork-bone soup! I'm okay with soup stock made from chicken bones and meat.)

When I'm working, meals are what I look forward to most of all. ♥

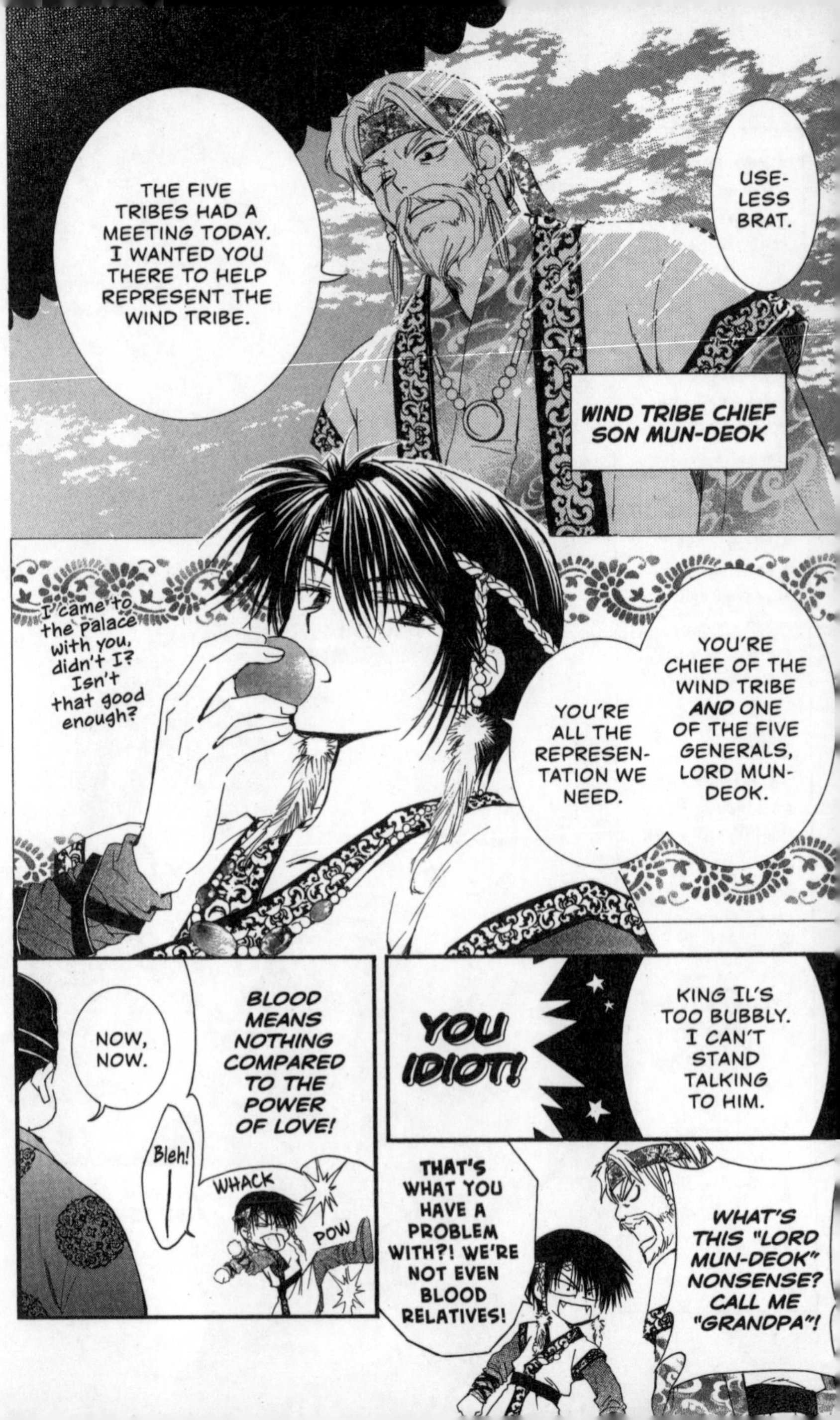
USE-LESS BRAT.
THE FIVE TRIBES HAD A MEETING TODAY. I WANTED YOU THERE TO HELP REPRESENT THE WIND TRIBE.
WIND TRIBE CHIEF SON MUN-DEOK
YOU'RE CHIEF OF THE WIND TRIBE AND ONE OF THE FIVE GENERALS, LORD MUN-DEOK.
YOU'RE ALL THE REPRESEN-TATION WE NEED.
I came to the palace with you, didn't I? Isn't that good enough?
KING IL'S TOO BUBBLY. I CAN'T STAND TALKING TO HIM.
YOU IDIOT!
WHAT'S THIS "LORD MUN-DEOK" NONSENSE? CALL ME "GRANDPA"!
THAT'S WHAT YOU HAVE A PROBLEM WITH?! WE'RE NOT EVEN BLOOD RELATIVES!
BLOOD MEANS NOTHING COMPARED TO THE POWER OF LOVE!
NOW, NOW.
Bleh!
WHACK
POW

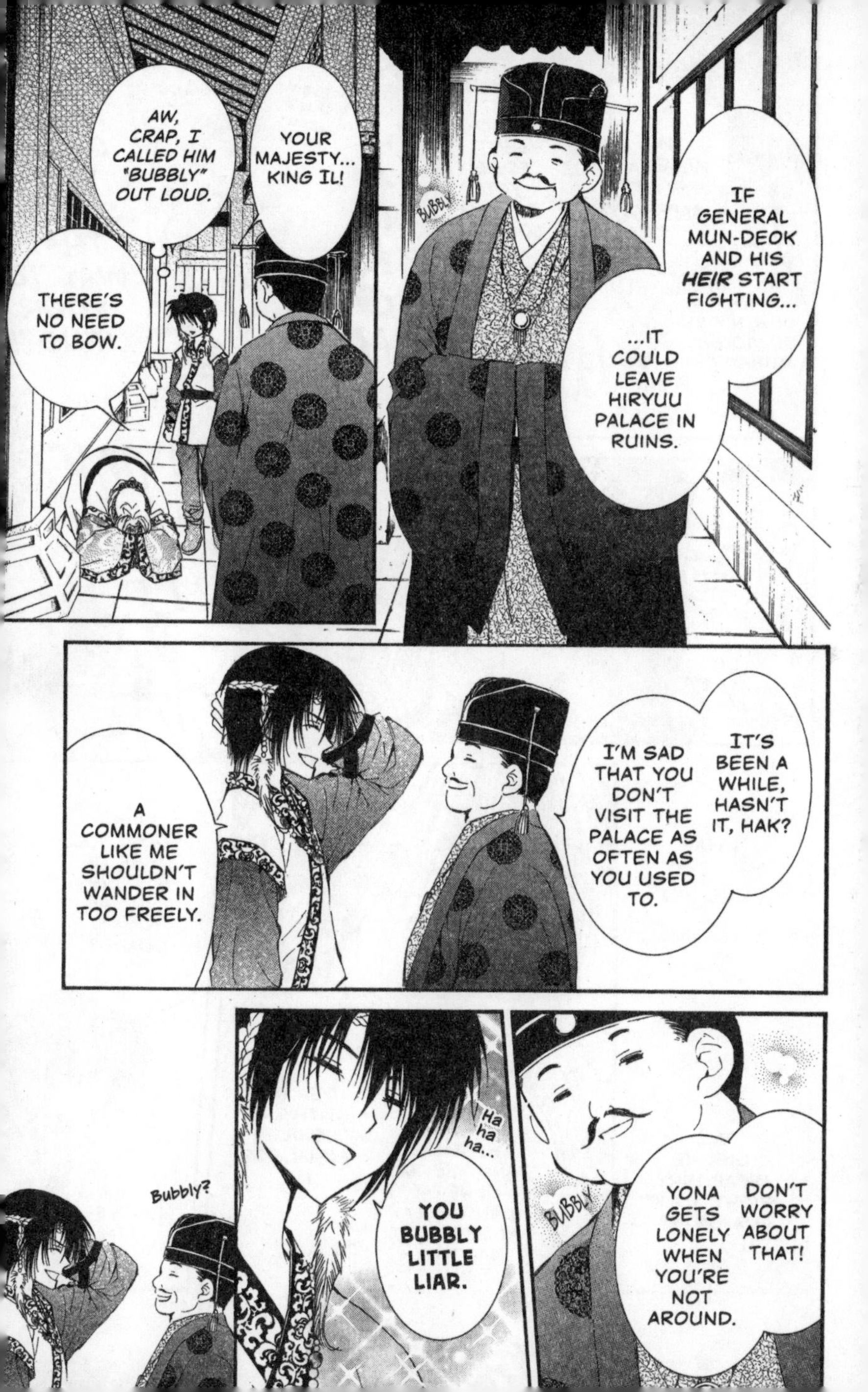
IF GENERAL MUN-DEOK AND HIS ***HEIR*** START FIGHTING...
...IT COULD LEAVE HIRYUU PALACE IN RUINS.
BUBBLY
YOUR MAJESTY... KING IL!
AW, CRAP, I CALLED HIM "BUBBLY" OUT LOUD.
THERE'S NO NEED TO BOW.
IT'S BEEN A WHILE, HASN'T IT, HAK?
I'M SAD THAT YOU DON'T VISIT THE PALACE AS OFTEN AS YOU USED TO.
A COMMONER LIKE ME SHOULDN'T WANDER IN TOO FREELY.
DON'T WORRY ABOUT THAT!
YONA GETS LONELY WHEN YOU'RE NOT AROUND.
BUBBLY
Ha ha ha...
YOU BUBBLY LITTLE LIAR.
Bubbly?

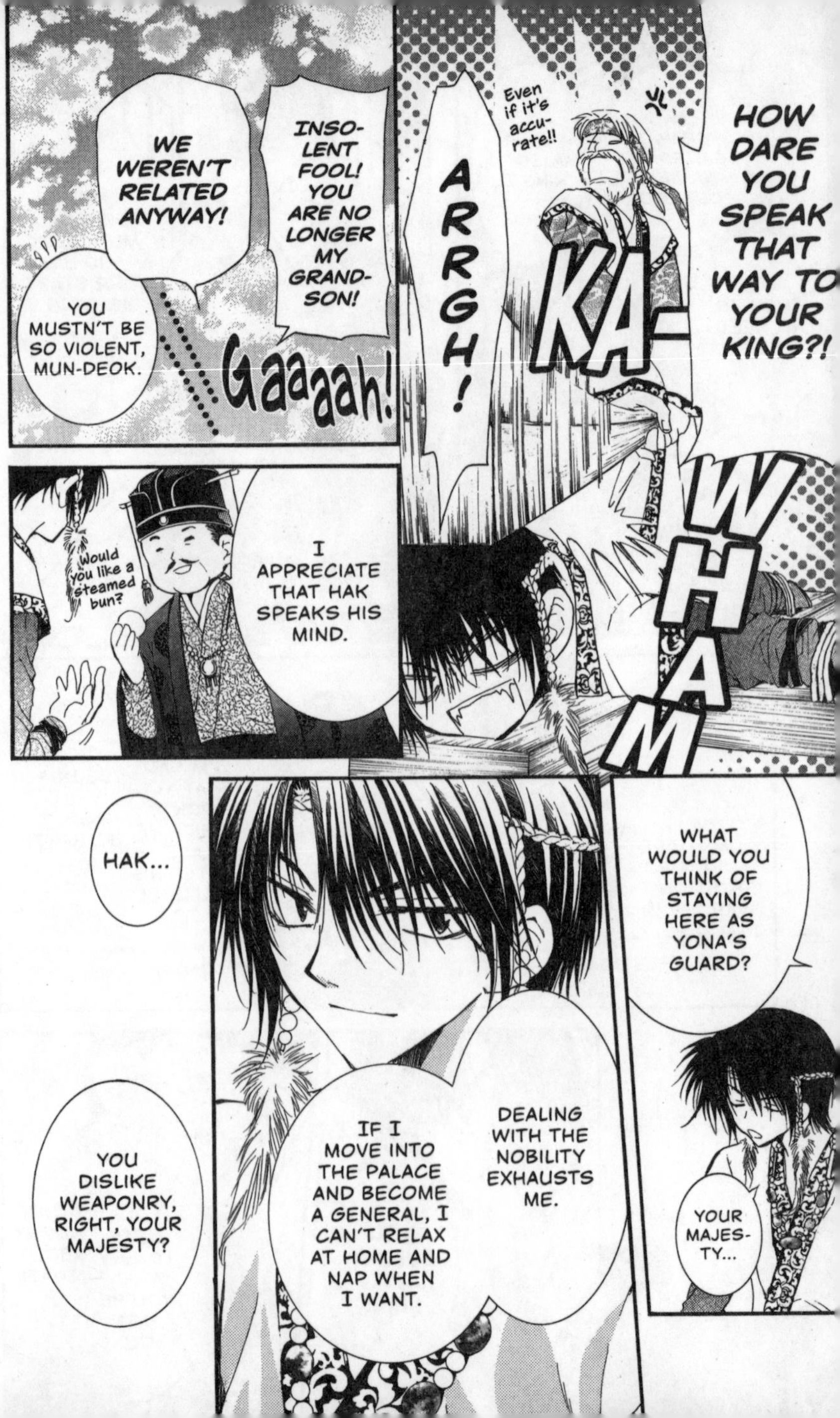
HOW DARE YOU SPEAK THAT WAY TO YOUR KING?!
Even if it's accurate!!
KA-
ARRGH!
WHAM
INSOLENT FOOL! YOU ARE NO LONGER MY GRANDSON!
WE WEREN'T RELATED ANYWAY!
Gaaaah!
YOU MUSTN'T BE SO VIOLENT, MUN-DEOK.
I APPRECIATE THAT HAK SPEAKS HIS MIND.
Would you like a steamed bun?
WHAT WOULD YOU THINK OF STAYING HERE AS YONA'S GUARD?
YOUR MAJESTY...
DEALING WITH THE NOBILITY EXHAUSTS ME.
IF I MOVE INTO THE PALACE AND BECOME A GENERAL, I CAN'T RELAX AT HOME AND NAP WHEN I WANT.
HAK...
YOU DISLIKE WEAPONRY, RIGHT, YOUR MAJESTY?

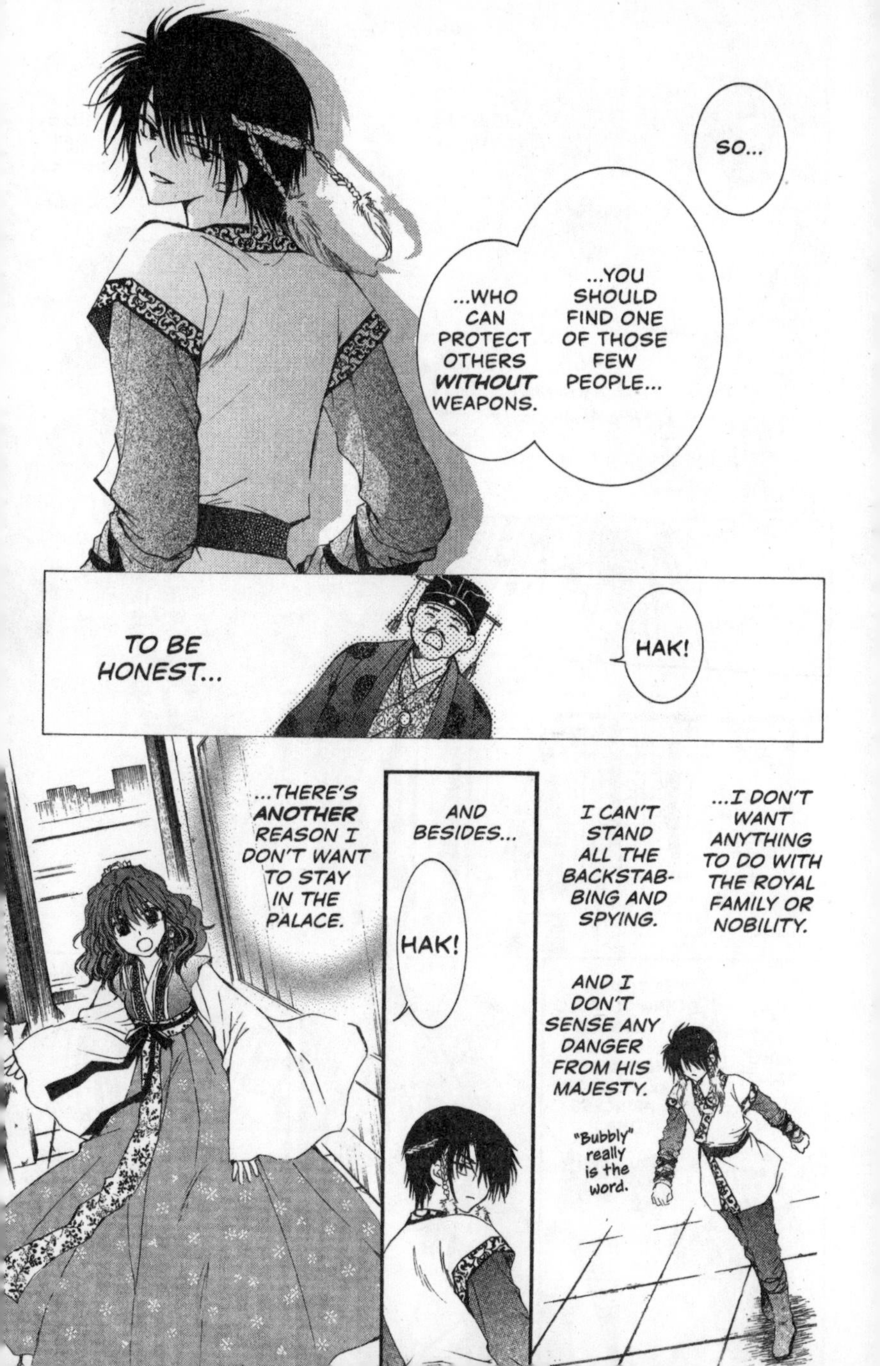
SO...
...YOU SHOULD FIND ONE OF THOSE FEW PEOPLE...
...WHO CAN PROTECT OTHERS WITHOUT WEAPONS.
HAK!
TO BE HONEST...
...I DON'T WANT ANYTHING TO DO WITH THE ROYAL FAMILY OR NOBILITY.
I CAN'T STAND ALL THE BACKSTAB-BING AND SPYING.
AND I DON'T SENSE ANY DANGER FROM HIS MAJESTY.
"Bubbly" really is the word.
AND BESIDES...
HAK!
...THERE'S ANOTHER REASON I DON'T WANT TO STAY IN THE PALACE.

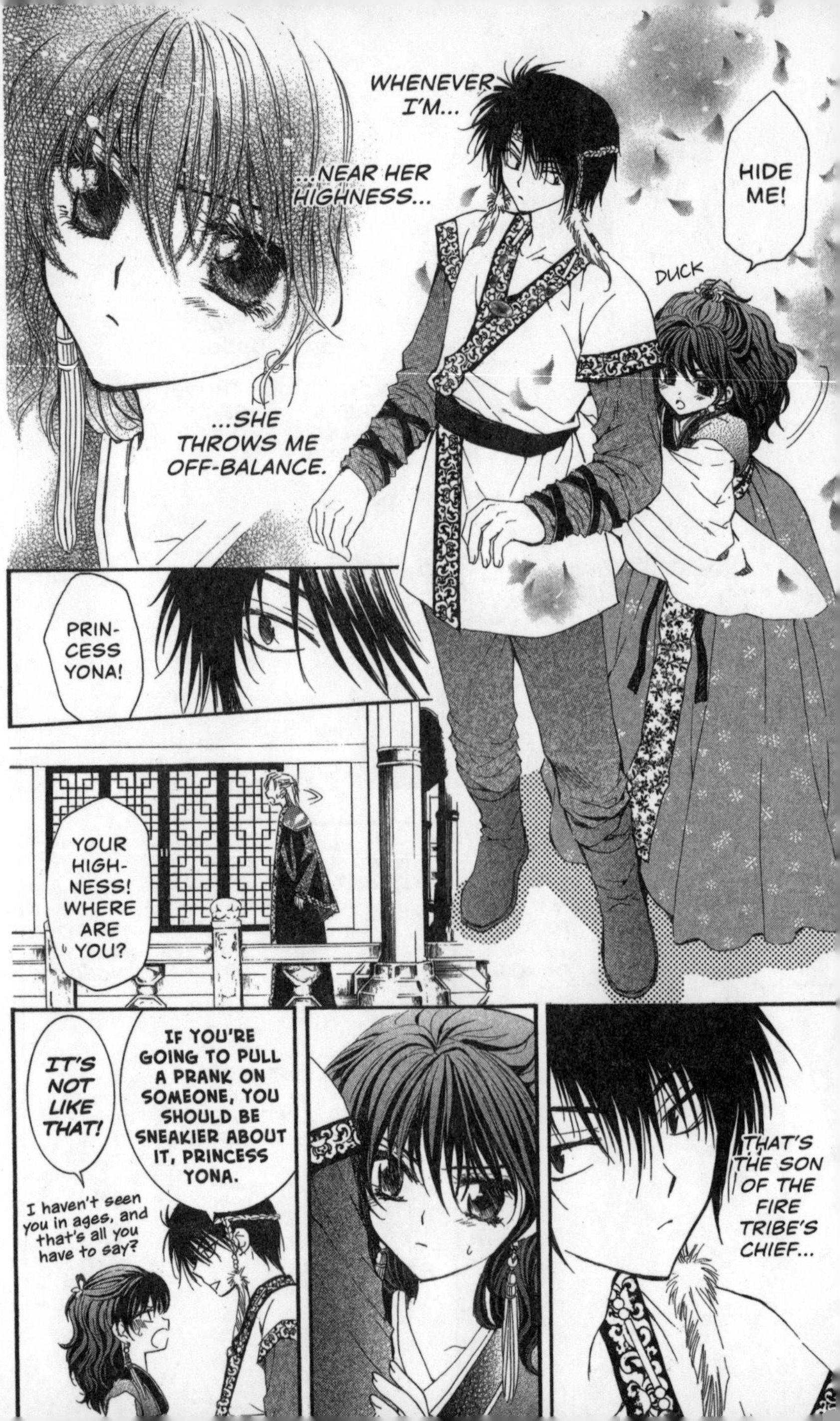
HIDE ME!
DUCK
WHENEVER I'M...
...NEAR HER HIGHNESS...
...SHE THROWS ME OFF-BALANCE.
PRIN-CESS YONA!
YOUR HIGH-NESS! WHERE ARE YOU?
THAT'S THE SON OF THE FIRE TRIBE'S CHIEF...
IF YOU'RE GOING TO PULL A PRANK ON SOMEONE, YOU SHOULD BE SNEAKIER ABOUT IT, PRINCESS YONA.
IT'S NOT LIKE THAT!
I haven't seen you in ages, and that's all you have to say?

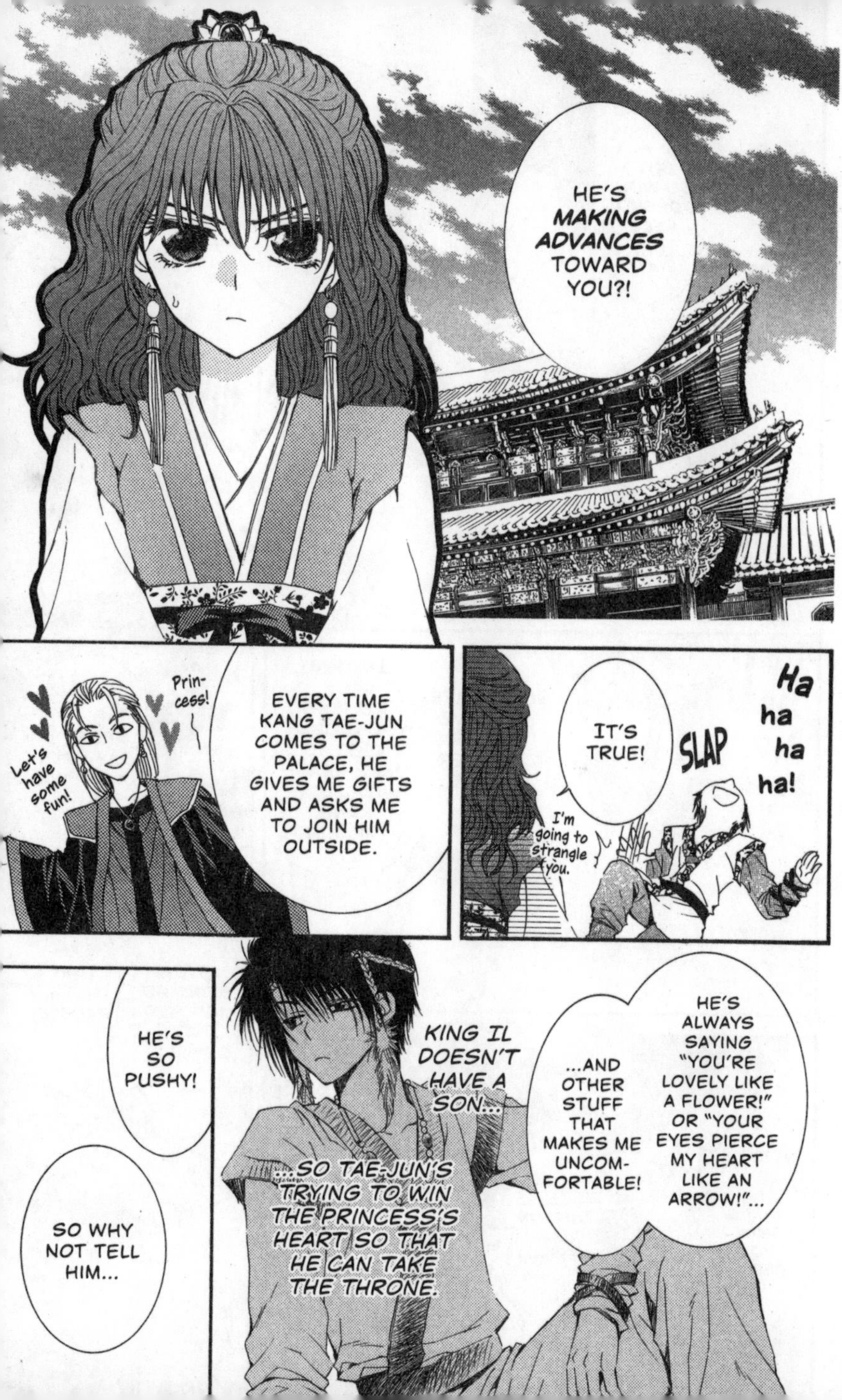
HE'S MAKING ADVANCES TOWARD YOU?!
Ha ha ha ha!
SLAP
IT'S TRUE!
I'm going to strangle you.
EVERY TIME KANG TAE-JUN COMES TO THE PALACE, HE GIVES ME GIFTS AND ASKS ME TO JOIN HIM OUTSIDE.
Prin-cess!
Let's have some fun!
HE'S ALWAYS SAYING "YOU'RE LOVELY LIKE A FLOWER!" OR "YOUR EYES PIERCE MY HEART LIKE AN ARROW!"...
...AND OTHER STUFF THAT MAKES ME UNCOM-FORTABLE!
KING IL DOESN'T HAVE A SON...
...SO TAE-JUN'S TRYING TO WIN THE PRINCESS'S HEART SO THAT HE CAN TAKE THE THRONE.
HE'S SO PUSHY!
SO WHY NOT TELL HIM...

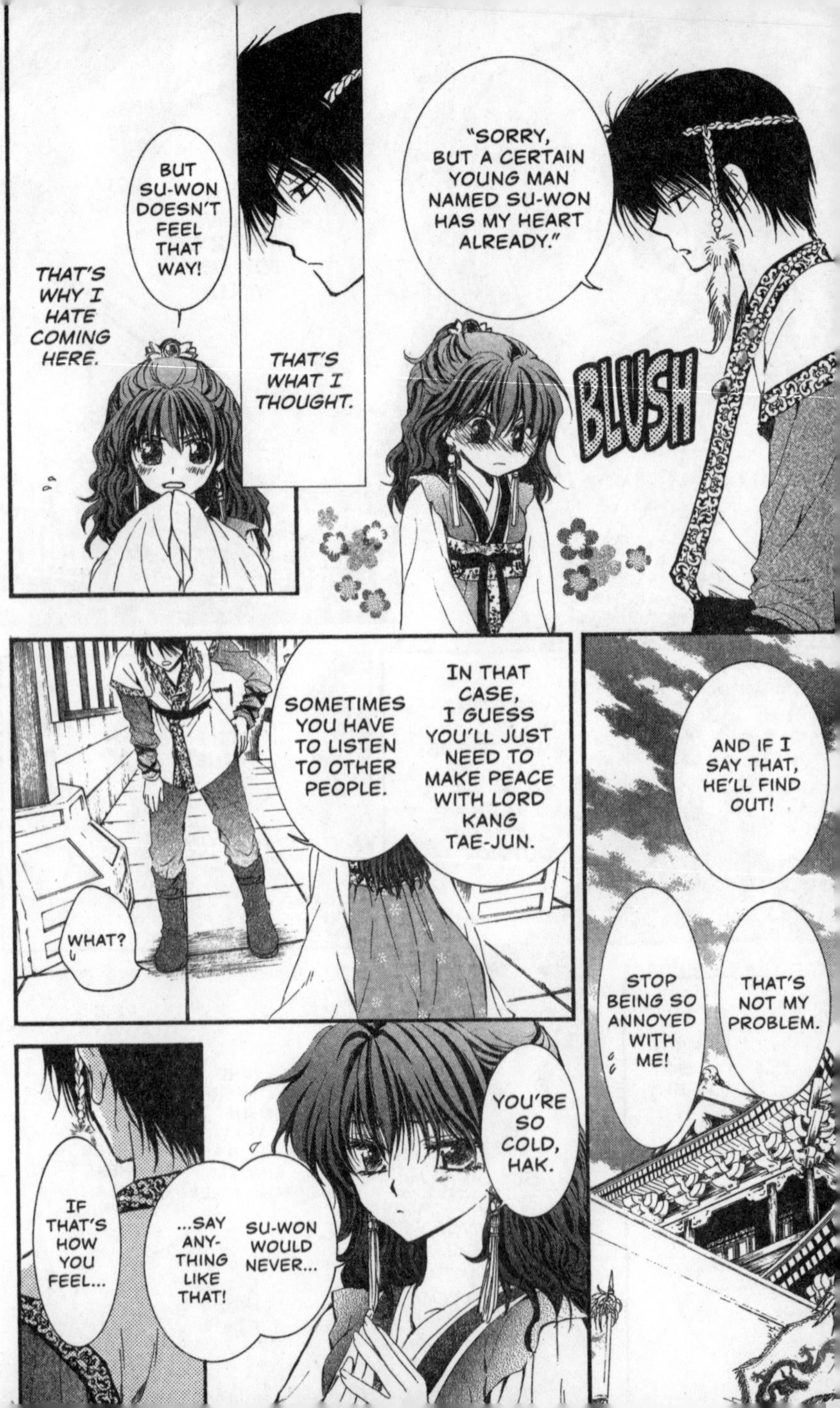
"SORRY, BUT A CERTAIN YOUNG MAN NAMED SU-WON HAS MY HEART ALREADY."
BLUSH
THAT'S WHAT I THOUGHT.
BUT SU-WON DOESN'T FEEL THAT WAY!
THAT'S WHY I HATE COMING HERE.
AND IF I SAY THAT, HE'LL FIND OUT!
THAT'S NOT MY PROBLEM.
STOP BEING SO ANNOYED WITH ME!
IN THAT CASE, I GUESS YOU'LL JUST NEED TO MAKE PEACE WITH LORD KANG TAE-JUN.
SOMETIMES YOU HAVE TO LISTEN TO OTHER PEOPLE.
WHAT?
YOU'RE SO COLD, HAK.
SU-WON WOULD NEVER...
...SAY ANYTHING LIKE THAT!
IF THAT'S HOW YOU FEEL...

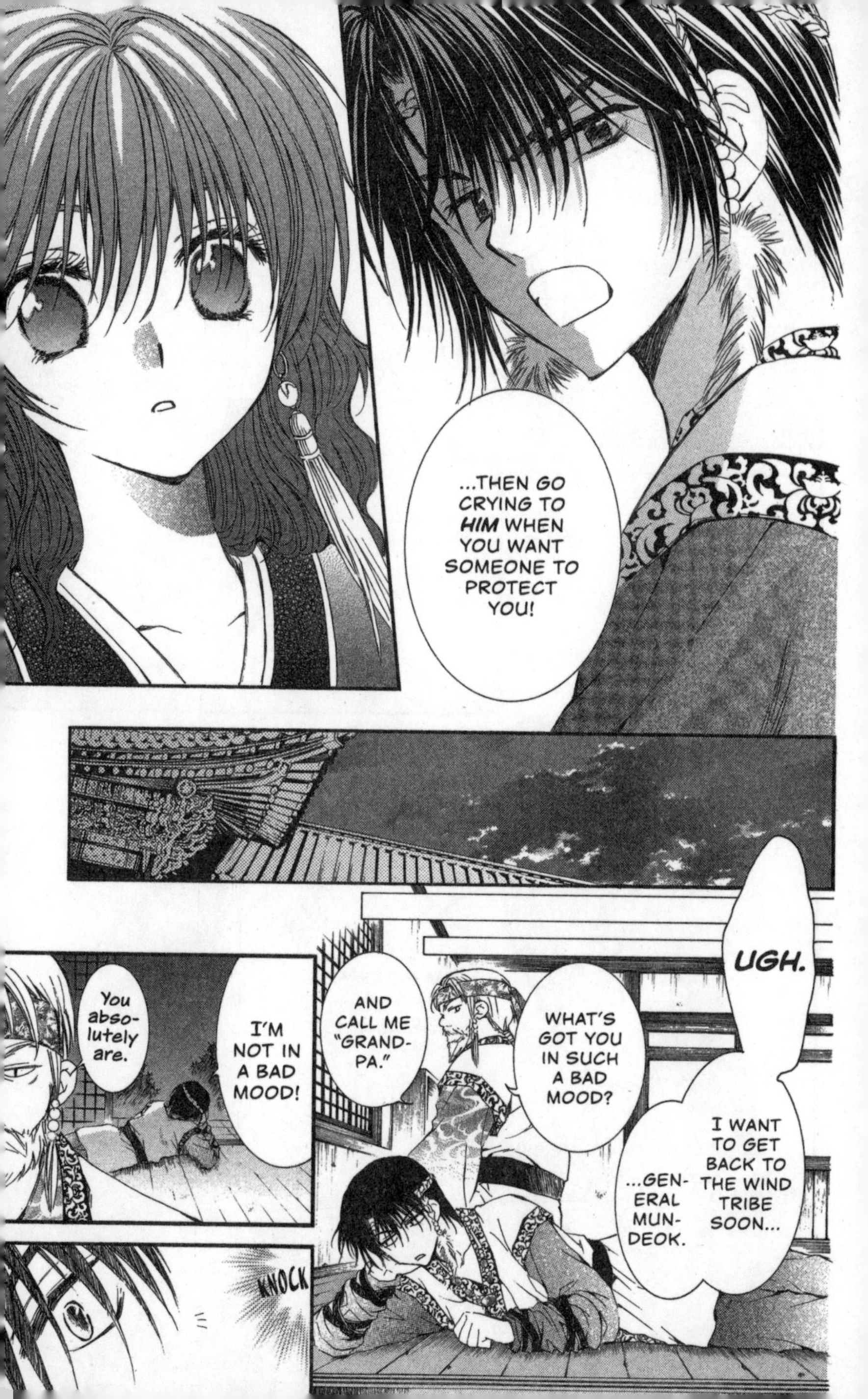
...THEN GO CRYING TO *HIM* WHEN YOU WANT SOMEONE TO PROTECT YOU!
UGH.
I WANT TO GET BACK TO THE WIND TRIBE SOON...
...GEN-ERAL MUN-DEOK.
WHAT'S GOT YOU IN SUCH A BAD MOOD?
AND CALL ME "GRAND-PA."
I'M NOT IN A BAD MOOD!
You abso-lutely are.
KNOCK

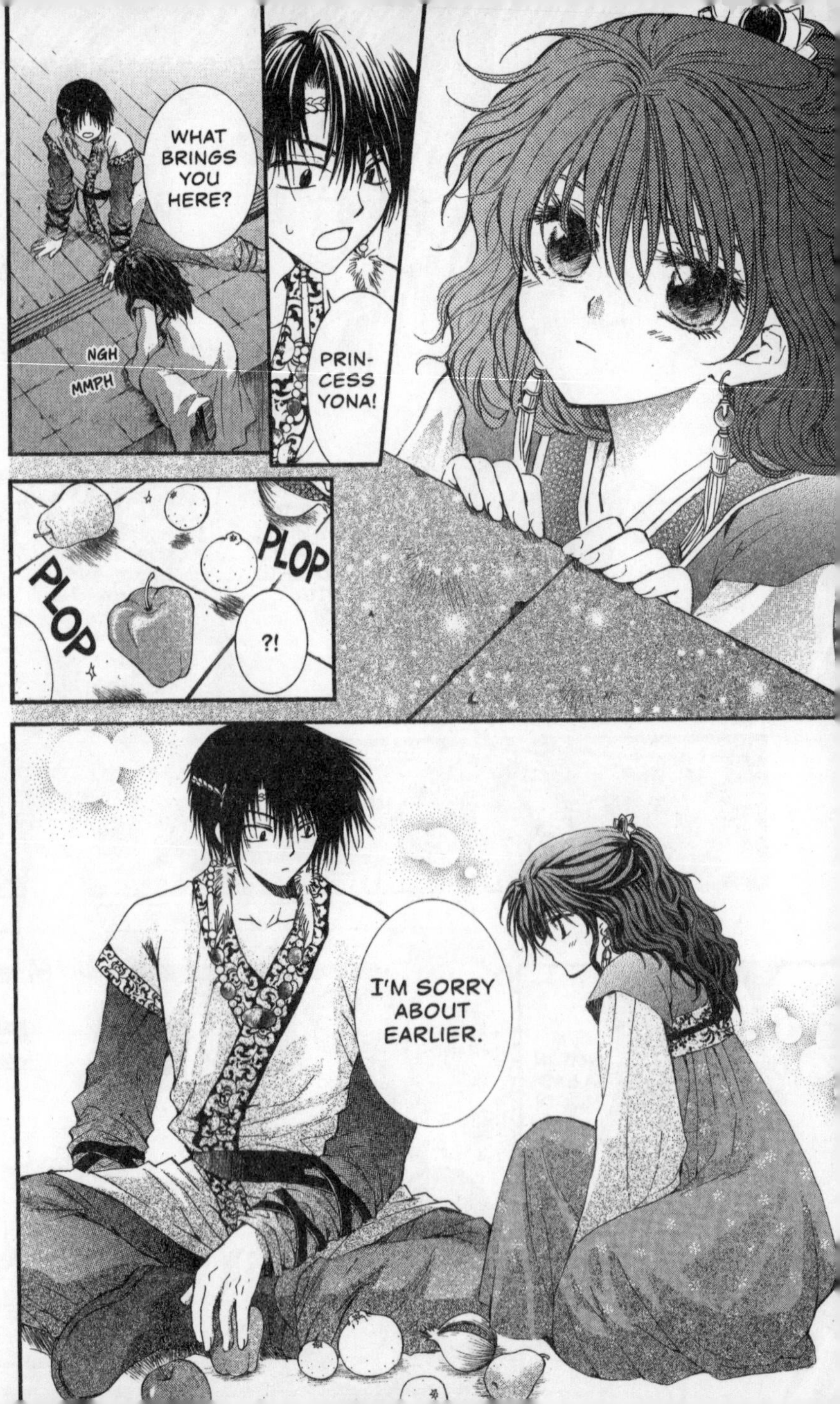

WHAT BRINGS YOU HERE?
PRIN-CESS YONA!
NGH
MMPH
PLOP
PLOP
?!
I'M SORRY ABOUT EARLIER.

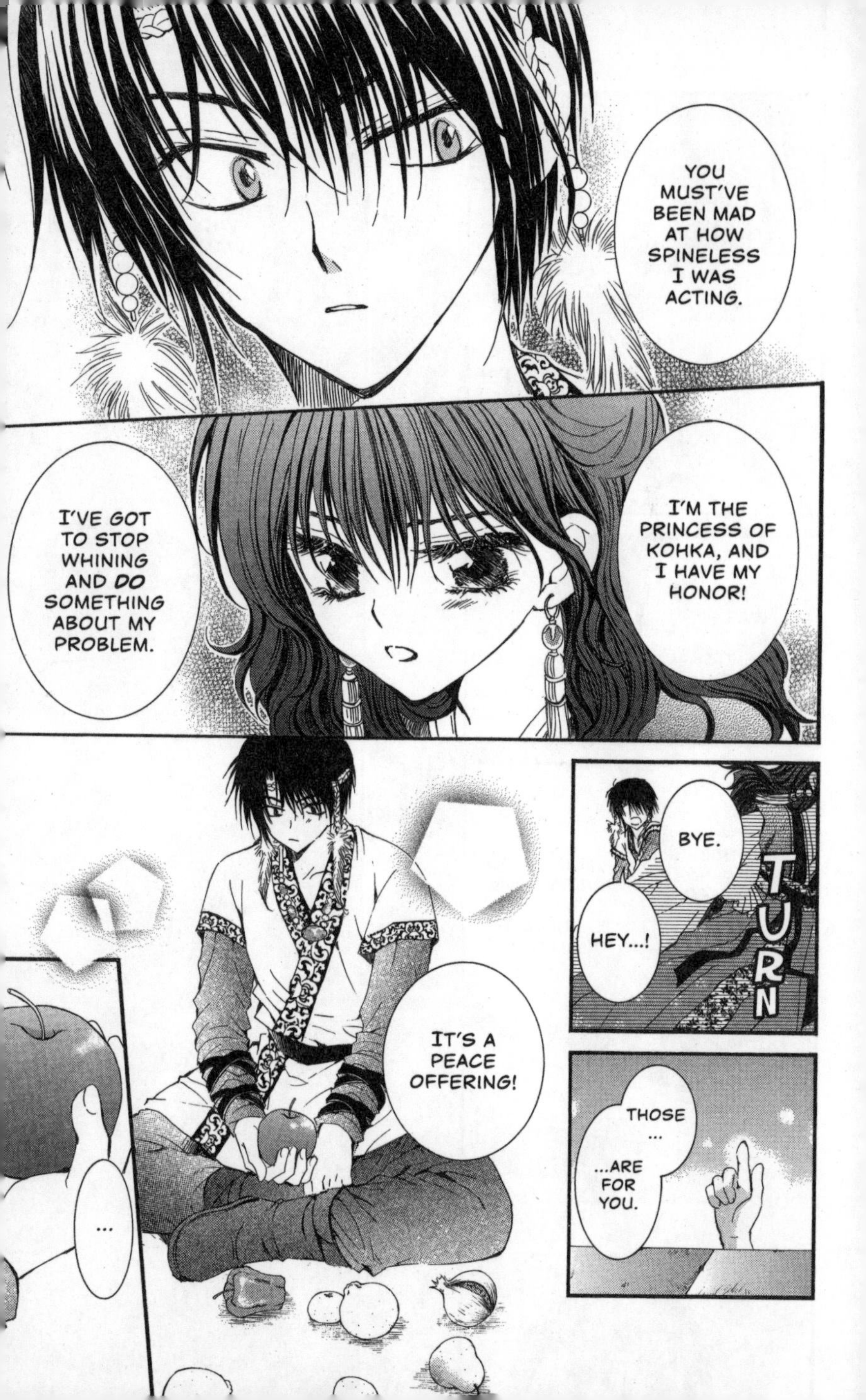
YOU MUST'VE BEEN MAD AT HOW SPINELESS I WAS ACTING.
I'M THE PRINCESS OF KOHKA, AND I HAVE MY HONOR!
I'VE GOT TO STOP WHINING AND *DO* SOMETHING ABOUT MY PROBLEM.
BYE.
TURN
HEY...!
THOSE... ...ARE FOR YOU.
IT'S A PEACE OFFERING!
...

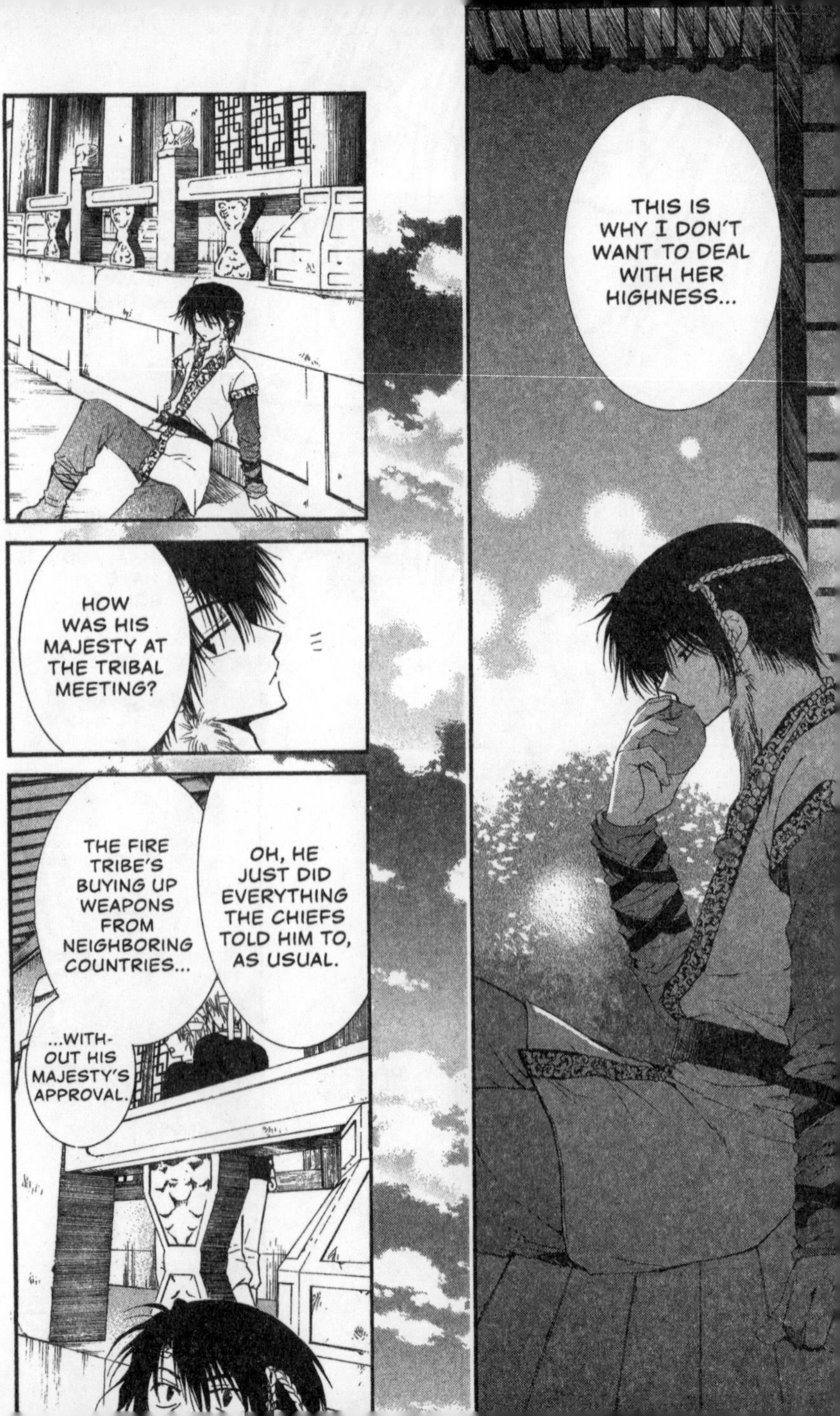
THIS IS WHY I DON'T WANT TO DEAL WITH HER HIGHNESS...
HOW WAS HIS MAJESTY AT THE TRIBAL MEETING?
OH, HE JUST DID EVERYTHING THE CHIEFS TOLD HIM TO, AS USUAL.
THE FIRE TRIBE'S BUYING UP WEAPONS FROM NEIGHBORING COUNTRIES...
...WITH-OUT HIS MAJESTY'S APPROVAL.

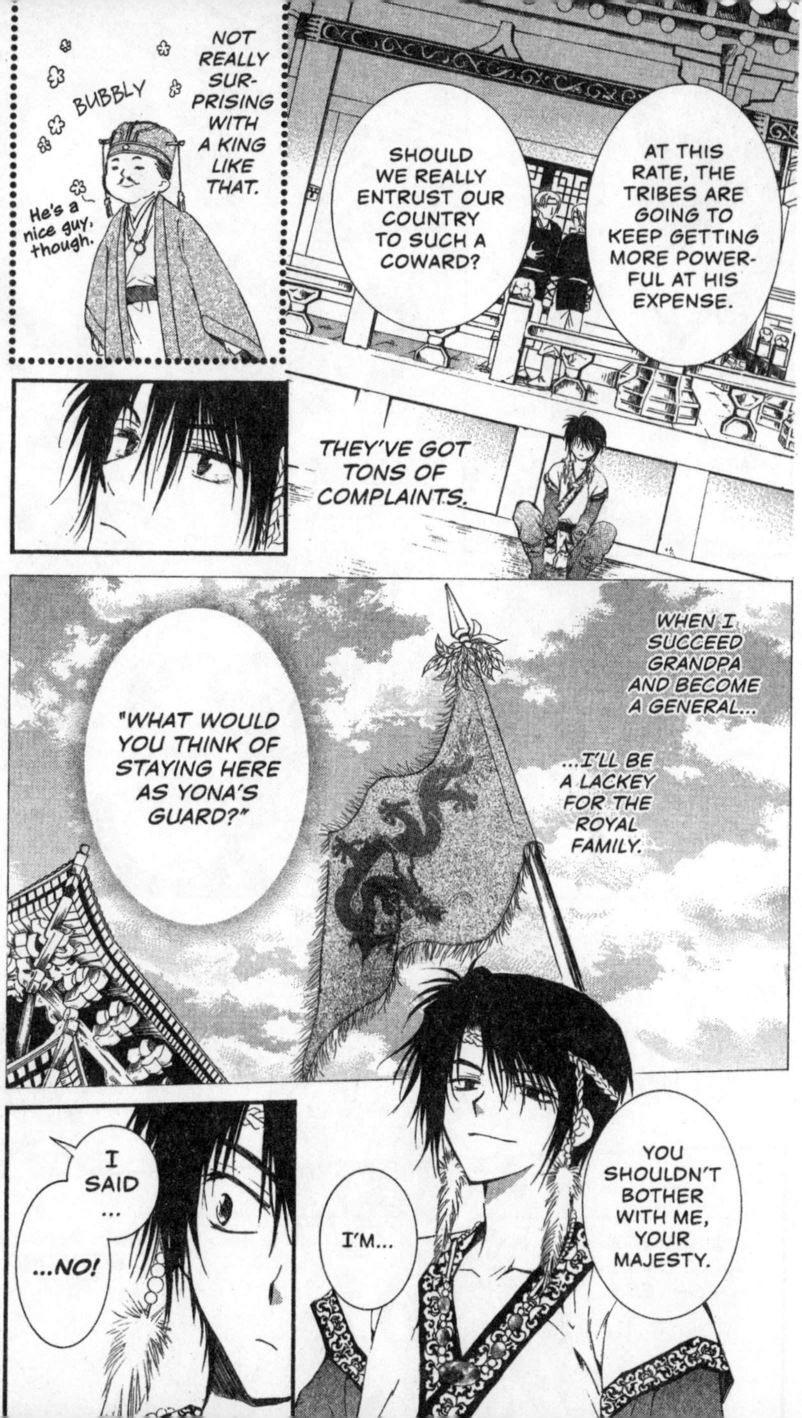
AT THIS RATE, THE TRIBES ARE GOING TO KEEP GETTING MORE POWERFUL AT HIS EXPENSE.
SHOULD WE REALLY ENTRUST OUR COUNTRY TO SUCH A COWARD?
NOT REALLY SURPRISING WITH A KING LIKE THAT.
BUBBLY
He's a nice guy, though.
THEY'VE GOT TONS OF COMPLAINTS.
WHEN I SUCCEED GRANDPA AND BECOME A GENERAL...
...I'LL BE A LACKEY FOR THE ROYAL FAMILY.
"WHAT WOULD YOU THINK OF STAYING HERE AS YONA'S GUARD?"
YOU SHOULDN'T BOTHER WITH ME, YOUR MAJESTY.
I'M...
I SAID... ...NO!

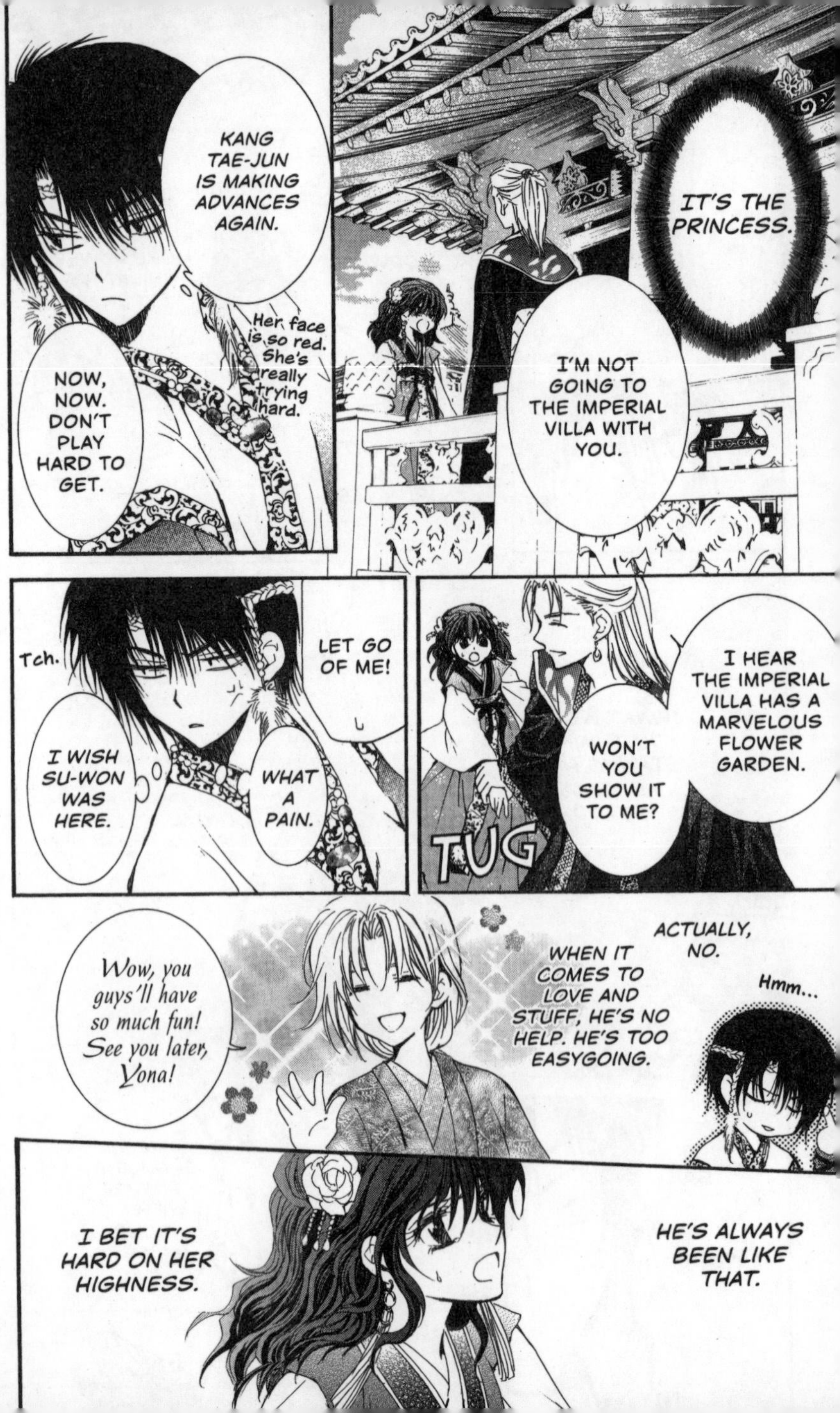
IT'S THE PRINCESS.
I'M NOT GOING TO THE IMPERIAL VILLA WITH YOU.
KANG TAE-JUN IS MAKING ADVANCES AGAIN.
Her face is so red. She's really trying hard.
NOW, NOW. DON'T PLAY HARD TO GET.
I HEAR THE IMPERIAL VILLA HAS A MARVELOUS FLOWER GARDEN.
WON'T YOU SHOW IT TO ME?
TUG
LET GO OF ME!
Tch.
WHAT A PAIN.
I WISH SU-WON WAS HERE.
ACTUALLY, NO.
Hmm...
WHEN IT COMES TO LOVE AND STUFF, HE'S NO HELP. HE'S TOO EASYGOING.
Wow, you guys'll have so much fun! See you later, Yona!
HE'S ALWAYS BEEN LIKE THAT.
I BET IT'S HARD ON HER HIGHNESS.

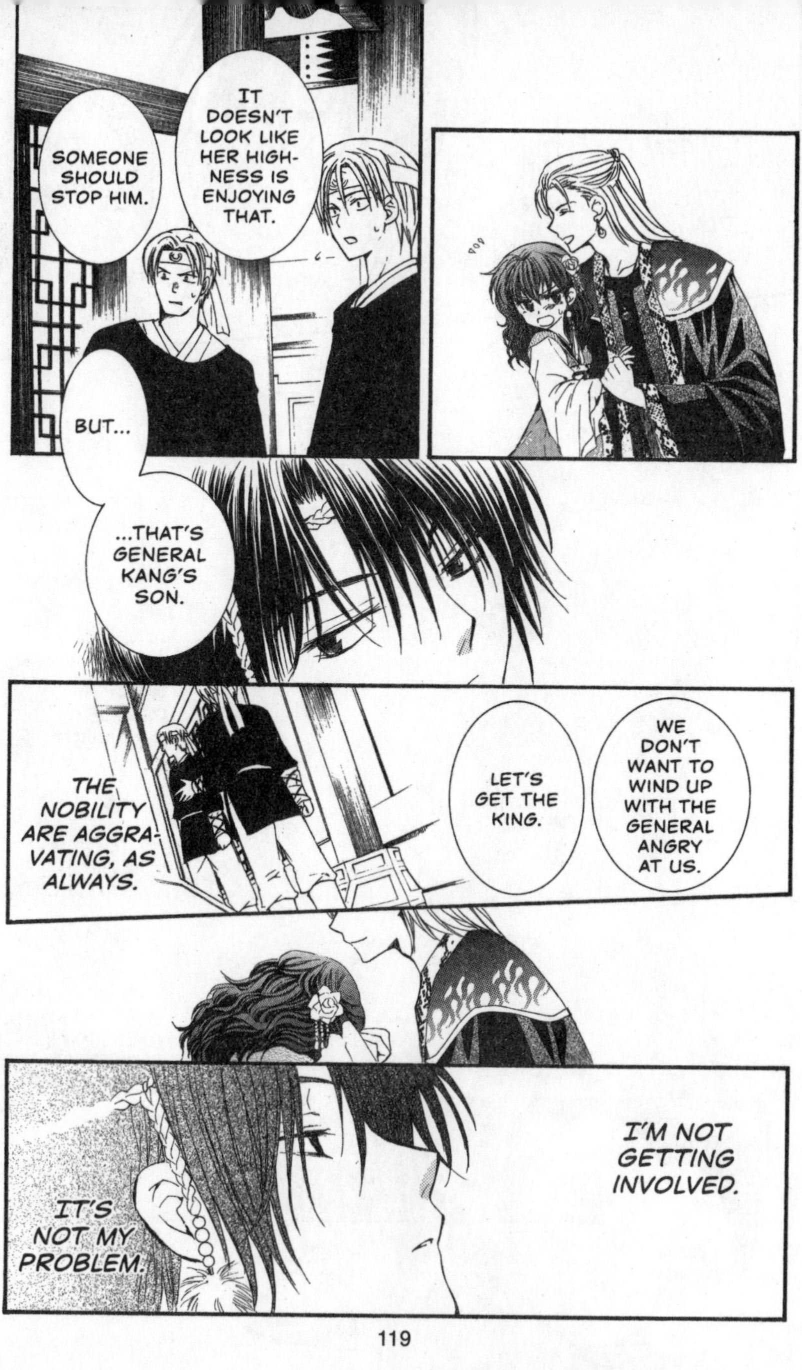
IT DOESN'T LOOK LIKE HER HIGH-NESS IS ENJOYING THAT.
SOMEONE SHOULD STOP HIM.
BUT...
...THAT'S GENERAL KANG'S SON.
WE DON'T WANT TO WIND UP WITH THE GENERAL ANGRY AT US.
LET'S GET THE KING.
THE NOBILITY ARE AGGRA-VATING, AS ALWAYS.
I'M NOT GETTING INVOLVED.
IT'S NOT MY PROBLEM.

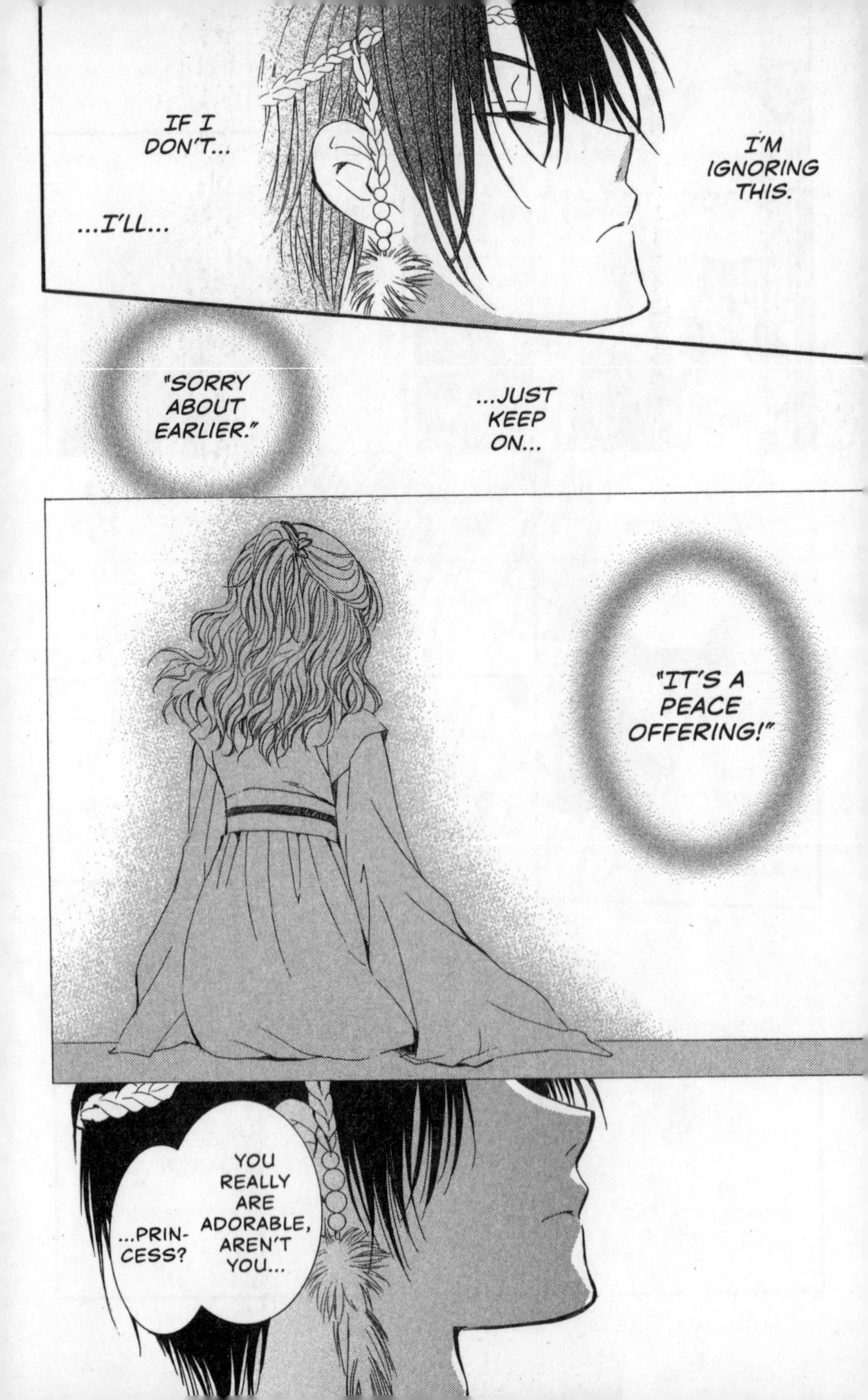
I'M IGNORING THIS.
IF I DON'T...
...I'LL...
...JUST KEEP ON...
"SORRY ABOUT EARLIER."
"IT'S A PEACE OFFERING!"
YOU REALLY ARE ADORABLE, AREN'T YOU...
...PRINCESS?

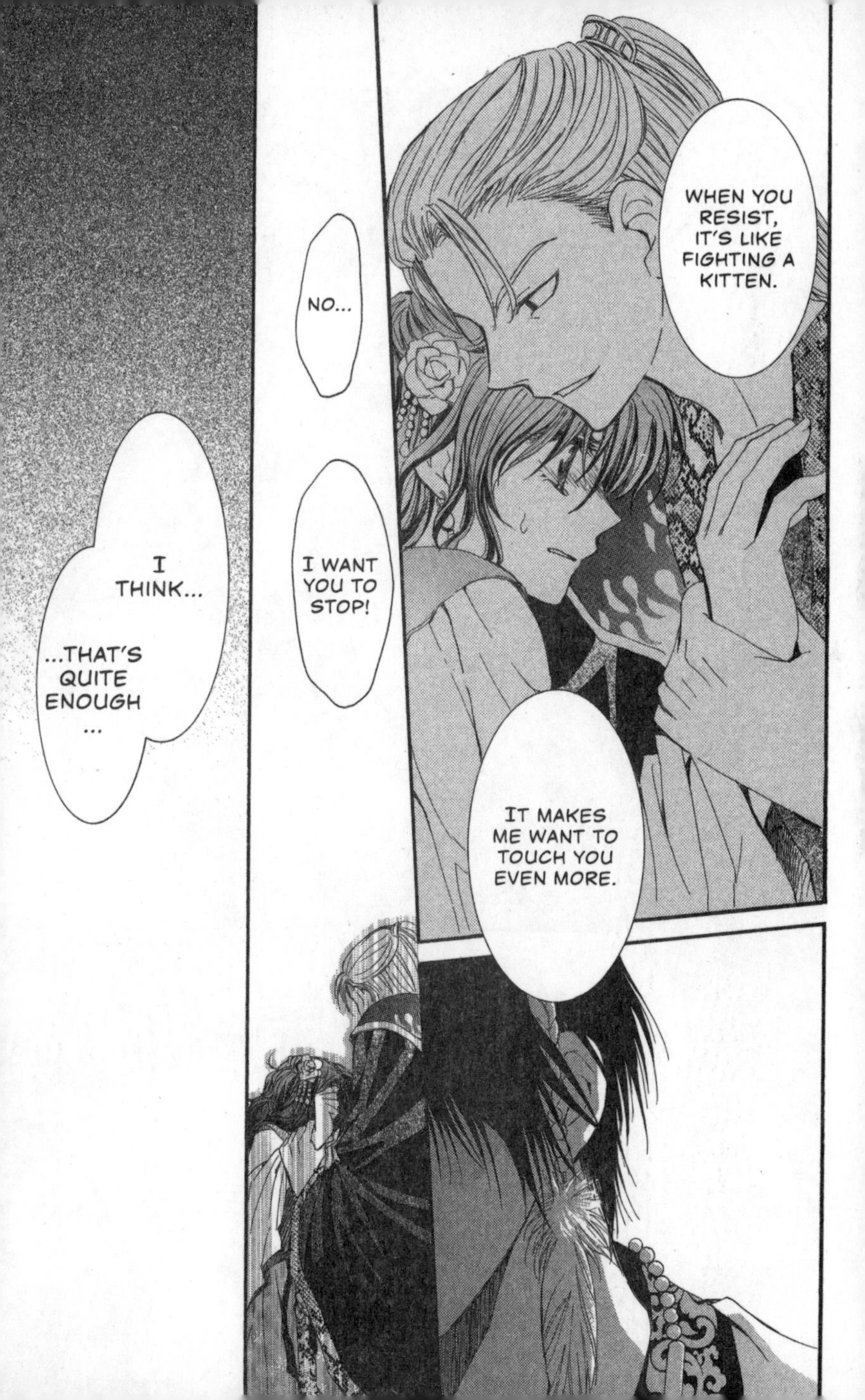
WHEN YOU RESIST, IT'S LIKE FIGHTING A KITTEN.
NO...
I WANT YOU TO STOP!
IT MAKES ME WANT TO TOUCH YOU EVEN MORE.
I THINK...
...THAT'S QUITE ENOUGH...

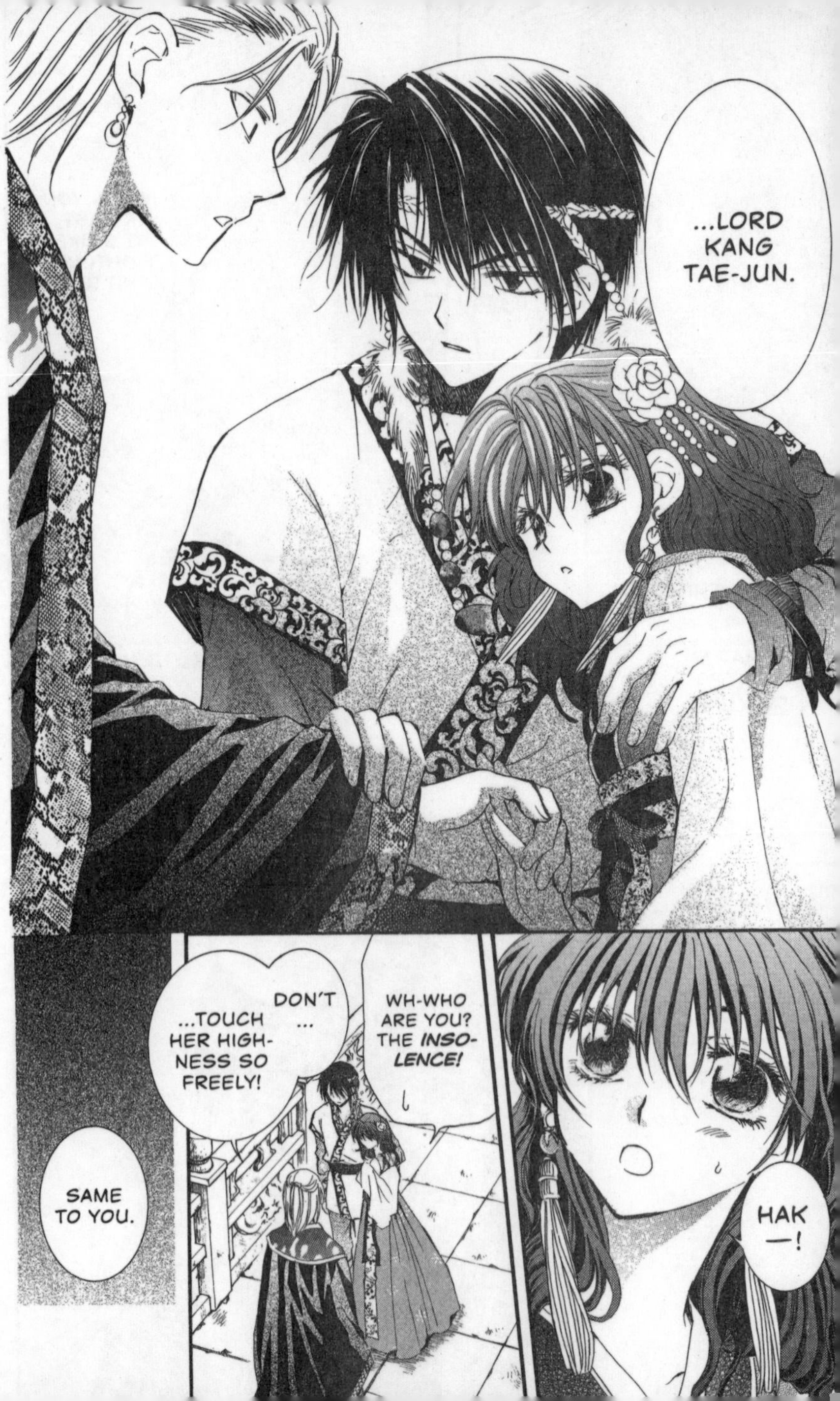
...LORD KANG TAE-JUN.
HAK—!
WH-WHO ARE YOU? THE *INSOLENCE!*
DON'T ...
...TOUCH HER HIGHNESS SO FREELY!
SAME TO YOU.

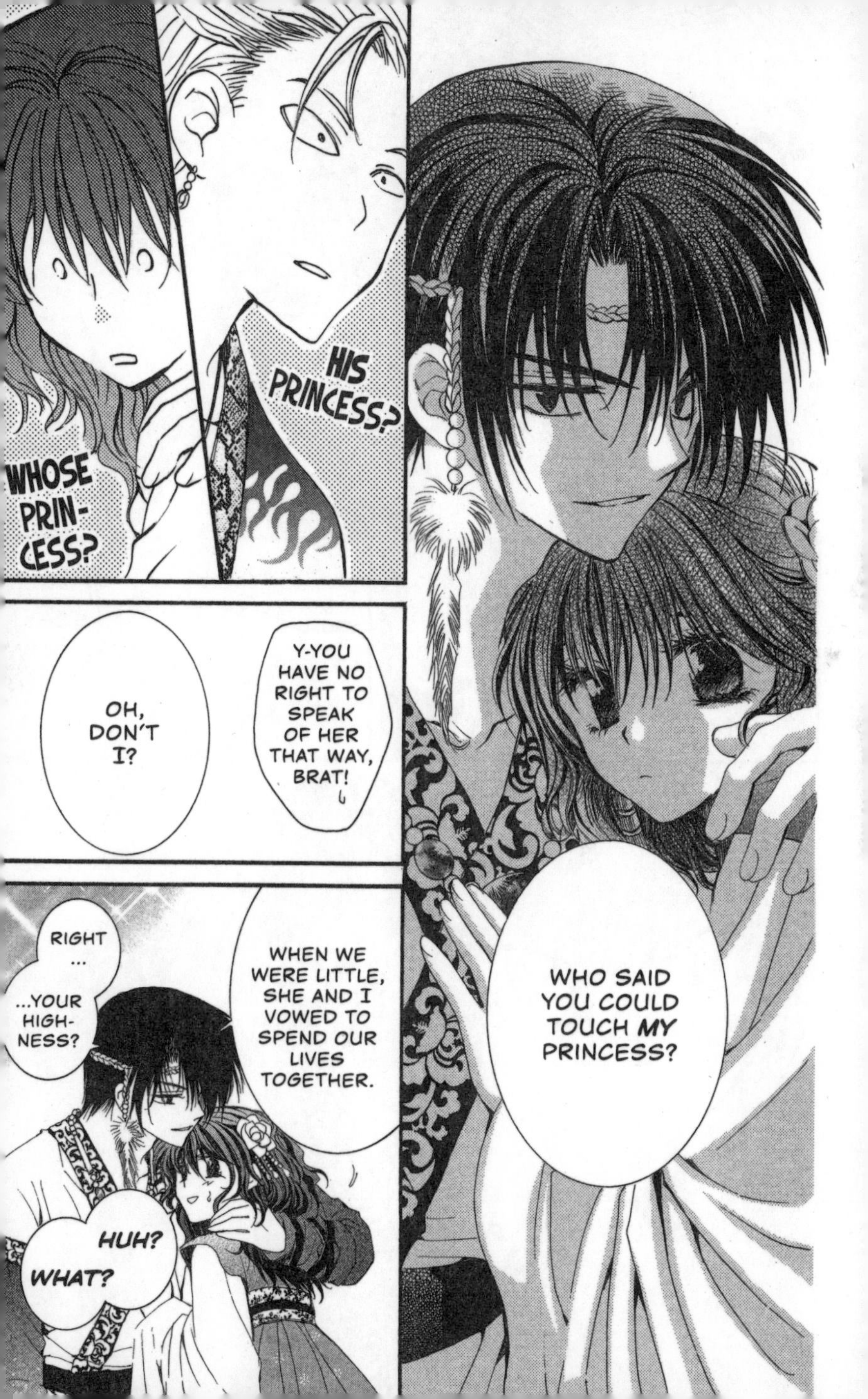
WHO SAID YOU COULD TOUCH *MY* PRINCESS?
HIS PRINCESS?
WHOSE PRIN-CESS?
Y-YOU HAVE NO RIGHT TO SPEAK OF HER THAT WAY, BRAT!
OH, DON'T I?
WHEN WE WERE LITTLE, SHE AND I VOWED TO SPEND OUR LIVES TOGETHER.
RIGHT ...
...YOUR HIGH-NESS?
HUH?
WHAT?

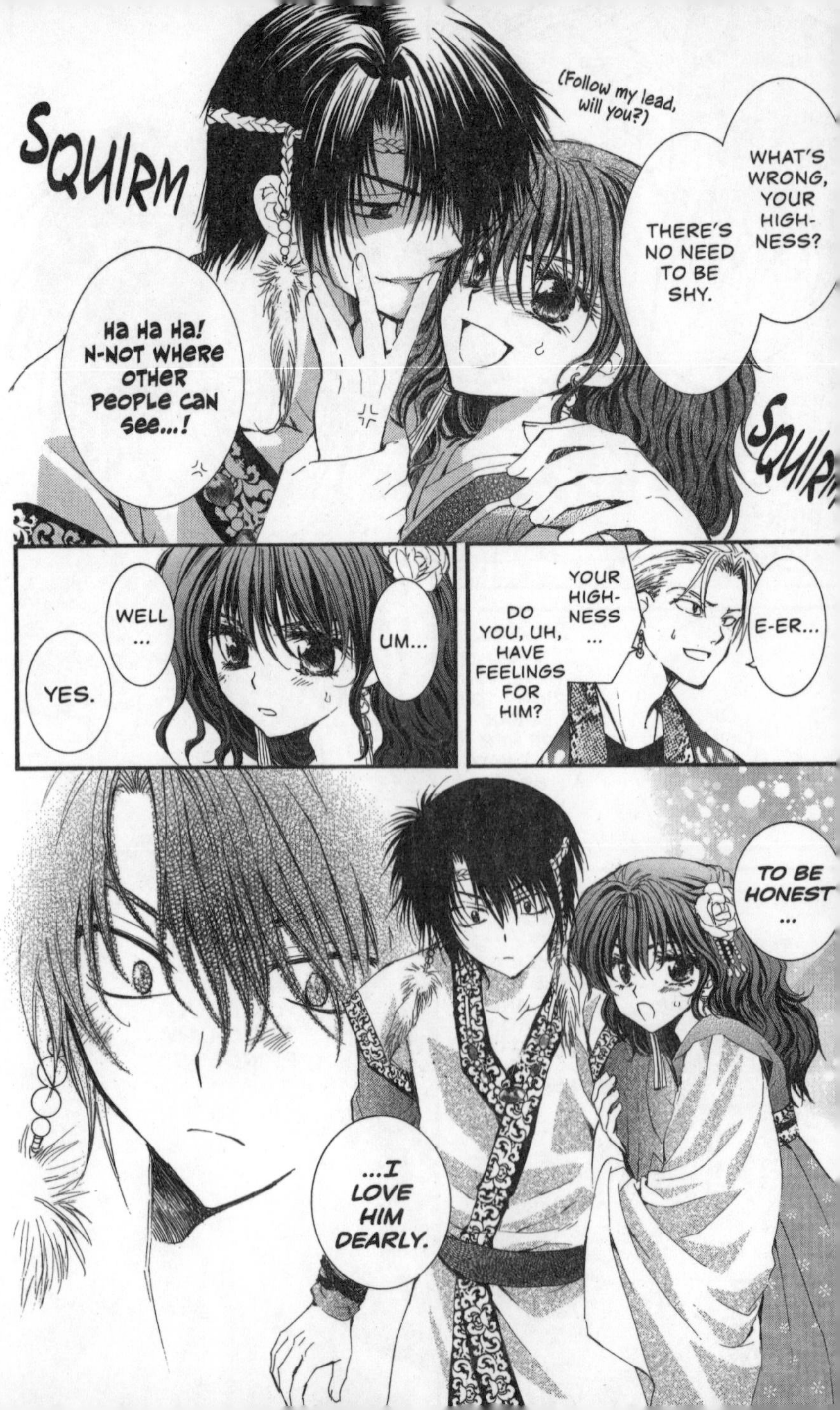
(Follow my lead, will you?)
WHAT'S WRONG, YOUR HIGHNESS? THERE'S NO NEED TO BE SHY.
SQUIRM
Ha ha ha! N-not where other people can see...!
SQUIRM
E-ER...
YOUR HIGHNESS...
DO YOU, UH, HAVE FEELINGS FOR HIM?
UM...
WELL...
YES.
TO BE HONEST...
...I LOVE HIM DEARLY.

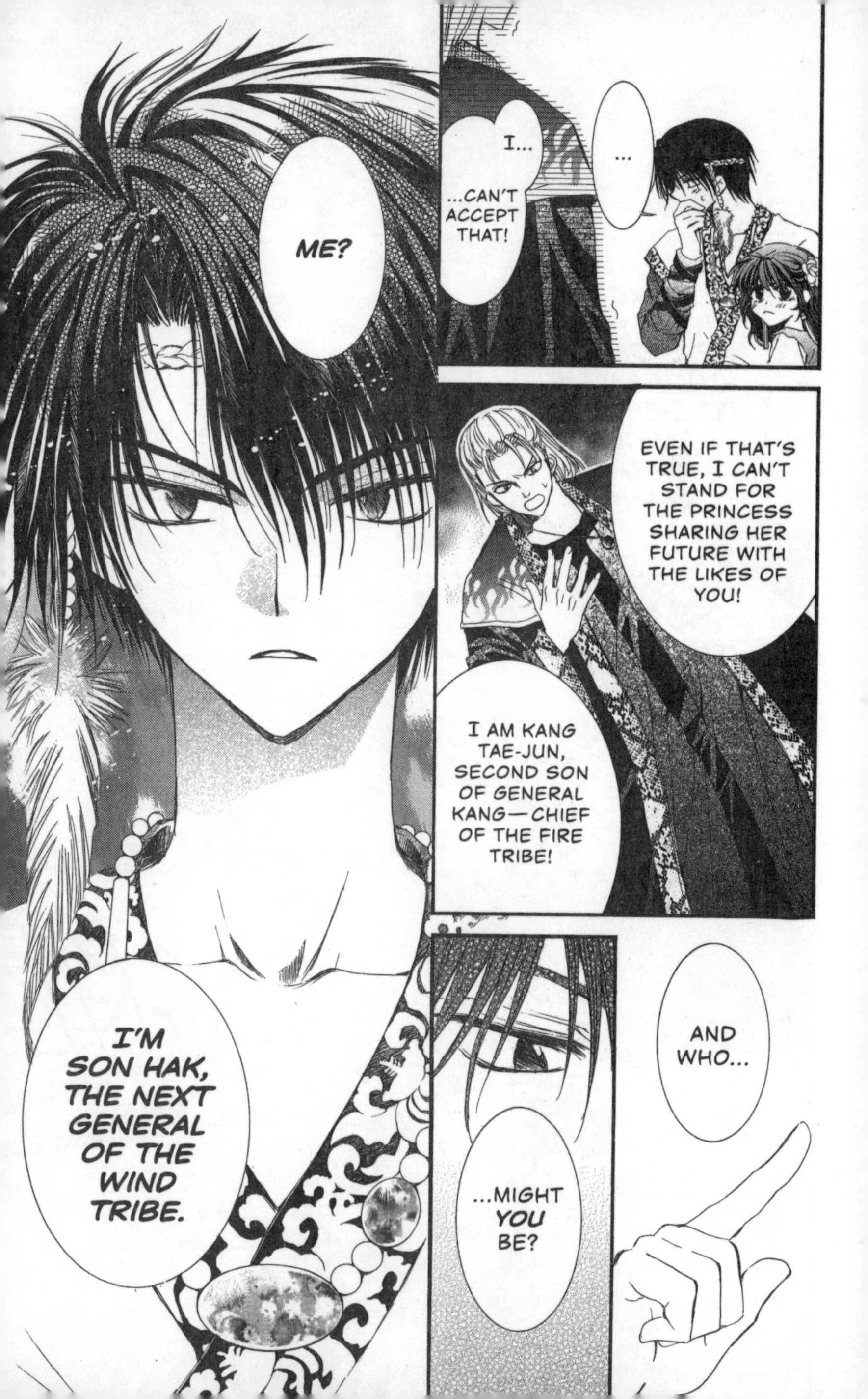

...
I...
...CAN'T ACCEPT THAT!
EVEN IF THAT'S TRUE, I CAN'T STAND FOR THE PRINCESS SHARING HER FUTURE WITH THE LIKES OF YOU!
I AM KANG TAE-JUN, SECOND SON OF GENERAL KANG—CHIEF OF THE FIRE TRIBE!
AND WHO...
...MIGHT *YOU* BE?
ME?
I'M SON HAK, THE NEXT GENERAL OF THE WIND TRIBE.

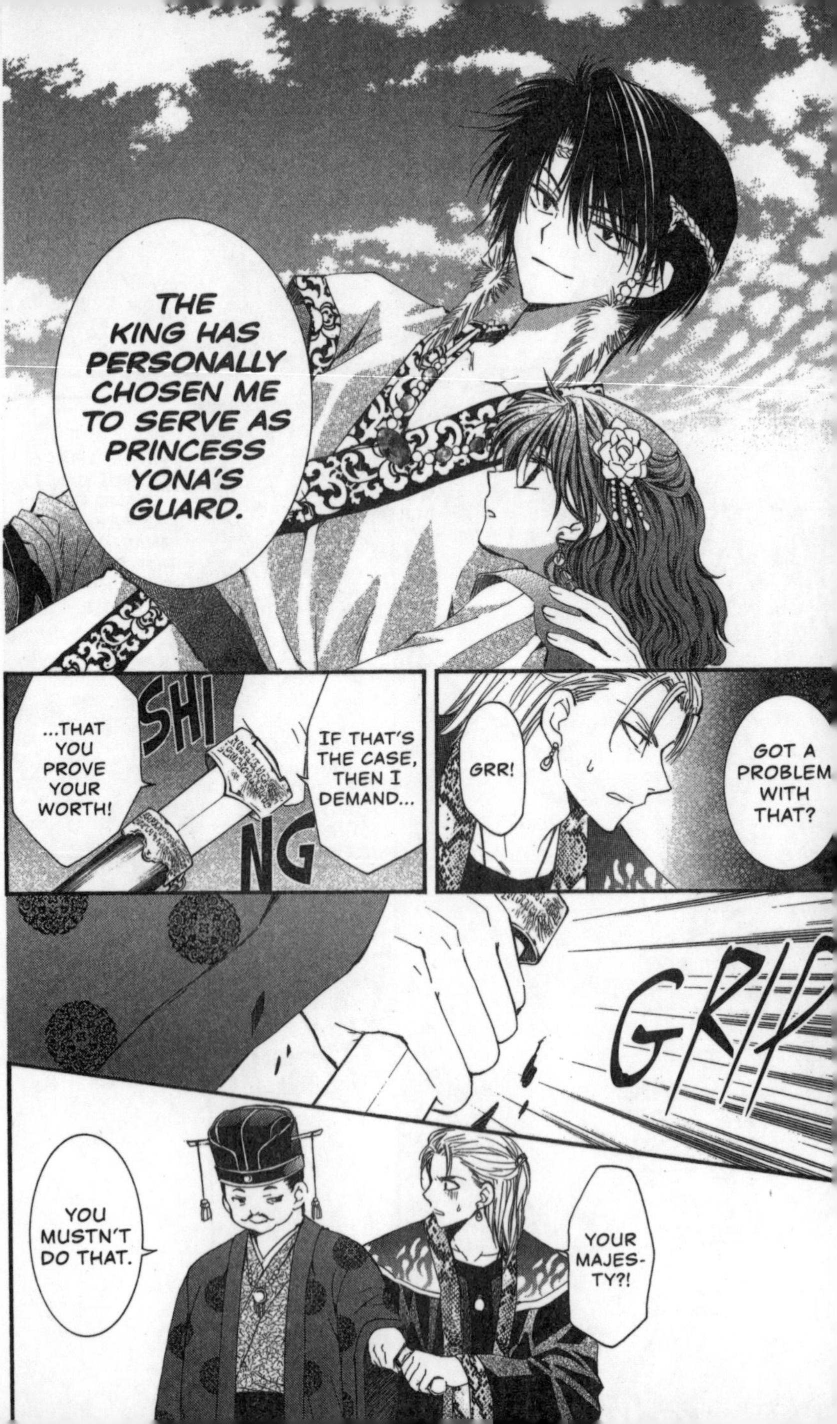
THE KING HAS PERSONALLY CHOSEN ME TO SERVE AS PRINCESS YONA'S GUARD.
GOT A PROBLEM WITH THAT?
GRR!
IF THAT'S THE CASE, THEN I DEMAND...
SHING
...THAT YOU PROVE YOUR WORTH!
GRIP
YOUR MAJES-TY?!
YOU MUSTN'T DO THAT.

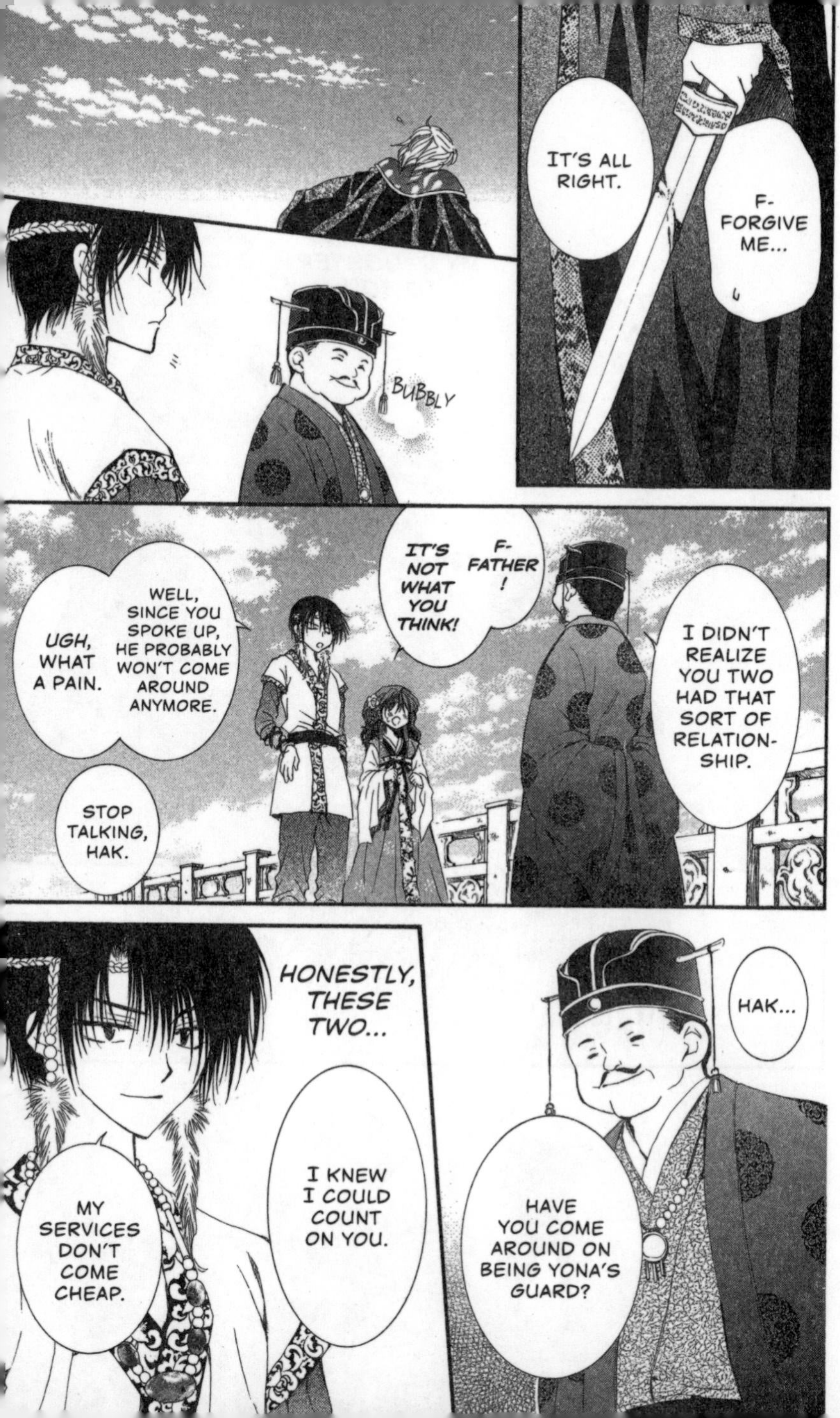
F- FORGIVE ME...
IT'S ALL RIGHT.
BUBBLY
I DIDN'T REALIZE YOU TWO HAD THAT SORT OF RELATION-SHIP.
F- FATHER!
IT'S NOT WHAT YOU THINK!
WELL, SINCE YOU SPOKE UP, HE PROBABLY WON'T COME AROUND ANYMORE.
UGH, WHAT A PAIN.
STOP TALKING, HAK.
HAK...
HAVE YOU COME AROUND ON BEING YONA'S GUARD?
I KNEW I COULD COUNT ON YOU.
HONESTLY, THESE TWO...
MY SERVICES DON'T COME CHEAP.

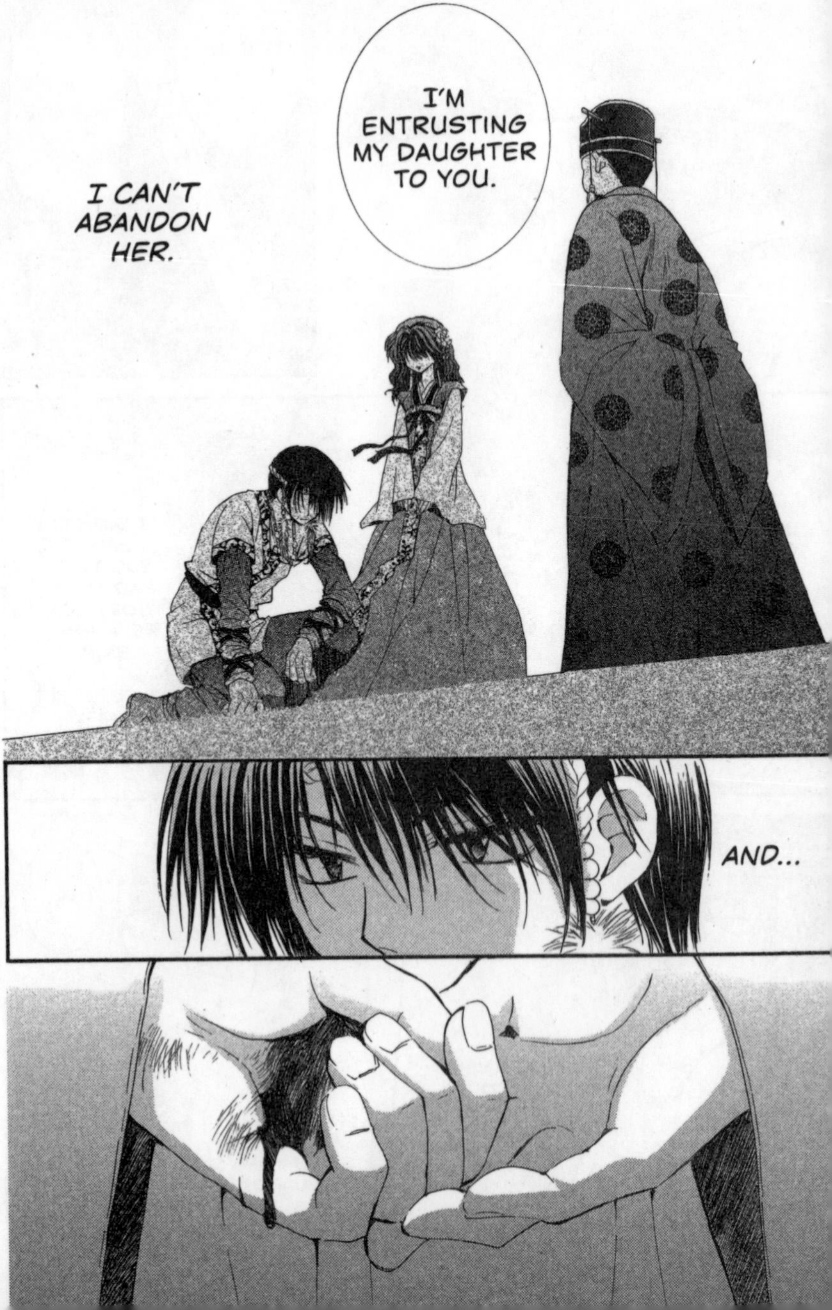
I'M ENTRUSTING MY DAUGHTER TO YOU.
I CAN'T ABANDON HER.
AND...

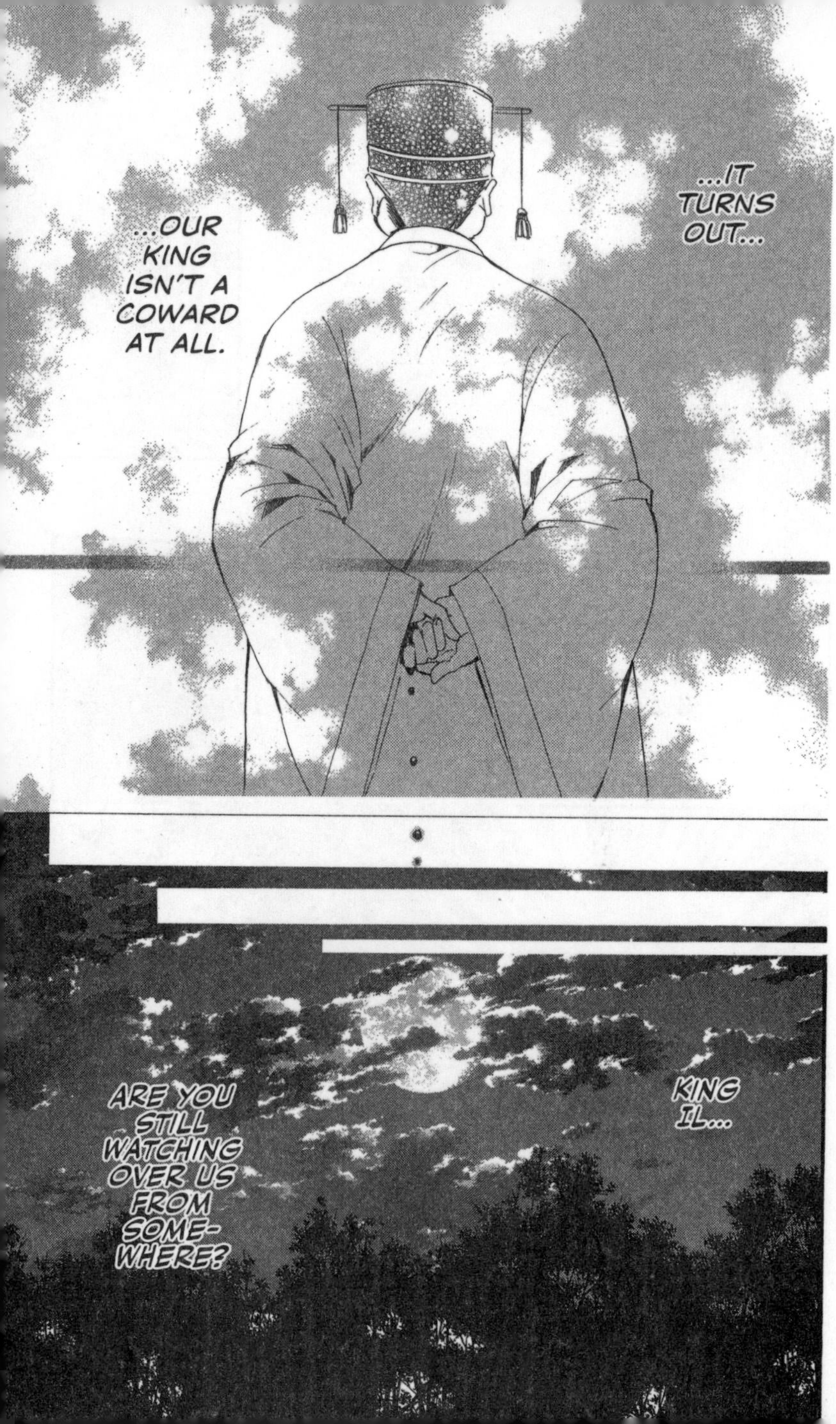
...IT TURNS OUT...
...OUR KING ISN'T A COWARD AT ALL.
KING IL...
ARE YOU STILL WATCHING OVER US FROM SOME-WHERE?

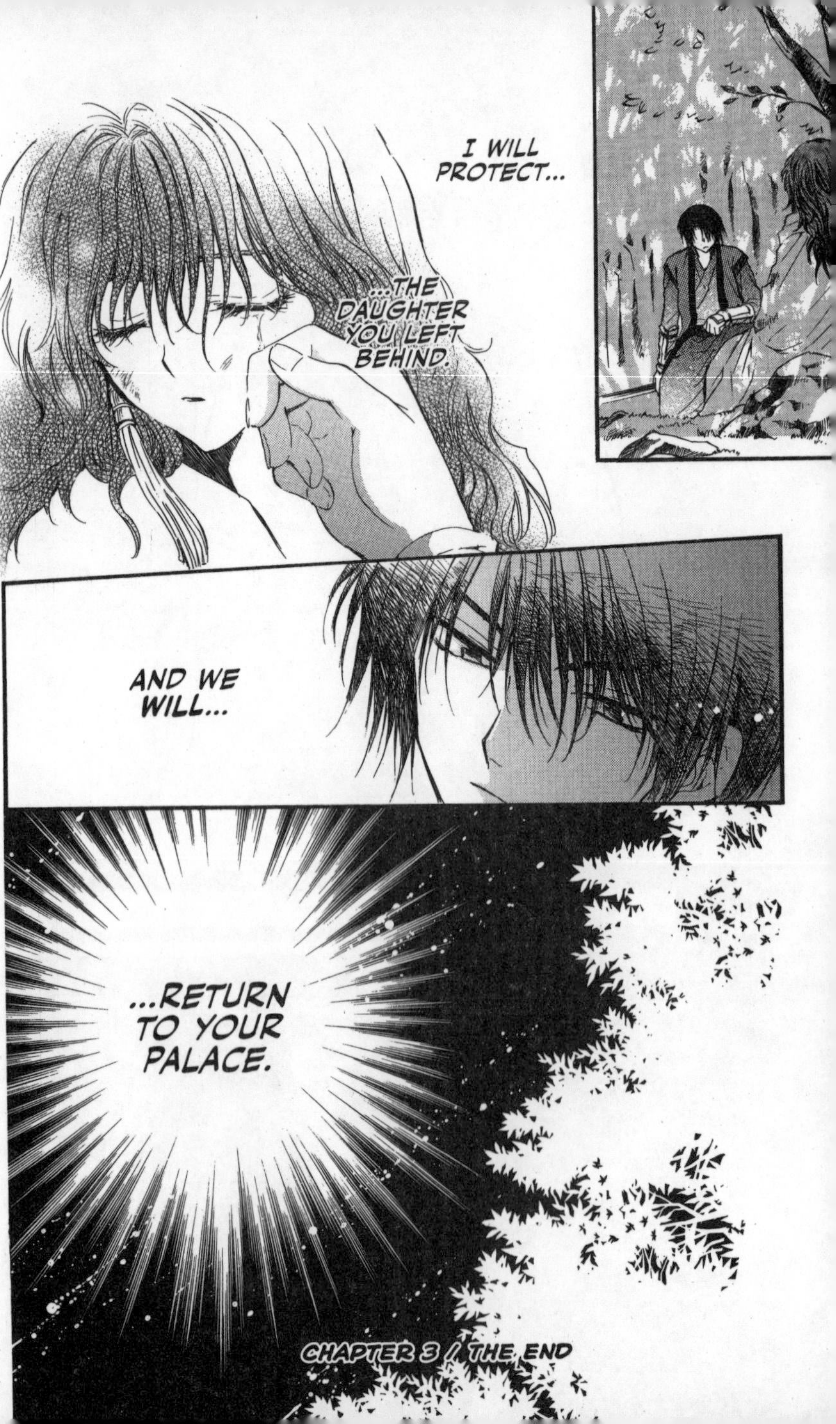
I WILL PROTECT...
...THE DAUGHTER YOU LEFT BEHIND.
AND WE WILL...
...RETURN TO YOUR PALACE.
CHAPTER 3 / THE END

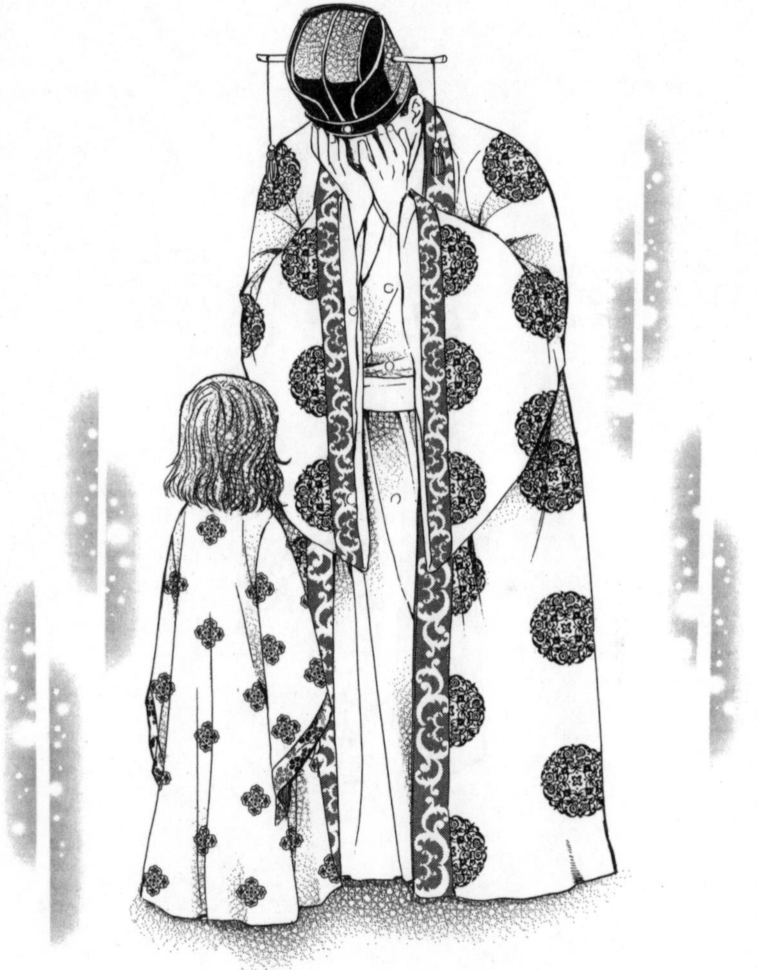

CHAPTER 4: DISTANT SKIES

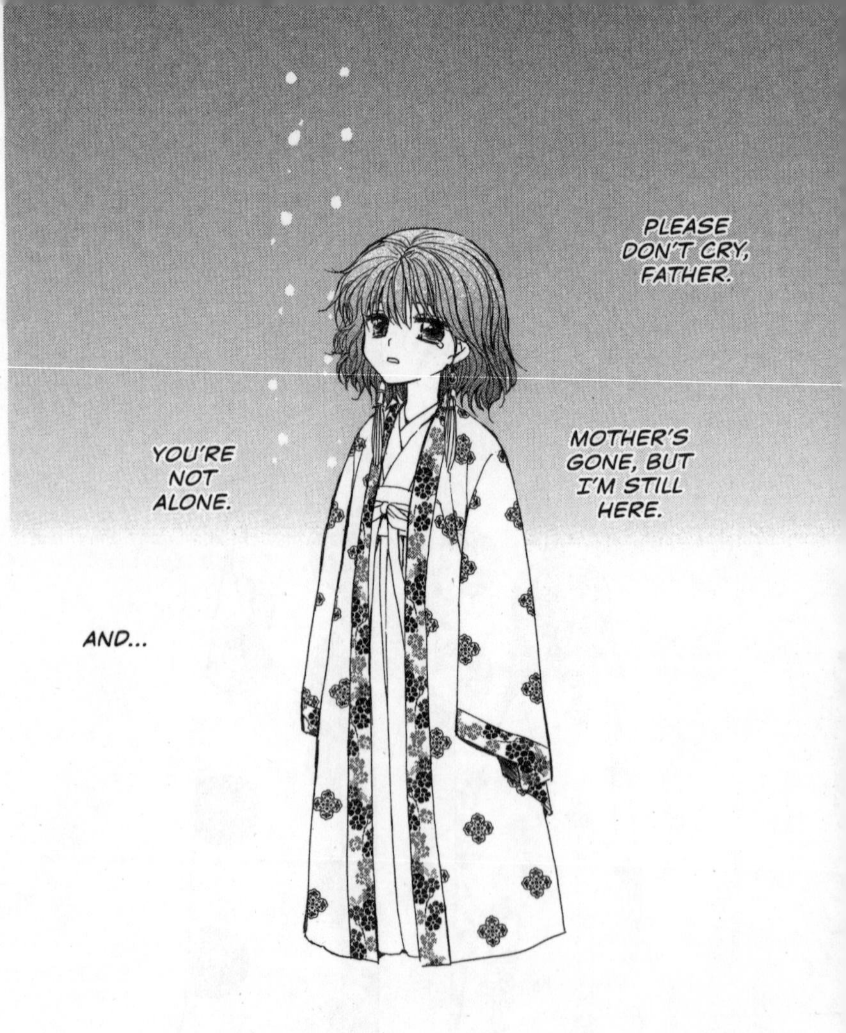
PLEASE DON'T CRY, FATHER.
MOTHER'S GONE, BUT I'M STILL HERE.
YOU'RE NOT ALONE.
AND...

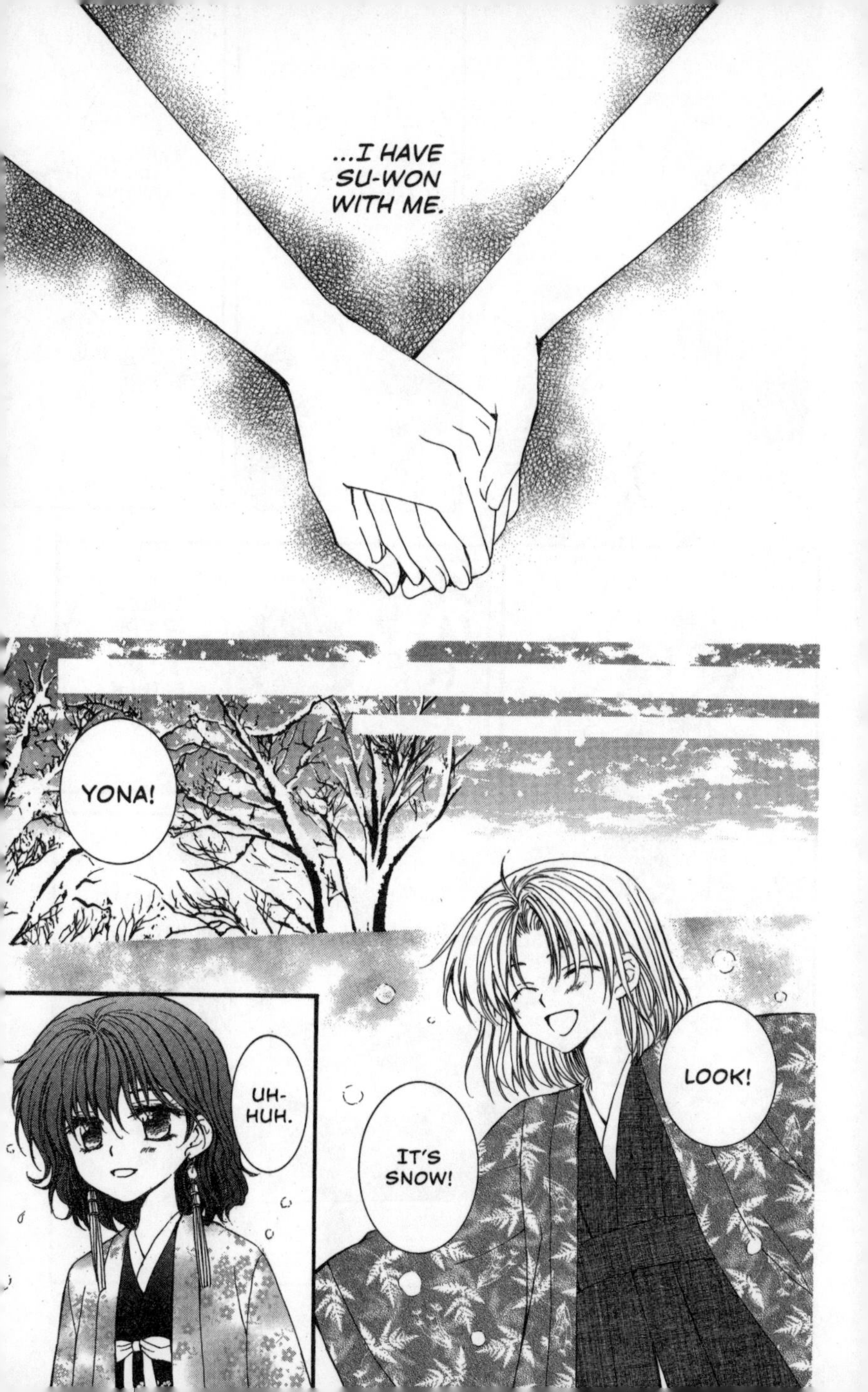
...I HAVE SU-WON WITH ME.
YONA!
LOOK!
IT'S SNOW!
UH-HUH.

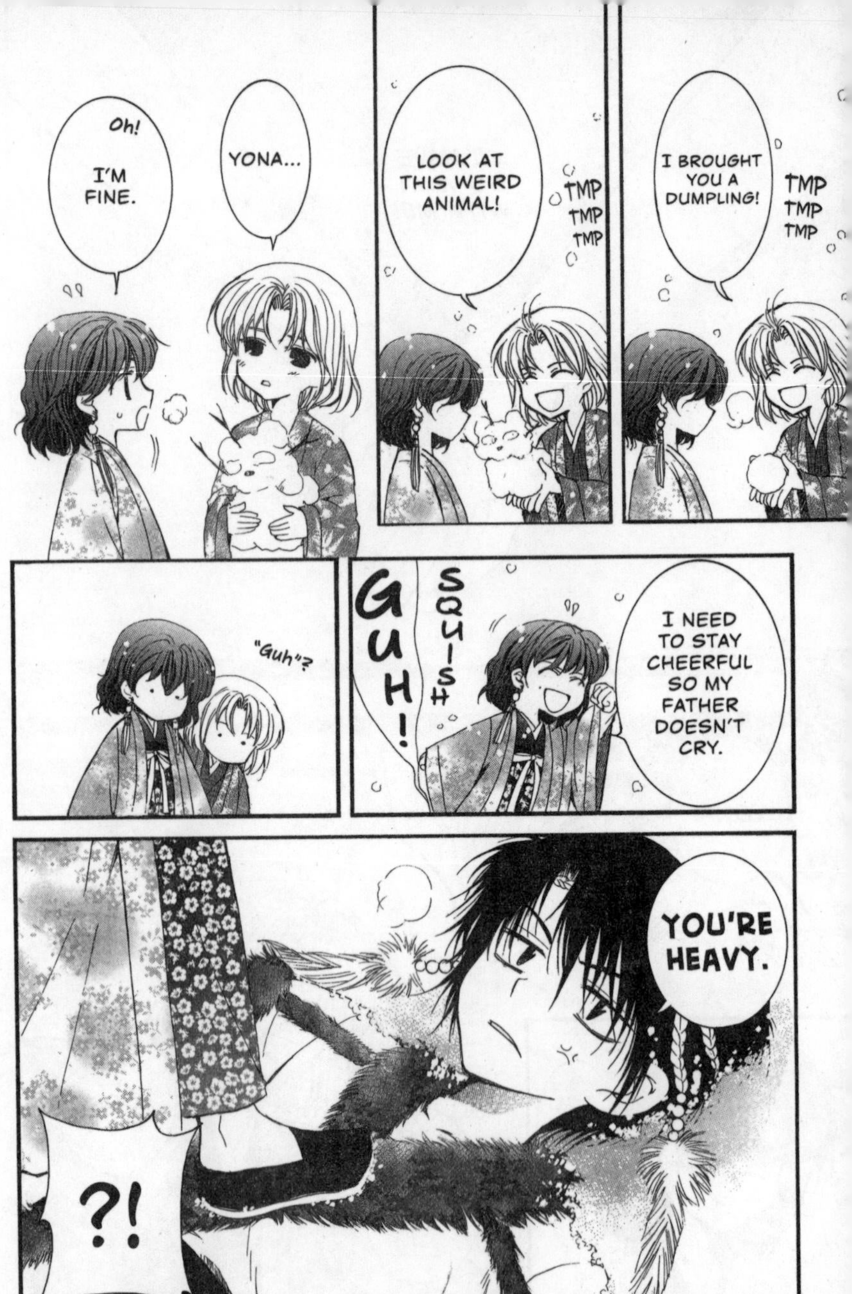
I BROUGHT YOU A DUMPLING!
TMP TMP TMP
LOOK AT THIS WEIRD ANIMAL!
TMP TMP TMP
YONA...
Oh! I'M FINE.
I NEED TO STAY CHEERFUL SO MY FATHER DOESN'T CRY.
SQUISH
GUH!
"Guh"?
YOU'RE HEAVY.
?!

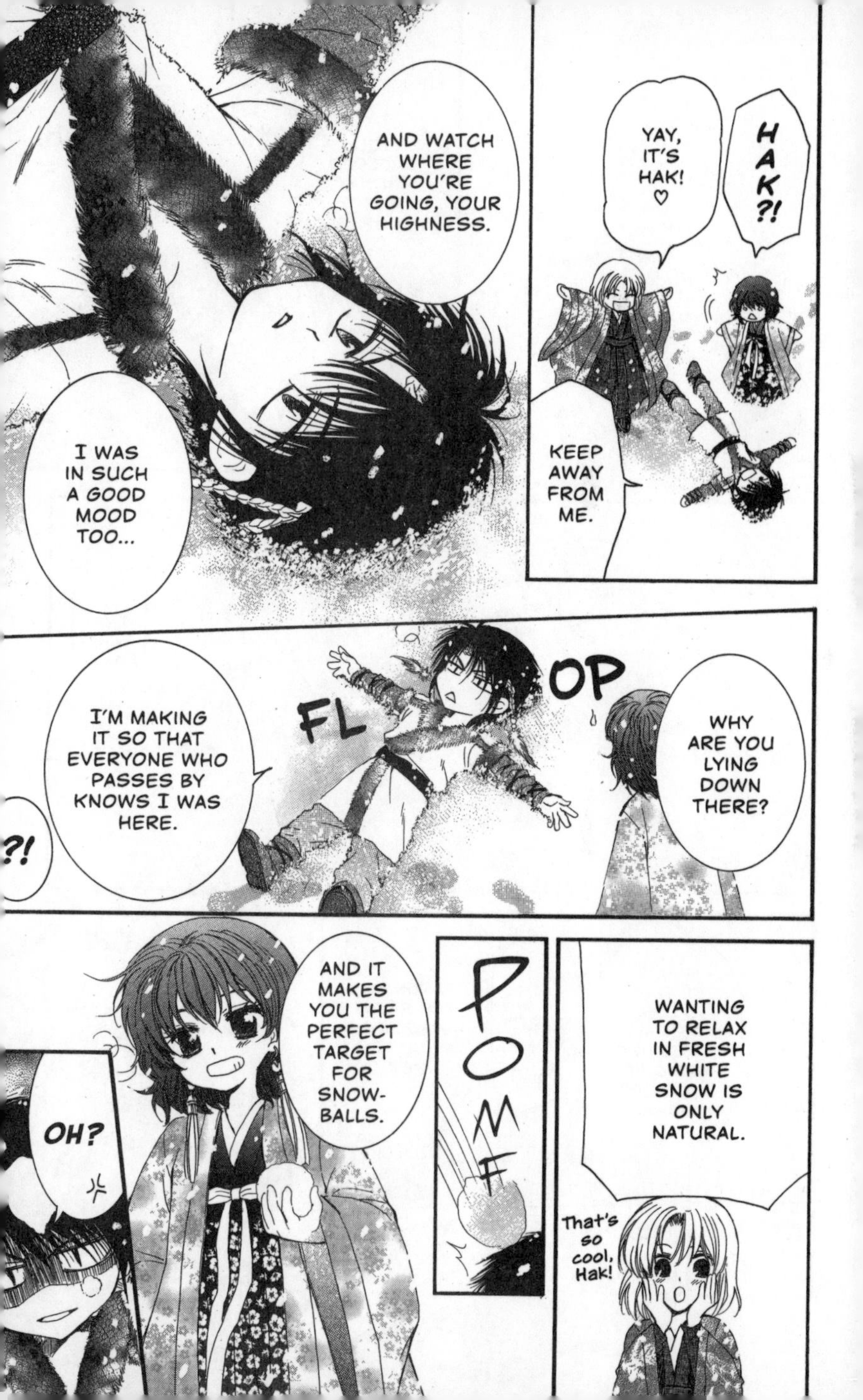
HAK?!
YAY, IT'S HAK! ♡
KEEP AWAY FROM ME.
AND WATCH WHERE YOU'RE GOING, YOUR HIGHNESS.
I WAS IN SUCH A GOOD MOOD TOO...
WHY ARE YOU LYING DOWN THERE?
FLOP
I'M MAKING IT SO THAT EVERYONE WHO PASSES BY KNOWS I WAS HERE.
?!
WANTING TO RELAX IN FRESH WHITE SNOW IS ONLY NATURAL.
That's so cool, Hak!
POMF
AND IT MAKES YOU THE PERFECT TARGET FOR SNOW-BALLS.
OH?

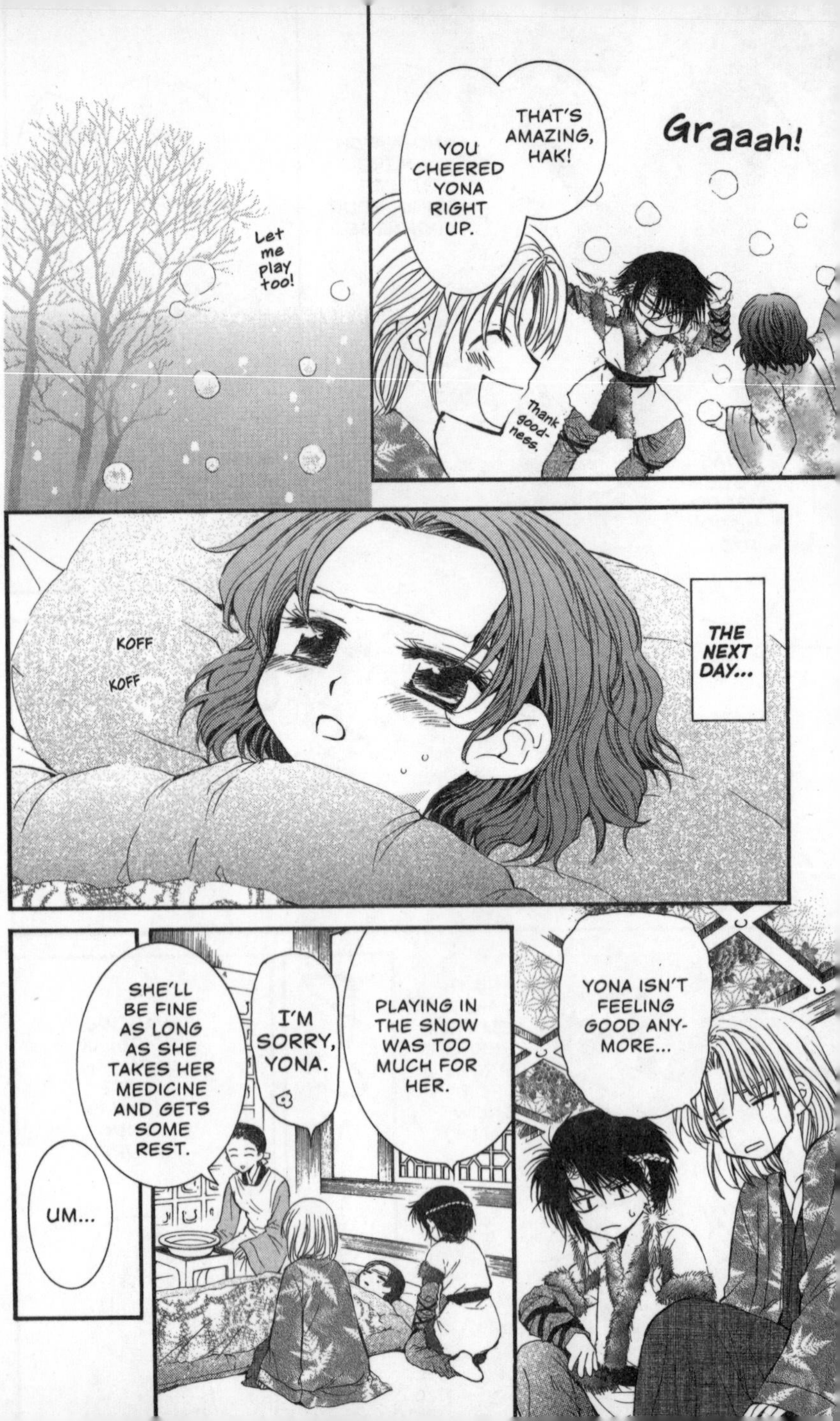
Graaah!
THAT'S AMAZING, HAK! YOU CHEERED YONA RIGHT UP.
Thank goodness.
Let me play too!
THE NEXT DAY...
KOFF
KOFF
YONA ISN'T FEELING GOOD ANYMORE...
PLAYING IN THE SNOW WAS TOO MUCH FOR HER.
I'M SORRY, YONA.
SHE'LL BE FINE AS LONG AS SHE TAKES HER MEDICINE AND GETS SOME REST.
UM...

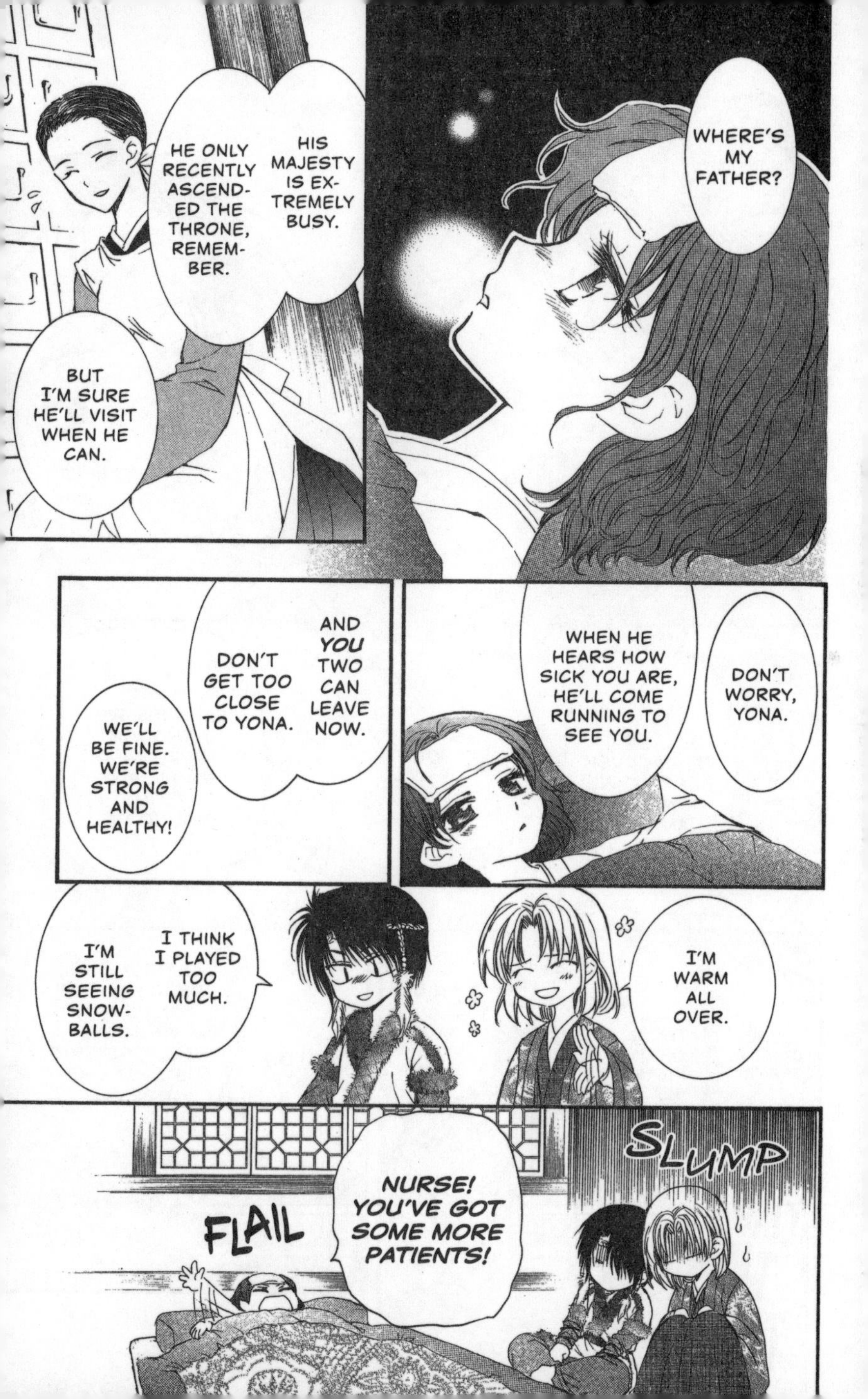
WHERE'S MY FATHER?
HIS MAJESTY IS EXTREMELY BUSY.
HE ONLY RECENTLY ASCENDED THE THRONE, REMEMBER.
BUT I'M SURE HE'LL VISIT WHEN HE CAN.
DON'T WORRY, YONA.
WHEN HE HEARS HOW SICK YOU ARE, HE'LL COME RUNNING TO SEE YOU.
AND *YOU* TWO CAN LEAVE NOW.
DON'T GET TOO CLOSE TO YONA.
WE'LL BE FINE. WE'RE STRONG AND HEALTHY!
I'M WARM ALL OVER.
I THINK I PLAYED TOO MUCH.
I'M STILL SEEING SNOWBALLS.
SLUMP
NURSE! YOU'VE GOT SOME MORE PATIENTS!
FLAIL

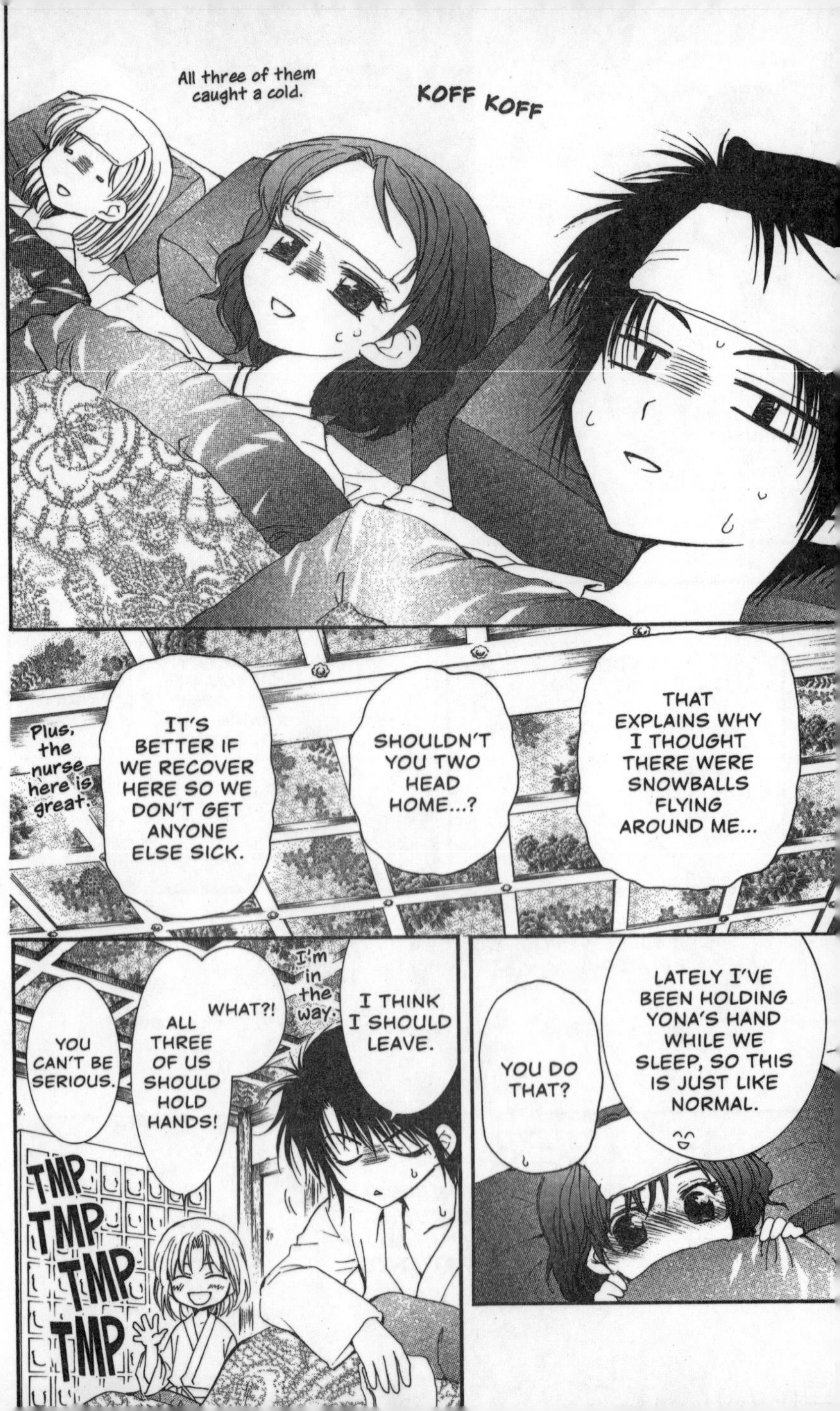
KOFF KOFF
All three of them caught a cold.
THAT EXPLAINS WHY I THOUGHT THERE WERE SNOWBALLS FLYING AROUND ME...
SHOULDN'T YOU TWO HEAD HOME...?
IT'S BETTER IF WE RECOVER HERE SO WE DON'T GET ANYONE ELSE SICK.
Plus, the nurse here is great.
LATELY I'VE BEEN HOLDING YONA'S HAND WHILE WE SLEEP, SO THIS IS JUST LIKE NORMAL.
YOU DO THAT?
I THINK I SHOULD LEAVE.
I'm in the way.
WHAT?!
ALL THREE OF US SHOULD HOLD HANDS!
YOU CAN'T BE SERIOUS.
TMP TMP TMP TMP

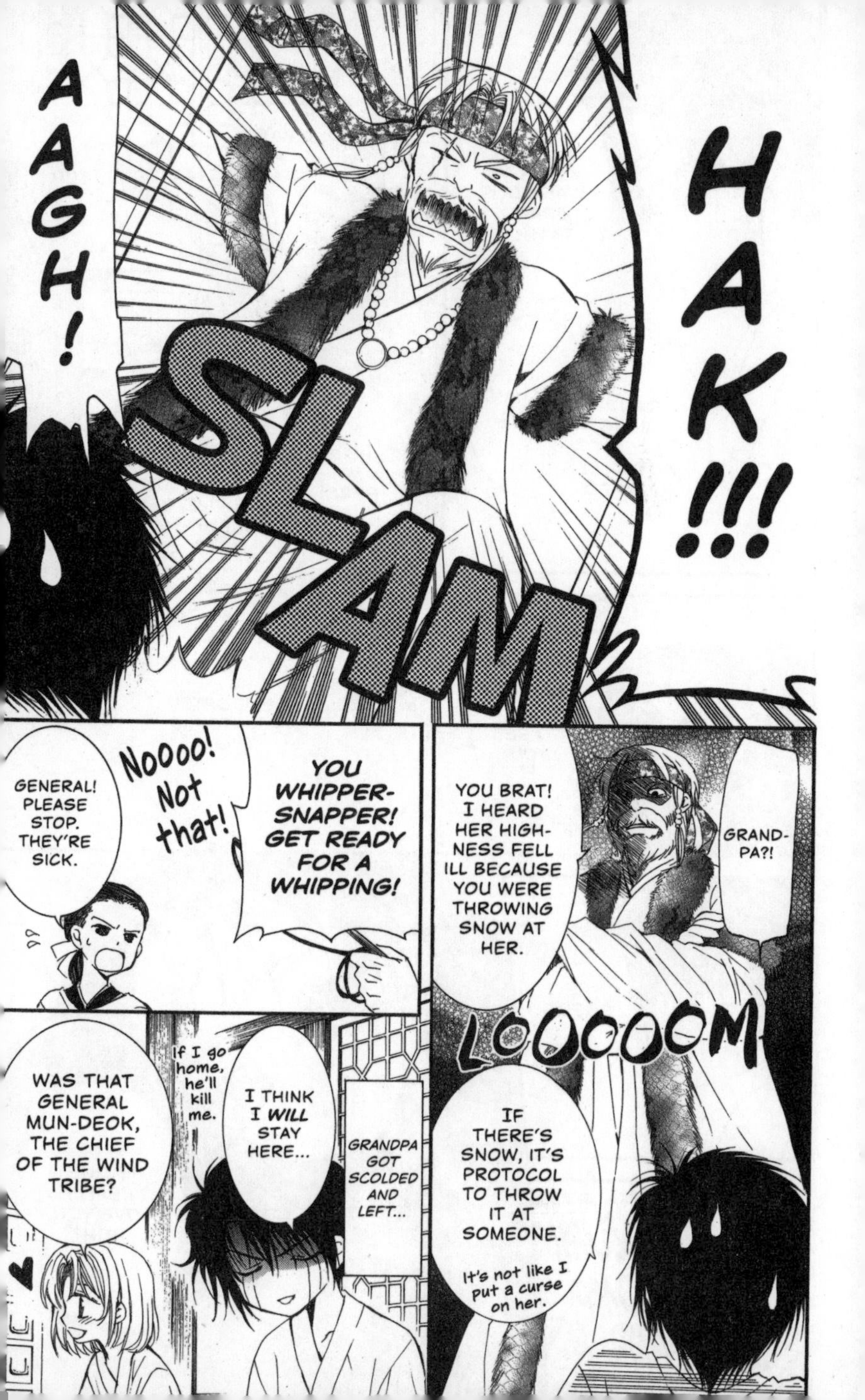
HAK!!!
SLAM
AAGH!
GRAND-PA?!
YOU BRAT! I HEARD HER HIGH-NESS FELL ILL BECAUSE YOU WERE THROWING SNOW AT HER.
YOU WHIPPER-SNAPPER! GET READY FOR A WHIPPING!
Noooo! Not that!
GENERAL! PLEASE STOP. THEY'RE SICK.
LOOOOOM
IF THERE'S SNOW, IT'S PROTOCOL TO THROW IT AT SOMEONE.
It's not like I put a curse on her.
GRANDPA GOT SCOLDED AND LEFT...
I THINK I *WILL* STAY HERE...
If I go home, he'll kill me.
WAS THAT GENERAL MUN-DEOK, THE CHIEF OF THE WIND TRIBE?

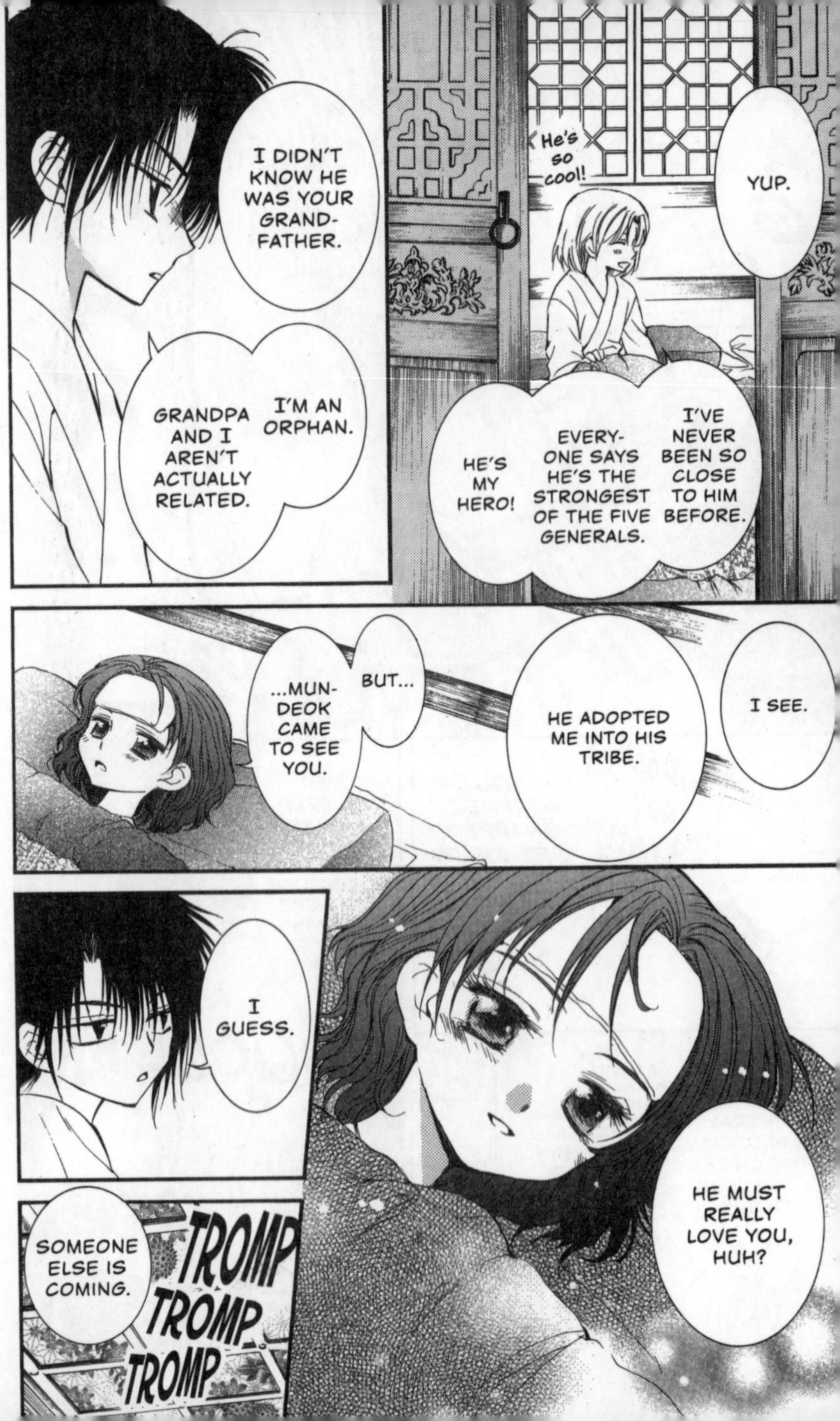
YUP.
He's so cool!
I'VE NEVER BEEN SO CLOSE TO HIM BEFORE.
EVERYONE SAYS HE'S THE STRONGEST OF THE FIVE GENERALS.
HE'S MY HERO!
I DIDN'T KNOW HE WAS YOUR GRANDFATHER.
I'M AN ORPHAN.
GRANDPA AND I AREN'T ACTUALLY RELATED.
I SEE.
HE ADOPTED ME INTO HIS TRIBE.
BUT...
...MUN-DEOK CAME TO SEE YOU.
HE MUST REALLY LOVE YOU, HUH?
I GUESS.
SOMEONE ELSE IS COMING.
TROMP
TROMP
TROMP

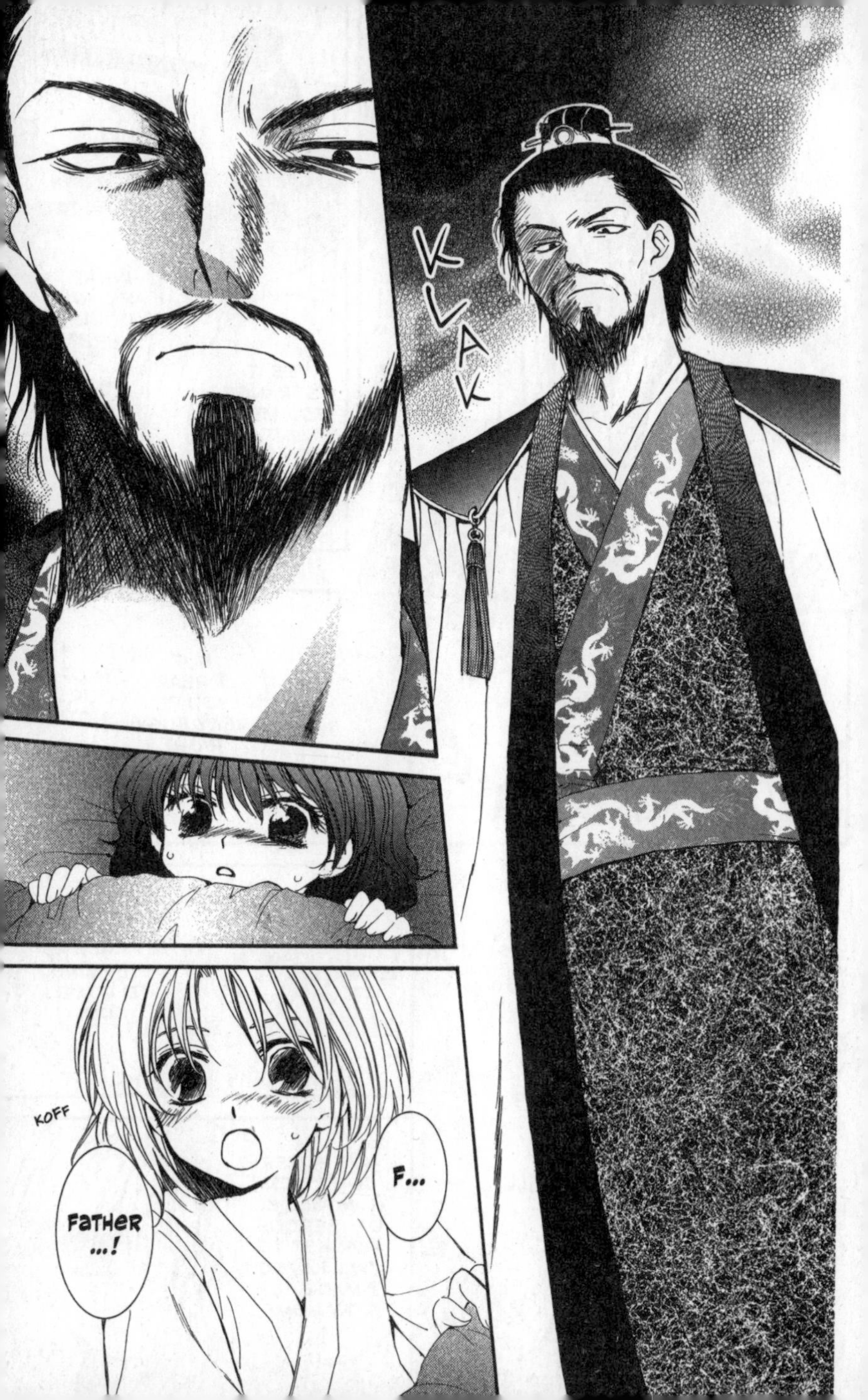
KLAK
KOFF
F...
FATHER ...!

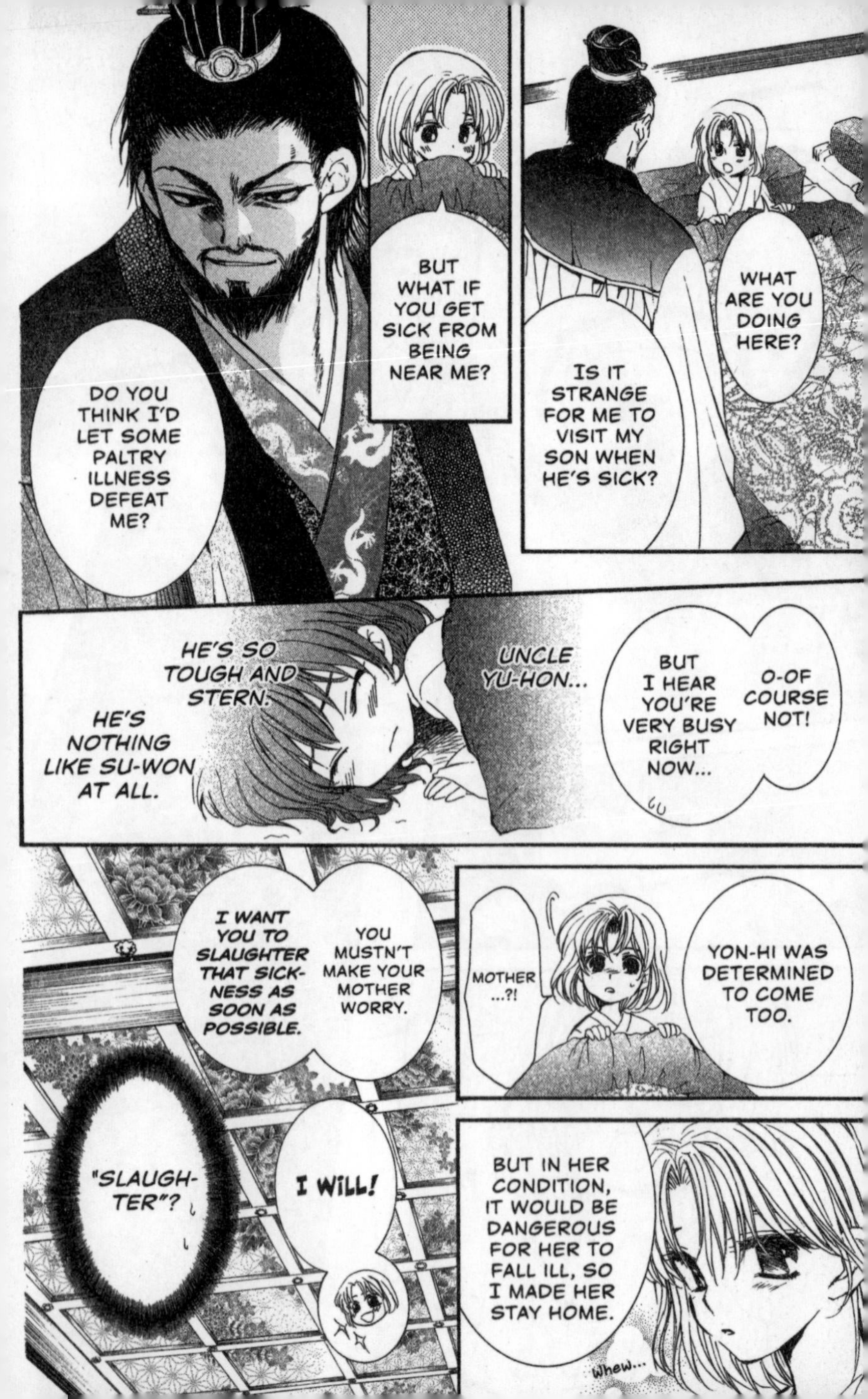
WHAT ARE YOU DOING HERE?
IS IT STRANGE FOR ME TO VISIT MY SON WHEN HE'S SICK?
BUT WHAT IF YOU GET SICK FROM BEING NEAR ME?
DO YOU THINK I'D LET SOME PALTRY ILLNESS DEFEAT ME?
O-OF COURSE NOT!
BUT I HEAR YOU'RE VERY BUSY RIGHT NOW...
UNCLE YU-HON...
HE'S SO TOUGH AND STERN.
HE'S NOTHING LIKE SU-WON AT ALL.
YON-HI WAS DETERMINED TO COME TOO.
MOTHER ...?!
BUT IN HER CONDITION, IT WOULD BE DANGEROUS FOR HER TO FALL ILL, SO I MADE HER STAY HOME.
Whew...
YOU MUSTN'T MAKE YOUR MOTHER WORRY.
I WANT YOU TO SLAUGHTER THAT SICKNESS AS SOON AS POSSIBLE.
I WILL!
"SLAUGHTER"?

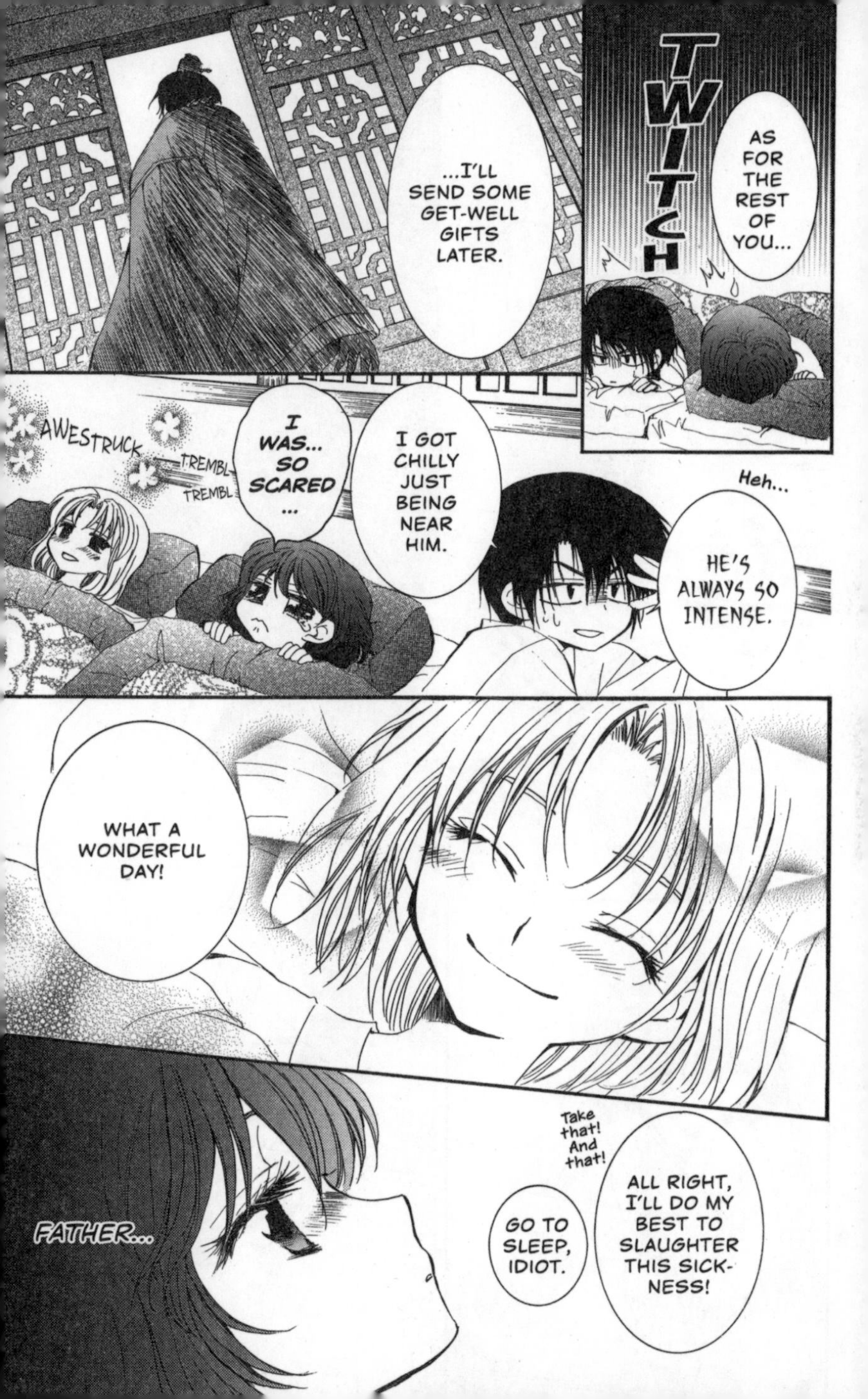
TWITCH
AS FOR THE REST OF YOU...
...I'LL SEND SOME GET-WELL GIFTS LATER.
Heh...
HE'S ALWAYS SO INTENSE.
I GOT CHILLY JUST BEING NEAR HIM.
I WAS... SO SCARED...
TREMBL TREMBL
AWESTRUCK
WHAT A WONDERFUL DAY!
Take that! And that!
ALL RIGHT, I'LL DO MY BEST TO SLAUGHTER THIS SICKNESS!
GO TO SLEEP, IDIOT.
FATHER...

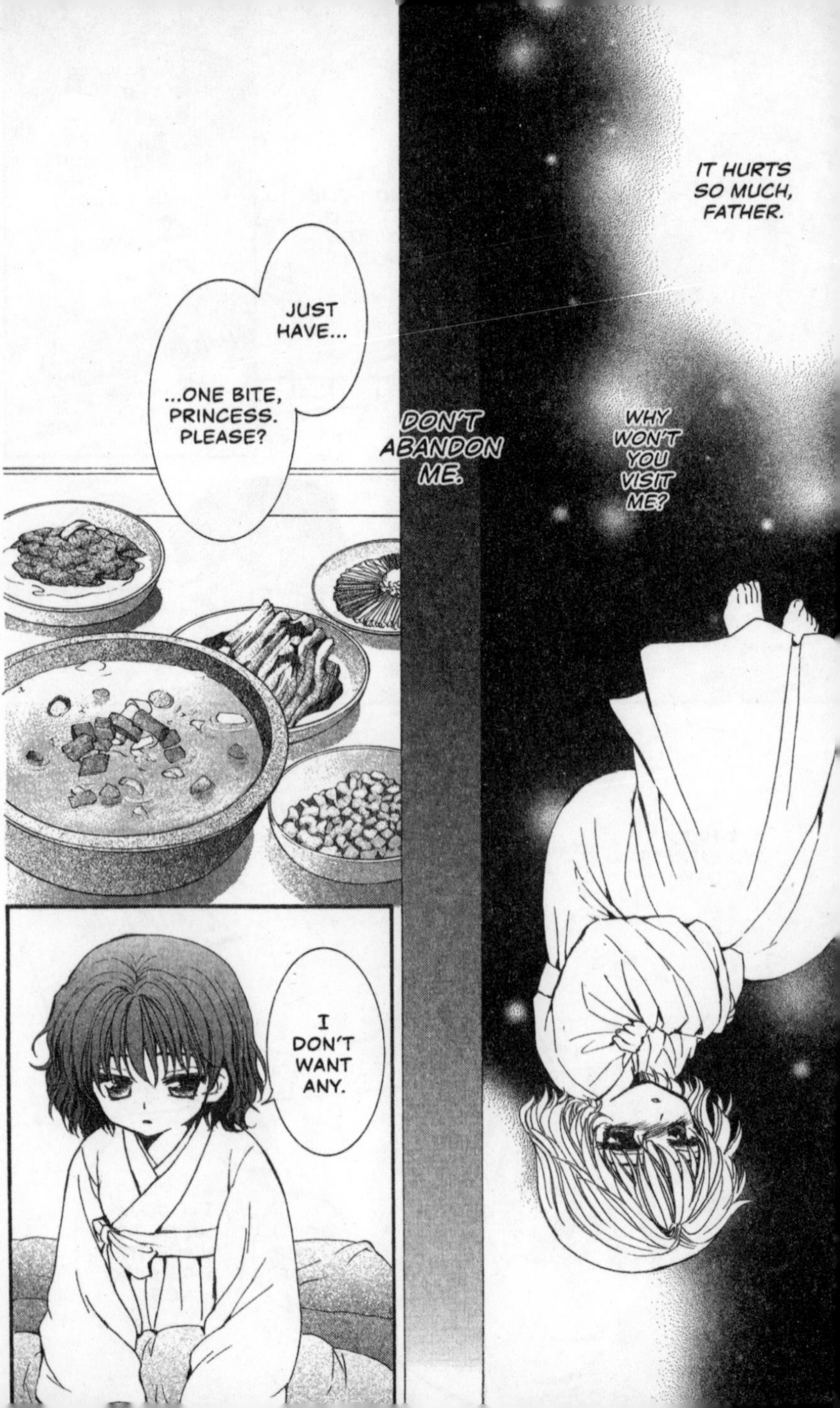
IT HURTS SO MUCH, FATHER.
WHY WON'T YOU VISIT ME?
DON'T ABANDON ME.
JUST HAVE...
...ONE BITE, PRINCESS. PLEASE?
I DON'T WANT ANY.

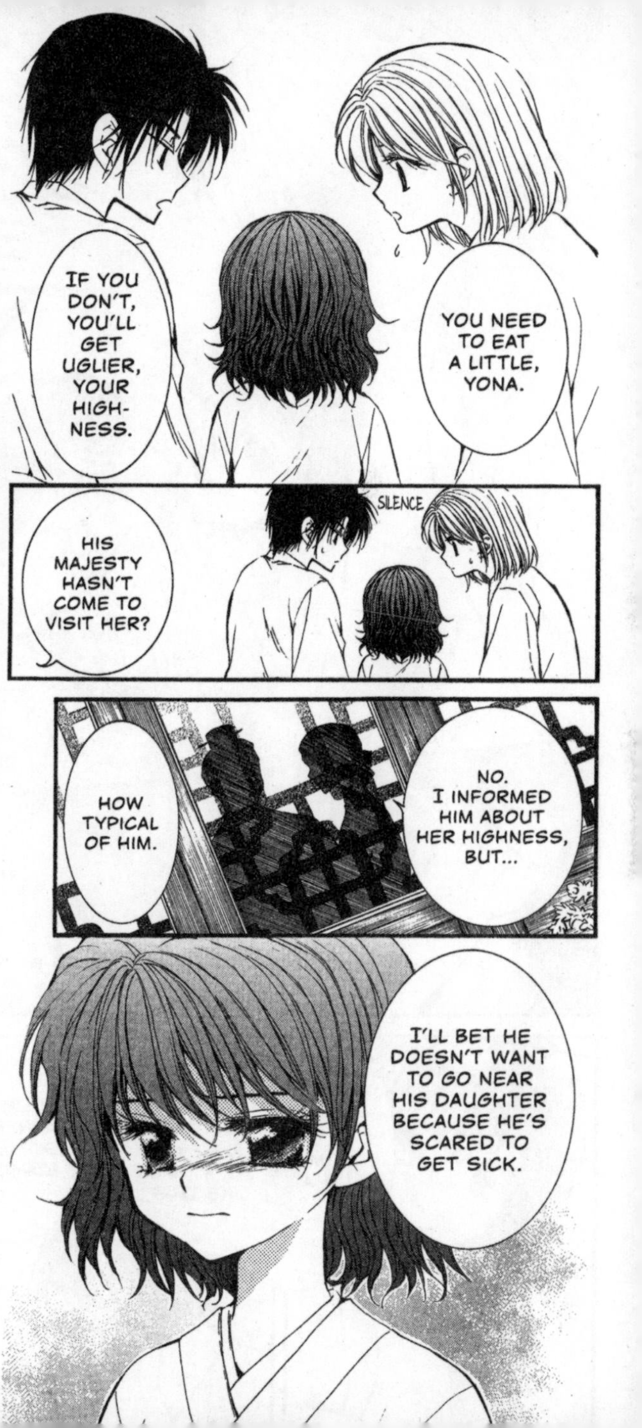
YOU NEED TO EAT A LITTLE, YONA.
IF YOU DON'T, YOU'LL GET UGLIER, YOUR HIGH-NESS.
SILENCE
HIS MAJESTY HASN'T COME TO VISIT HER?
NO. I INFORMED HIM ABOUT HER HIGHNESS, BUT...
HOW TYPICAL OF HIM.
I'LL BET HE DOESN'T WANT TO GO NEAR HIS DAUGHTER BECAUSE HE'S SCARED TO GET SICK.
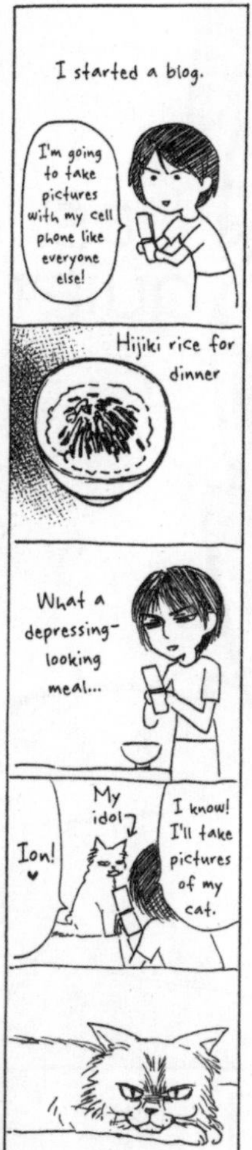
I started a blog.
I'm going to take pictures with my cell phone like everyone else!
Hijiki rice for dinner
What a depressing-looking meal...
I know! I'll take pictures of my cat.
My idol
Ion! ♥
Scary...

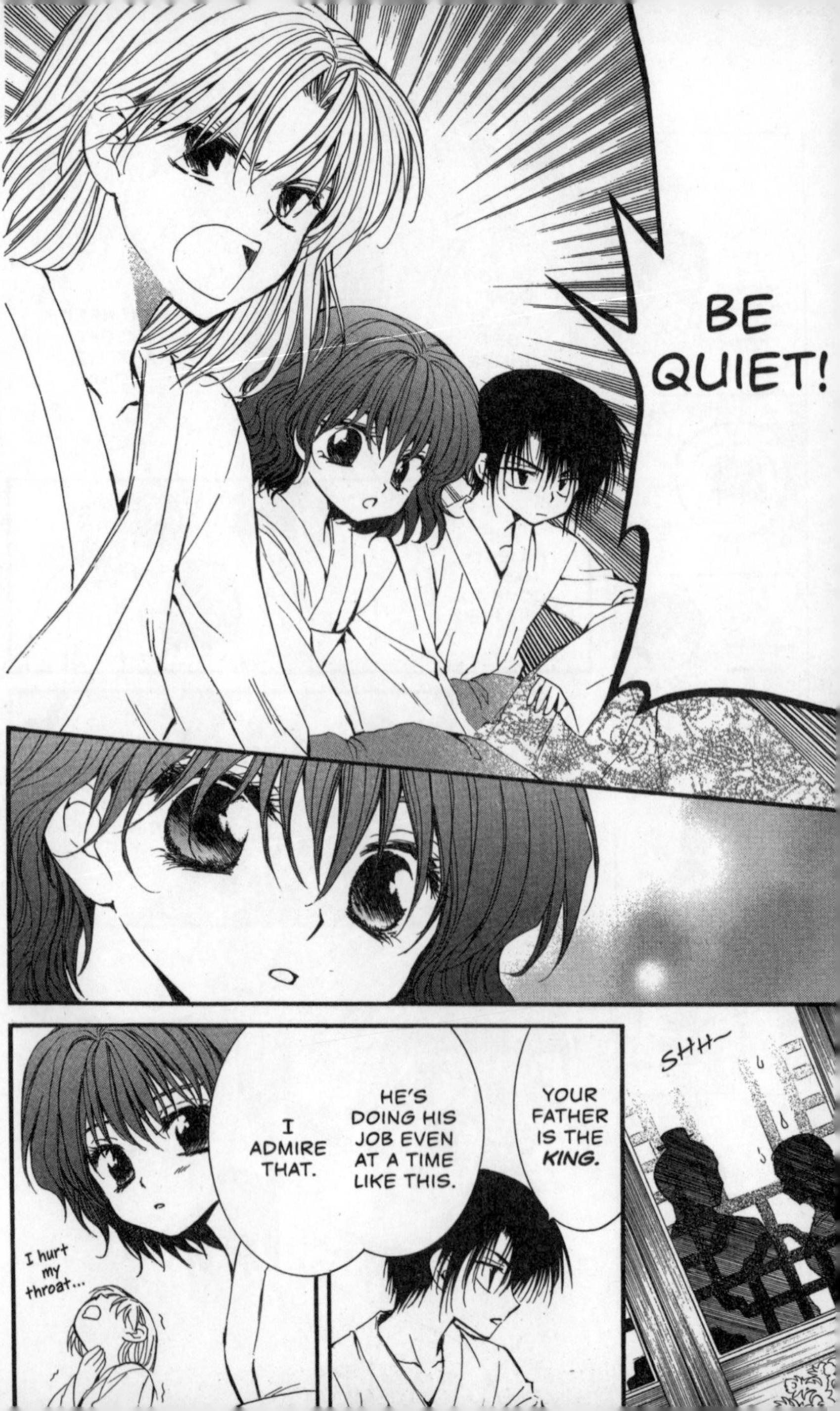
BE QUIET!
SHH—
YOUR FATHER IS THE KING.
HE'S DOING HIS JOB EVEN AT A TIME LIKE THIS.
I ADMIRE THAT.
I hurt my throat...

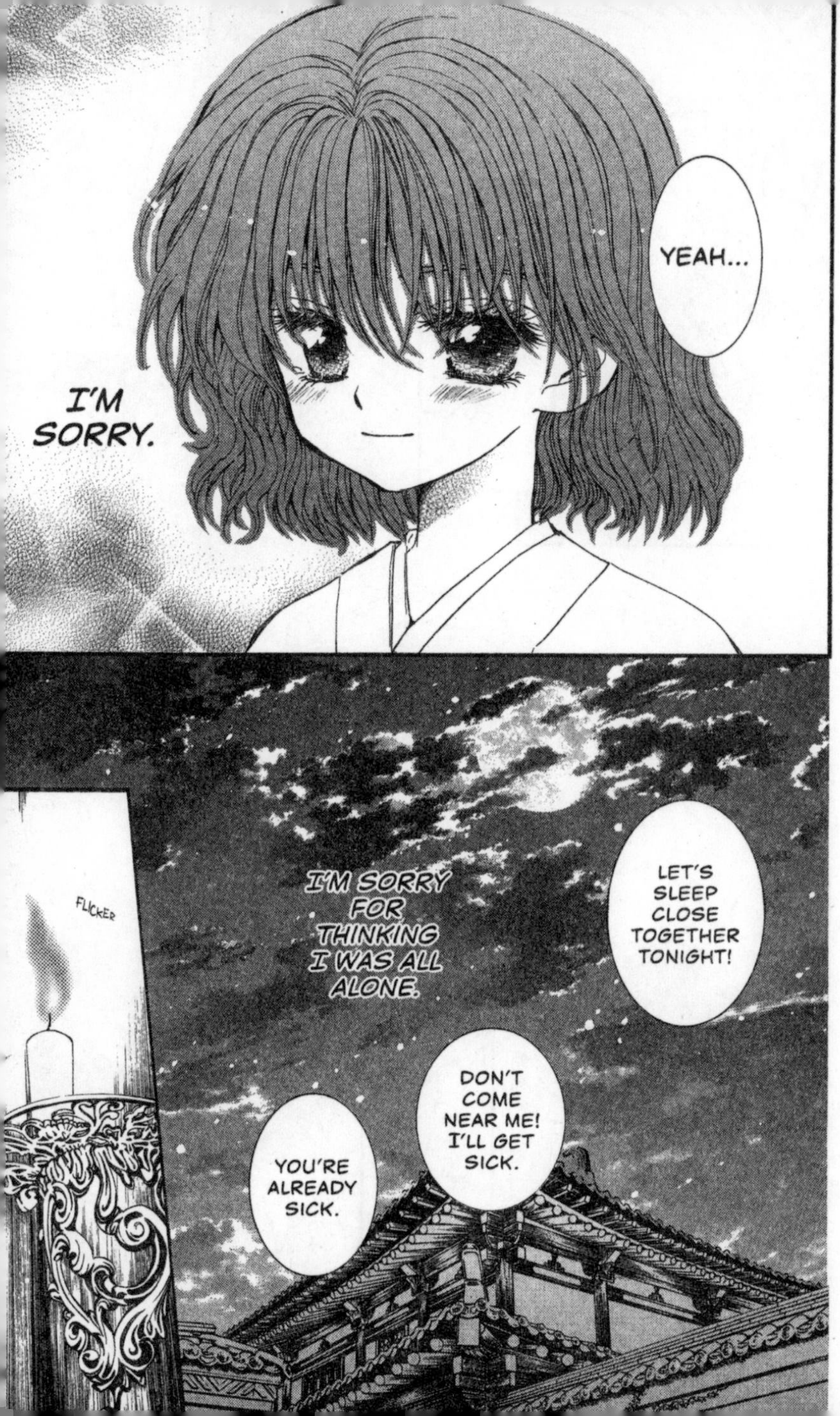
YEAH...
I'M SORRY.
LET'S SLEEP CLOSE TOGETHER TONIGHT!
I'M SORRY FOR THINKING I WAS ALL ALONE.
DON'T COME NEAR ME! I'LL GET SICK.
YOU'RE ALREADY SICK.
FLICKER

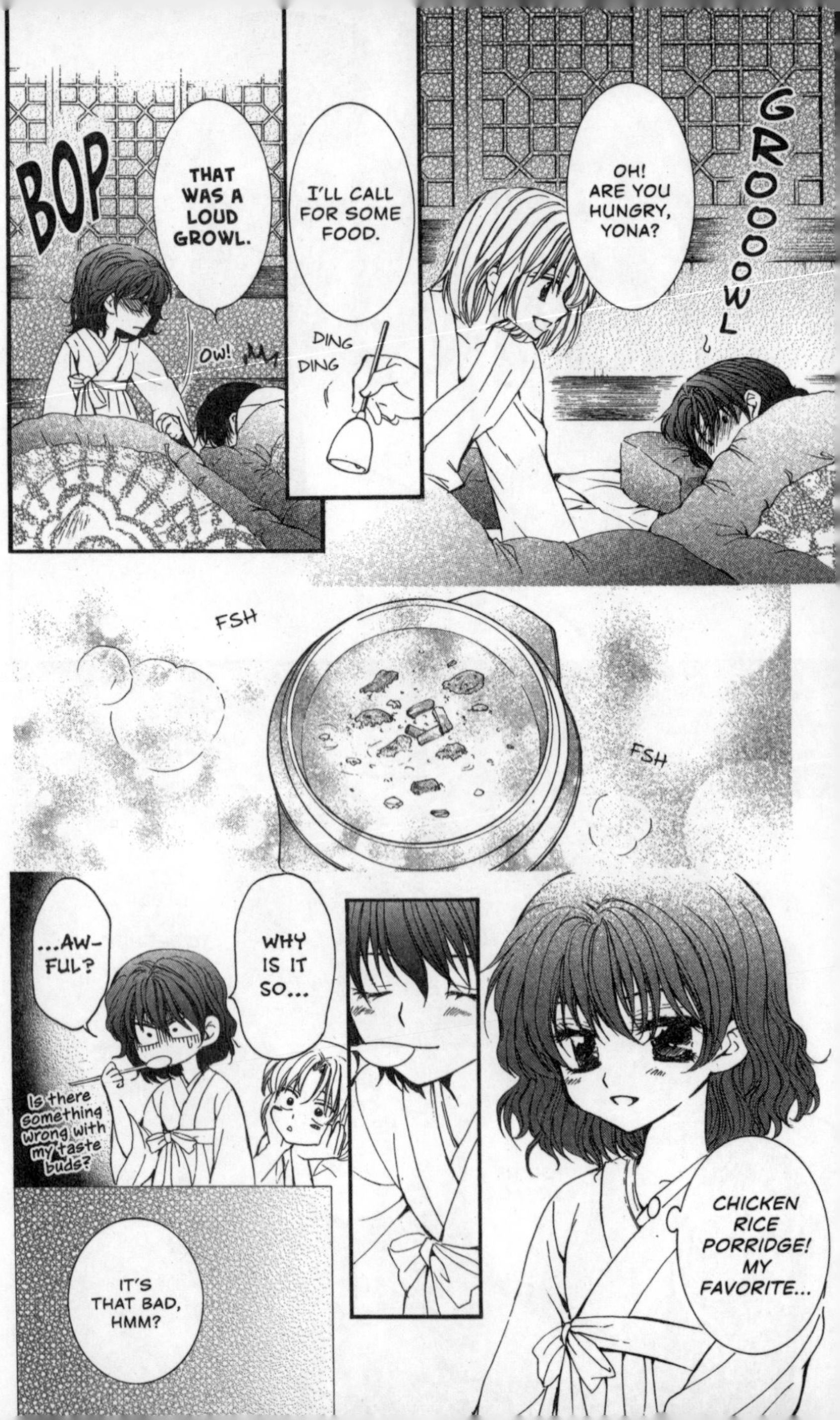
GROOOOWL
OH! ARE YOU HUNGRY, YONA?
I'LL CALL FOR SOME FOOD.
DING DING
BOP
THAT WAS A LOUD GROWL.
OW!
FSH
FSH
CHICKEN RICE PORRIDGE! MY FAVORITE...
WHY IS IT SO...
...AW-FUL?
Is there something wrong with my taste buds?
IT'S THAT BAD, HMM?

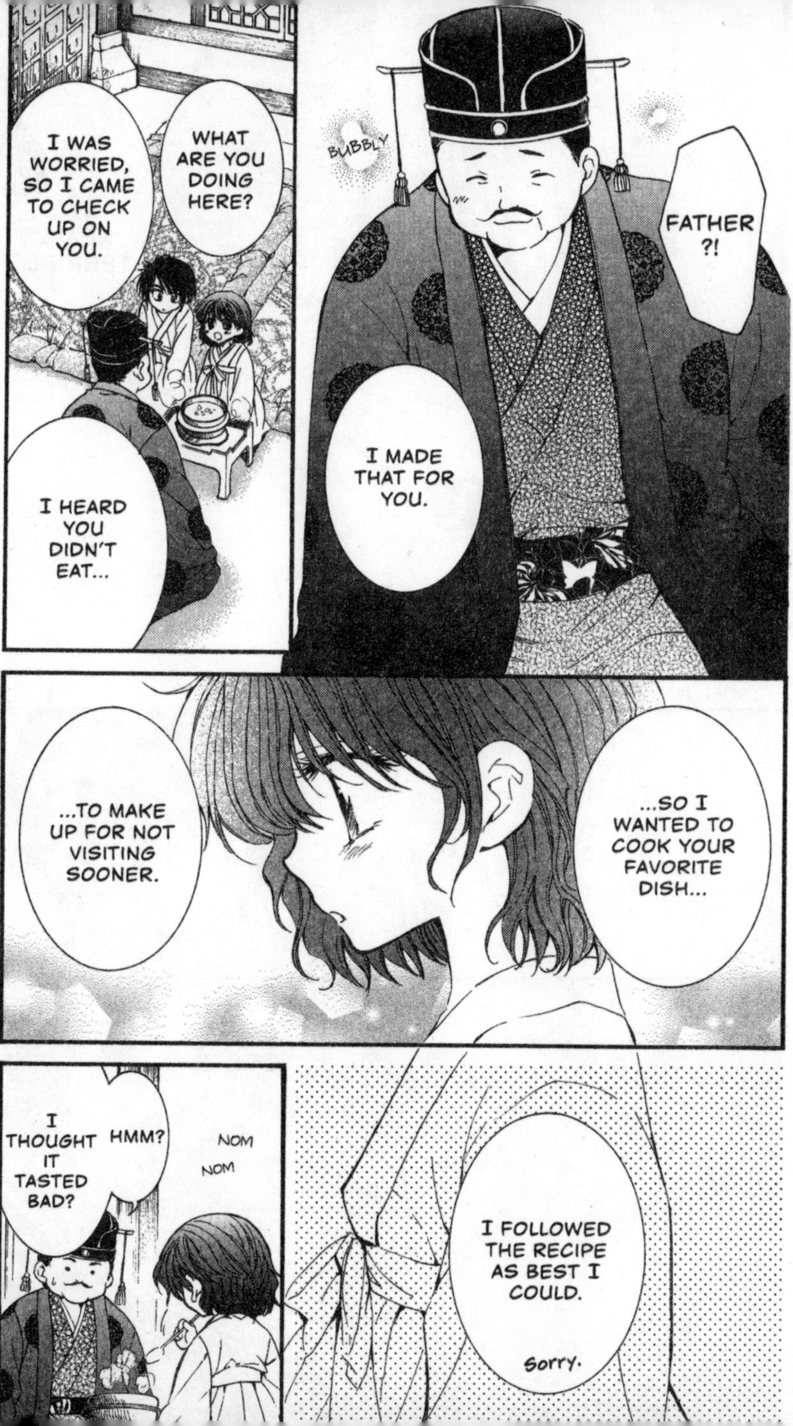
FATHER?!
BUBBLY
I MADE THAT FOR YOU.
WHAT ARE YOU DOING HERE?
I WAS WORRIED, SO I CAME TO CHECK UP ON YOU.
I HEARD YOU DIDN'T EAT...
...SO I WANTED TO COOK YOUR FAVORITE DISH...
...TO MAKE UP FOR NOT VISITING SOONER.
I FOLLOWED THE RECIPE AS BEST I COULD.
Sorry.
NOM
NOM
HMM?
I THOUGHT IT TASTED BAD?

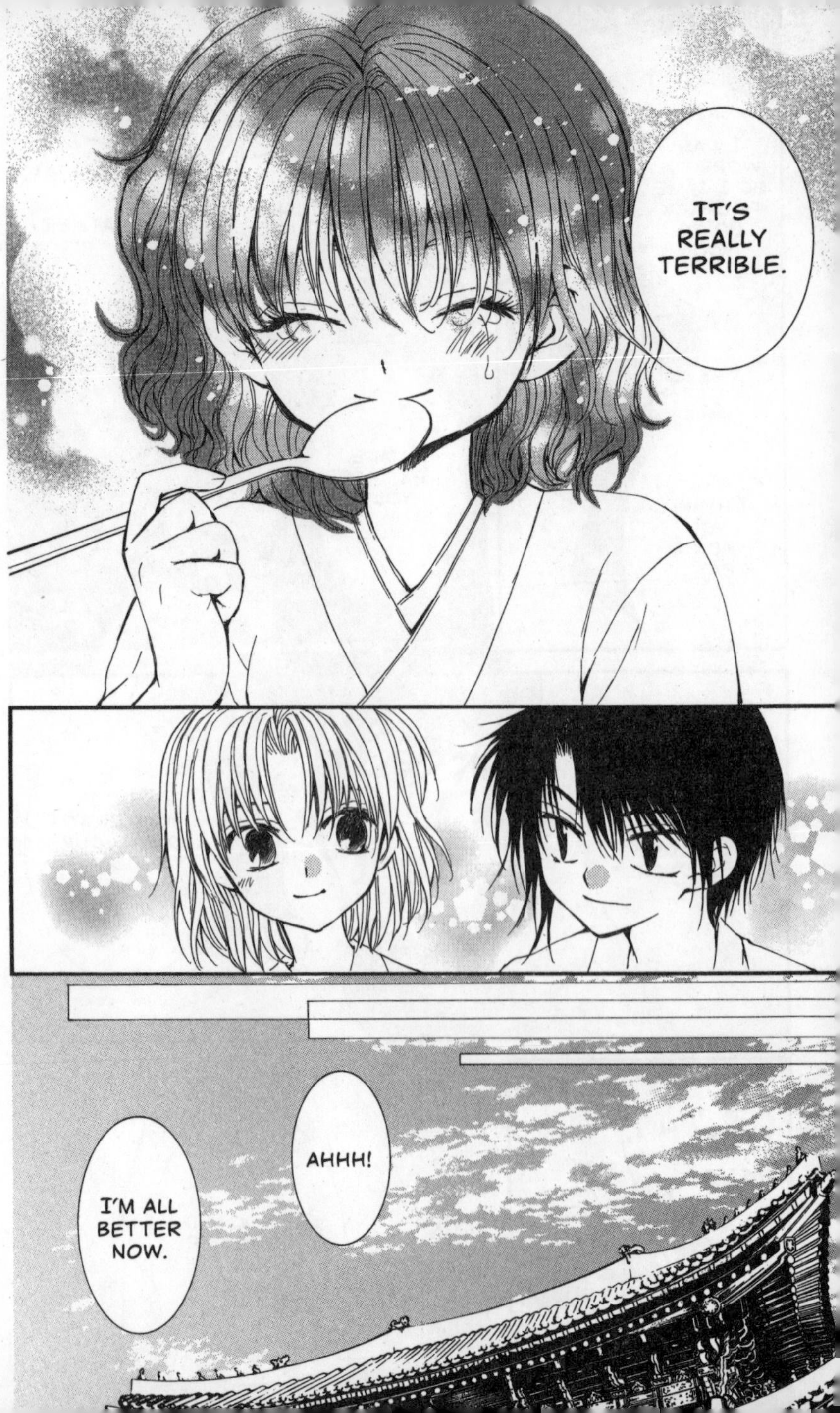
IT'S REALLY TERRIBLE.
AHHH!
I'M ALL BETTER NOW.

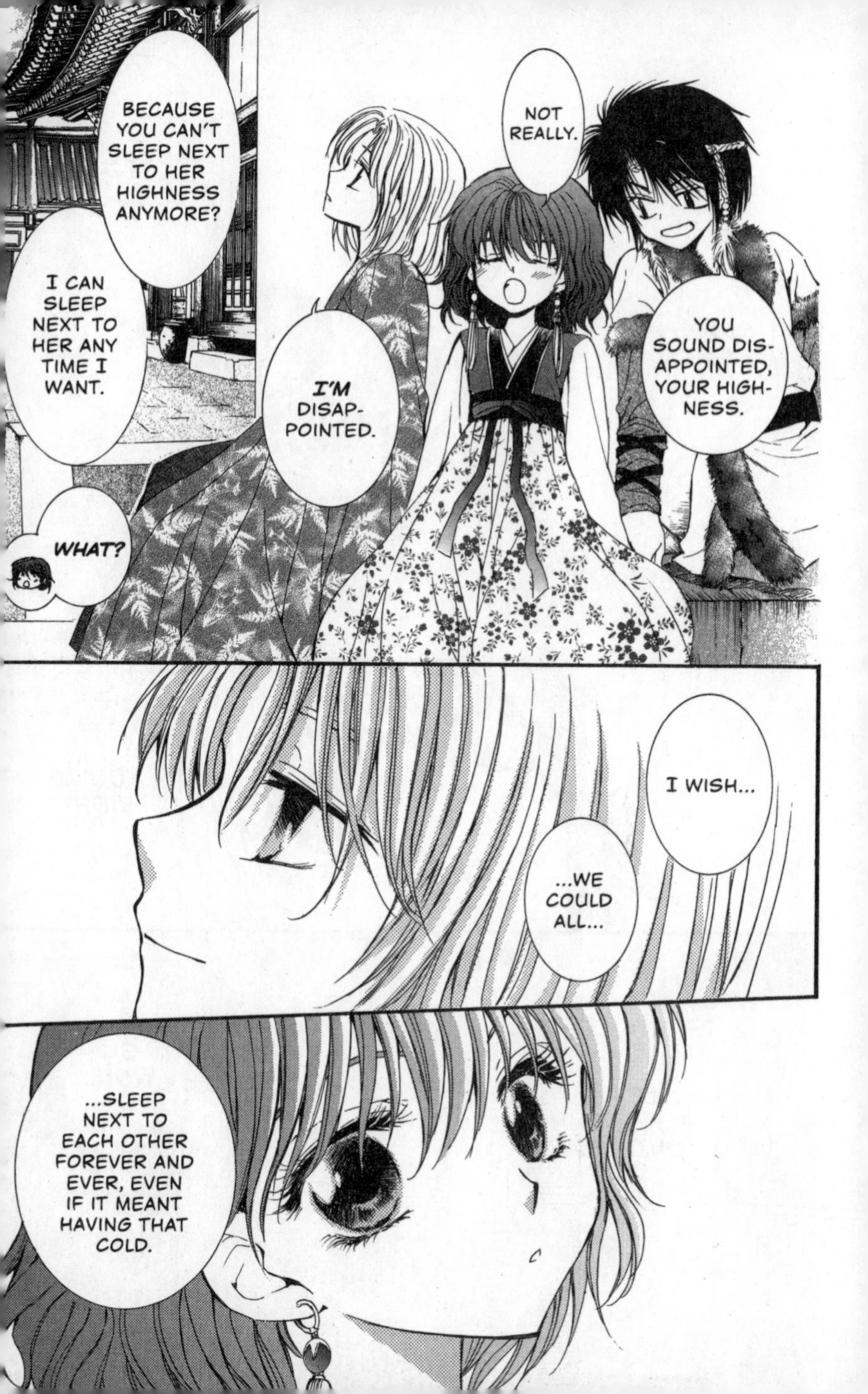
YOU SOUND DIS-APPOINTED, YOUR HIGH-NESS.
NOT REALLY.
BECAUSE YOU CAN'T SLEEP NEXT TO HER HIGHNESS ANYMORE?
I CAN SLEEP NEXT TO HER ANY TIME I WANT.
I'M DISAP-POINTED.
WHAT?
I WISH...
...WE COULD ALL...
...SLEEP NEXT TO EACH OTHER FOREVER AND EVER, EVEN IF IT MEANT HAVING THAT COLD.

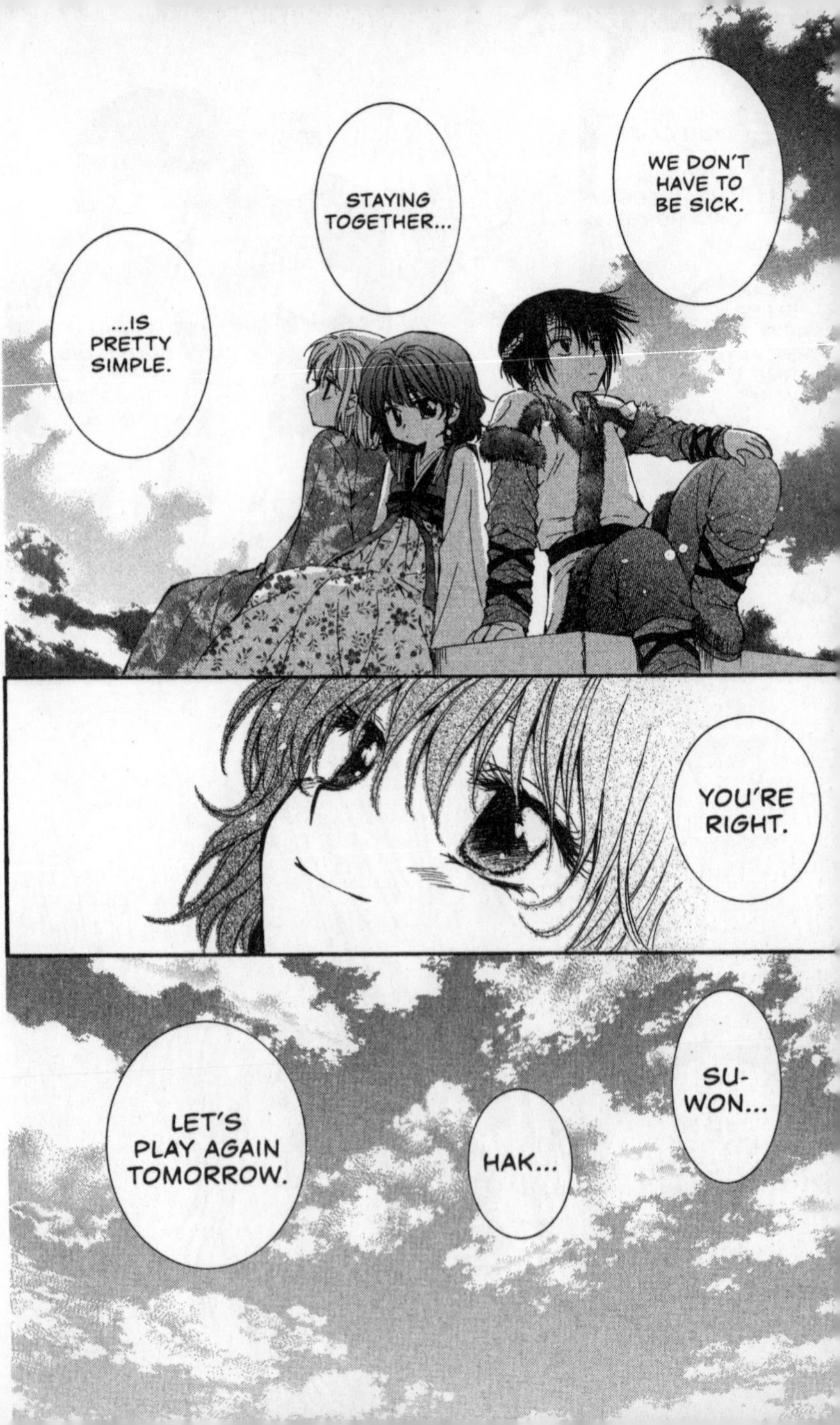
WE DON'T HAVE TO BE SICK.
STAYING TOGETHER...
...IS PRETTY SIMPLE.
YOU'RE RIGHT.
SU-WON...
HAK...
LET'S PLAY AGAIN TOMORROW.

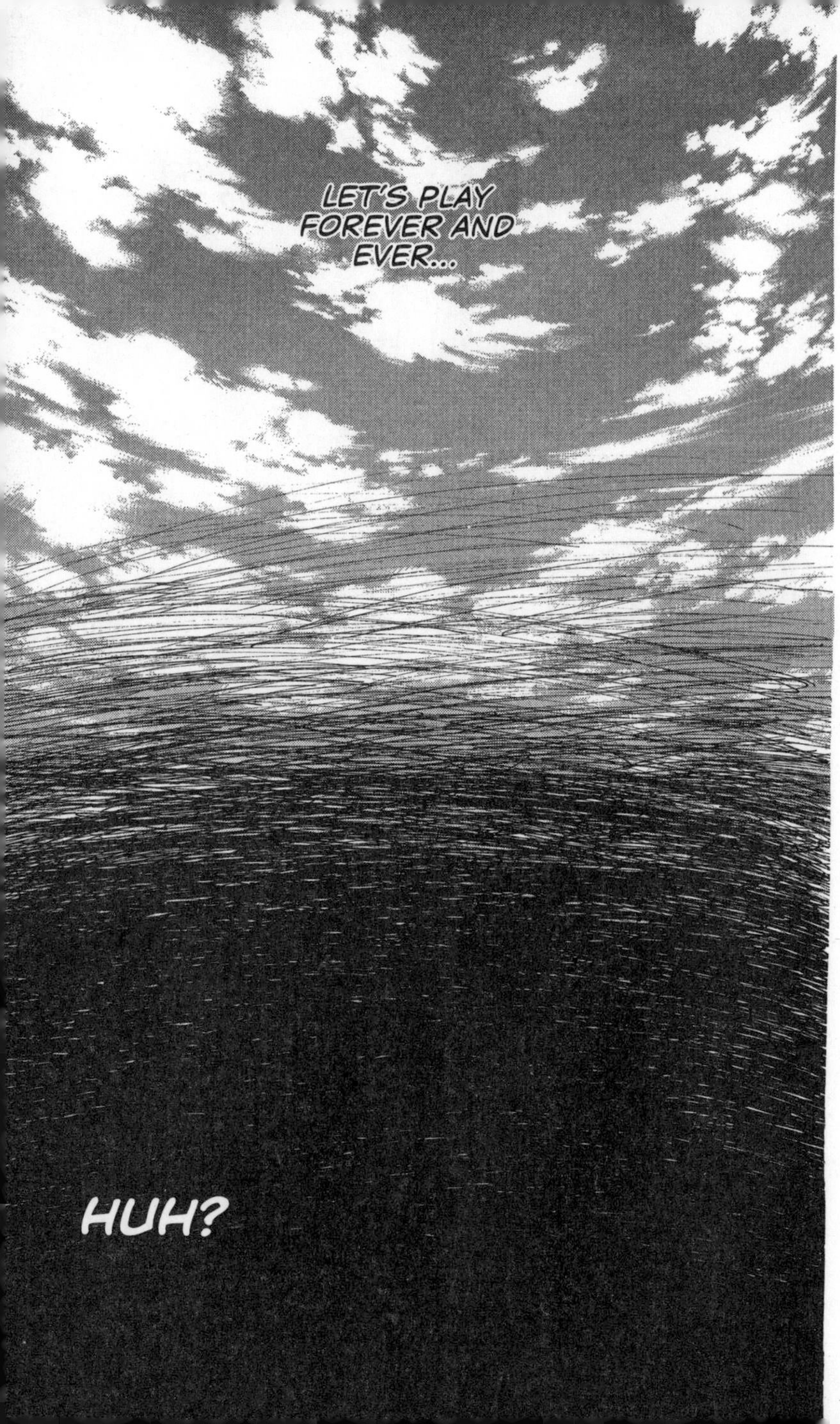
LET'S PLAY FOREVER AND EVER...
HUH?

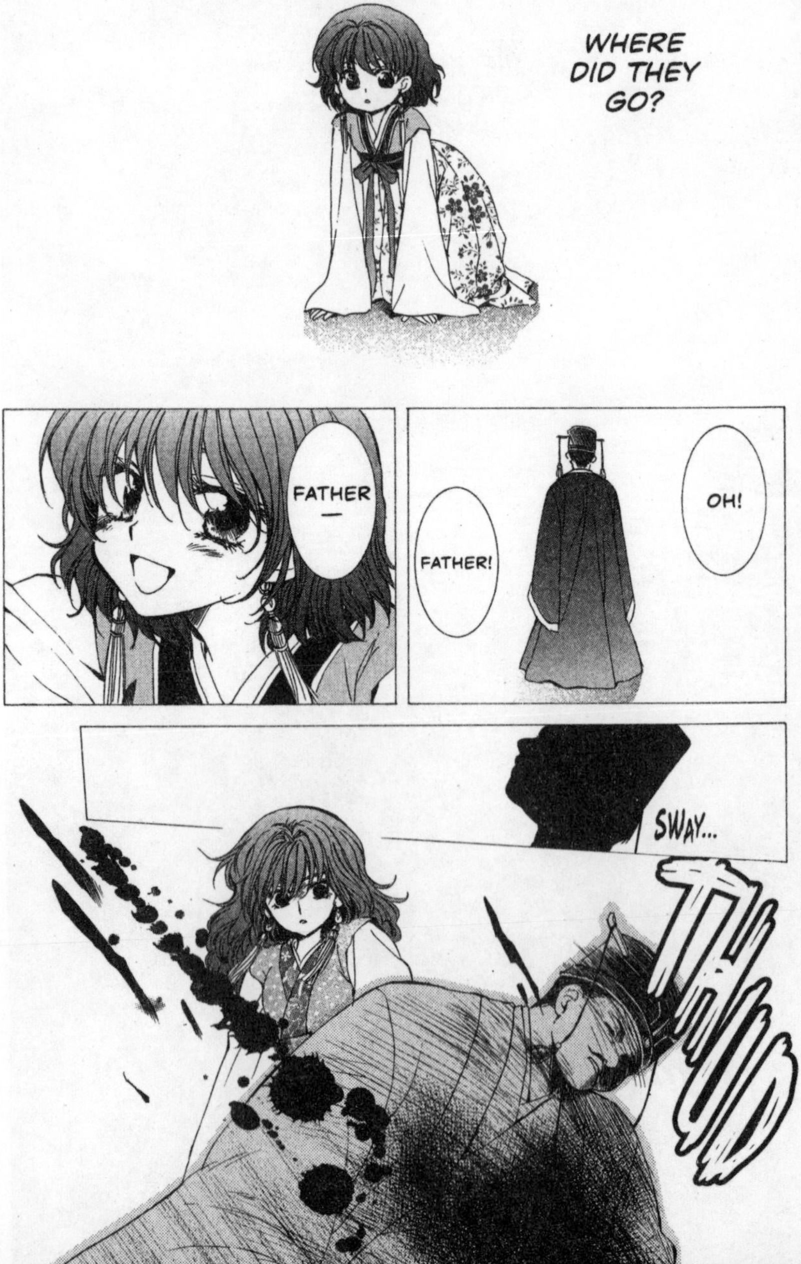
WHERE DID THEY GO?
OH!
FATHER!
FATHER —
SWAY...
THUD

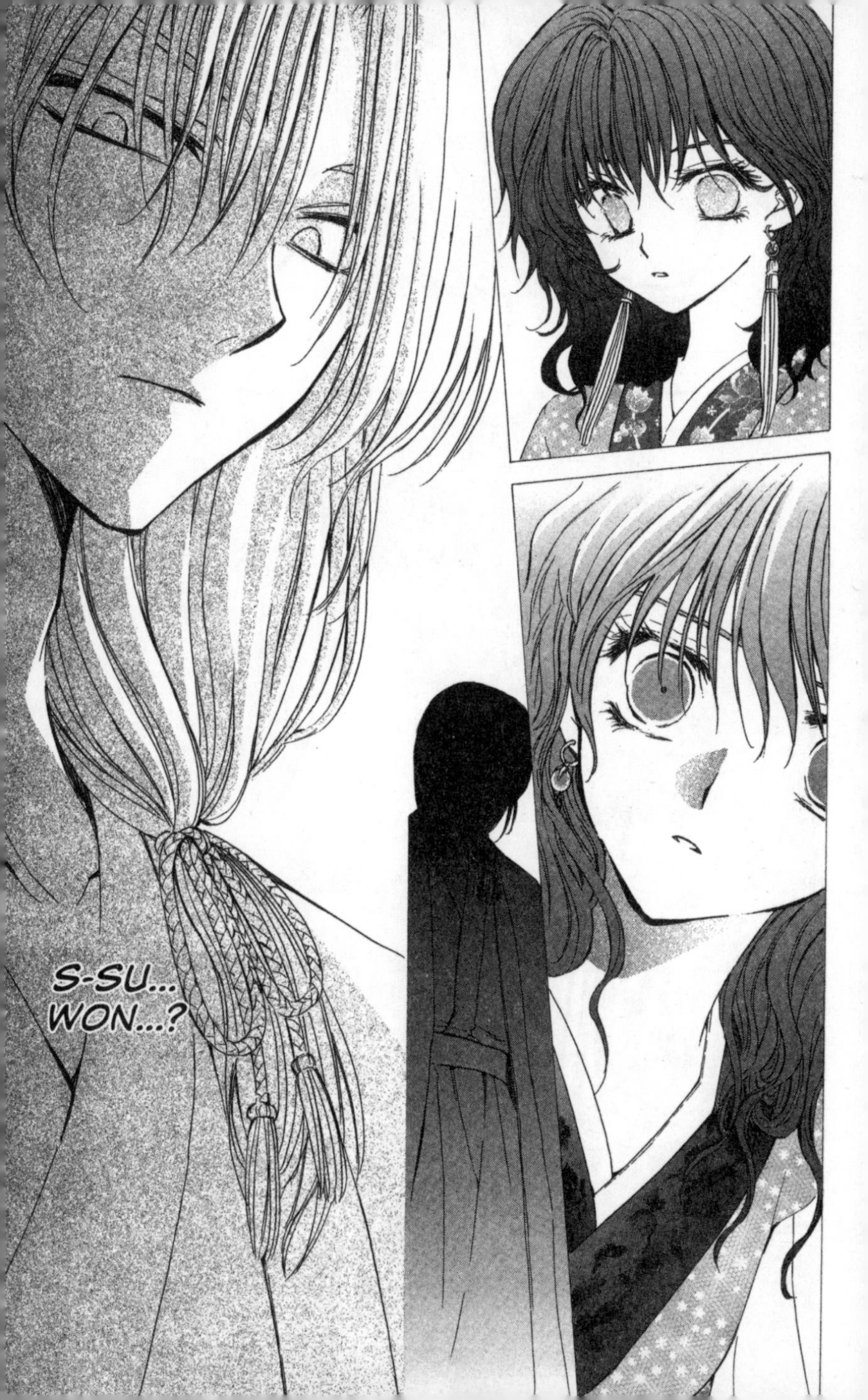
S-SU...
WON...?

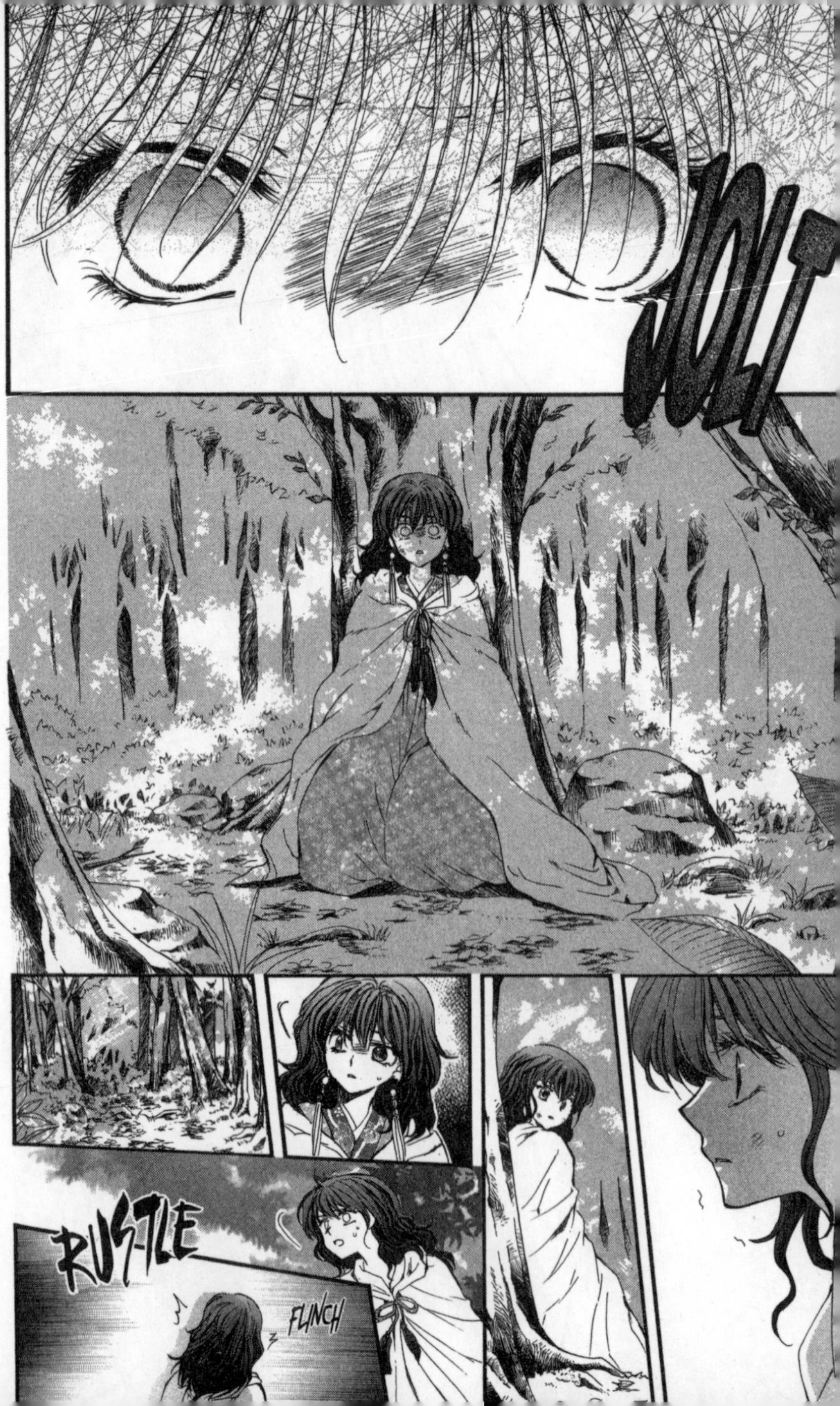
JOLT
RUSTLE
FLINCH

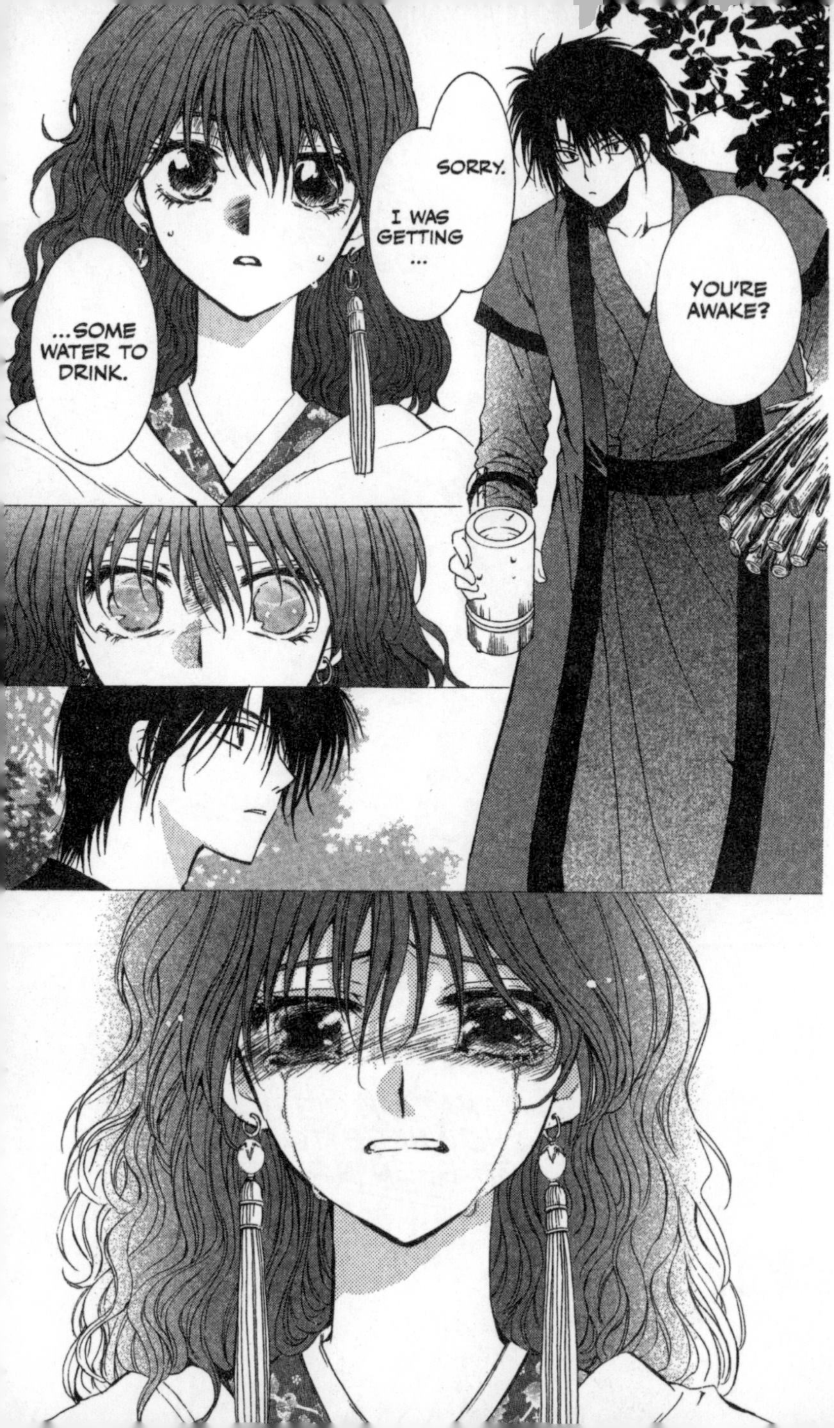
YOU'RE AWAKE?
SORRY.
I WAS GETTING ...
...SOME WATER TO DRINK.

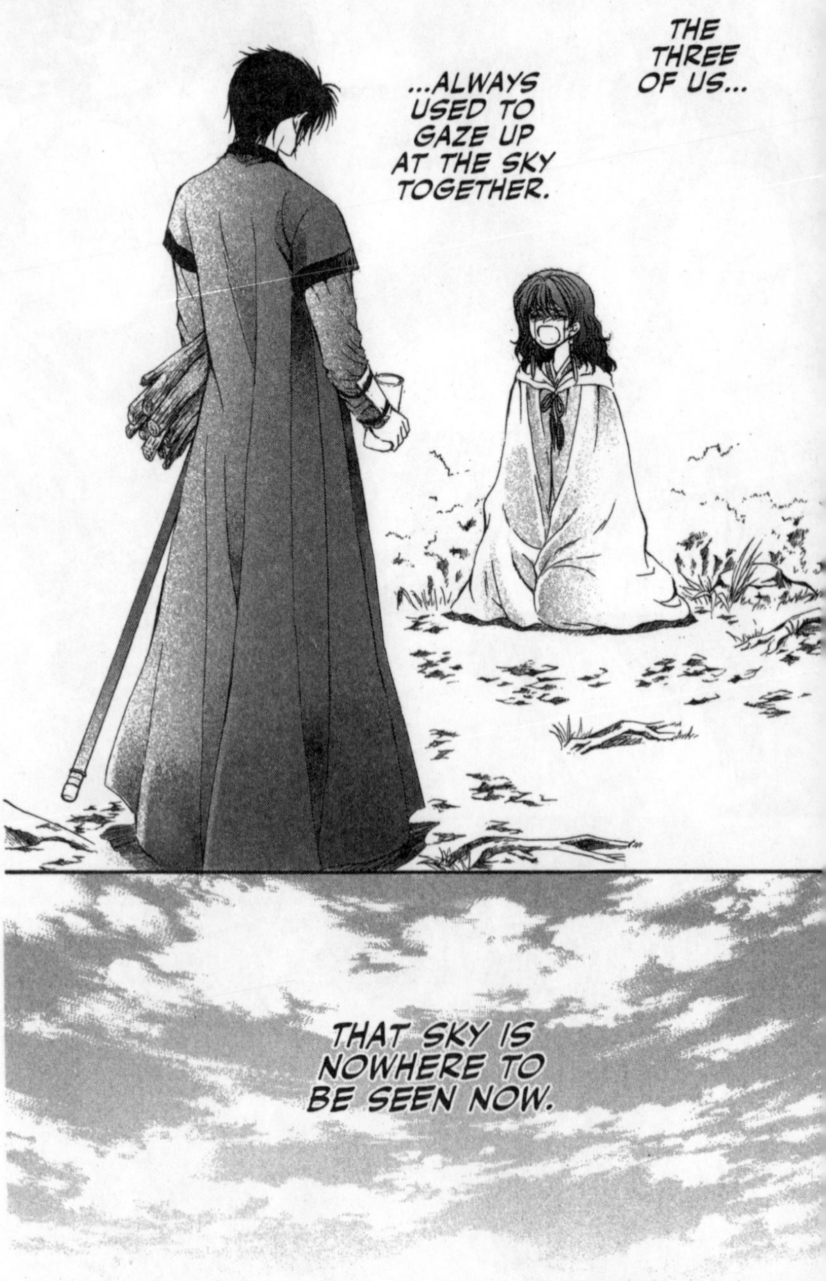
THE THREE OF US...
...ALWAYS USED TO GAZE UP AT THE SKY TOGETHER.
THAT SKY IS NOWHERE TO BE SEEN NOW.

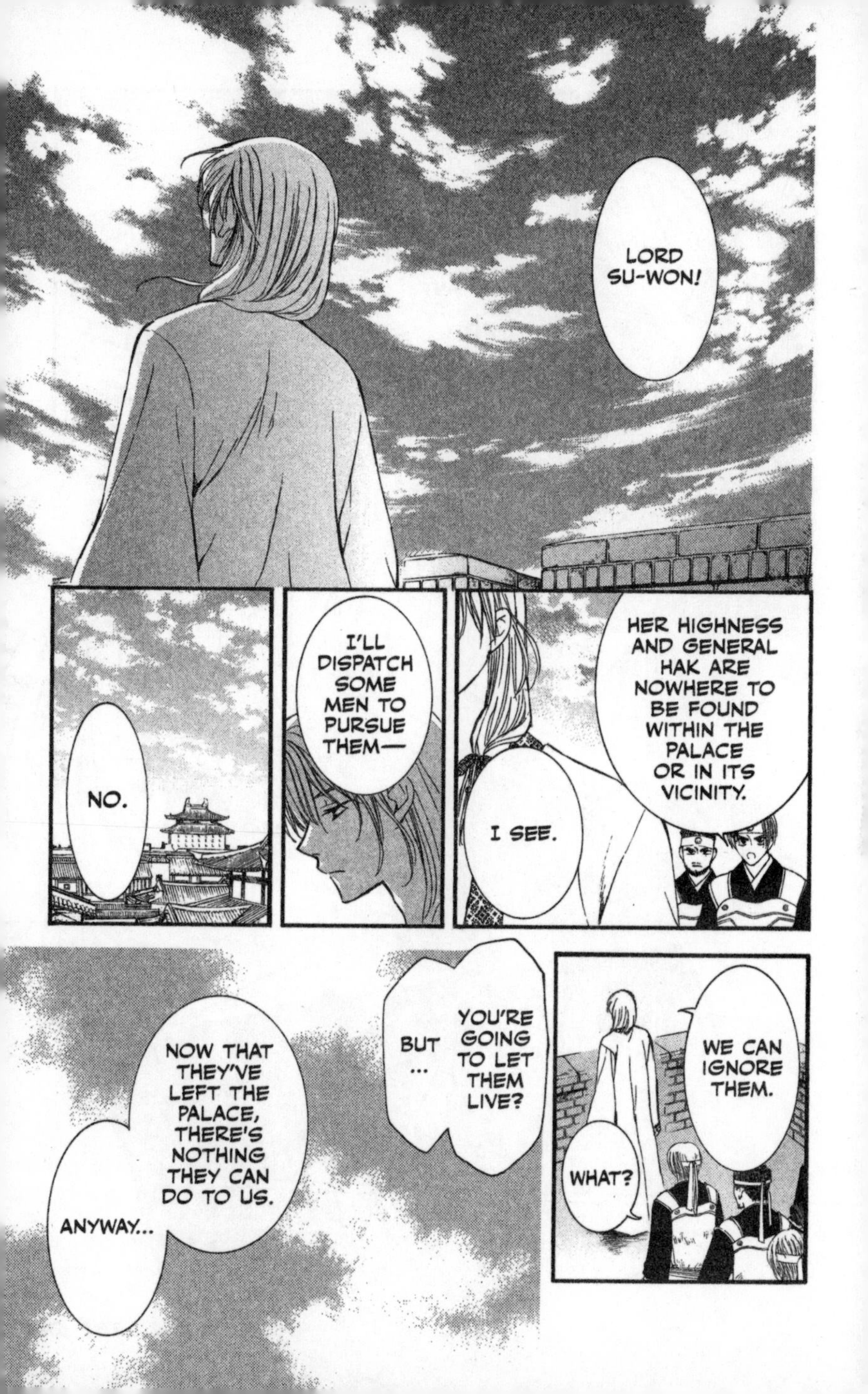
LORD SU-WON!
HER HIGHNESS AND GENERAL HAK ARE NOWHERE TO BE FOUND WITHIN THE PALACE OR IN ITS VICINITY.
I SEE.
I'LL DISPATCH SOME MEN TO PURSUE THEM—
NO.
WE CAN IGNORE THEM.
WHAT?
YOU'RE GOING TO LET THEM LIVE?
BUT ...
NOW THAT THEY'VE LEFT THE PALACE, THERE'S NOTHING THEY CAN DO TO US.
ANYWAY...

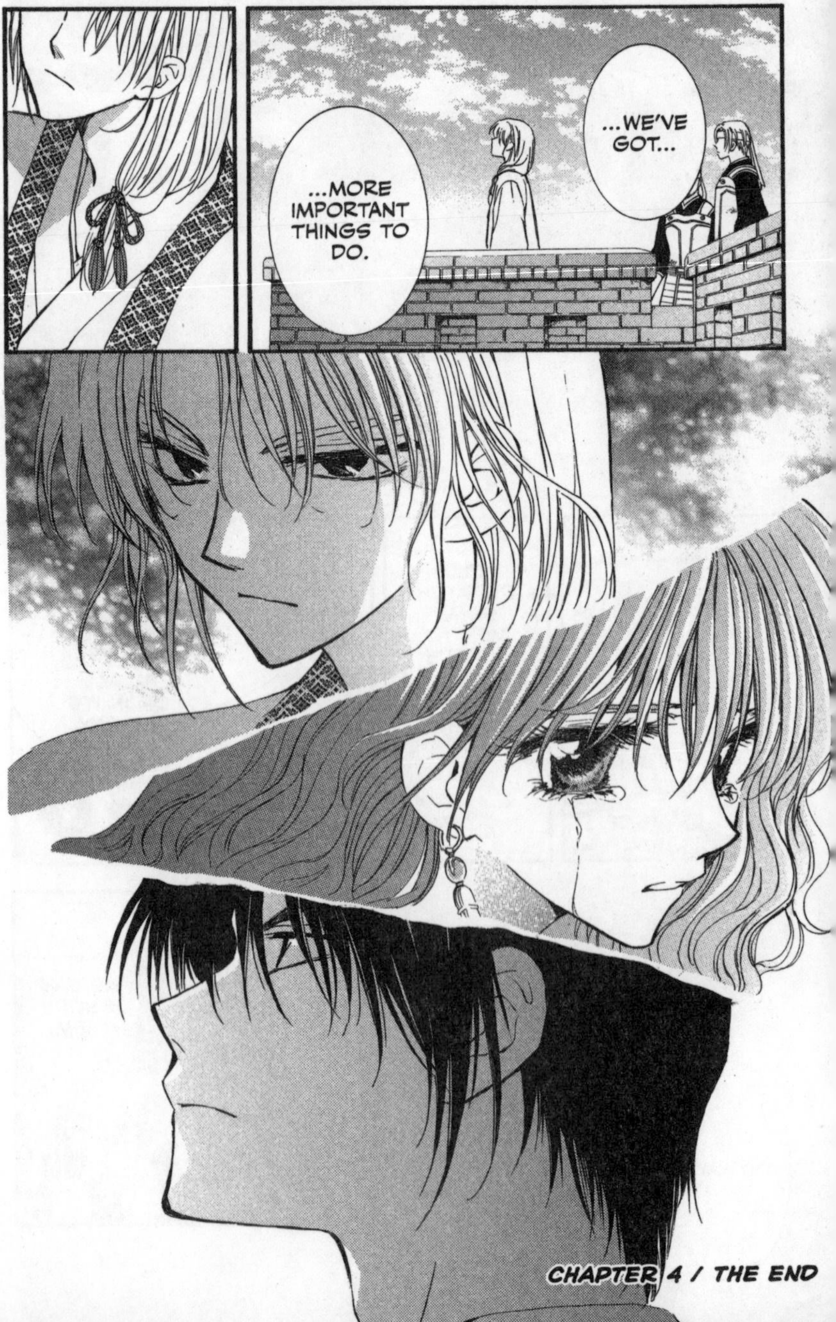
...WE'VE GOT...
...MORE IMPORTANT THINGS TO DO.
CHAPTER 4 / THE END

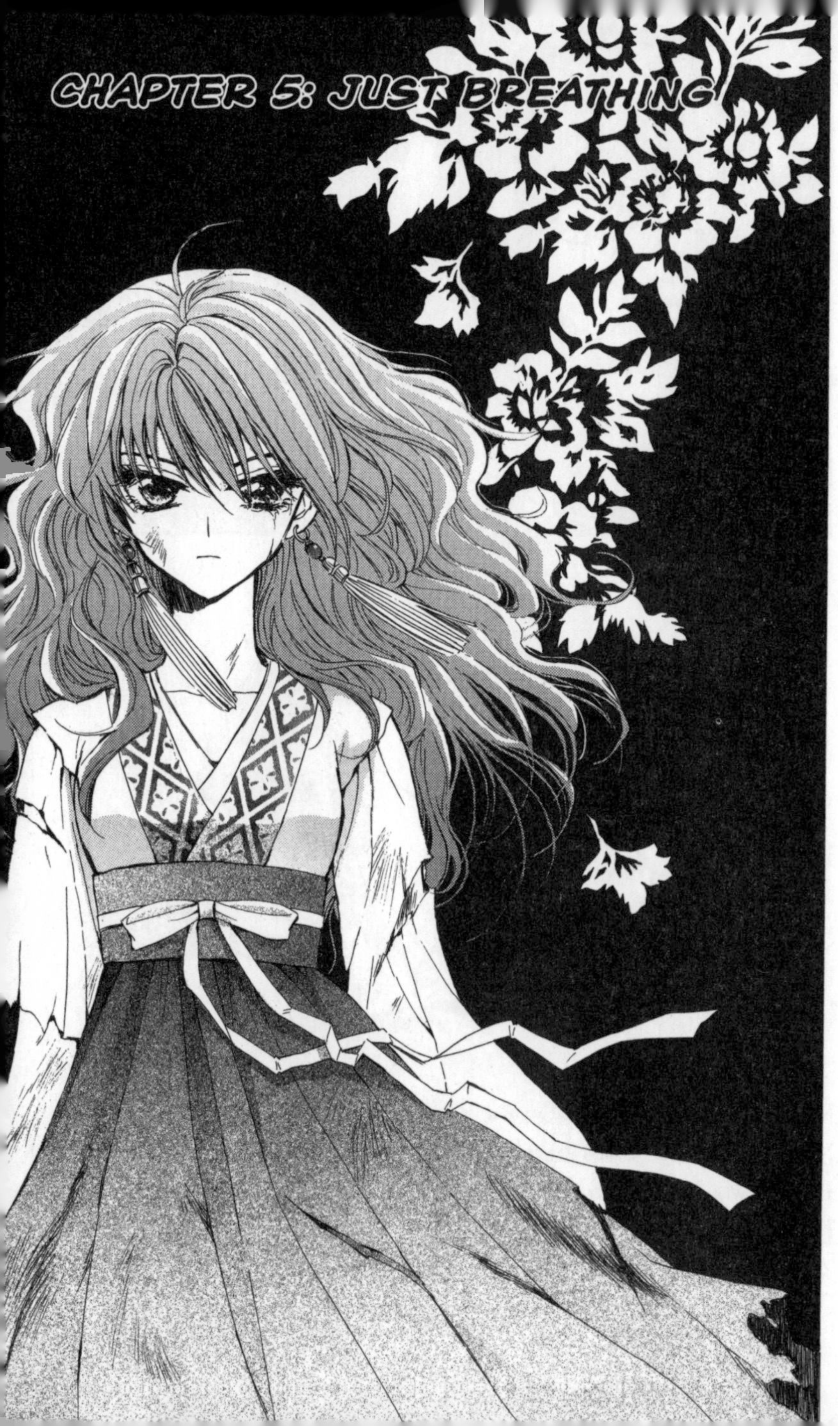
CHAPTER 5: JUST BREATHING

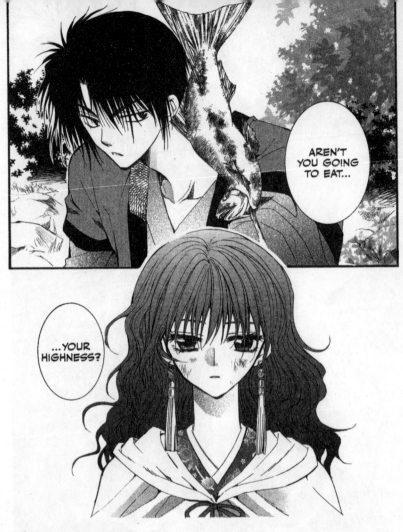

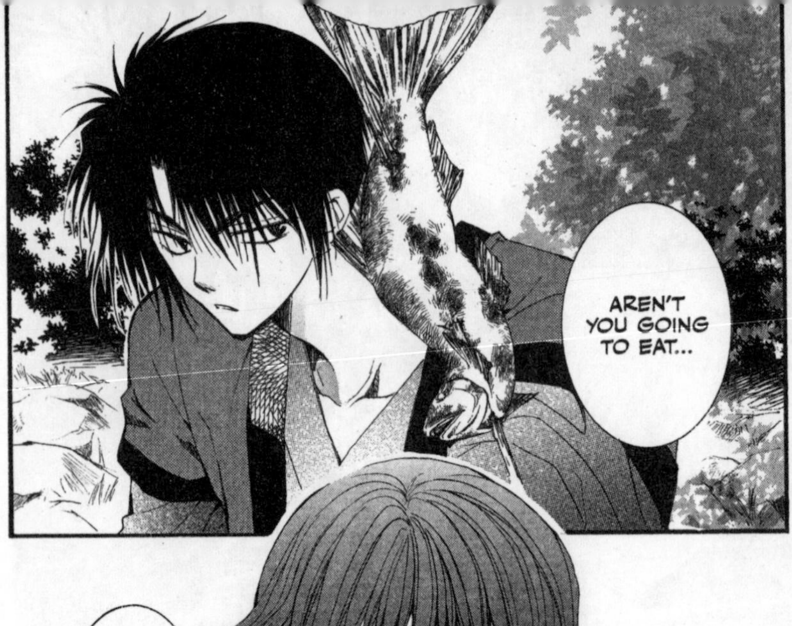
AREN'T YOU GOING TO EAT...
...YOUR HIGHNESS?

Special thanks go out to...

My assistants: Mikorun, Ryo Sakura, Rurunga, Kyoko and my little sister...

My editor Yamashita, and the *Hana to Yume* editorial office...

Everyone who helped me create and sell this manga...

Family and friends who supported me...

And my readers! Thank you so very much.

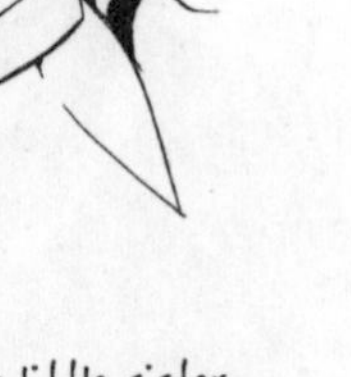

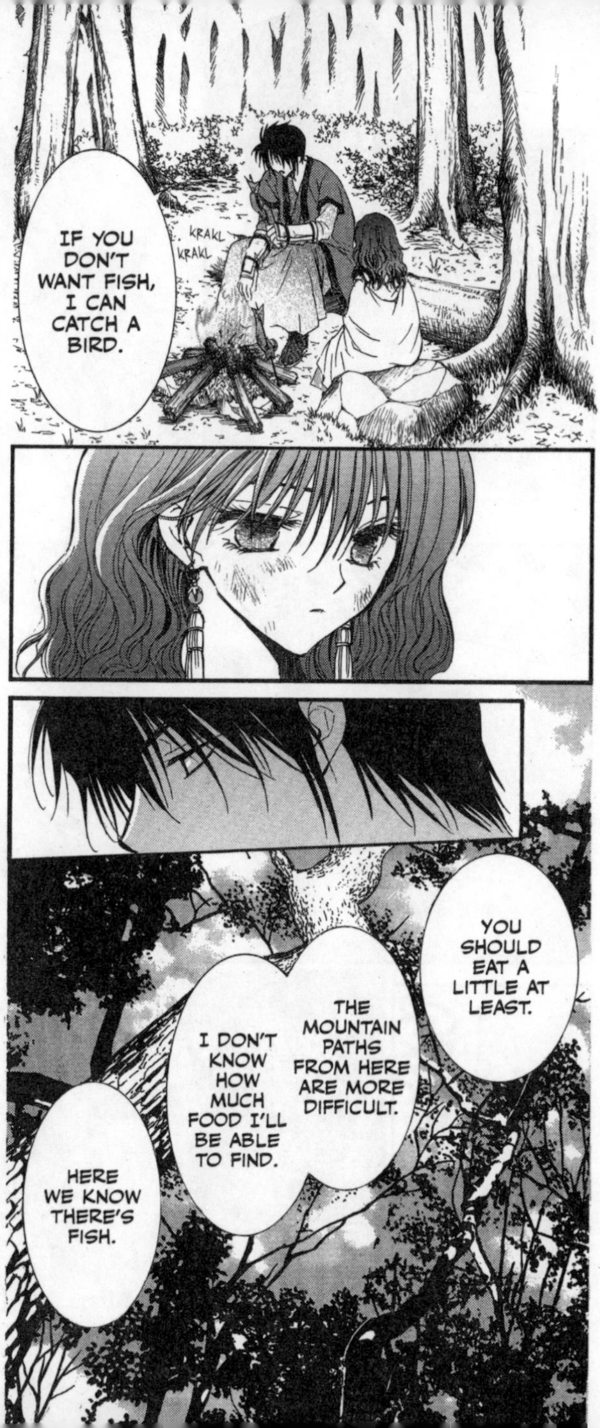
IF YOU DON'T WANT FISH, I CAN CATCH A BIRD.
KRAKL KRAKL
YOU SHOULD EAT A LITTLE AT LEAST.
THE MOUNTAIN PATHS FROM HERE ARE MORE DIFFICULT.
I DON'T KNOW HOW MUCH FOOD I'LL BE ABLE TO FIND.
HERE WE KNOW THERE'S FISH.

Just before *Yona* was serialized, I attended an autograph session. It was in a nearby prefecture, so it was a relaxing experience.♥

Kinokuniya Books was very welcoming. I'd like to thank everyone who came!

I'd also like to thank everyone who writes letters or answers magazine surveys. I can create manga because of all of you!

Yona of the Dawn has only just started, but I hope you'll keep checking it out!

Stay tuned for volume 2!

Send mail to this address: ↓

Mizuho Kusanagi
c/o Yona of the Dawn Editor
Viz Media
P.O. Box 77010
San Francisco, CA 94107

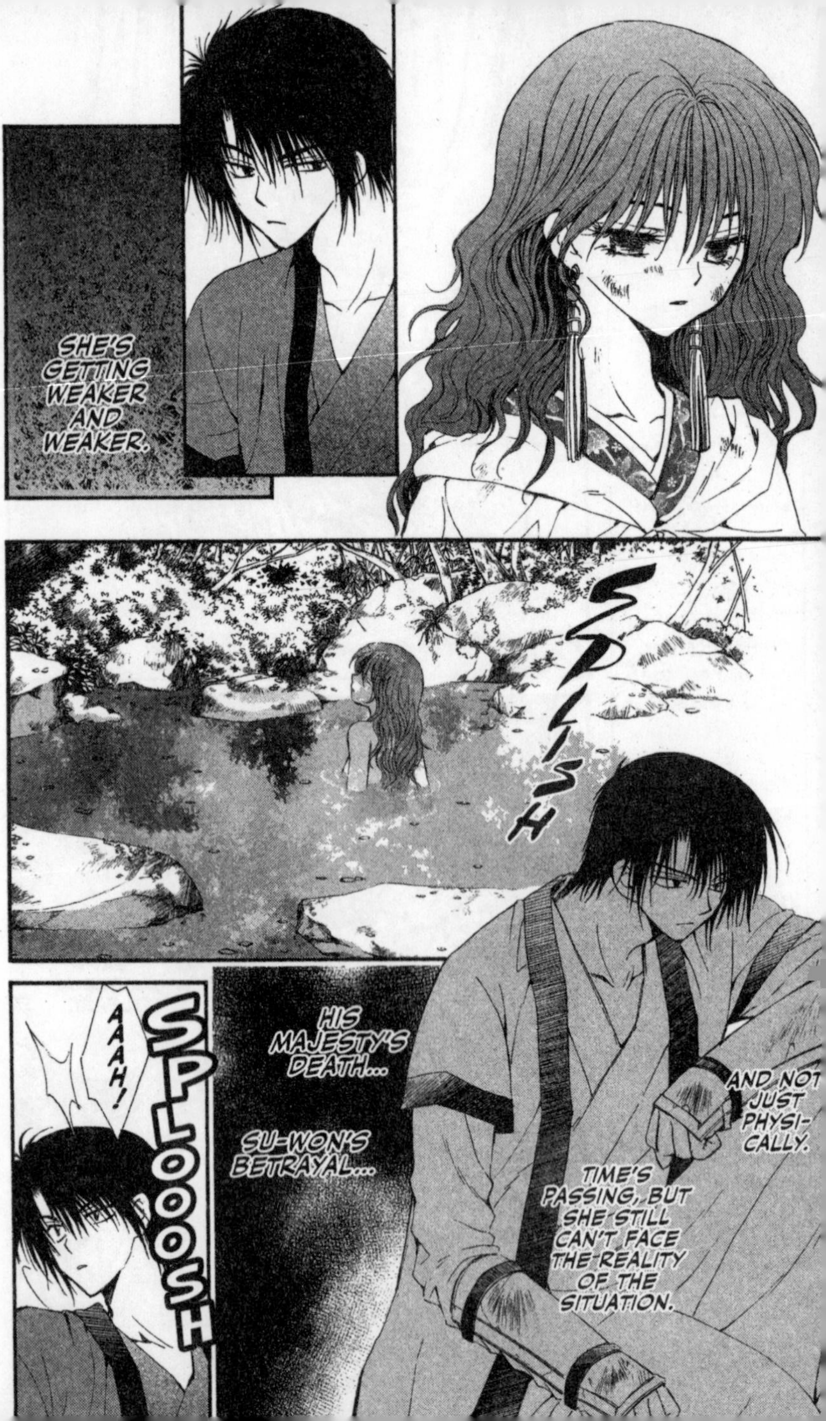
SHE'S GETTING WEAKER AND WEAKER.
SPLISH
AND NOT JUST PHYSI-CALLY.
TIME'S PASSING, BUT SHE STILL CAN'T FACE THE REALITY OF THE SITUATION.
HIS MAJESTY'S DEATH...
SU-WON'S BETRAYAL...
SPLOOOOSH
AAAH!

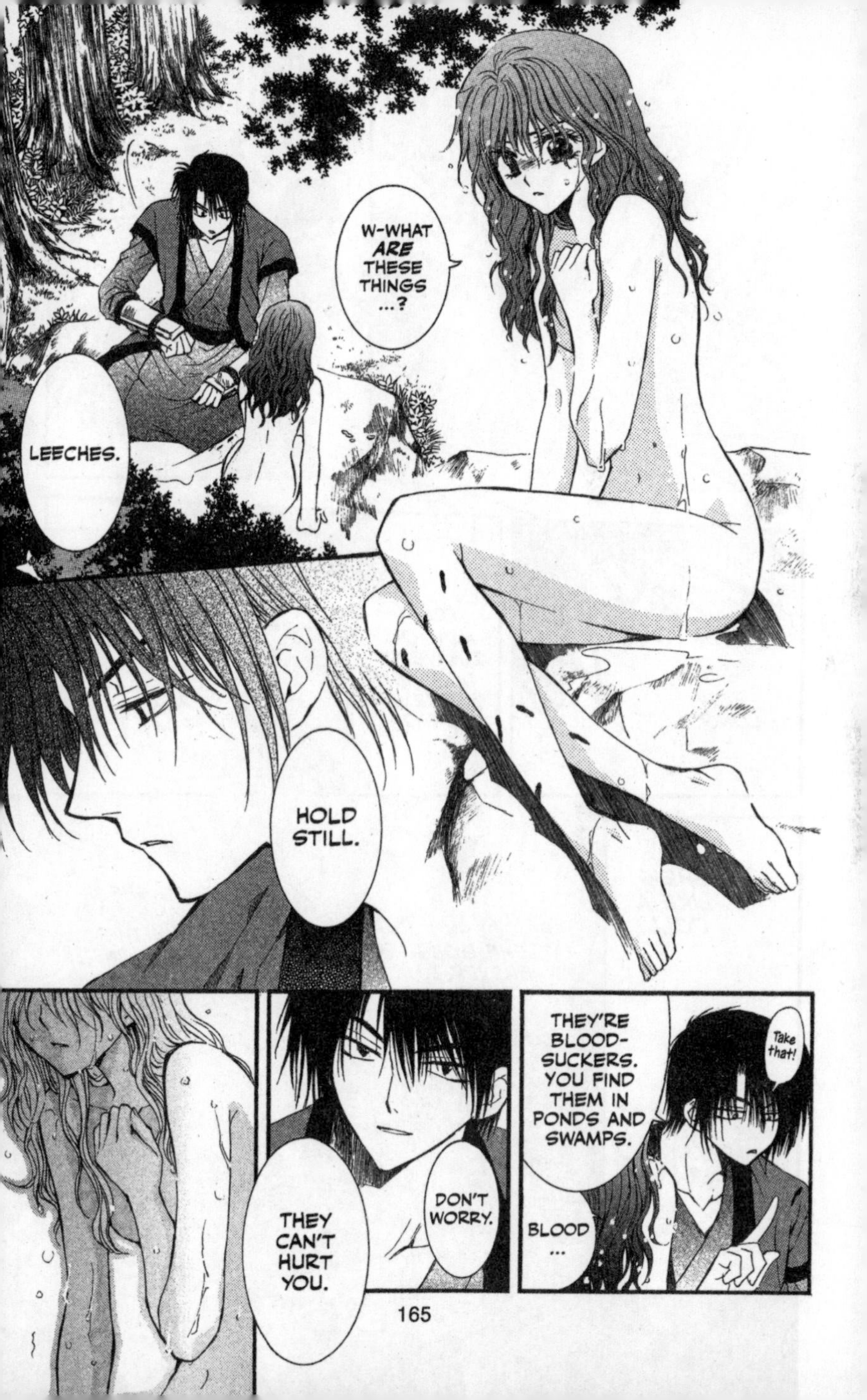
W-WHAT *ARE* THESE THINGS ...?
LEECHES.
HOLD STILL.
Take that!
THEY'RE BLOOD-SUCKERS. YOU FIND THEM IN PONDS AND SWAMPS.
BLOOD ...
DON'T WORRY.
THEY CAN'T HURT YOU.

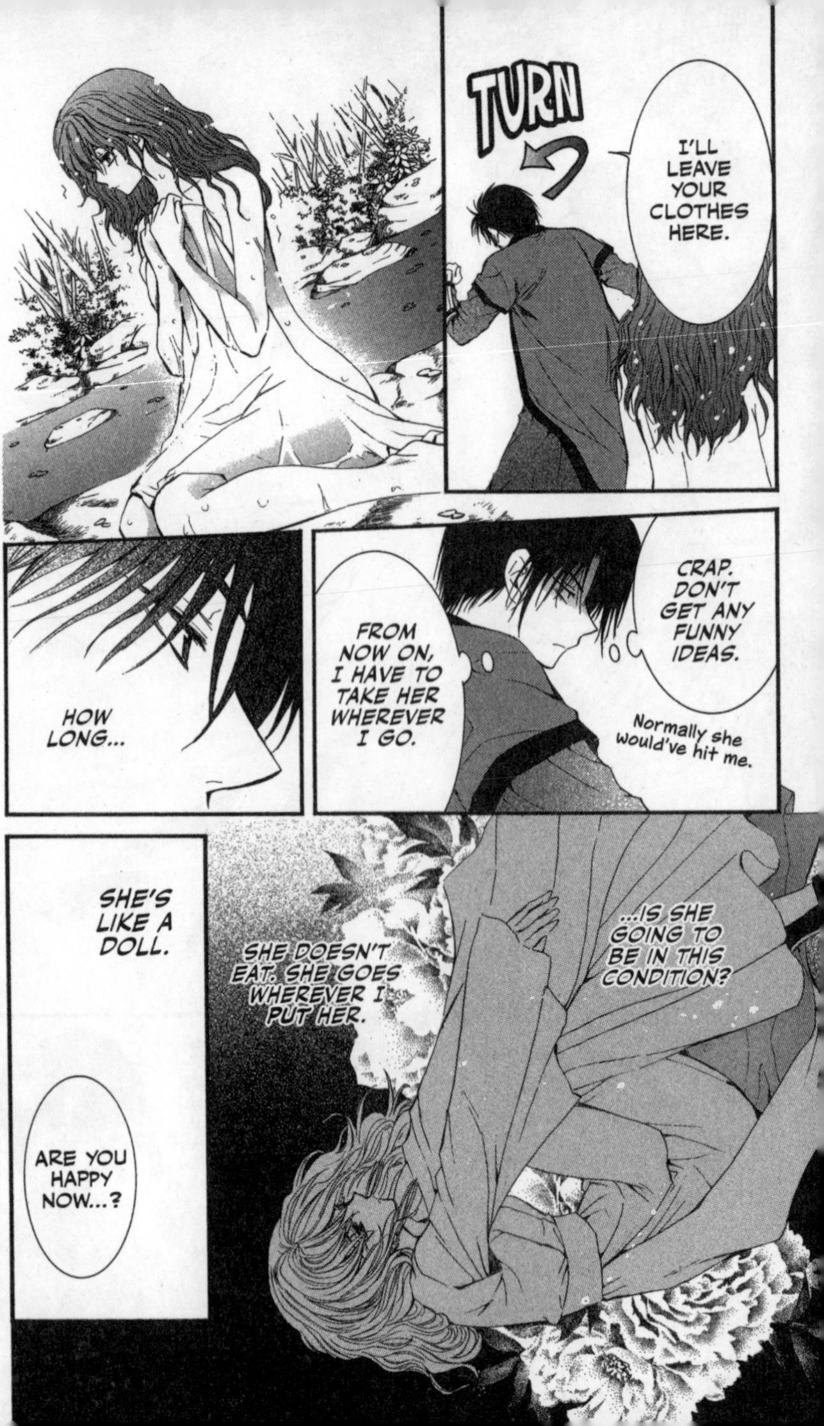
TURN
I'LL LEAVE YOUR CLOTHES HERE.
CRAP. DON'T GET ANY FUNNY IDEAS.
Normally she would've hit me.
FROM NOW ON, I HAVE TO TAKE HER WHEREVER I GO.
HOW LONG...
...IS SHE GOING TO BE IN THIS CONDITION?
SHE DOESN'T EAT. SHE GOES WHEREVER I PUT HER.
SHE'S LIKE A DOLL.
ARE YOU HAPPY NOW...?

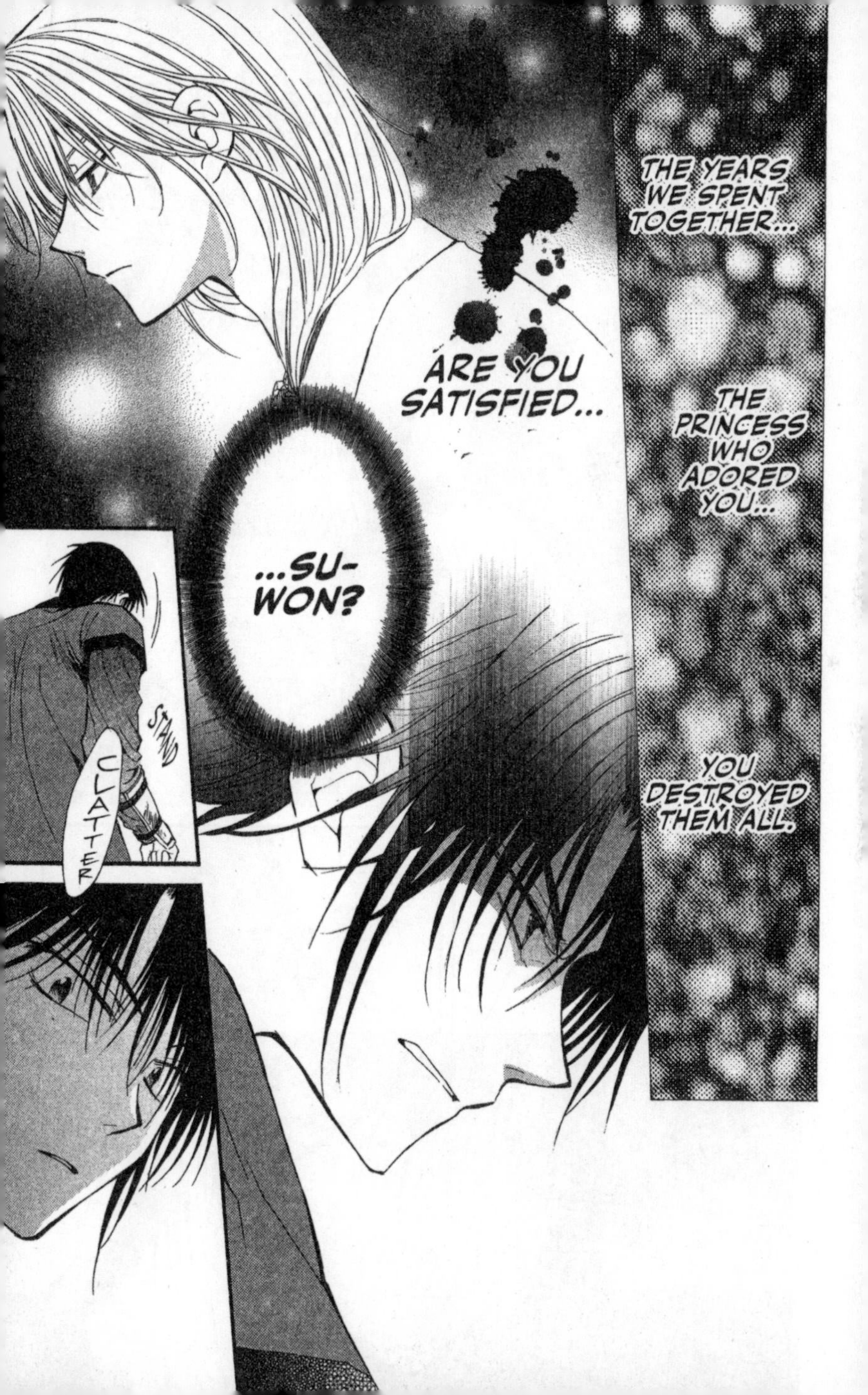
THE YEARS WE SPENT TOGETHER...
THE PRINCESS WHO ADORED YOU...
YOU DESTROYED THEM ALL.
ARE YOU SATISFIED...
...SU-WON?
STAND
CLATTER

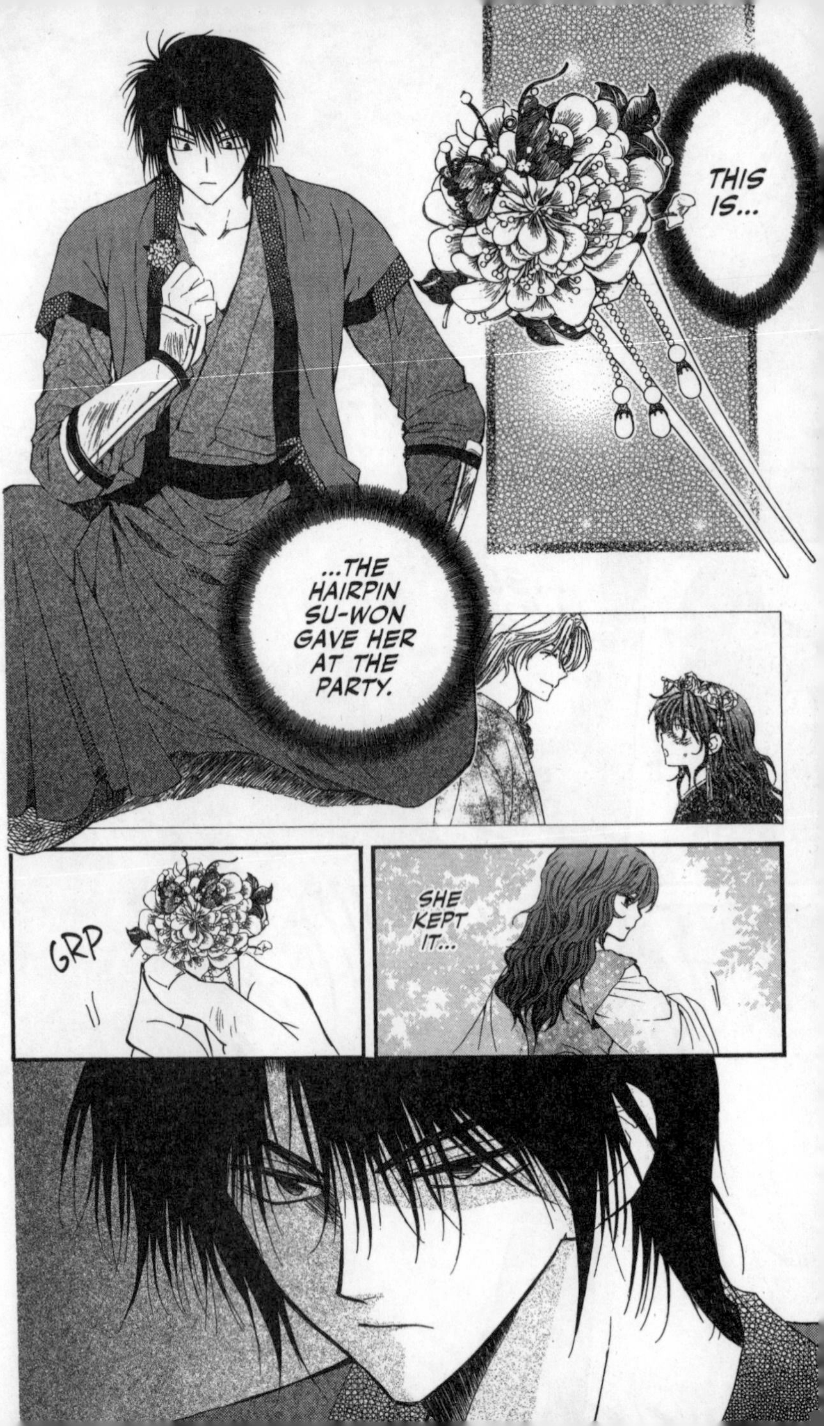
THIS IS...
...THE HAIRPIN SU-WON GAVE HER AT THE PARTY.
SHE KEPT IT...
GRP

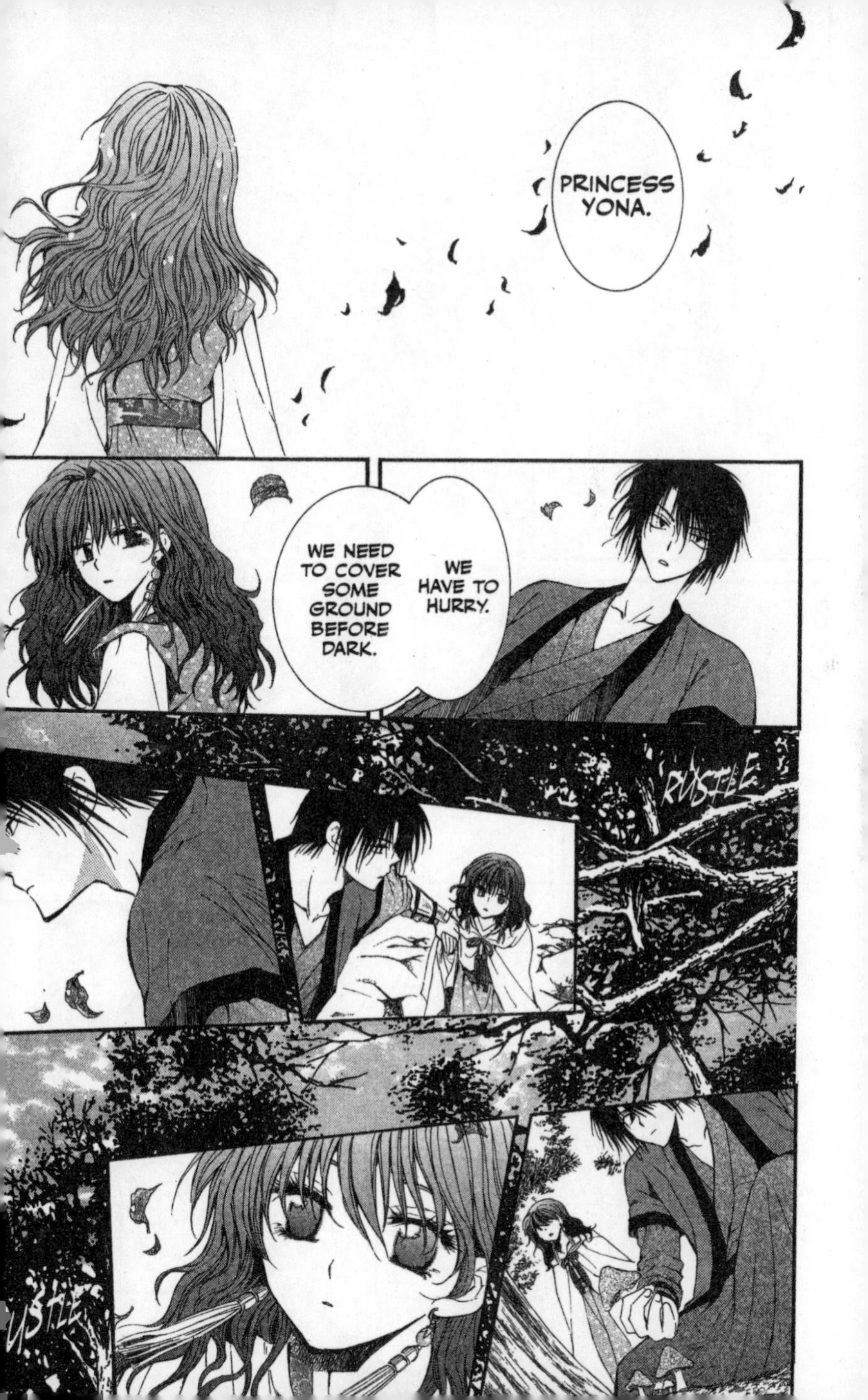
PRINCESS YONA.
WE HAVE TO HURRY.
WE NEED TO COVER SOME GROUND BEFORE DARK.
RUSTLE

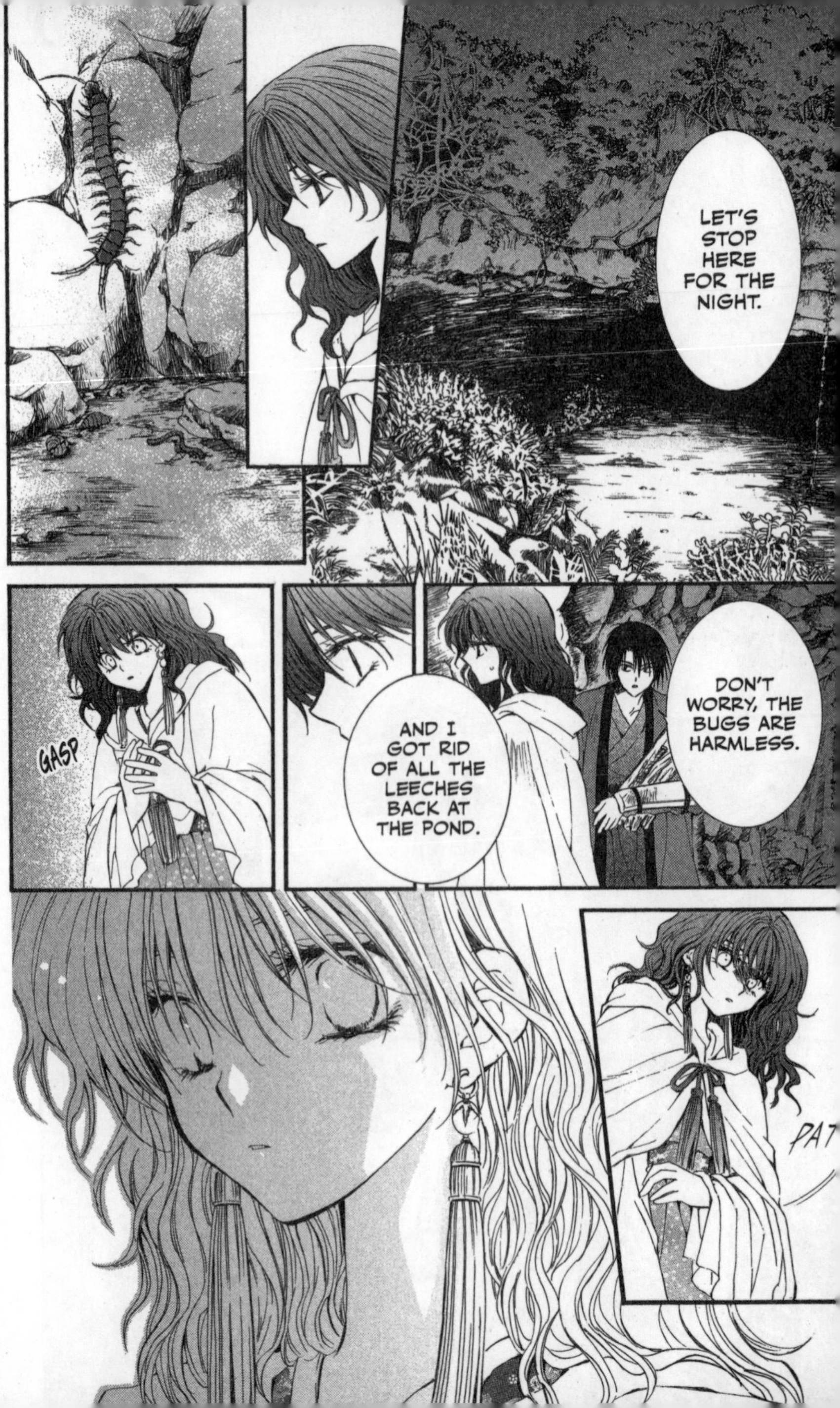
LET'S STOP HERE FOR THE NIGHT.
DON'T WORRY, THE BUGS ARE HARMLESS.
AND I GOT RID OF ALL THE LEECHES BACK AT THE POND.
GASP
PAT

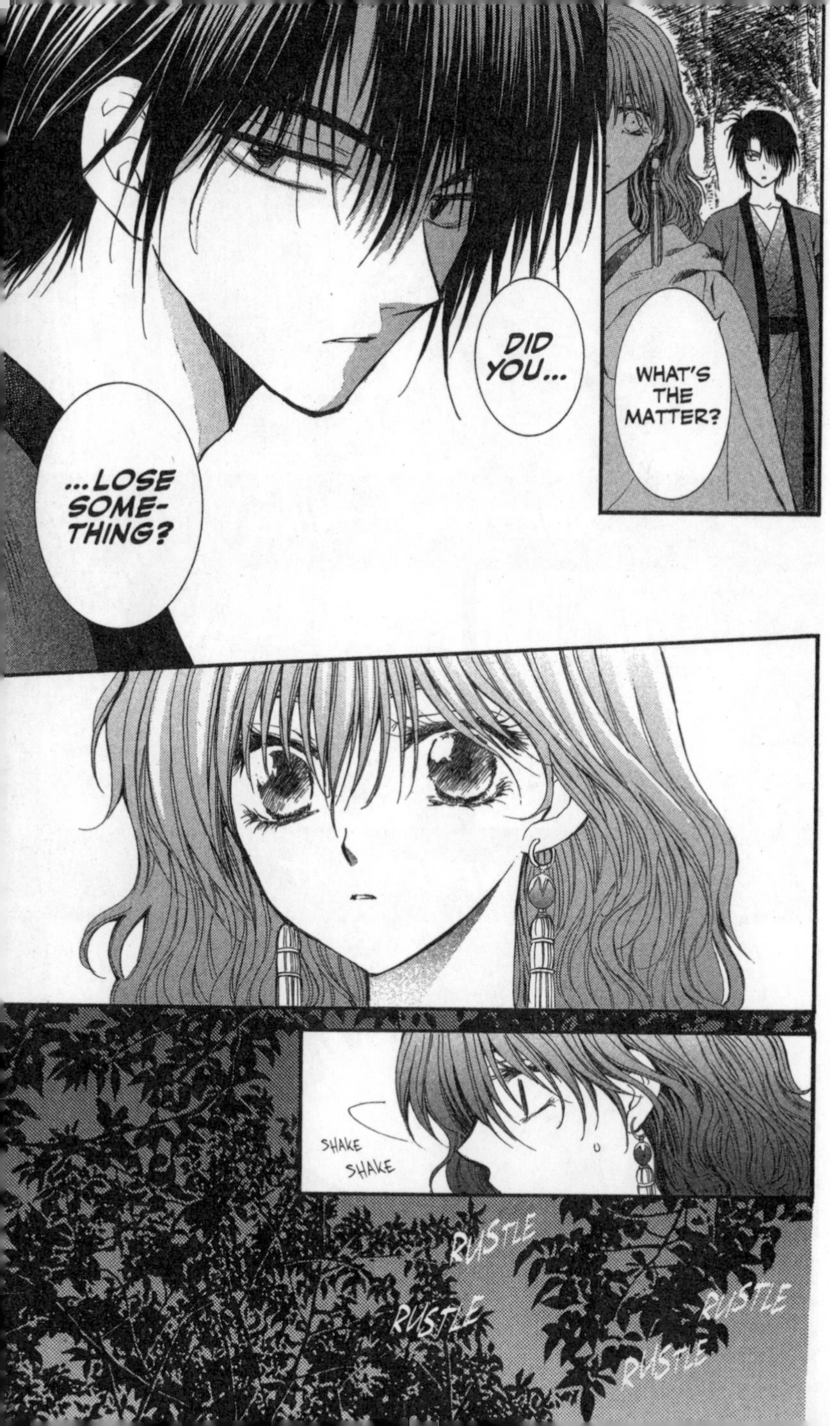
WHAT'S THE MATTER?
DID YOU...
...LOSE SOME-THING?
SHAKE
SHAKE
RUSTLE
RUSTLE
RUSTLE
RUSTLE

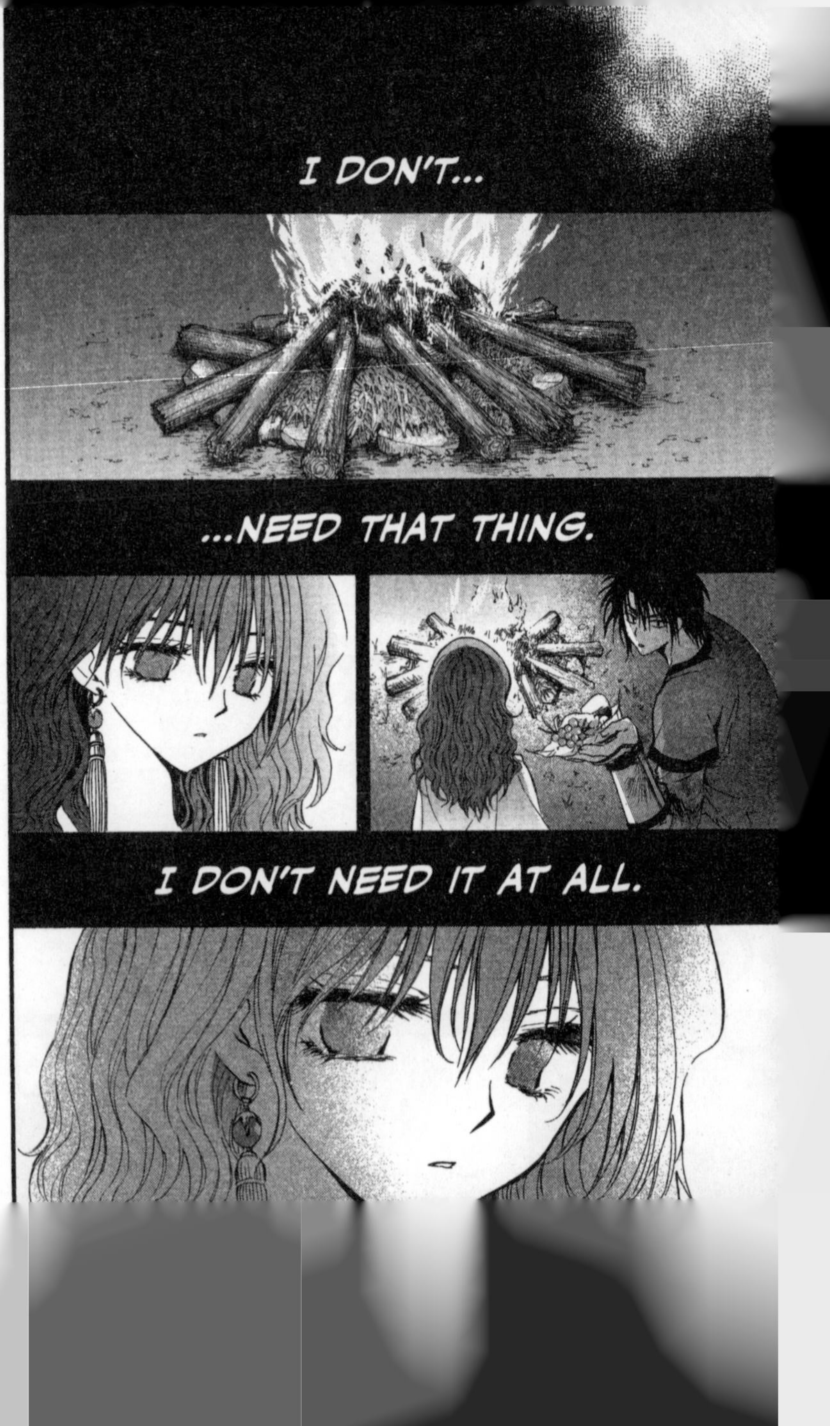
I DON'T...
...NEED THAT THING.
I DON'T NEED IT AT ALL.

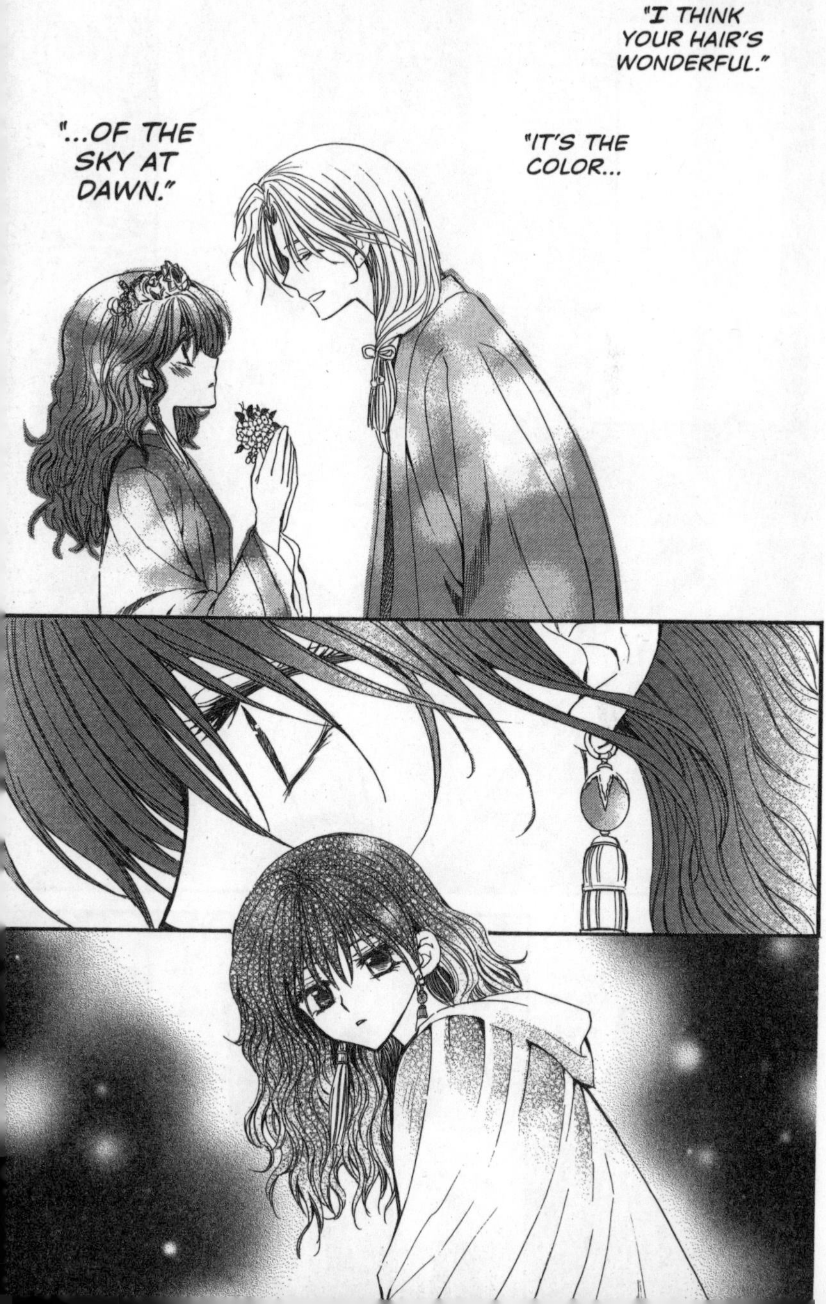
"I THINK YOUR HAIR'S WONDERFUL."
"IT'S THE COLOR...
"...OF THE SKY AT DAWN."

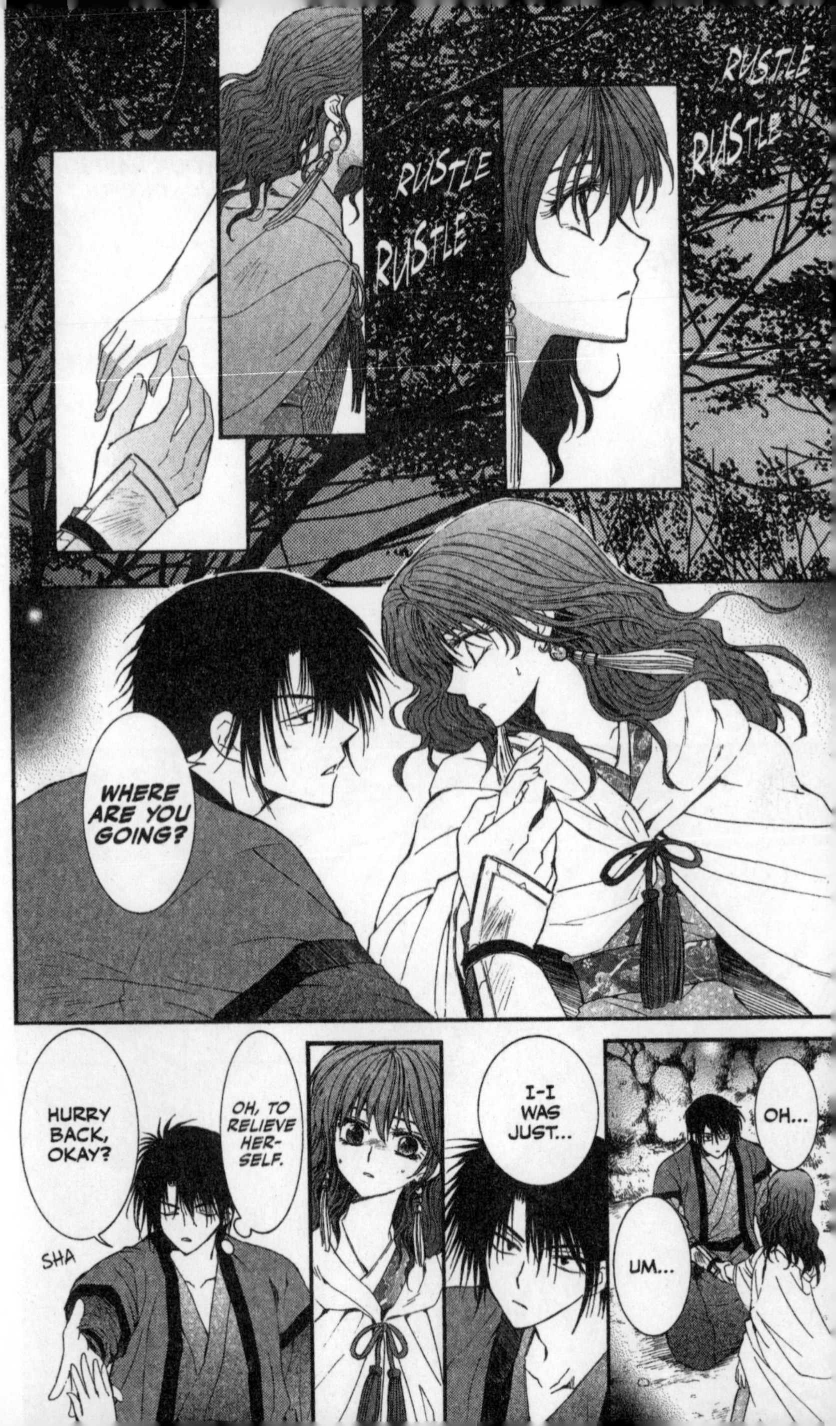
RUSTLE
RUSTLE
RUSTLE
RUSTLE
WHERE ARE YOU GOING?
OH...
UM...
I-I WAS JUST...
OH, TO RELIEVE HER-SELF.
HURRY BACK, OKAY?
SHA

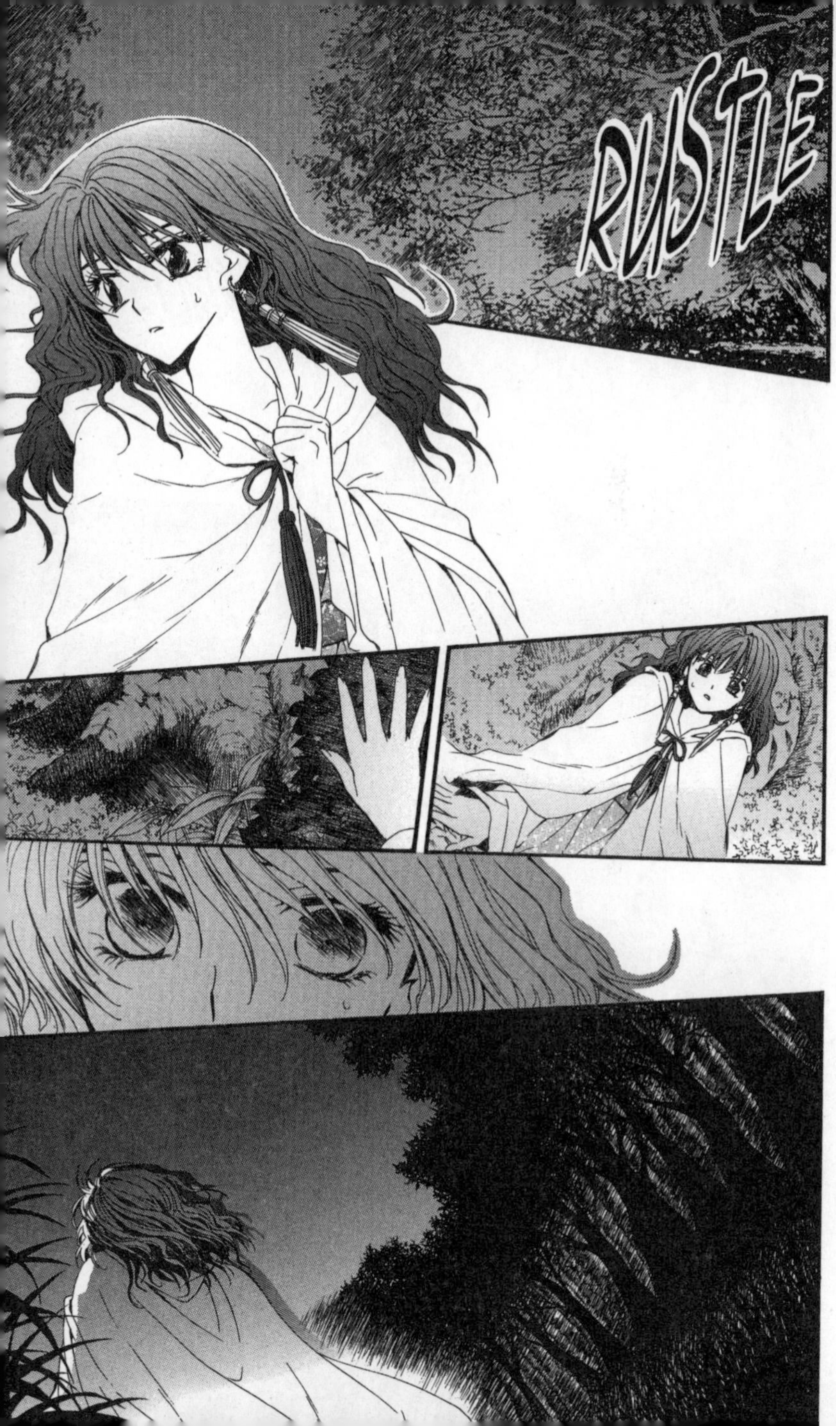
RUSTLE

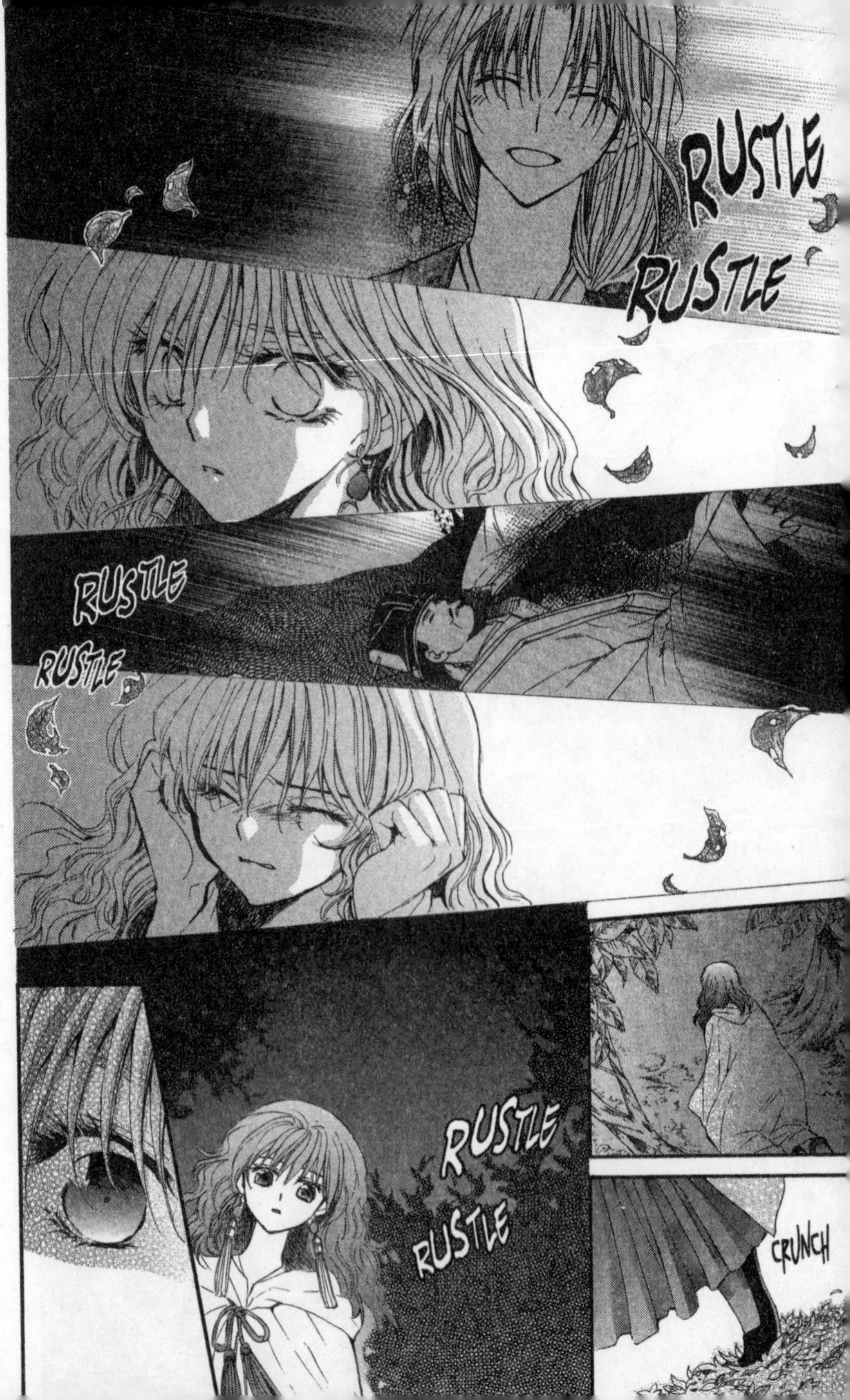
RUSTLE
RUSTLE
RUSTLE
RUSTLE
CRUNCH
RUSTLE
RUSTLE

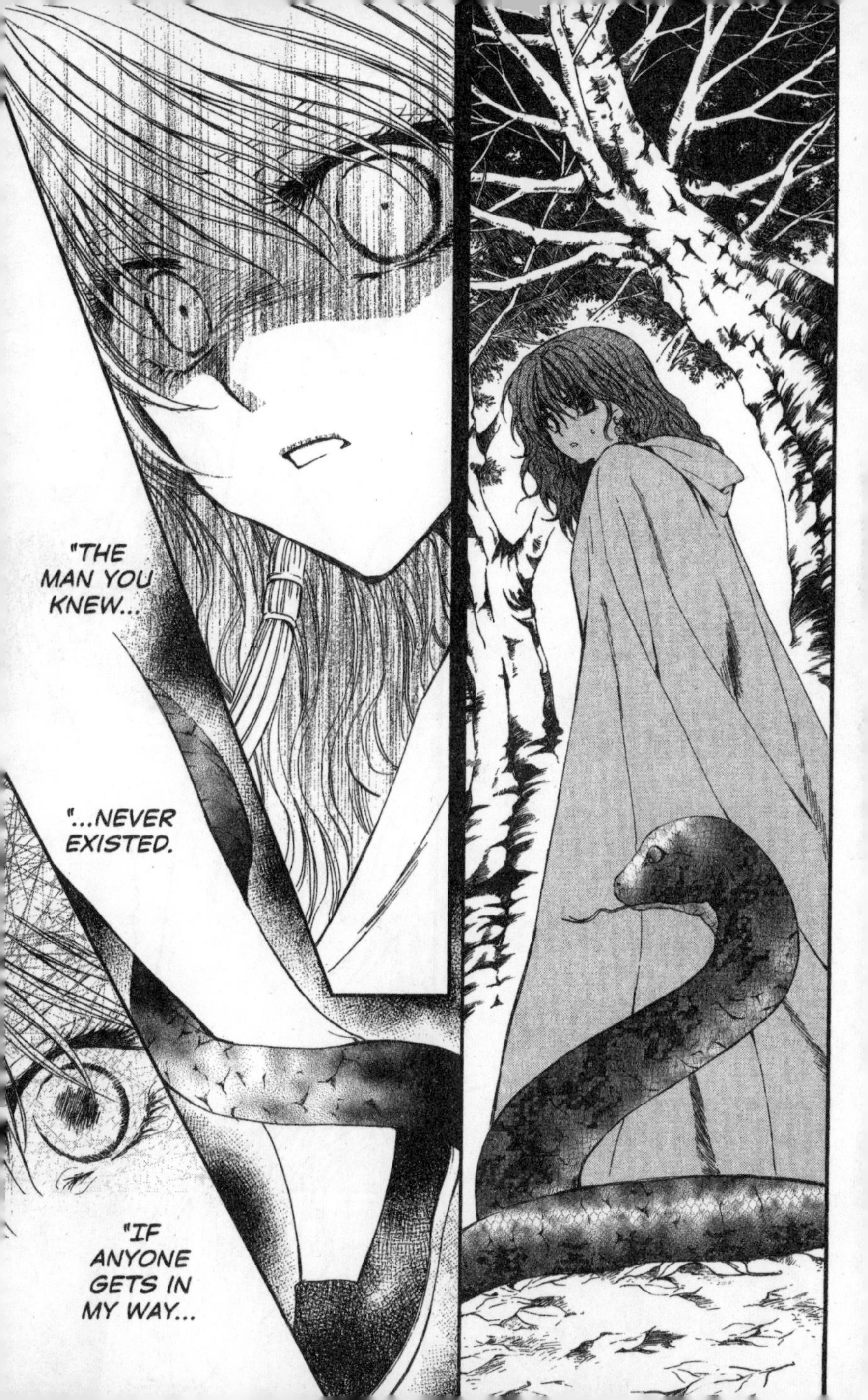
"THE MAN YOU KNEW...
"...NEVER EXISTED.
"IF ANYONE GETS IN MY WAY...

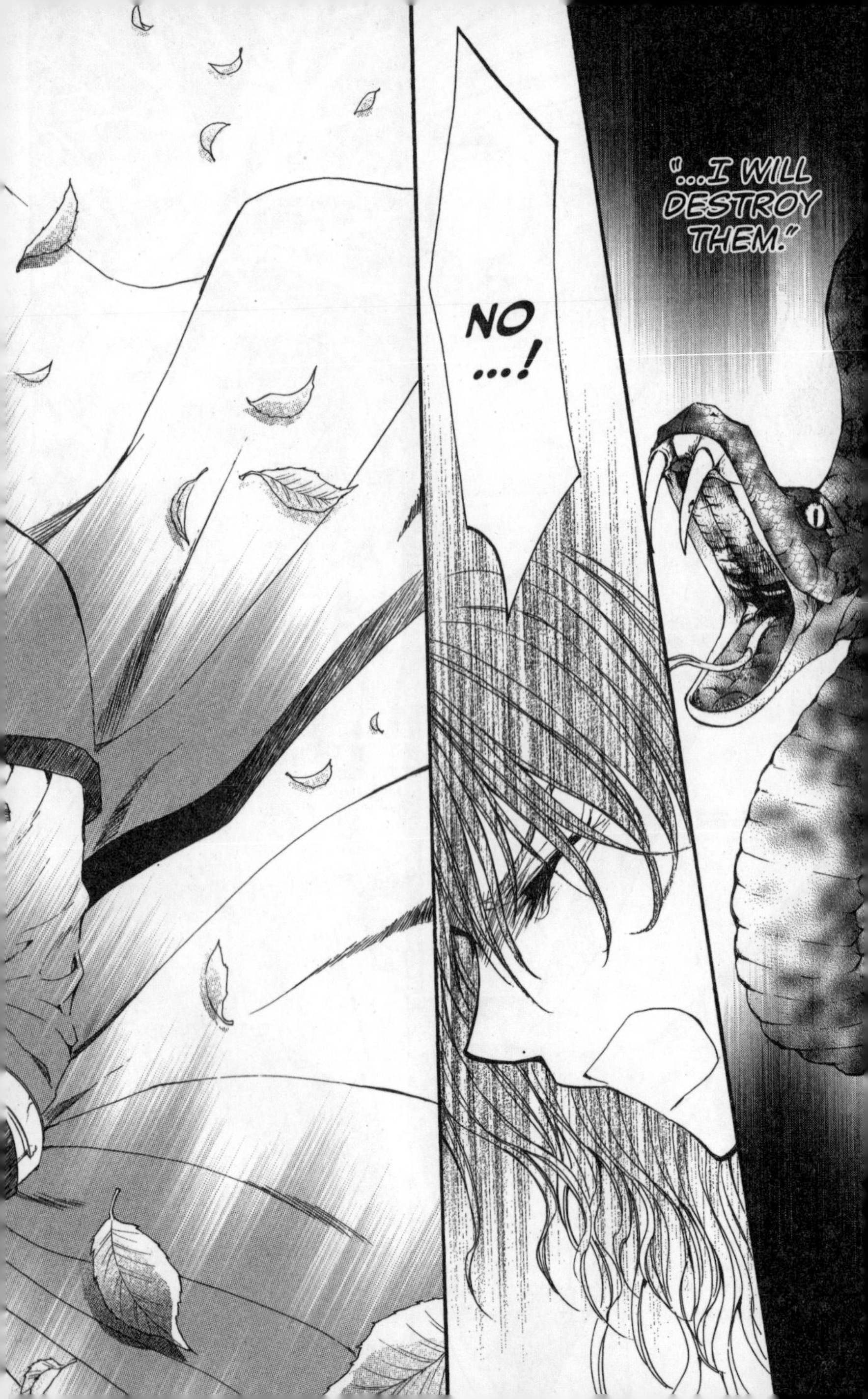
"...I WILL DESTROY THEM."
NO ...!

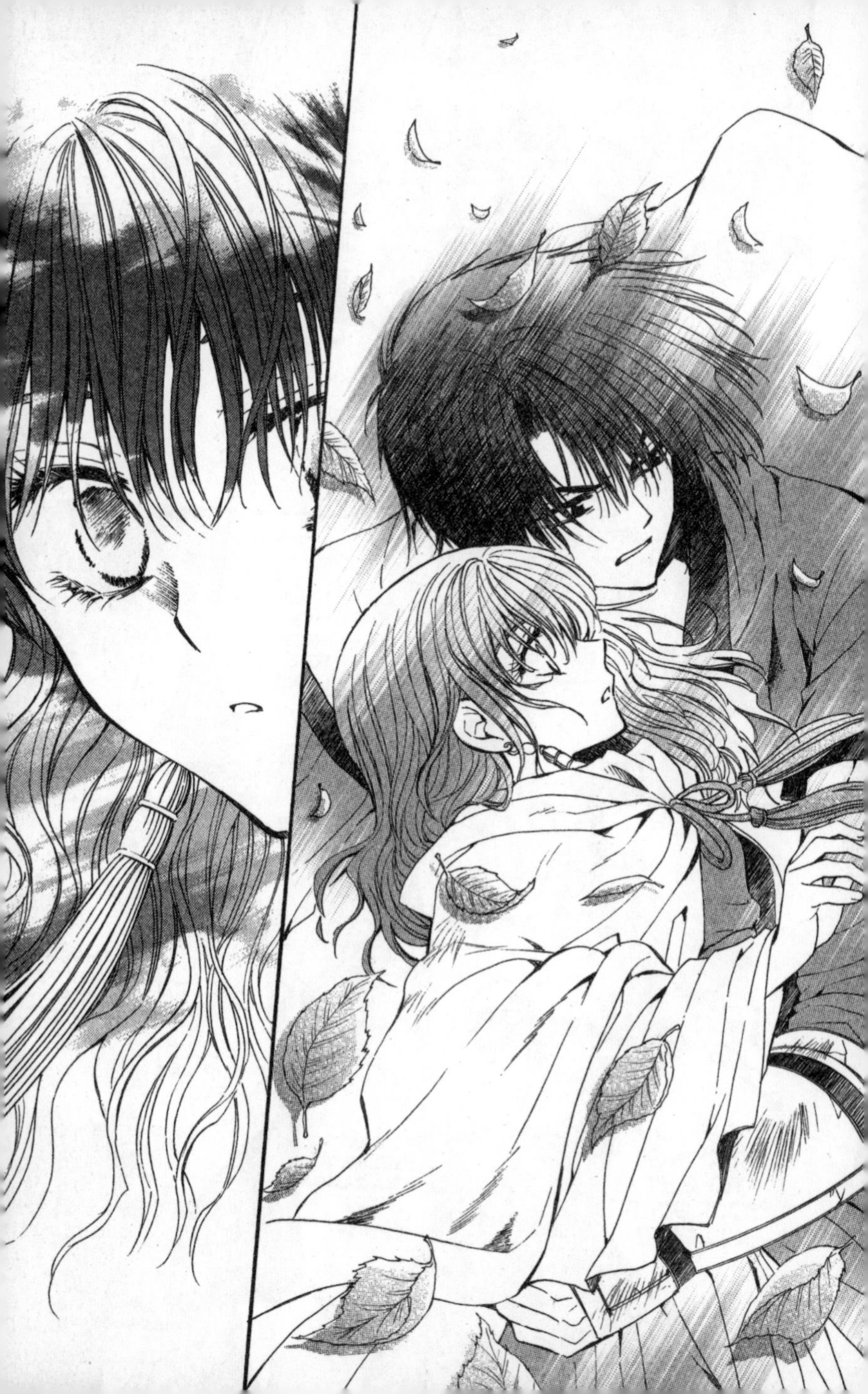

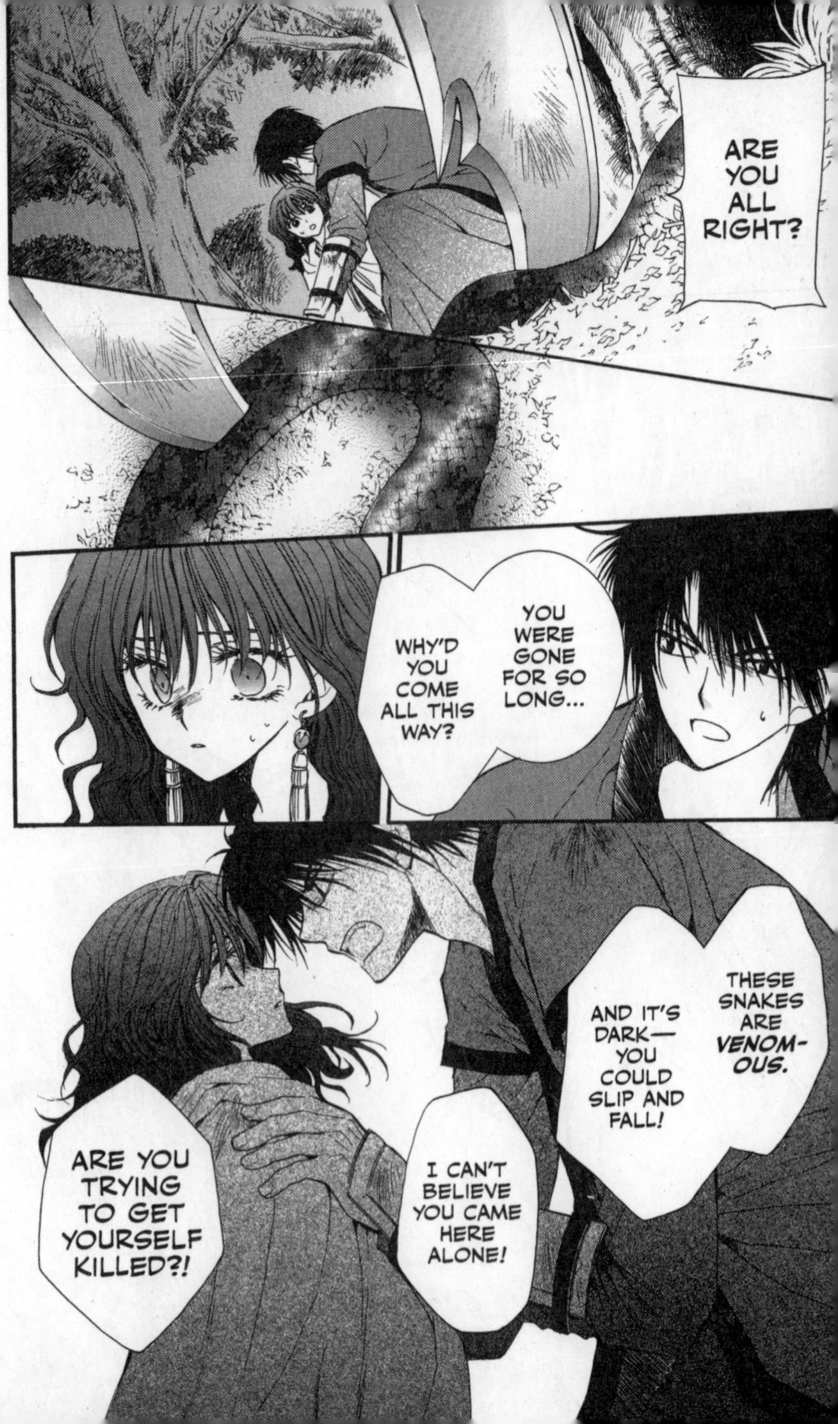
ARE YOU ALL RIGHT?
YOU WERE GONE FOR SO LONG...
WHY'D YOU COME ALL THIS WAY?
THESE SNAKES ARE *VENOMOUS.*
AND IT'S DARK—YOU COULD SLIP AND FALL!
I CAN'T BELIEVE YOU CAME HERE ALONE!
ARE YOU TRYING TO GET YOURSELF KILLED?!

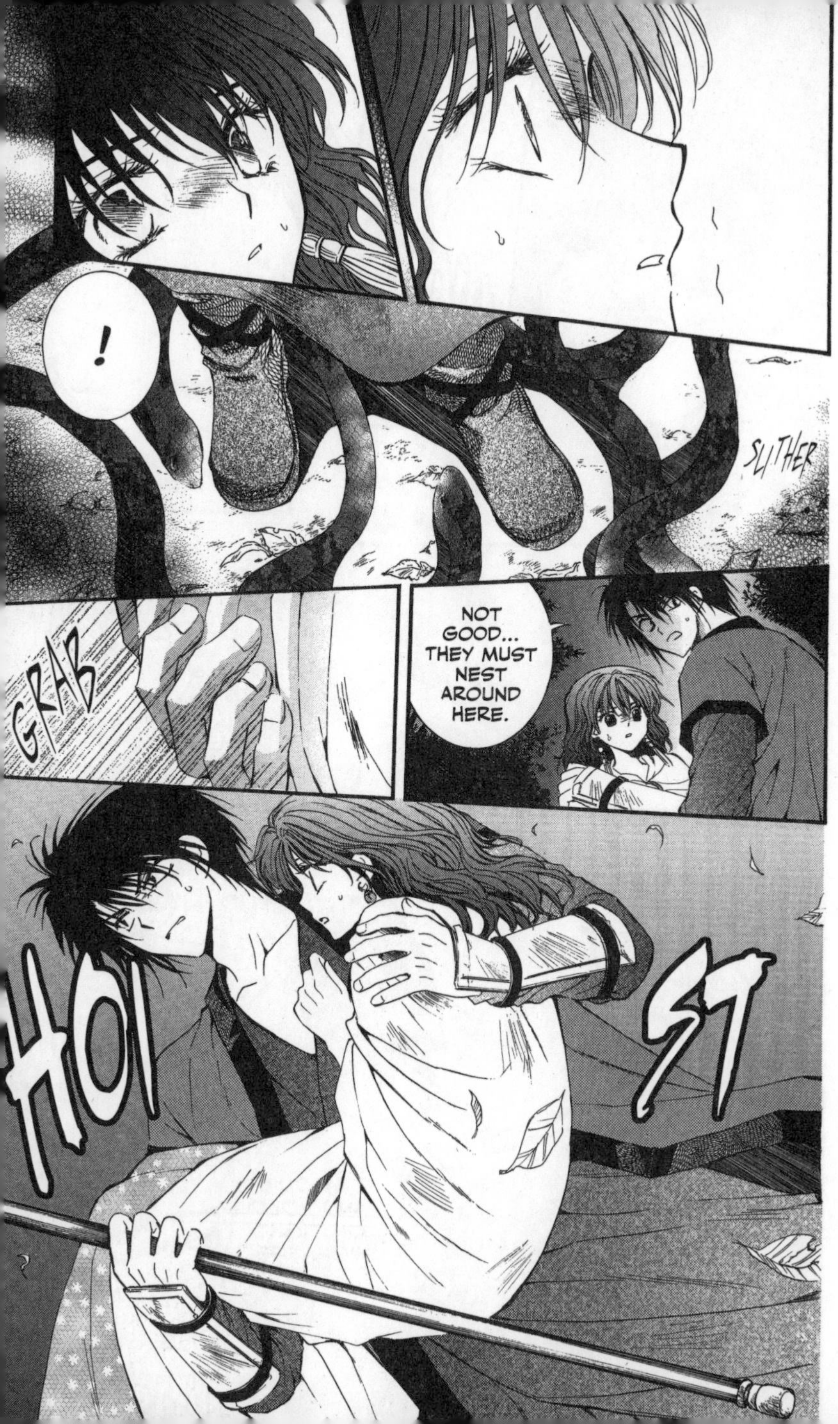
!
SLITHER
NOT GOOD... THEY MUST NEST AROUND HERE.
GRAB
ST
HOI

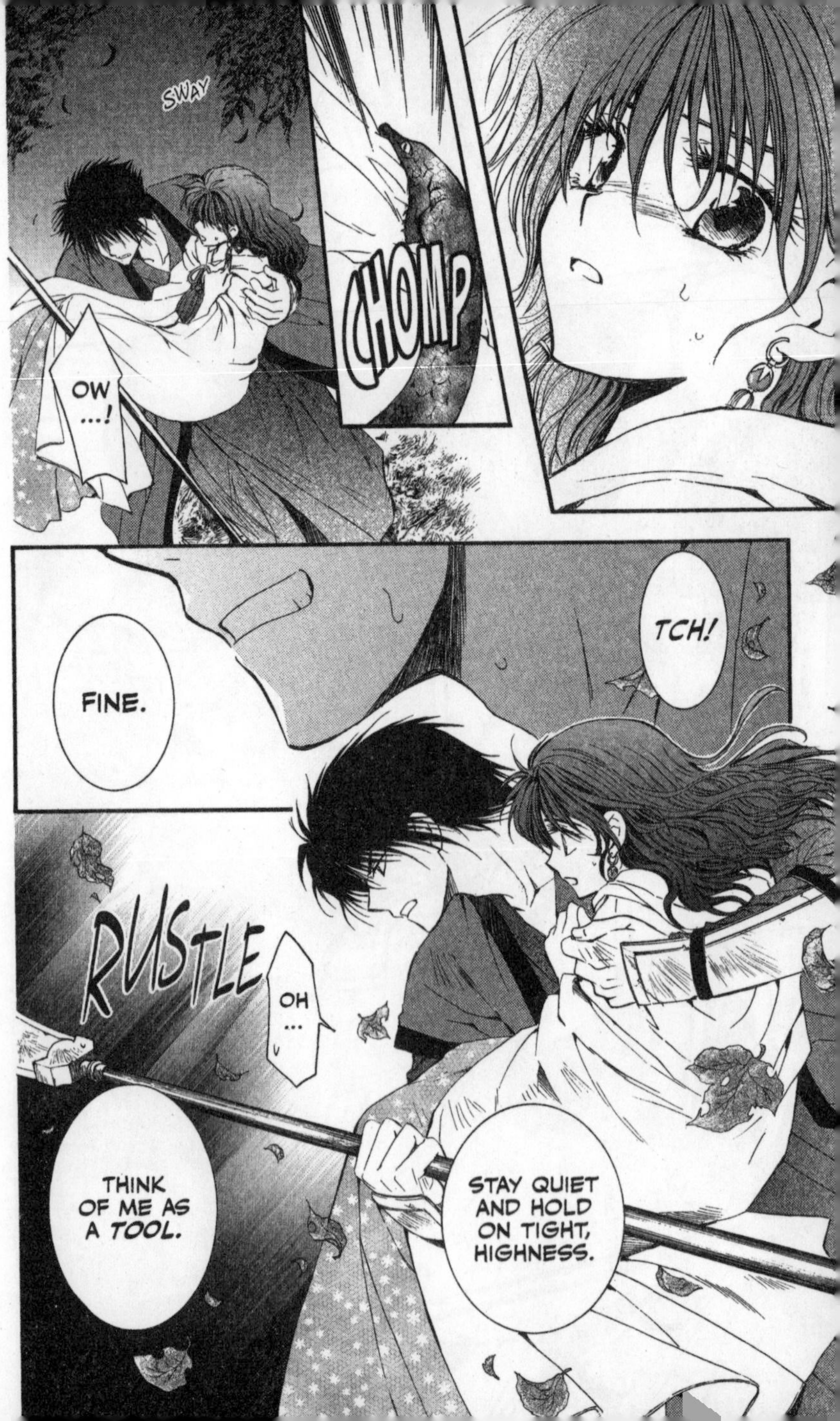
CHOMP
SWAY
OW ...!
TCH!
FINE.
RUSTLE
OH ...
STAY QUIET AND HOLD ON TIGHT, HIGHNESS.
THINK OF ME AS A *TOOL*.

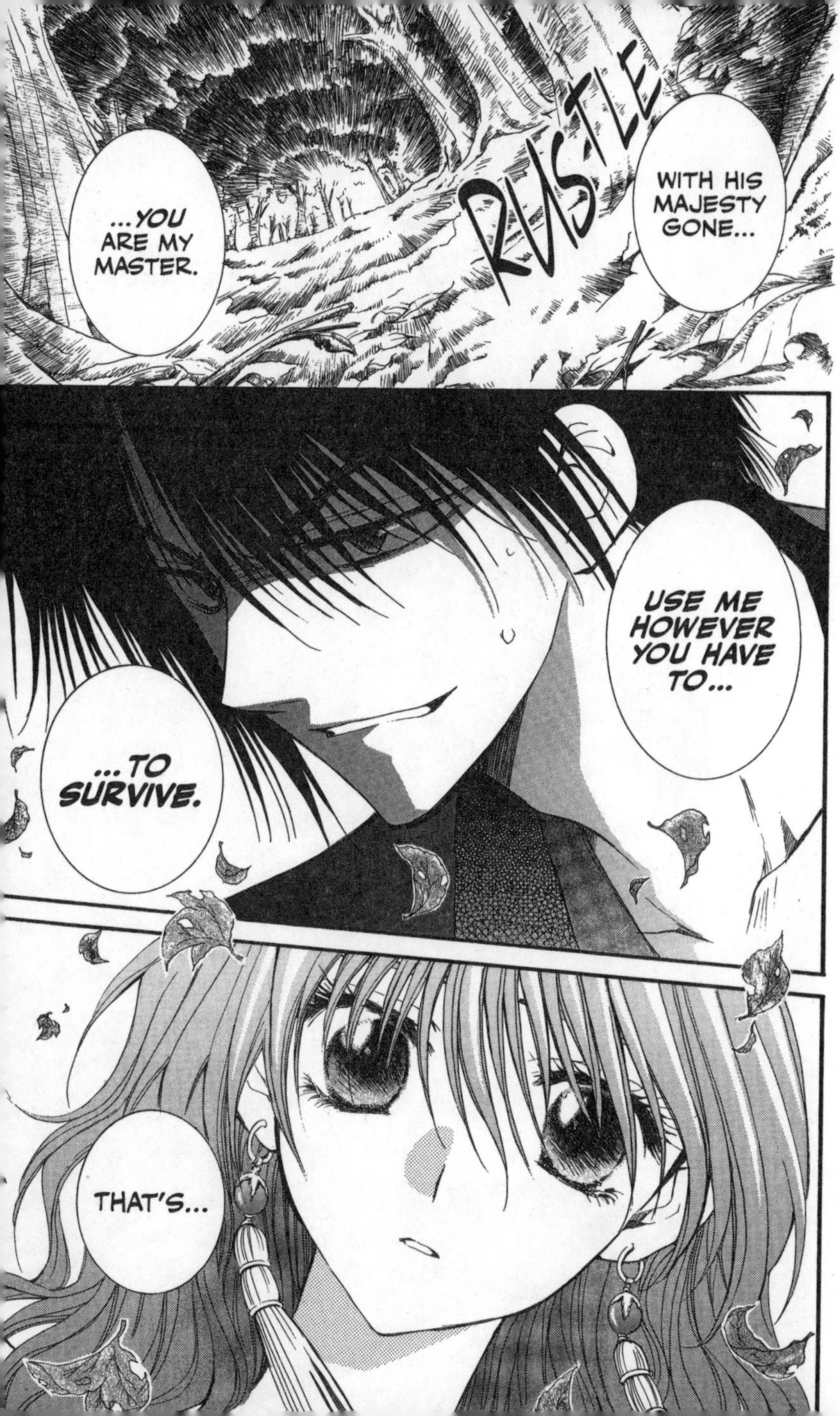
WITH HIS MAJESTY GONE...
RUSTLE
...YOU ARE MY MASTER.
USE ME HOWEVER YOU HAVE TO...
...TO SURVIVE.
THAT'S...

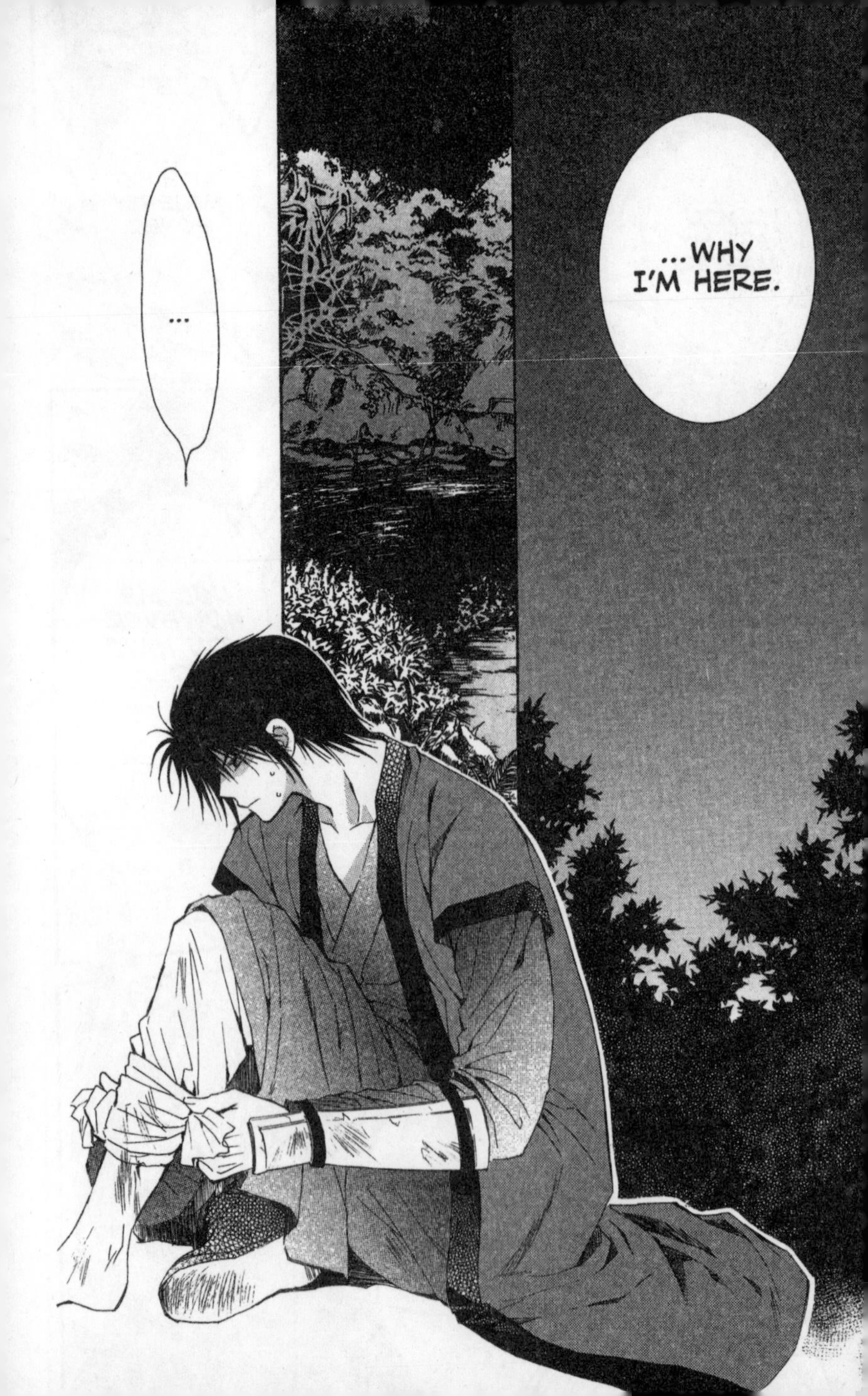
...WHY I'M HERE.
...

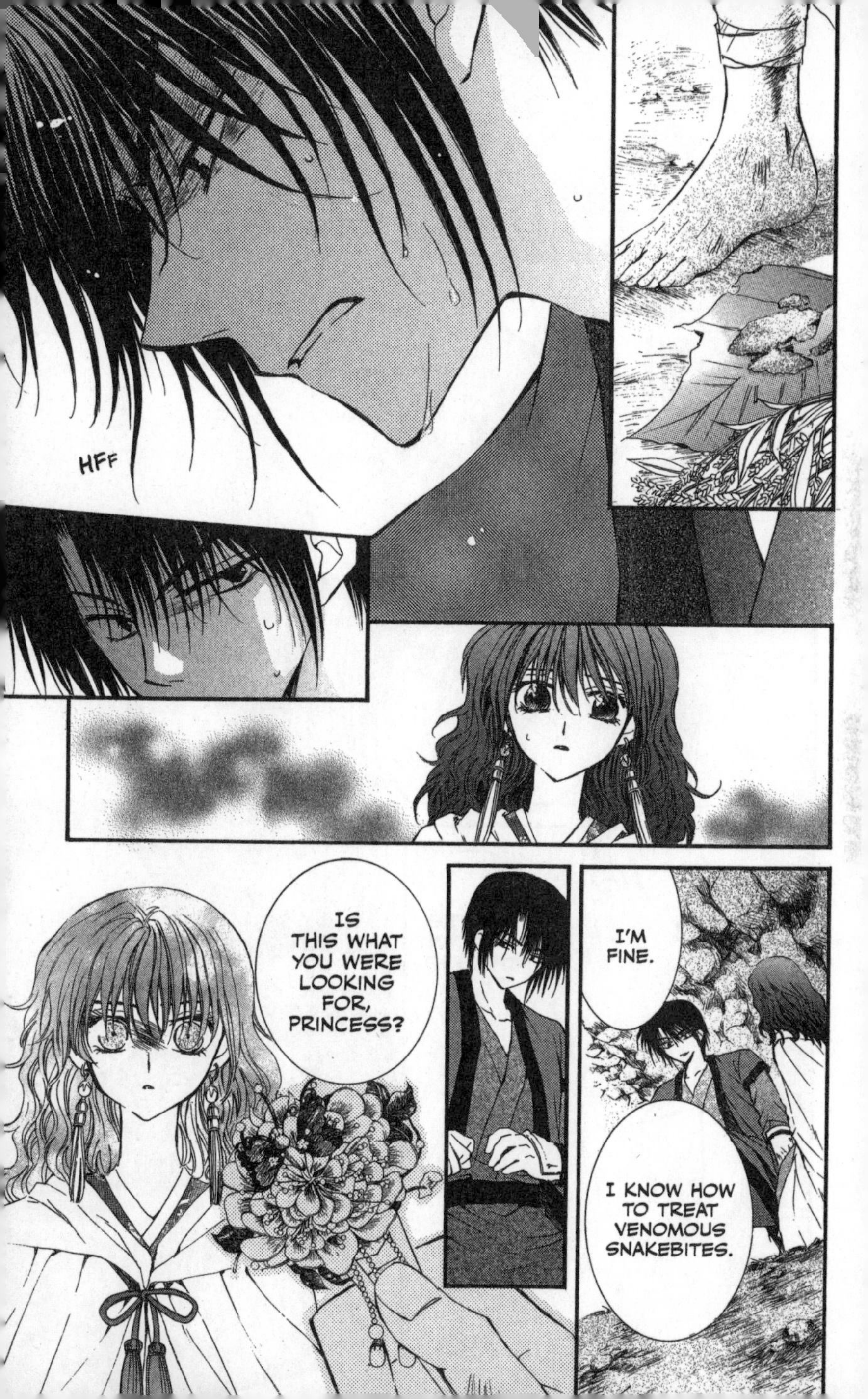
HFF
I'M FINE.
I KNOW HOW TO TREAT VENOMOUS SNAKEBITES.
IS THIS WHAT YOU WERE LOOKING FOR, PRINCESS?

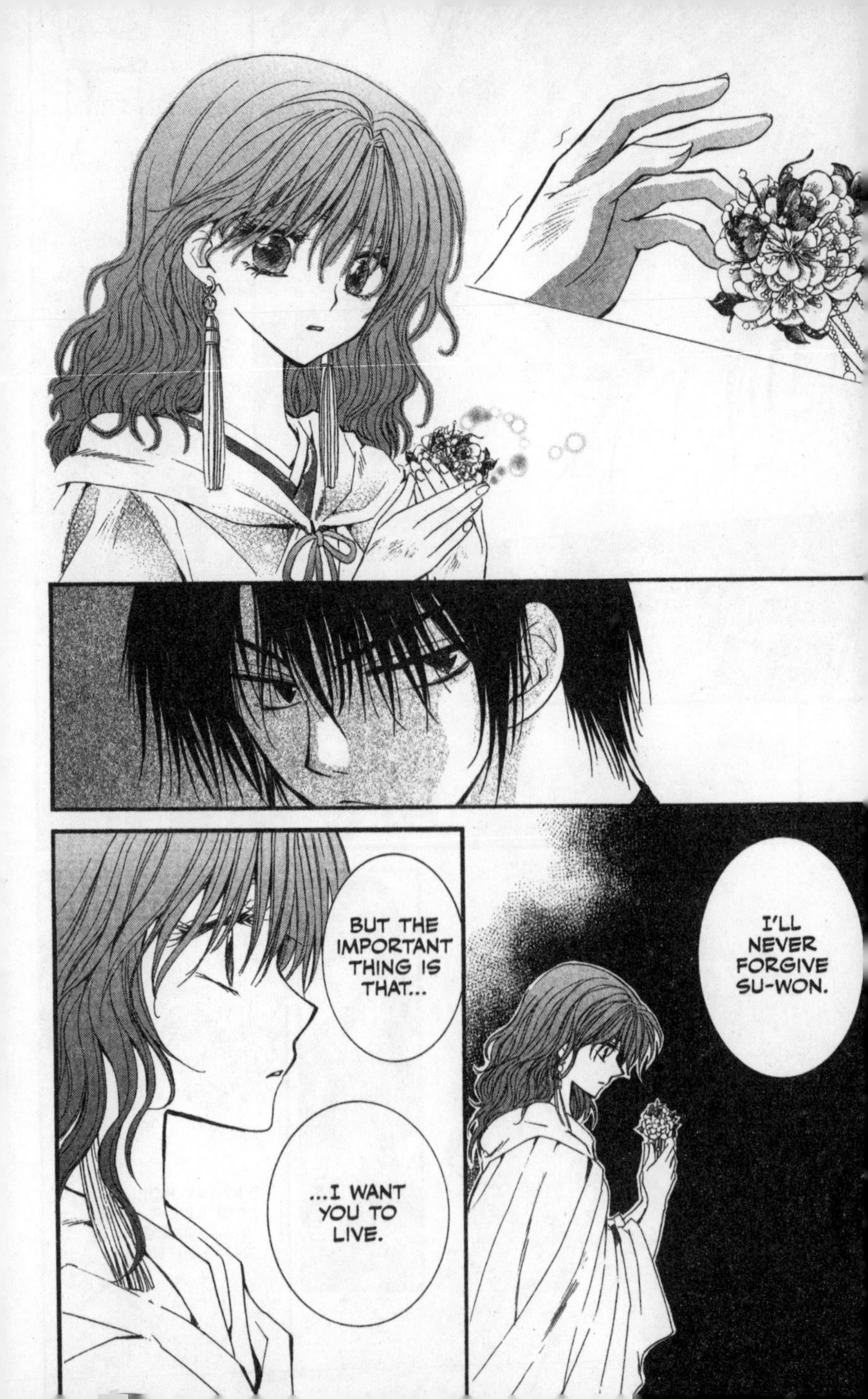
I'LL NEVER FORGIVE SU-WON.
BUT THE IMPORTANT THING IS THAT...
...I WANT YOU TO LIVE.

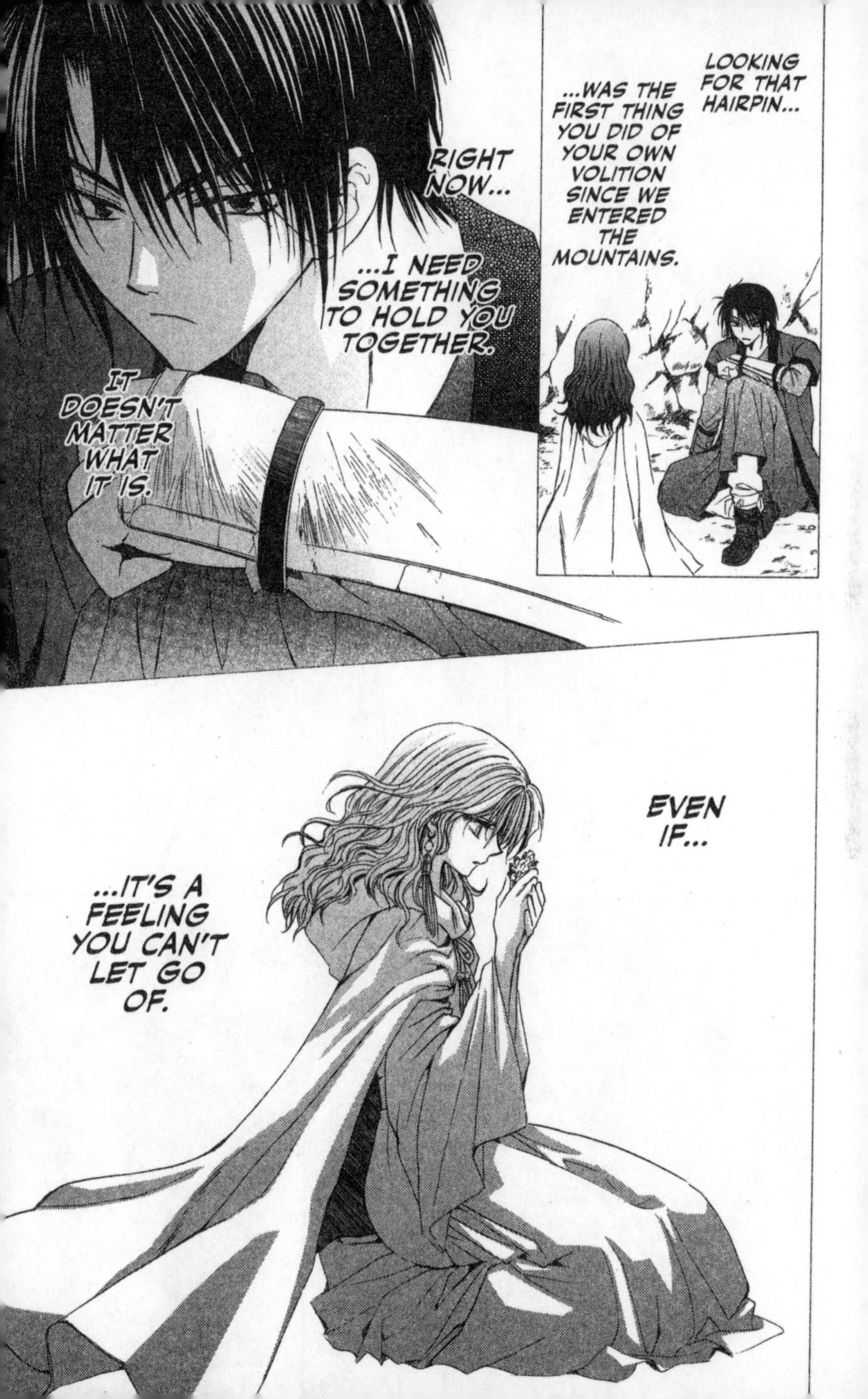
LOOKING FOR THAT HAIRPIN...
...WAS THE FIRST THING YOU DID OF YOUR OWN VOLITION SINCE WE ENTERED THE MOUNTAINS.
RIGHT NOW...
...I NEED SOMETHING TO HOLD YOU TOGETHER.
IT DOESN'T MATTER WHAT IT IS.
EVEN IF...
...IT'S A FEELING YOU CAN'T LET GO OF.

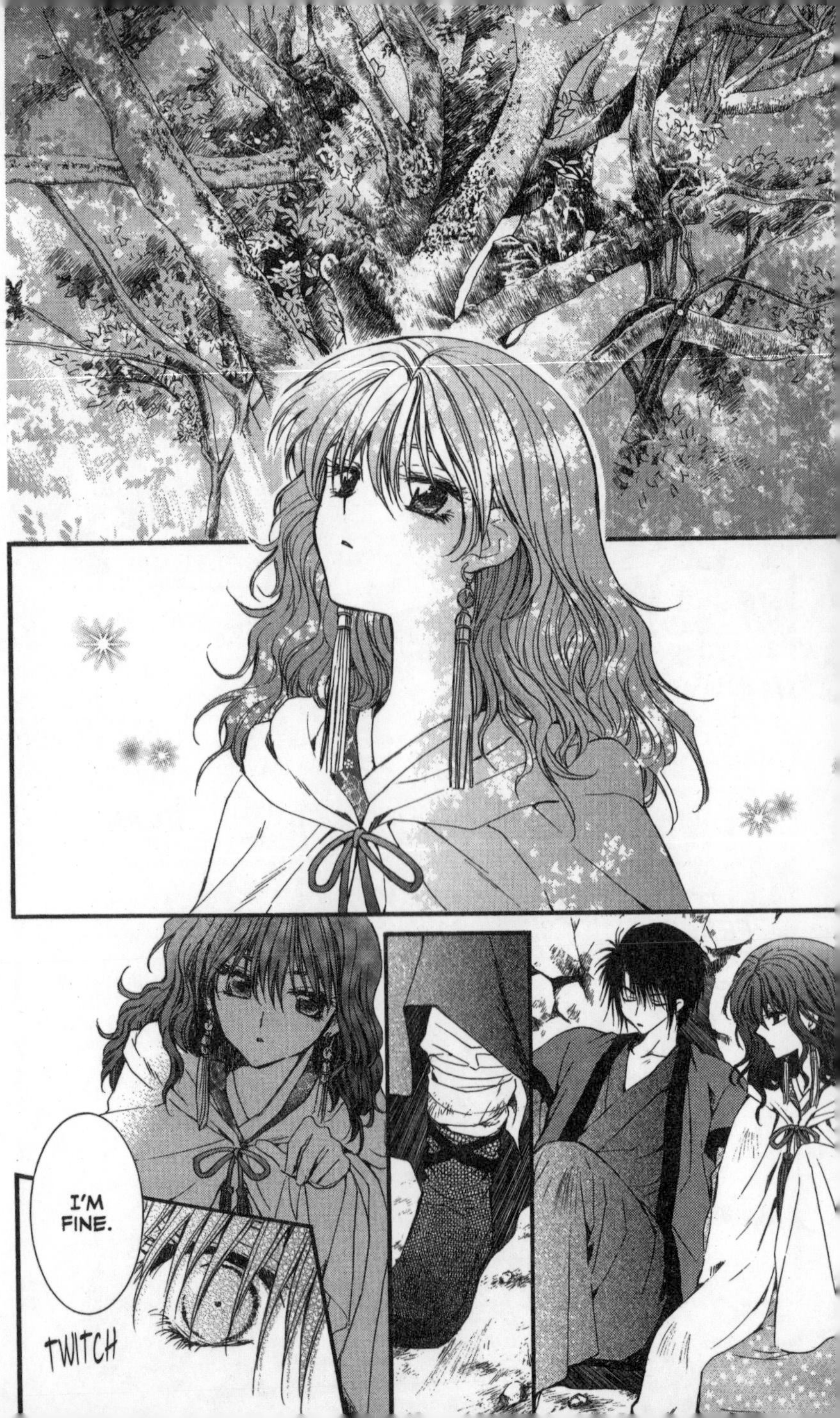
I'M FINE.
TWITCH

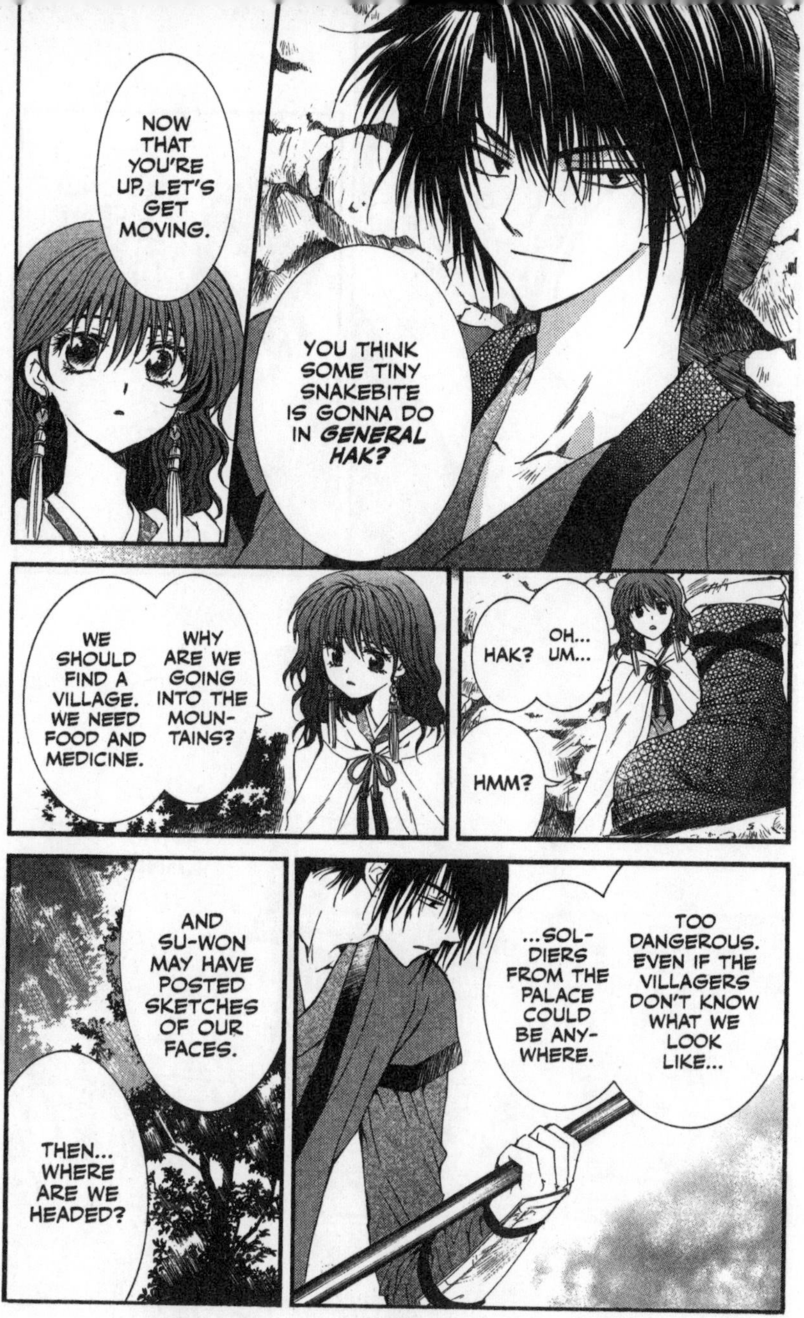
YOU THINK SOME TINY SNAKEBITE IS GONNA DO IN *GENERAL HAK?*
NOW THAT YOU'RE UP, LET'S GET MOVING.
OH... UM...
HAK?
HMM?
WHY ARE WE GOING INTO THE MOUNTAINS?
WE SHOULD FIND A VILLAGE. WE NEED FOOD AND MEDICINE.
TOO DANGEROUS. EVEN IF THE VILLAGERS DON'T KNOW WHAT WE LOOK LIKE...
...SOLDIERS FROM THE PALACE COULD BE ANYWHERE.
AND SU-WON MAY HAVE POSTED SKETCHES OF OUR FACES.
THEN... WHERE ARE WE HEADED?

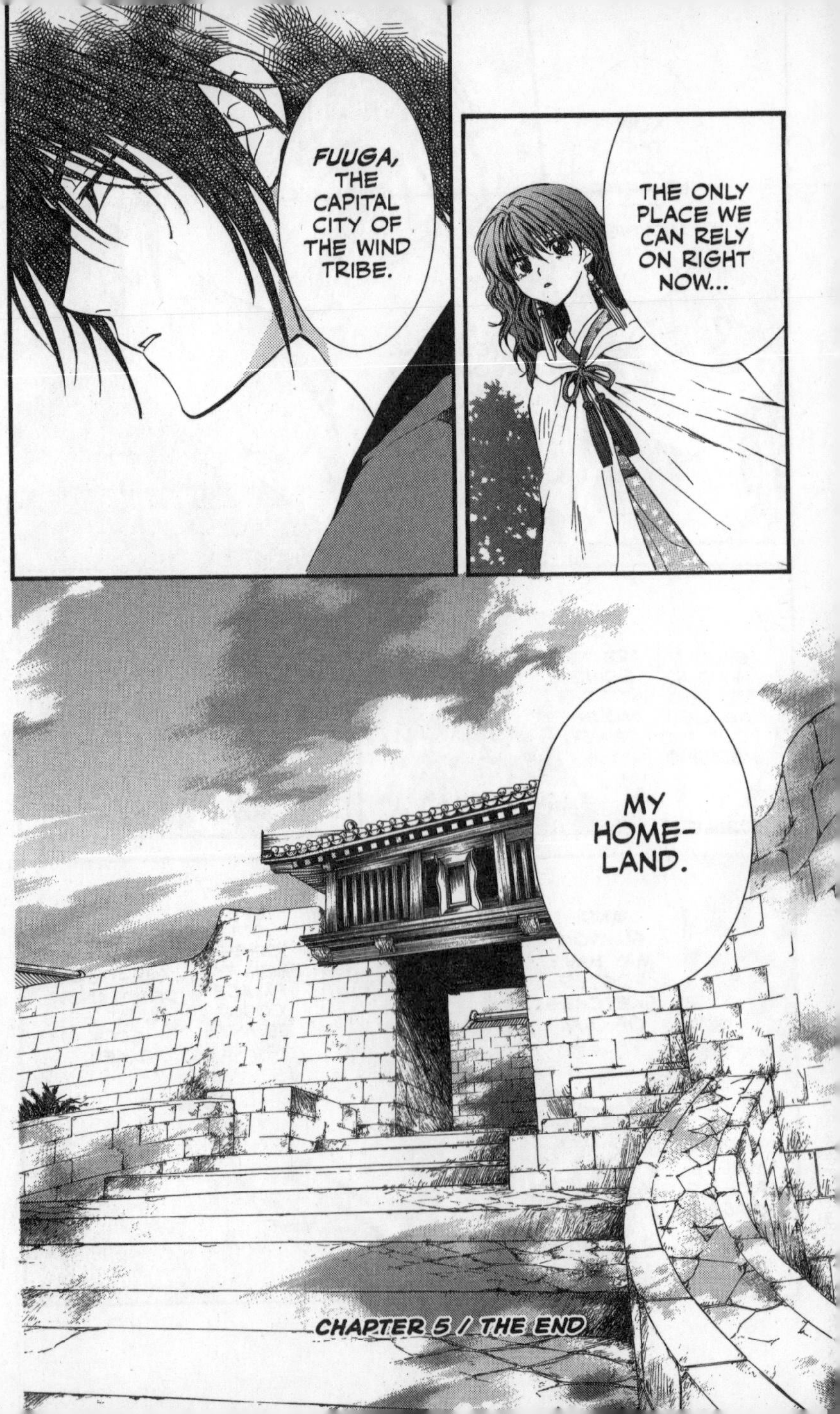
THE ONLY PLACE WE CAN RELY ON RIGHT NOW...
FUUGA, THE CAPITAL CITY OF THE WIND TRIBE.
MY HOME-LAND.
CHAPTER 5 / THE END

Born on February 3 in Kumamoto
Prefecture in Japan, Mizuho Kusanagi
began her professional manga
career with *Yoiko no Kokoroe* (The
Rules of a Good Child) in 2003. Her
other works include *NG Life*, which
was serialized in *Hana to Yume* and
The Hana to Yume magazines and
published by Hakusensha in Japan.
Yona of the Dawn was adapted into an
anime in 2014.

YONA OF THE DAWN

VOL. 1
Shojo Beat Edition

STORY AND ART BY
MIZUHO KUSANAGI

English Adaptation/Ysabet Reinhardt MacFarlane
Translation/JN Productions
Touch-Up Art & Lettering/Lys Blakeslee
Design/Yukiko Whitley, Izumi Evers
Editor/Amy Yu

Akatsuki no Yona by Mizuho Kusanagi
© Mizuho Kusanagi 2010
All rights reserved.
First published in Japan in 2010 by HAKUSENSHA, Inc., Tokyo.
English language translation rights arranged with
HAKUSENSHA, Inc., Tokyo.

The stories, characters and incidents mentioned in this publication
are entirely fictional.

No portion of this book may be reproduced or transmitted in
any form or by any means without written permission from the
copyright holders.

Printed in Italy

Published by VIZ Media, LLC
P.O. Box 77010
San Francisco, CA 94107

10 9 8 7 6
First printing, August 2016
Sixth printing, March 2022

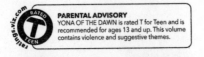

PARENTAL ADVISORY
YONA OF THE DAWN is rated T for Teen and is
recommended for ages 13 and up. This volume
contains violence and suggestive themes.

 MEDIA

viz.com   shojobeat.com

Kamisama Kiss

Story and art by **Julietta Suzuki**

What's a newly fledged godling to do?

Now a hit anime series!

Nanami Momozono is alone and homeless after her dad skips town to evade his gambling debts and the debt collectors kick her out of her apartment. So when a man she's just saved from a dog offers her his home, she jumps at the opportunity. But it turns out that his place is a shrine, and Nanami has unwittingly taken over his job as a local deity!

Available now!

viz.com

Kamisama Hajimemashita © Julietta Suzuki 2008/HAKUSENSHA, Inc.

Now available in 2-in-1 edition!

Maid-sama!

Story & Art by
Hiro Fujiwara

As if being student council president of a predominantly male high school isn't hard enough, Misaki Ayuzawa has a major secret—she works at a maid café after school! How is she supposed to keep her image of being ultrasmart, strong and overachieving intact once school heartthrob Takumi Usui discovers her double life?!

Kaicho wa Maid Sama! © Hiro Fujiwara 2006/HAKUSENSHA, Inc.

www.viz.com

Don't Hide What's *Inside*

OTOMEN

by AYA KANNO

Despite his tough jock exterior, Asuka Masamune harbors a secret love for sewing, shojo manga, and all things girly. But when he finds himself drawn to his domestically inept classmate Ryo, his carefully crafted persona is put to the test. Can Asuka ever show his true self to anyone, much less to the girl he's falling for?

Find out in the *Otomen* manga—buy yours today!

www.shojobeat.com

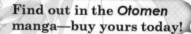
Available at your local bookstore or comic store.

OTOMEN © Aya Kanno 2006/HAKUSENSHA, Inc.

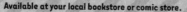

RATED
TEEN
ratings.viz.com

VIZ MEDIA
www.viz.com

Ouran High School

Host Club

BOX SET

Story and Art by
Bisco Hatori

Escape to the world of the young, rich and sexy

**All 18 volumes
in a collector's box
with an Ouran High
School stationery
notepad!**

In this screwball romantic
comedy, Haruhi, a poor girl at
a rich kids' school, is forced to
repay an $80,000 debt by working
for the school's swankiest, all-
male club—as a boy! There she
discovers just how wealthy the six
members are and how different
the rich are from everybody else...

VIZ MEDIA
www.viz.com

Shojo Beat

Ouran Koko Host Club © Bisco Hatori 2002/HAKUSENSHA, Inc.

From the creator of Ouran High School Host Club!

Millennium Snow

By Bisco Hatori

Seventeen-year-old Chiyuki has heart problems, and her doctors say she won't live to see the next snow. Touya is a young vampire who hates blood and refuses to make the traditional partnership with a human, whose life-giving blood would keep them both alive for a thousand years. Can Chiyuki teach Touya to feel a passion for life, even as her own is ending?

Shojo Beat Manga

Millennium Snow

Bisco Hatori

Only $9.99

www.shojobeat.com
MANGA from the HEART

Also available at your local bookstore and comic store.   Sennen no Yuki © Bisco Hatori 1998/HAKUSENSHA, Inc.

www.viz.com

...and STILL kick some butt?!

ORESAMA TEACHER

Story & art by Izumi Tsubaki

Determined to make the best of the situation and make her mother proud, Mafuyu decides to turn over a new, feminine, well-behaved leaf. But her fighting spirit can't be kept down, and the night before school starts she finds herself defending some guy who's getting beaten up. One slip wouldn't have been a problem, except the guy is **...her teacher?!** How can Mafuyu learn to be a good girl if her teacher won't let her forget her wicked past?

Oresama Teacher, Vol. 1
ISBN: 978-1-4215-3863-1 • $9.99 US / $12.99 CAN

IN STORES NOW!

ORESAMA TEACHER © Izumi Tsubaki 2008/HAKUSENSHA, Inc.

www.viz.com

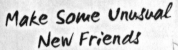

Natsume's BOOK of FRIENDS

STORY and ART by Yuki Midorikawa

Make Some Unusual New Friends

The power to see hidden spirits has always felt like a curse to troubled high schooler Takashi Natsume. But he's about to discover he inherited a lot more than just the Sight from his mysterious grandmother!

Available at your local bookstore or comic store.

www.shojobeat.com

Natsume Yujincho © Yuki Midorikawa 2005/HAKUSENSHA, Inc.

www.viz.com

This is the last page.

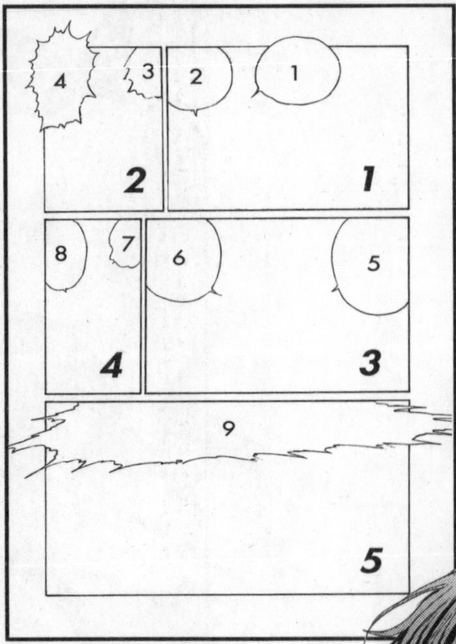
1
1
2
2
3
4
3
5
6
4
7
8
5
9

In keeping with the original Japanese comic format, this book reads from right to left—so action, sound effects, and word balloons are completely reversed. This preserves the orientation of the original artwork—plus, it's fun! Check out the diagram shown here to get the hang of things, and then turn to the other side of the book to get started!

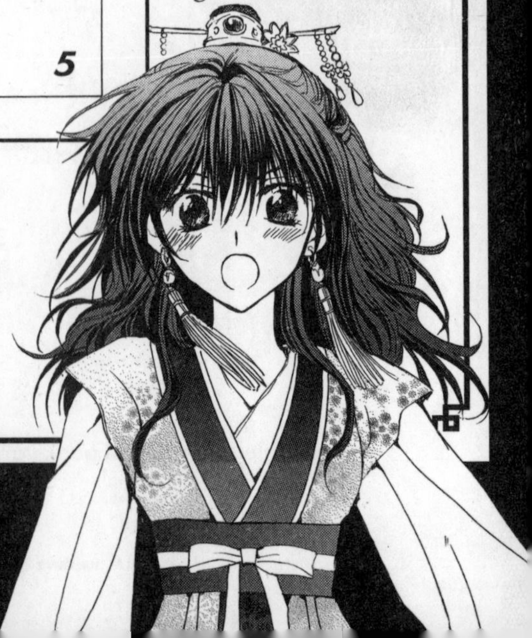